About the Author

Stan Fischler, whom some have called "The Hockey Man," has been covering the ice game longer and more actively than any living journalist. He began working professionally as a hockey journalist in 1954 and is a Lester Patrick Award winner "for contributions to hockey in the United States." Currently appearing on MSG Network's *Hockey Night Live* weekly program, he made his television debut in 1973 as an announcer working in Boston and covering the World Hockey Association's New England Whalers. His NHL debut took place two years later, when he began doing telecasts for the New York Islanders. Fischler still does Islanders telecasts for the Madison Square Garden Networks, and he has no less than seven Emmy Awards to his credit, also winning a writing award for his work on *Subway Series,* which was carried on MSG's Metro Channel. He wrote his first of more than 90 hockey books in 1968, an autobiography of Hall of Famer Gordie Howe. Fischler has ghost written autobiographies, too, for such notables as Brad Park, Don Cherry, and Derek Sanderson. His *Bobby Orr and the Big, Bad Bruins* was a bestseller, as was *Hammer,* the autobiography of Philadelphia Flyers tough guy Dave Schultz. Before his wife, Shirley, died in May 2014, she collaborated with her husband on two definitive hockey encyclopedias, as well as other NHL books. Fischler is a Brooklyn native.

Also from Visible Ink Press

The Handy African American History Answer Book
by Jessie Carnie Smith
ISBN: 978-1-57859-452-8

The Handy Anatomy Answer Book, 2nd edition
by Patricia Barnes-Svarney and Thomas E. Svarney
ISBN: 978-57859-542-6

The Handy Answer Book for Kids (and Parents), 2nd edition
by Gina Misiroglu
ISBN: 978-1-57859-219-7

The Handy Art History Answer Book
by Madelynn Dickerson
ISBN: 978-1-57859-417-7

The Handy Astronomy Answer Book, 3rd edition
by Charles Liu
ISBN: 978-1-57859-190-9

The Handy Bible Answer Book
by Jennifer Rebecca Prince
ISBN: 978-1-57859-478-8

The Handy Biology Answer Book, 2nd edition
by Patricia Barnes Svarney and Thomas E. Svarney
ISBN: 978-1-57859-490-0

The Handy Chemistry Answer Book
by Ian C. Stewart and Justin P. Lamont
ISBN: 978-1-57859-374-3

The Handy Civil War Answer Book
by Samuel Willard Crompton
ISBN: 978-1-57859-476-4

The Handy Dinosaur Answer Book, 2nd edition
by Patricia Barnes-Svarney and Thomas E. Svarney
ISBN: 978-1-57859-218-0

The Handy English Grammar Answer Book
by Christine A. Hult, Ph.D.
ISBN: 978-1-57859-520-4

The Handy Geography Answer Book, 2nd edition
by Paul A. Tucci
ISBN: 978-1-57859-215-9

The Handy Geology Answer Book
by Patricia Barnes-Svarney and Thomas E. Svarney
ISBN: 978-1-57859-156-5

The Handy History Answer Book, 3rd edition
by David L. Hudson, Jr.
ISBN: 978-1-57859-372-9

The Handy Investing Answer Book
by Paul A. Tucci
ISBN: 978-1-57859-486-3

The Handy Islam Answer Book
by John Renard Ph.D.
ISBN: 978-1-57859-510-5

The Handy Law Answer Book
by David L. Hudson Jr.
ISBN: 978-1-57859-217-3

The Handy Math Answer Book, 2nd edition
by Patricia Barnes-Svarney and Thomas E. Svarney
ISBN: 978-1-57859-373-6

The Handy Military History Answer Book
by Samuel Willard Crompton
ISBN: 978-1-57859-509-9

The Handy Mythology Answer Book,
by David A. Leeming, Ph.D.
ISBN: 978-1-57859-475-7

The Handy Nutrition Answer Book
by Patricia Barnes-Svarney and Thomas E. Svarney
ISBN: 978-1-57859-484-9

The Handy Ocean Answer Book
by Patricia Barnes-Svarney and Thomas E. Svarney
ISBN: 978-1-57859-063-6

The Handy Personal Finance Answer Book
by Paul A. Tucci
ISBN: 978-1-57859-322-4

The Handy Philosophy Answer Book
by Naomi Zack
ISBN: 978-1-57859-226-5

The Handy Physics Answer Book, 2nd edition
by Paul W. Zitzewitz, Ph.D.
ISBN: 978-1-57859-305-7

The Handy Politics Answer Book
by Gina Misiroglu
ISBN: 978-1-57859-139-8

The Handy Presidents Answer Book, 2nd edition
by David L. Hudson
ISB N: 978-1-57859-317-0

The Handy Psychology Answer Book
by Lisa J. Cohen
ISBN: 978-1-57859-223-4

The Handy Religion Answer Book, 2nd edition
by John Renard
ISBN: 978-1-57859-379-8

The Handy Science Answer Book, 4th edition
by The Carnegie Library of Pittsburgh
ISBN: 978-1-57859-321-7

The Handy Supreme Court Answer Book
by David L Hudson, Jr.
ISBN: 978-1-57859-196-1

The Handy Technology Answer Book
by Naomi Balaban and James Bobick
ISBN: 978-1-57859-563-1

The Handy Weather Answer Book, 2nd edition
by Kevin S. Hile
ISBN: 978-1-57859-221-0

Please visit the "Handy" series website at www.handyanswers.com.

THE
HANDY
HOCKEY
ANSWER
BOOK

Stan Fischler

VISIBLE
INK
PRESS

Detroit

THE HANDY HOCKEY ANSWER BOOK

Visible Ink Press®
43311 Joy Rd., #414
Canton, MI 48187–2075
Visible Ink Press is a registered trademark of Visible Ink Press LLC.

Most Visible Ink Press books are available at special quantity discounts when purchased in bulk by corporations, organizations, or groups. Customized printings, special imprints, messages, and excerpts can be produced to meet your needs. For more information, contact Special Markets Director, Visible Ink Press, www.visibleink.com, or 734–667–3211.

Managing Editor: Kevin S. Hile
Art Director: Mary Claire Krzewinski
Typesetting: Marco DiVita
Proofreaders: Larry Baker, Janet Hile, and Shoshana Hurwitz
Indexer: Larry Baker

Cover images: Front cover images: (background) Shutterstock; all other images, Associated Press.

Back cover images (top to bottom): courtesy of Montreal Hockey Club archives, David Perlmutter, Stan Fischler, Troy Parla.

Library of Congress Cataloging–in–Publication Data

Fischler, Stan.
  The handy hockey answer book / by Stan Fischler.
    pages cm. — (The handy ... answer book)
  Includes bibliographical references and index.
  ISBN 978-1-57859-513-6 (paperback : alk. paper)
  1. Hockey—History. 2. National Hockey League—History. 3. Hockey players—Statistics. 4. Hockey players—Rating of. I. Title. II. Title: Hockey.
  GV846.5.F55 2016
  796.962—dc23   2015022547

Printed in the United States of America

10 9 8 7 6 5 4 3 2 1

Contents

Acknowledgments

In the National Hockey League, the coach's mantra often boils down to three little words: Keep it simple.

That's what we tried to accomplish in this first-of-its-kind guide, *The Handy Hockey Answer Book*—Keep it simple.

When it comes to a volume of this kind that is both unique and comprehensive, fulfilling those three little words was not as easy as it sounds. It required a team that specialized in journalistic teamwork; the kind you find in a Stanley Cup-winning organization or behind the bench, where often as many as three coaches collaborate at the same time.

In this case the "coaches" each performed nobly, energetically and meticulously to produce a winning product. Mikka Burrell, Rakhee Kulkarni, and Matthew Gaffney blended their literary tools like perfectly meshed gears.

But they couldn't do it alone. They were accompanied by a dedicated cast without whom this book would not be possible. The starry lineup includes Michael Cotton, Joe Kozlowski, Adrian Szkolar, Jake Becker, and Noah Pelletieri.

No less thanks to my wonderful agent, Agnes Birnbaum, for steering me in the direction of this project, as well as publisher Roger Jänecke of Visible Ink Press and his redoubtable managing editor, Kevin Hile.

To one and all—I'll try to keep it simple—THANKS!

Stan Fischler, New York City

Photo Sources

Alaney2k (Wikicommons): p. 77.

Alarico/Shutterstock: p. 165.

American Hockey League: p. 62.

Arnold C (User:Buchanan-Hermit — Wikicommons): p. 220.

Aspen Photo: p. 10.

Christophe Badoux: p. 192 (bottom left and bottom right).

Boston Bruins: p. 144.

Centpacrr (Wikicommons): pp. 173, 284.

Bruce C. Cooper: p. 185.

Czwerling (Wikicommons): p. 163.

dan4th (Wikicommons): pp. 199, 212.

Håkan Dahlström: pp. 178, 208, 301.

Paul Darling: p. 226.

Rick Dikeman: p. 186.

Edward F. Dolan: p. 40.

Stan Fischler: pp. 69, 80, 91, 93, 98, 102, 107,120, 128, 149, 153, 155, 159, 160, 161, 172, 175, 190, 206, 213, 217, 225, 274, 294, 310.

5of7 (Wikicommons): p. 231.

Francesca (Wikicommons): p. 268.

Aaron Frutman: p. 116.

Lisa Gansky: p. 307.

Sean Hagen: p. 140.

Hockey Hall of Fame: pp. 5, 48, 50, 72, 264.

Hockey Hall of Fame/Imperial Oil-Turofsky Collection: p. 75.

Hockeybroad/Cheryl Adams: p. 237.

Dedication

This book is dedicated to the late Shirley Walton Fischler, my wife of 46 years, who adored the game of hockey as much as I did.

Too often, Shirley's modesty as both writer and broadcaster overshadowed her major contributions as a journalist.

It was only after her death in May 2014 that the general public came to realize that she not only was a pioneering female hockey writer but also paved the way for women to work side by side in press boxes throughout the NHL.

Such was not the case in 1971, when women reporters were explicitly barred from sitting in the Madison Square Garden among other places.

One year prior, Shirley tried to join the Professional Hockey Writers' Association to get access to the Madison Square Garden's press box, but the group's constitution stated otherwise. She promptly filed a discrimination complaint with the New York Human Rights Commission.

Apart from her gender, Shirley told the Associated Press in February 1971: "I am sure that I am fully qualified in every other way."

Shirley either wrote or co-wrote more hockey books than any of the many men who desperately tried to thwart her press work. *The Macmillan Encyclopedia*—considered the definitive work of its kind in the field—was a product of my wife's tenacity as a researcher and her ability to solve the frustrations of the early computer era.

Her love of the game spanned our entire marriage, and until her late sixties she was a regular, attending New Jersey Devil games at Continental Airlines Arena. She also shared the four Islanders Stanley Cups and watched the Rangers win their 1994 Championship. Shirley's friends ran the gamut, both in and out of hockey, and this was evident at her memorial service. Hall of Famers Pat LaFontaine, Rod Gilbert, and Lou Lamoriello were in attendance because they respected her work and loved her as a friend.

Anything more I say about Shirley would be like gilding the rose or painting the lily.

Stan Fischler, New York City

Introduction

The very first hockey book I ever read was penned by New York Rangers patriarch Lester Patrick. I discovered it at the Tompkins Park Library in the Bedford-Stuyvesant section of Brooklyn in 1941.

I was ten years old at the time and already a confirmed hockey nut. Devouring every word in the book, I couldn't wait to read more about my favorite sport. In time, I found the likes of a hockey manual by Dartmouth coach Eddie Jeremiah from which, among other things, I learned what "The Quick Wide Lateral Dribble" was all about.

Wherever possible, I sought hockey literature and saved same. When I received a large scrapbook for my tenth birthday, I immediately put it to good use and started what would be a ten-year collection of clippings about not only the National Hockey League but the Eastern Amateur Hockey League and assorted other areas of puck interest.

It was then that I began gravitating to certain writers such as James Burchard of the *New York World-Telegram* and Kerr N. Petrie of the *New York Herald-Tribune*. Instinctively, I began writing short summations of every game I witnessed at Madison Square Garden on Manhattan's Eighth Avenue between 49th and 50th Streets.

I didn't realize it at the time, but not only was hockey well-ensconced in my blood but somewhere in my subconscious there was an inevitable pursuit of life as a hockey writer. Naturally, it didn't happen overnight but rather over a period of time.

After graduating from Brooklyn College in 1954, I went to work for the Rangers in the publicity department as an aide de camp to chief publicist Herb Goren. Just by watching this former hockey writer knock off stories at about a mile a minute, I learned some of the writing craft. Observing top journalists such as Stan Saplin—my primary mentor—I made pivotal contacts.

My one-year (1954–55) Rangers stint enabled me to get my first full-time newspaper job with Hearst's flagship evening broad sheet, *The New York Journal-American*. I spent more than a dozen years at the J-A, highlighted—among other gigs—by coverage of the Rangers.

Ironically, at no time during this writing period—which included New York coverage for *The Hockey News*—did I ever contemplate writing a book. That challenge simply seemed too long and arduous a process for me nor did I expect anyone to arrive on the scene to offer me such a deal.

Then it happened. A buddy, Jack Zanger, who also happened to be an editor at *Sport* magazine, had been doing baseball profile books for an outfit named Grosset and Dunlap. When Zanger was asked to write one about Gordie Howe of the Detroit Red Wings, he declined the offer and instead suggested that I do the biography.

With enormous compunctions, I took on the assignment, not really knowing a heck of a lot what I was doing, but plodding ahead nonetheless. The result was a lot better than I had expected; the book was done and published. Never in my wildest dreams—nightmares included—could I have contemplated that it would be the first of 100 books written by Your's Truly; most of them about hockey.

The game of hockey has dramatically changed—in some cases for the better and some not so good. As a youth I reveled in the fact that stick handlers rushed up and down the rink bareheaded and that goaltenders never wore masks nor were there barriers along the side boards.

It was a simpler, more personal game, bereft of annoying agents, players so wealthy they are practically cartels, and the advent of helmets, face masks, and every other annoyance short of ads on jerseys. Nevertheless, the contemporary game has compensated well for the absence of "Old-Time Hockey."

The game is faster, the players are bigger (not necessarily better), hits are harder, concussions more prevalent, and novelties such as the overtime shootout have spiced up the action. Expansion, which began in 1967—from The Original Six to a Dozen—spread the NHL across the continent.

With a current 30-franchise roster, the league considers further expansion but prefers strengthening weaker franchises such as the Panthers in Sunrise, Florida, and the Coyotes in Phoenix.

Technological advances in television—especially high-definition—have made the NHL product more easily understood to new fans, while outdoor games have produced crowds in excess of 100,000. As a result, the NHL has made record profits, while player salaries have reached stratospheric proportions.

My challenge as an author is to present a comprehensive history that is easy to read from cover to cover. Hence, I've chosen the question-and-answer form. Answers require no more than four paragraphs, enabling me to cover all significant aspect of hockey's growth while speeding the reader through ice tales from 1900 to the present.

Come to think of it, I've come a long way from the Tompkins Park Library to working for Madison Square Garden Networks at hockey games. It's been an exciting ride, and I hope this history comfortably seats you in the hockey's driver's seat.

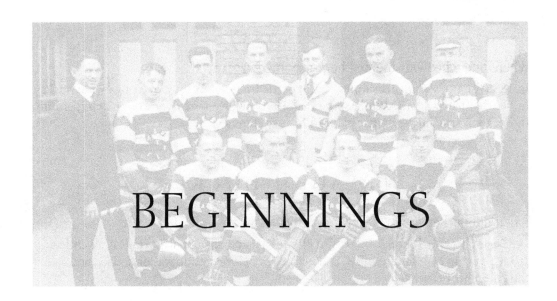

BEGINNINGS

FIRST GAMES

Where does hockey come from?

There are many examples of games throughout history that incorporate hitting a ball on ice. IJscolf, a game resembling on-ice golf, was popular throughout the Middle Ages and the Dutch Golden Age.

Modern ice hockey, however, is believed to have evolved from outdoor stick-and-ball games adapted to the icy conditions in Canada during the 19th century. The games played by British soldiers and people who immigrated to Canada may have influenced the game played on ice skates with sticks.

Another theory is that the game was introduced by immigrants from Iceland after they were forced to immigrate to Canada and the United States after a volcanic eruption in 1875.

Stick-and-ball games date back to pre-Christian times. In Europe, these games included the Irish sport of hurling, the closely related Scottish sport of shinny, and versions of field hockey. It is not totally clear from where modern ice hockey obtained its modern form, because it has been influenced by so many different cultures.

Who organized the first publicized hockey game?

The organizer of the first publicized game in Montreal was a man from Halifax, Nova Scotia, named James Creighton. When a local exhibition of ice lacrosse proved to be a failure, Creighton proposed ice hockey instead and even had sticks shipped from Halifax to Montreal.

Where and when was the first hockey game ever played?

In 1885 the Royal Canadian Rifles, a unit of the Imperial Army, played a game of hockey in Halifax, Nova Scotia. While some historians believe that they were playing shinny rather than true hockey, their place in history stands.

SPREAD OF HOCKEY

When did hockey arrive in New York City?

On December 14, 1894, a rink called the Ice Palace opened at Lexington Avenue and 101st Street in Manhattan. In 1895, the New York Hockey Club was organized and called the Palace its home.

Which NHL publicist created a false derivation of the name "hockey" as a press agent's gimmick?

Hockey has had its share of classic press agents, and one of the best was Jack Filman, a native of Hamilton, Ontario, who became the New York Rangers' publicist in their first season. Filman was given to poetic license. Like many of his ilk during the Roarin' Twenties, Filman liked to exaggerate. In a publicity release, he once explained the origin of hockey, claiming that North American Indians invented the game and called it "hogee." Pressed about the veracity of the term, Filman insisted it was the correct word. "Hogee in English," said Filman, "means 'it hurts!'"

When was six-man hockey invented and who was its creator?

Hockey originally was a seven-man game—six skaters and a goaltender—with one of the skaters being called a "rover." The switch to a six-man game was inspired by Charlie McClurg and an unnamed co-conspirator from the Pittsburgh roster, who set into motion the new format on December 26, 1904. An injury forced McClurg out of the lineup early in the Sault Ste. Marie, Ontario–Pitt contest. The Ontario squad was compelled unwillingly to play the entire game with six men. Fortunately, a Pittsburgh player took off on what newspapers labeled as a "post-Christmas spree." The teams then agreed to use only six skaters, thereby eliminating the "rover."

BIRTH OF THE CUP

Who was Lord Stanley?

In 1888, Queen Victoria appointed Sir Frederick Arthur Stanley to be governor general of Canada. Lord Stanley of Preston, sixth governor general of Canada, donated a silver cup to the Canadians' amateur championship team in 1893. Back then, the trophy was referred to as "The Lord Stanley Challenge Trophy."

What was the Stanley Cup first called?

When the trophy was originally commissioned in 1892, it was called the Dominion Hockey Challenge Cup.

Which team was the first to win the Stanley Cup?

In 1893, one of Montreal's representatives in the Amateur Hockey Association of Canada won the trophy. The Montreal Athletic Association, one of three teams representing the city of Montreal in the league (others were the Crystals and Victorias), won the Cup. The winners included one

Lord Stanley of Preston (1841–1908) donated the silver cup trophy in 1893 that would later come to be known as the Stanley Cup.

goaltender, two defensemen, and six forwards. The schedule consisted of 20 games and the Montreal contingent's 7–1 record included a forfeit win over the Crystals.

Which was the first American team to win the Stanley Cup?

In 1917, the Seattle Metropolitans of the Pacific Coast Hockey Association (PCHA) topped the Montreal Canadiens three games to one to become the first American champs. However, toward the end of the 1915–16 season, the PCHA champion Portland Rosebuds prematurely engraved their names on the trophy before they played against the National Hockey Association (NHA) champion Montreal Canadiens. The Canadiens won the series three games to two, claiming the Cup.

BEST AMATEUR TEAMS

What was the first amateur hockey league in America?

The American Amateur Hockey League (AAHL) was organized in November 1896. Its teams included the St. Nicholas Hockey Club, the New York Athletic Club, the Crescent Athletic Club, and the Skating Club of Brooklyn. One year later, the Baltimore Hockey League was formed, as the game began to expand along the East Coast.

What trophy was considered America's answer to the Stanley Cup?

Not to be outdone by Canada's Stanley Cup, the AAHL winner received the McNaughton Cup, which was almost three feet tall and consisted of 40 pounds of silver.

In 1917 the Seattle Metropolitans (shown here c. 1920) was the first team from the United States to win the Stanley Cup.

Which national hockey championship final was played with two fans on one team dressed in ordinary street clothes?

Although uniformity of hockey apparel was established in the late 1880s, that trend was broken in 1890 when the Quebec Hockey Club played Montreal for the Canadian Amateur Hockey Association championship.

The break in uniformity of uniforms was unintentional on the part of the Quebec club, which arrived at the arena only to learn that they were missing two squad members. Undaunted, the Quebecers added two attending fans to their roster, and they played the national final in their ordinary street clothes.

Which Montreal player led the ECAHA in goals in the 1906–07 season?

Centerman Ernie Russell of the Montreal Wanderers scored an ECAHA-high of 42 goals in just a nine-game season. (The ECAHA was the Eastern Canada Amateur Hockey Association.) Get this: he scored five goals, twice; once he scored six goals; and twice he scored eight goals.

This explains why his team, the Wanderers, went 10–0 during the 1906–07 season and won the Stanley Cup. The Wanderers won the Stanley Cup four times (the 1905–06 season, the 1906–07 season, the 1907–08 season, and the 1909–10 season).

The Montreal Wanderers in 1907, which was in the middle of their three-year winning streak.

Which team interrupted the Montreal Wanderers' attempt to win four Stanley Cups in a row?

For three years in a row, from 1906 to 1908, the Montreal Wanderers won the Stanley Cup. However, in 1908, the ECAHA was renamed the Eastern Canada Hockey Association (ECHA), and because of a rule change, the winner in the ECHA in 1908–09 would automatically receive the Stanley Cup.

The Ottawa Senators had a 10–2 record and the Montreal Wanderers had only a 9–3 record. Therefore, since the Senators won the regular season title (the ECHA title), they won the Stanley Cup in the 1908–09 season. The Wanderers did, however, win the Stanley Cup the following season for their fourth Cup.

THE (OTHER) ALLAN CUP

How did the Allan Cup come into play?

H. Montague Allan, a Montreal businessman and the president of the Montreal Amateur Athletic Association, donated the trophy bearing his name in 1909. In 1908 a split had occurred in Canadian ice hockey competition. Many of the top amateur teams left the Eastern Canada Amateur Hockey Association to form the Intra-Provincial Hockey Union, a league purely for amateurs. It was the decision of the Stanley Cup trustees to award the Cup to the professional ice champion. This meant that there was no trophy for the amateur championship of Canada. Thus, the Allan Cup would become that trophy. Like the Stanley Cup, it would be passed on from champion to champion every year.

Which team was the first to win the Allan Cup?

In 1909 the Ottawa Cliffsides became the first team to be awarded the Allan Cup. The Cliffsides only played for three seasons in the league but briefly reappeared in the Ottawa City Senior League before disappearing for good.

Which teams are permitted to play for the Allan Cup in present-day hockey?

Since 1984, teams in the Senior AAA category have competed for the Allan Cup. Despite the diminishing popularity of senior hockey, the Cup retains an important place in Canadian history. The Cup championship is determined in an annual tournament in the city or town of the host team, playing against regional champions. The original Allan Cup has been retired to the Hockey Hall of Fame. A replica is awarded to the winner now.

Which Canadian area has captured the most Allan Cups?

The twin cities of Port Arthur and Fort William, Ontario, merged to become Thunder Bay, Ontario. Teams from that area have won the Allan Cup ten times. This included four as Port Arthur before the city's amalgamation.

HIGH SCHOOL
AND COLLEGE HOCKEY

How many schools currently offer college hockey?

There are 138 NCAA hockey programs, 59 of which play in Division I. Those 59 teams are spread across six conferences: Atlantic Hockey, Big 10, ECAC Hockey, Hockey East, the National Collegiate Hockey Conference, and the Western Collegiate Hockey Association.

What famous college hockey tournament takes place in Boston each year?

Once a year, four prominent Boston teams (Boston College, Boston University, Northeastern, and Harvard) face off in the Beanpot tournament. B.U. has claimed the trophy 29 times, followed by B.C. with 19 titles, Harvard with 10, and Northeastern with 4.

What are some other notable college hockey rivalries?

College hockey has several intense rivalries. They are:

- The Battle for the Golden Pan—This pits the Colorado College Tigers against the University of Denver Pioneers. The squads have played at least four times a season since 1950.
- Cornell–Harvard—As two rival Ivy League schools and two of the top teams in the ECAC, the Bears and the Crimson have developed an on-ice rivalry as well.
- The Green Line Rivalry—This local match-up pits Boston College against Boston University. It is also known as the Battle of Commonwealth Avenue and dates back to 1918.
- The Holy War on Ice—While the football game between Notre Dame and Boston College is dubbed the Holy War, the teams actually met on the ice before they clashed on the gridiron.

Fierce rivalries also exist between Michigan and Michigan State, New Hampshire and Dartmouth, and New Hampshire and Maine.

Which state is famous for its massive high school hockey tournament?

The Minnesota State High School League Tournament has drawn more than 100,000 fans more than 20 times in its history, making it the largest state sports tournament in the country in terms of attendance and viewership.

For whom is college hockey's most outstanding player award named?

The award is named for Hobey Baker, who learned hockey at St. Paul's School in New Hampshire before playing for the Princeton Tigers. He became recognized as one of the best amateur hockey players of the era. During World War I, Baker became a member of the 141st Aero Squadron. Shortly after the war, Baker received his orders to return home but wanted to take one final flight before leaving his men. There was a plane on the airfield that had just been repaired and was in need of a test flight, which Baker volunteered to fly. A few hundred yards off the runway, the plane crashed; Baker survived the crash but died in the ambulance shortly after. In 1981, the Hobey Baker Award was created to honor both his legacy and his natural skill on the ice.

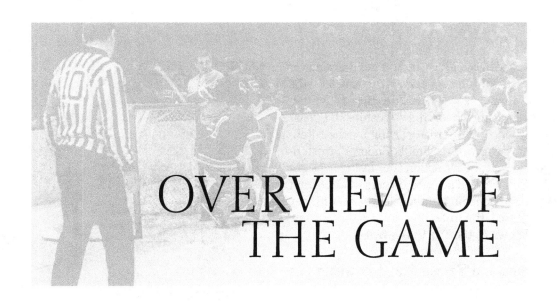

OVERVIEW OF THE GAME

THE RULES
AND RULE CHANGES

What is the position known as the "rover"?

The rover was a term used for a player without a set position. His job was to roam the ice and go where needed. In 1910 the rover position was removed from some but not all leagues. Instead of there being seven players, a few leagues switched to six players on the ice at one time (three forwards, two defensemen, and a goalie). In contemporary hockey the term "rover" is used to informally describe fast, rushing offensive defensemen, such as former NHL star Scott Niedermayer. That type of player leaves his normal position to create offensive scoring chances.

During the 1918–19 season, the NHL revolutionized the game by introducing what form of rule changes?

During the 1918–19 season, the NHL introduced the two blue lines, 20 feet from the center of the ice. This created three playing zones and allowed forward passing in the 40-foot neutral, or center, ice area. Suddenly, by painting two lines on the surface of the ice, the sport changed from an "onside" game to an "offside" game. The game had been transformed from a sport of mostly stickhandling to a game that included passing. That same year the NHL began crediting players with assists, and not just goals.

What is the "Trushinski Bylaw" and how did it get its name?

In March 1939 Toronto Maple Leafs left wing George Parsons was injured in a game against the Chicago Blackhawks. As a result he lost his left eye. NHL president Frank Calder in-

9

voked bylaw 12:6, which states that a player with only one eye cannot participate in the National Hockey League. Bylaw 12:6 became known as the "Trushinski Bylaw" when a defenseman playing for the Kitchener Greenshirts, Frank "Snoozer" Trushinski, returned to action after losing the sight in one eye. The NHL owners did not want this happening in their league and so they passed the rule that informally became known as the Trushinski Bylaw.

A Zamboni is a large ice-scraping and cleaning machine used to smooth out and resurface the ice for safe play.

What is a "Zamboni" and for whom was it named?

A Zamboni is a combined ice-scraper-cleaner that also resurfaces the ice with a new water cover. In most leagues it is put into use after each period. As a result, ice blemishes disappear before your eyes as the vehicle makes its way around and around the rink.

The name comes from the inventor, Frank J. Zamboni, who began his experiments in 1942 in hopes of finding a quick, efficient way to resurface the ice at his skating rink in Paramount, California. The Zamboni takes the snow off the rink's surface while it lays down a thin coat of hot water. The water then freezes, leaving a fresh, even layer of shimmering ice. The first single-driver Zamboni made its debut in 1949. It is now possible for one man to lay down a new ice surface in ten minutes, where it once took half a dozen men an hour and a half to do the job with hoses and swabs.

What year was the red line introduced in NHL play?

In 1943–44, the center red line made its debut. It was introduced at the urging of New York Rangers manager Frank Boucher, who was a member of the NHL's Rules Committee. Boucher believed that the red line would speed up the game by allowing longer passes than previously allowed with only two blue lines.

What was the Gretzky Rule?

The Gretzky Rule was a nickname affixed to an addition made in the NHL rule book. Its primary purpose after adoption in the late 1980s was to prevent the powerhouse Edmonton Oilers, whose star was NHL great Wayne Gretzky, from having more open ice. The Oilers were so dominant in four-on-four situations that the league changed the rules on offsetting minor penalties. Instead of teams facing offsetting penalties playing four-on-four, they would continue to play at full strength. The rule was eventually changed back to teams playing four-on-four during offsetting penalties.

What was imposed prior to the start of the 2005–6 season that limited how much a team could pay their players per year?

The negotiations for the 2005–12 Collective Bargaining Agreement revolved primarily around player salaries. About 75 percent of the teams' revenues were spent on salaries for its players, which was a percentage far higher than any other sport in North America. NHL commissioner Gary Bettman presented many concepts to the National Hockey League Players Association (NHLPA), all of which revolved around the idea of imposing a salary cap, something the NHLPA was strongly against. The owners imposed a lockout, which forced the NHL to cancel the entire 2004–5 season. The lockout finally ended when the NHLPA agreed on a hard salary cap based on the revenues of the league. The NHL did, however, implement revenue sharing, which would allow for a higher cap figure. At the start of the 2005–6 season, the NHL's first salary cap was set at $39 million per team and no more than $7.8 million or 20 percent of the cap for a single player. Since then, the cap has fluctuated on a year-to-year basis.

What major part of today's game was introduced at the start of the 2005–6 season?

The NHL owners decided that rather than having a game decided with a tie after the overtime period, they would adopt a more melodramatic finish—the shootout. In its original form, the shootout consisted of three players from each team who would each skate one-on-one against the opposition's goalie and try to score a goal. After both teams' players took their shots, the team with the most goals would be awarded the victory. If necessary, the teams would use more than three shooters and never the same shooter twice. The winning team would be awarded two points in the standings (same as any victory), and the losing team would be awarded one point. If a player scored in the shootout, it did not count towards his personal season statistics. For example, if a player scored twice in regulation and once in the shootout, only the two goals in regulation count towards his stats. He would not have recorded a hat trick. From its inception, a bloc of purists opposed the shootout. By the end of the 2014–15 season, opponents of the shootout forced changes that in the future would limit use of the shootout.

How did the penalty shot and the delayed penalty become a part of hockey?

The idea for the penalty shot was inspired by Lester and Frank Patrick while the hockey-playing brothers and, later, operators of the Pacific Coast Hockey League visited England. They had gone to a soccer match and were enthralled by the excitement produced by the penalty shot in that game. Upon their return to the Pacific Coast League, the penalty shot became a part of their ice hockey rules.

Then, speeding the flow of a hockey game became an obsession with the Patricks. They were particularly appalled by the way a referee could slow the game down to a virtual halt by an endless series of penalties. At times, each side could be reduced to two men including the goaltenders, and the games would become a bore. As a result, the Patricks invented the delayed-penalty system that ensured four skaters on the ice no

11

In a penalty shot a player is allowed to take a shot at the goal with no opposing players in the way with the exception of the goalie.

matter how many infractions were called. There is also the delayed penalty, in which a team is called for a penalty but play continues so long as the penalized team doesn't touch the puck. In those cases, the team that will soon have a man advantage will pull its goalie, giving it a temporary 6-on-5 advantage, so long as the penalized team hasn't yet touched the puck.

For which change in officiating can we credit ice hockey referee Fred C. "Old Wag" Waghorne Sr.?

Fred Waghorne was born in England and then moved to Canada. He was interested in rugby, lacrosse, and ice hockey and is best known for his career as a referee. Many of the decisions he made on the ice rink became long-term rules in both amateur and professional ice hockey. Waghorne is credited with several changes and innovations to ice hockey rules, such as:

- The use of a whistle instead of the customary cow bell to stop play when fans started bringing their own cowbells to disrupt game play.

- The acceptance of professional referees in amateur hockey games.

- The practice of dropping the puck from a few feet up at face-off rather than placing it directly on the ice, which limited player contact with the referee's shins and ankles during face-offs.

• The ruling that if half of a broken hockey puck entered the net, no goal was counted—a rule that led to the development of one-piece pucks.

Prior to 1900, a face-off began when the puck was placed on the ice by the referee, who then had to make certain each center was lined up correctly. However, this often led to sticks hitting tender areas of the official's anatomy. Waghorne debuted a new method in 1900. He simply dropped the puck, and soon the new face-off method was eventually adopted.

In 1900, Waghorne had a situation where a puck split in two, and only one half ended up in the goal. After much deliberation, he ruled it as "no goal" because the official definition of a puck included specific dimensions, and since the piece of rubber in the goal did not meet these specifications, it could not be a puck. He then instituted the rule that the entire puck must cross the line for a goal to count.

How did the blue line come into being?

In addition to legalizing kicking the puck in certain areas of the rink, hockey entrepreneurs Lester and Frank Patrick decided that the addition of blue lines would enhance play in their Pacific Coast Hockey League during the 1914–15 season.

To preview the fans, Lester provided the local newspapers with detailed explanations of the purposes of blue lines, and the cities in each league printed them.

Some confusion about the rules resulted, and Lester liked to joke about it. He frequently told the story of the day a fan asked his crack defenseman, Ernie "Moose" Johnson, to explain the blue-line rules. Johnson laughed. "What's the blue line all about?" he repeated. "Don't ask me, bud. As far as I'm concerned there's only *one* rule in hockey—you take the puck on your stick and you shoot it in the net!"

How did Lester Patrick change the rules for the manner in which a goalie could make saves?

Although Lester was basically a defenseman and also played rover in the seven-man game, it was his affection for goaltending that would occasion a handful of remarkable exploits between the pipes. The earliest of these occurred in Victoria when Patrick's goalie, Hec Fowler, was ejected from a game. Lester decided to replace him but chose not to wear the traditional pads because he found them too cumbersome.

Lester went to the nets with the simple defenseman's attire and foiled all shots hurled by the Vancouver team. When it was over, Patrick dismissed the feat with typi-

---

What rule change altered the way hockey was played in 1928?

In 1928, forward passing within each zone (offensive, defensive, and neutral) was allowed for the first time. This created a more free-flowing, open game.

cal logic. "I worked on a simple principle—only one puck could come at a time. I stopped each shot and we won!"

After gaining some practical experience in the nets, Lester decided it was ill-advised to retain a rule that forced goaltenders to remain on their feet when making saves. The Patricks promptly changed the regulation, and from that point on goaltenders began flopping, splitting, and doing *anything* possible to keep the puck out of the net.

In the modern game, players rarely take shifts of more than two to three minutes. How was it different in the early days when stars such as Joe Malone played?

Joe Malone remembered that in the early days of the NHL, some players remained on the ice for up to 50 to 55 minutes. "They didn't bother too much about changing lines, only individuals," Malone remembered. "There were only about nine or ten players on each team. I used to stickhandle in close and beat the goalie with a wrist shot. There was no forward passing allowed in the offensive zone and not as much scrambling as there was later. We wore shoulder and elbow pads, but the equipment wasn't too heavy and this was a good thing considering the number of minutes we had to play each game. The goalkeepers stood up a lot more. There were no slapshots, but much more passing and stickhandling than in the modern era."

What rule changes were enacted at the start of the 2005–6 season?

After experimenting with many rule changes in 2004–5 in the American Hockey League, many of the rule changes from the previous year were adopted. For example:

- The league introduced shootouts at the end of overtime if the score remained tied.
- If a team ices the puck, it is not allowed to make a line change afterwards.
- The "two-line offside pass" rule was abolished.

New Jersey Devils player John Madden takes a shot at Rangers goalie Kevin Weekes in a 2005 shootout.

- Goaltender equipment was reduced in size by 11 percent.
- All referees are now equipped with wireless microphones so they can announce penalties over the public address system, similar to NFL referees.
- Any player who shoots the puck over the glass (without deflection) from his own defensive zone will be penalized for delay of game.

EQUIPMENT

How did the hockey puck develop its present shape?

The hockey puck has not always looked the way we know it today. In the second half of the 1800s, hockey was still being played with a hard rubber ball. The problem with the rubber ball was that it frequently bounced over the low end boards and into the crowd, or high out of the rink and through an arena window. One night, after about $350 worth of his windows had been broken, an irate rink owner got ahold of a stray ball and, using a knife borrowed from a fan, cut off the top and bottom parts and returned the middle section to the players.

The game continued with the newly shaped puck. Instead of bouncing around wildly, the puck slid smoothly across the ice. The idea caught on quickly and was adopted around the world of hockey.

Which culture is credited with the invention of the ice skate?

The Dutch are most often credited with the invention of the ice skate.

STRATEGIES

What are the strategies of hockey?

The objective of both teams in an ice hockey game is to advance the puck into the opposing team's defensive zone and get it into the net, or goal. There are several methods and strategies that a team will use to score and to prevent the opponent from scoring.

On offense, the players move the puck towards the offensive zone by passing the puck to each other or by skating and carrying it themselves, using a skill called stickhandling. Using these skills, a team can creatively get past the opposing team's defenders.

Another common tactic is to shoot the puck to the end of the opponent's defensive zone once past the center line and then retrieve the puck. This is known as a dump-and-chase, or chip-and-chase, and is often used when the opponent clogs the neutral zone with defenders and makes it difficult to carry the puck over the blue line. However,

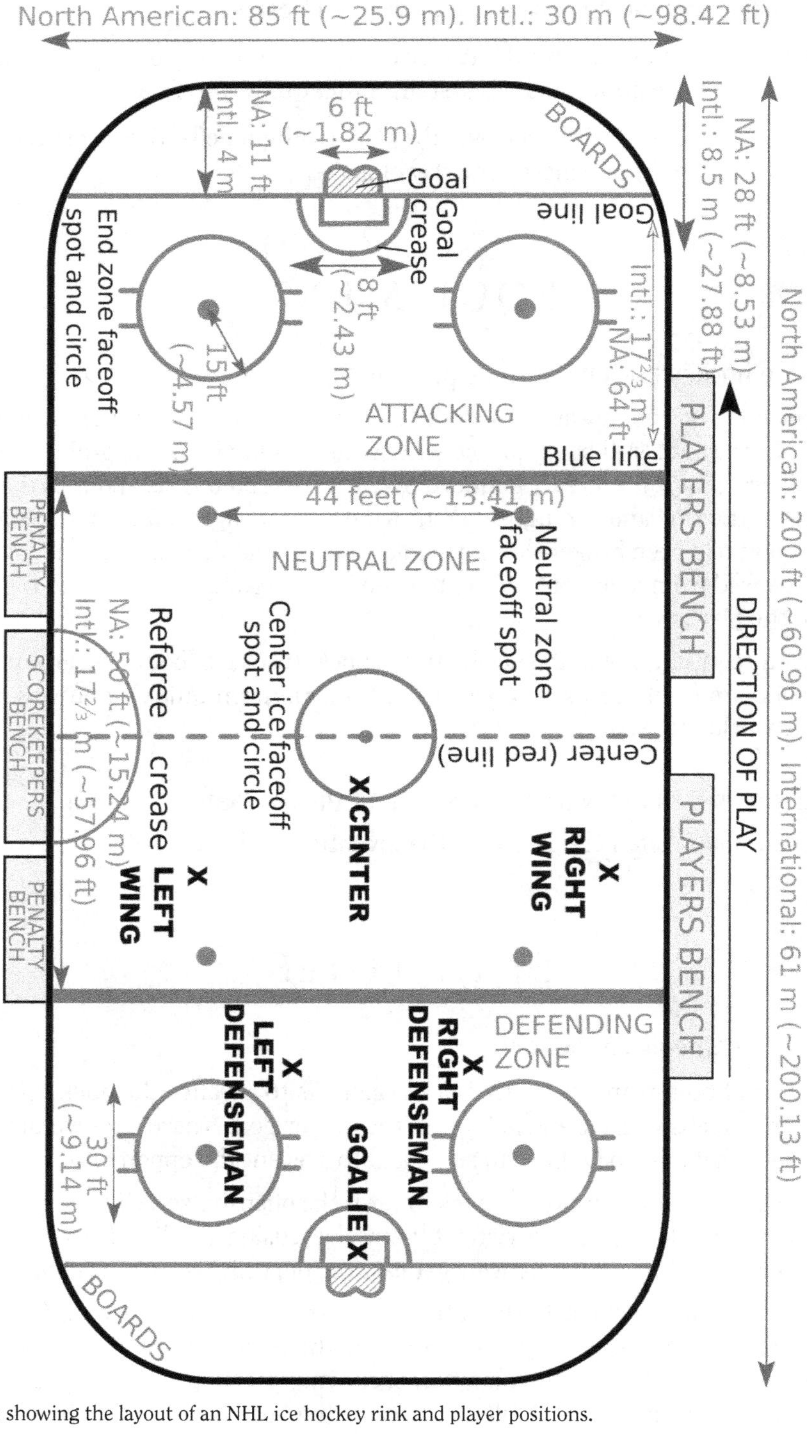

North American: 85 ft (~25.9 m). Intl.: 30 m (~98.42 ft)

6 ft (~1.82 m)

NA: 11 ft Intl.: 4 m

Goal crease

Goal crease

8 ft (~2.43 m)

15 ft (~4.57 m)

End zone faceoff spot and circle

BOARDS

Goal line

Intl.: 17⅔ m NA: 64 ft

ATTACKING ZONE

Blue line

NA: 28 ft (~8.53 m) Intl.: 8.5 m (~27.88 ft)

North American: 200 ft (~60.96 m). International: 61 m (~200.13 ft)

PLAYERS BENCH

DIRECTION OF PLAY

44 feet (~13.41 m)

NEUTRAL ZONE

Neutral zone faceoff spot

Center ice faceoff spot and circle

PENALTY BENCH

SCOREKEEPERS BENCH

PENALTY BENCH

NA: 50 ft (~15.24 m) Intl.: 17⅔ m (~57.96 ft)

Referee crease

Center (red line)

X CENTER

X RIGHT WING

X LEFT WING

PLAYERS BENCH

30 ft (~9.14 m)

X LEFT DEFENSEMAN

X RIGHT DEFENSEMAN

DEFENDING ZONE

GOALIE X

BOARDS

16   A diagram showing the layout of an NHL ice hockey rink and player positions.

if the puck is shot in before crossing the center line, icing will be called, and a face-off will take place in the offensive team's defensive zone.

Once inside the offensive zone, a team will try to create a scoring opportunity. This can be done by shooting the puck on goal, or passing the puck to someone who is open for a better shot. Often, a team will work the puck along the boards and perimeter and try to keep possession until the puck-carrier finds an unmarked player, preferably in the slot, or until he finds a good opportunity to shoot. This is called cycling the puck.

Teams will often try to send at least one player to play near the front of the net. Most goals are scored in a small area only a few feet in front of the goal, often on rebounds from previous shots. A common tactic teams will use is to have players rush the net after a shot, looking for a loose puck. This is called "crashing the net."

The defensive team has several methods to regain possession of the puck. If the offensive team is still behind its own blue line, the defensive team will often send at least one player to pursue the puck and try to retrieve it. This is called forechecking.

If a team is defending within its own defensive zone, it will typically try to keep the opponent to the outside, where it is more difficult to score. Defensive players will pursue the puck and either try to poke-check the puck away, or hit the puck away with their own sticks, or body check the puck-carrier to try to separate him from the puck.

A priority of the defense is to make sure the front of the net is covered. If the puck winds up in this area after a rebound, the defense will often try to get to the puck first and shoot the puck away.

POSITIONS

What are the positions of ice hockey?

There are four different positions in contemporary hockey. They are: center, winger, defenseman, and goaltender.

Centers cover the middle areas of the ice and often shoulder the heaviest responsibilities of any of the forwards. On offense, since they tend to handle the puck the most, centers usually function as the playmaker and typically rack up more assists than goals. Defensively, they are responsible for covering the slot area, as well as helping out the defensemen on the perimeter.

Wingers play the perimeter of the rink, flanking the center. There are two wingers on the ice, taking the left and right sides. On offense, the wingers typically skate down their respective sides and try to "stretch" the defense with their speed. On defense, they are responsible for covering the opposing defensemen on the points and making themselves available for a pass once possession is won back.

Defensemen are primarily responsible for preventing the opposition from scoring and getting shots on goal. There are two defensemen on the ice, taking the left and right **17** sides. On defense, they cover lower areas of the defensive zone and the front of the net. They try to pressure the opposing forwards and keep them to the outside. On offense, they play just inside the blue line or the point, and are responsible for keeping the puck inside the zone and taking hard shots to the net. While a lot of defensemen are "stay-at-home" types and focus on their defensive responsibilities, some defensemen are more offensive-minded and will often rush the puck themselves and set up forwards for goals.

Goaltenders provide the last line of defense for the team. They are responsible for stopping shots taken on goal. They wear heavier equipment, such as chest protectors and pads, to protect themselves from heavy shots. While goaltenders of the past often played a "stand-up" style and made saves on their feet, today's goaltenders rely on the "butterfly" style, dropping down to their knees to cover the lower parts of the ice. Goaltenders also often come out of the net to play the puck to support the defensemen when necessary.

Name the defenseman who changed hockey's style by actually trying to score goals?

As a defenseman in the early days of professional hockey, Lester Patrick could never understand why forwards and *only* forwards were the puck-carriers. In 1902, for example, defensemen had only one assignment—stop the attack.

"In Brandon, Manitoba, where Lester had signed with the local team, Patrick was expected to behave like a defense player," wrote hockey historian Elmer Ferguson, "but instinct and temperament proved too strong."

Rather than resort to the prosaic and boring technique of lifting the puck into the enemy's end of the rink when he captured it, Lester stunned the Brandon spectators by digging his skates into the ice and rushing headlong toward the goal. Although he missed the shot, he left both the opposition and his teammates awed by his unorthodox performance, and at the end of the period, he was summoned to the Board of Directors' room, where he was questioned about his antics.

Lester replied with impeccable logic that was his hallmark in later years: "Why not let defensemen rush if it works—and if the fans like it?" In the next period, Lester promptly scored a goal, the crowd loved it, and from that point on, defensemen have had as much a part of the attack as the two wings and the center. Conceivably, if Lester had not decided to make that rush in Brandon, Bobby Orr might never have been more than a defenseman who hurled the puck from one end of the Boston Garden to the other.

GOALTENDING

When was the butterfly style of goaltending prohibited in the NHL?

Believe it or not, there was a rule in the books during the NHL's first season (1917–18) that prohibited a goalie from lying on the ice to make a save. Clint Benedict even picked

> ## Who was the shortest goaltender in NHL history?
>
> **R**oy Worters. Nicknamed "Shrimp" for being only 5'3" and 130 lbs., Worters played twelve successful seasons in the NHL backstopping the Pittsburgh Pirates, Montreal Canadiens, and New York Americans. Worters won the Hart and Vezina trophies for his efforts during the 1929 and 1931 seasons, respectively. He was inducted into the Hockey Hall of Fame in 1969.

up the disparaging nickname "Now I Lay Me Down." Thankfully for him, the rule was repealed in January 1918.

Who was the goaltender for the first U.S.-based team to win the Stanley Cup?

Harry "Hap" Holmes was in goal for the Seattle Metropolitans when they defeated the Montreal Canadiens to win the Stanley Cup in 1917. Holmes posted a 3–1 record in the best-of-five series against the Habs. He was inducted into the Hockey Hall of Fame in 1972.

Who holds the NHL record for most shots faced and saves made in one game?

Chicago Blackhawks goaltender Sam LoPresti faced a whopping 83 shots against the Boston Bruins in 1941. Though the Hawks ended up losing 3–2 to the Bruins, LoPresti still managed to make 80 saves for his club.

Which two goalies faced off in the first NHL game to ever be played on Christmas Day?

Ivan Mitchell backstopped the Toronto St. Pats to a 5–4 win over Georges Vezina and the Montreal Canadiens in the first NHL game played on Christmas Day, 1920.

Who was the first goaltender to allow a player to score a hat trick in one period?

In 1934, Bill Beveridge of the St. Louis Eagles was the unfortunate goaltender who allowed Maple Leafs forward Harvey "Busher" Jackson to actually score four goals in the third period. The Leafs cruised to a 5–2 victory over Beveridge and the Eagles.

Who was the first goaltender to be pulled from a game to allow an extra attacker?

In 1940, head coach Paul Thompson of the Chicago Blackhawks pulled goaltender Sam LoPresti while losing to the Toronto Maple Leafs. It was the first time pulling the goaltender was used as a tactic in an NHL game. Ultimately, Toronto held on to win the game.

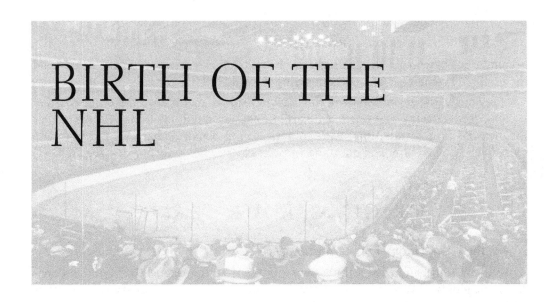

BIRTH OF THE NHL

NHA–NHL BACKROOM BATTLE

Which Bulldog was a Phantom?

Joe Malone's first major goal-scoring season came in 1912–13 with the Quebec Bulldogs. He netted 43 goals in 20 National Hockey Association (NHA) games, including
seven in one game against Toronto.

That spring, when Quebec played Sydney, Nova Scotia, in a Stanley Cup series, Malone scored nine goals in a single game. He was so quick on the ice that he was granted
the nickname "Phantom Joe."

Which team in 1912–13 blew away the competition with two of their most artistic and tough players?

The Quebec Bulldogs dominated the NHA in 1912–13. The Bulldogs went 16–4 and
scored 112 goals, allowing 75. Skillful Joe Malone and diminutive, but speedy Tommy
Smith led the offense. On defense, Quebec boasted two of the toughest stickhandlers of
any era. The most notorious was "Bad" Joe Hall. His sidekick, Harry Mummery, was no
less feared, and together they regularly intimidated the opposition.

Who was the first official scorer the National Hockey League ever had?

Jim Larkin of Ottawa, who had been a sportswriter with the *Ottawa Citizen* when the
NHL was organized, held that original statistical job. At the time the league was formed
(1917), scorekeepers were unnecessary since statistics were unheard of in the league
offices, operated by Frank Calder.

"Somebody suggested to Calder," Larkin recalled, "that hockey start keeping track
of things like they were doing in baseball. The coaches screamed. They said if we started

keeping track of who got the goals, there'd be no team play anymore. Every man would turn selfish. I remember one of them saying it would kill the game."

Previously, the sports editor of the local newspaper maintained the only record of scorers. "I became the first one," said Larkin, "because Ottawa had the first game after the idea was brought in. All we were told was to put down the name of the man who scored, who helped him, and not to name two helpers when only one deserved it."

ORIGINAL FOUR TEAMS

Why is the term "Original Six" a misnomer?

When the NHL began in 1917, there were four teams in the league: the Montreal Canadiens, the Montreal Wanderers, the Ottawa Senators, and the Toronto Arenas. The other teams considered part of the "Original Six" joined later (the Boston Bruins in 1924, the New York Rangers and Chicago Blackhawks in 1926, and Detroit in 1932). The Wanderers and Senators folded while the Arenas became the St. Pats and later the Maple Leafs. By the 1941–42 season, there were seven teams in the NHL: Boston, Toronto, Montreal, Chicago, and Detroit, plus two from New York—the Rangers and Americans. When the Americans dropped out in the summer of 1942, the NHL then had its "Original" Six.

What does the "H" in the Montreal Canadiens' logo stand for?

No, it does not connote "Habitants" as some people believe. The H stands for Hockey since the official French name for the team is Club de Hockey Canadien.

Which team won the first NHL Championship?

While the Stanley Cup was awarded in previous years, the Toronto Arenas claimed the first National Hockey League championship in the 1917–18 season. The Arenas took home the title after defeating the Montreal Canadiens in a two-game playoff. The Arenas then faced the Vancouver Millionaires of the Pacific Coast Hockey Association in the Stanley Cup Finals and took the series three games to two.

How did the Toronto Maple Leafs get their name?

The franchise in Toronto was first known as the Arenas, as they were owned by the Toronto Arena Company. In 1919, the club was sold to the owners of a team in the Ontario Hockey Association known as the St. Patricks and took on that name for themselves. In 1927, the team changed hands again and was purchased by Conn Smythe. Inspired by patriotism, he changed the team's name to the Maple Leafs and switched their colors to blue and white for the Canadian sky and snow respectively.

Why did the Montreal Wanderers only exist for one season?

In 1917, the Wanderers' two best players, Odie and Sprague Cleghorn, were forced to sit out a season due to a wartime exemption. The club, desperate to remain relevant, requested that the NHL provide them with replacement players from the other teams. Before the issue could be determined, however, the Montreal Arena burned down. While the Wanderers could have played in the Jubilee Rink in the French part of the city, they refused since they represented the English-speaking population. Consequently, the franchise folded.

FIRST NHL STARS

Which member of the Hockey Hall of Fame and Stanley Cup winner served as a pilot in World War I?

Frank Frederickson. One of the few big-leaguers of Icelandic descent, Frederickson was captain of the University of Manitoba hockey team at the outbreak of World War I and enlisted in the armed forces. Following the war, Frederickson returned to North America and played on the Canadian hockey team in the 1920 Winter Olympics in Antwerp, Belgium.

From there, he went on to NHL stardom but always spoke fondly of his war experiences. Professionally, Fredrickson played for the Victoria Cougars (in the Pacific Coast Hockey Association). He also played for the Boston Bruins, the Pittsburgh Pirates, and the Detroit Falcons in the NHL. He helped Victoria win the Stanley Cup in 1925.

He remembered it as follows: "Everything was moving along well in school and I would have graduated in 1918 except that World War I had broken out and a lot of my chums were joining the 196th University Battalion.

"I felt a duty to go along so I joined up, but before they sent me overseas I switched to the 223rd Scandinavian Battalion. When I got to the other side I joined the Air Force, which was really a laugh. In those days the planes were more like box kites. I'd climb in the front, peer around and see a rudder that looked like two organ pedals. The joy stick seemed like the top of a pair of scissors.

"My plane was a Maurice-Farman that had pusher-type engines and a total speed of about 75 miles per hour. We did our training in Egypt of all places and if we were good enough we graduated on to Bristol Scouts and Avros, which I did. Then, they transferred me back to Italy. I really was enjoying my trip across the Mediterranean at that time."

Which National Hockey League player scored seven goals in a game?

Joe Malone. Originally a star with Quebec, Malone joined the Canadiens—along with "Bad" Joe Hall—in time for the 1917–18 season. According to those who saw Malone in action, he was one of the greatest all-round scorers ever. "He might have been the most prolific scorer of all time if they had played more games in those days," said Frank J.

23

Selke Sr., the former Canadiens' managing director, who remembers Malone as a young professional.

"It was amazing the way Joe used to get himself in position to score." In that respect, his style was similar to Gordie Howe's. Joe was no Howie Morenz as far as speed was concerned. But he was a clean player like Dave Keon and Frank Boucher. On the other hand, though, centerman Joe never took a backward step from anybody and had one of the best pivots of all time.

Joe cracked the record book on the night of January 31, 1920, when he scored seven goals in a game in Quebec City. Three of the goals were scored within two minutes in the third period. Unfortunately, the game was played on a night when the temperature hovered around 25 degrees *below zero* and only a handful of fans turned up at the rink.

Joe Malone

Which Hall of Famer trained on champagne?

Didier (Pit) Pitre. One of the earliest of Canada's hockey stars and the first to sign with the Canadiens, the French-Canadian Pitre emerged as a hero of the Habs in the early 1920s. Weighing nearly 220 pounds, Pitre could skate at a tremendous clip, and his shots were so hard they were known to splinter the end boards.

Like many of the hell-for-leather skaters who played in the Roarin' Twenties, Pitre was not much for observing training rules. "When reinforced by a pint of ice-cold champagne, drained at a gulp, between periods," wrote veteran Montreal scribe Elmer Ferguson, "Pitre could step out and blaze around at an amazing pace."

EXPANSION

When did the NHL first begin to expand?

After battling many challenges in its infancy, including the dissolution of the Montreal Wanderers franchise and competing with other major leagues for players, the NHL found itself to be a very profitable four-team establishment. By the end of the 1923–24 season, it had thriving teams in Montreal, Ottawa, Toronto, and Hamilton. The men of the NHL decided that now was the time to grow.

The league got applications from many areas for franchises, including from Providence, New York, and Philadelphia. However, for the 1924–25 season, the league would add teams in Boston and Montreal. The Boston Bruins were owned by Charles Adams, a grocery store financier, and the Montreal Professional Hockey Club, later nicknamed by the press as the Maroons, would appeal to that city's English population.

Boston hired Art Ross, a prominent figure in Canadian sporting circles, to manage and coach the team. Despite his best efforts, which included recruiting expeditions as far as Sault Ste. Marie, Ontario, and Duluth, Minnesota, he did not find much talent. The team struggled in its first season, winning only six games and losing 24 times. Worse, the team struggled to draw fans, as the established amateur teams often drew better than the Bruins.

The Maroons, on the other hand, had an immediate following from the city's English population. The team called the Montreal Forum its home and drew 5,000 people for the opening game, and on December 27, the Maroons packed the Forum with 11,000 spectators in a contest against the Canadiens. Despite its box office success, the Maroons did not fare much better than the Bruins on the ice, winning only nine games that season.

Has a hockey team ever gone on strike?

Yes. In the spring of 1925, the Hamilton Tigers enjoyed the best record of any team in the National Hockey League. As league champions, they drew a bye in the playoffs and were slated to meet the winner of the Toronto–Montreal series.

Redvers Green, a star for the Tigers, claimed, however, that the Hamilton players had played more games than were called for in their contracts, and unless they were paid additional money, they would not compete in the playoffs.

When the players refused to compromise, league president Frank Calder fined and suspended them, thus making the winner of the Toronto–Montreal series league champions. As a result of the strike and suspension of the players, the Hamilton franchise was sold to New York City bootlegger "Big" Bill Dwyer. The team's name was changed to the New York Americans and became the first New York NHL club starting in the 1925–26 season.

Who were the Pittsburgh Pirates?

Prior to the NHL arriving, Pittsburgh had a rich hockey history. Hockey was firmly established as a popular winter activity, and Pittsburgh had previously hosted a pro hockey

Which team was the NHL's first expansion team?

This distinction goes to the Quebec Bulldogs, which joined the league for its 1919–20 season. They struggled for one season before relocating to Hamilton and becoming the Tigers. The same team became the New York Americans in 1925 but continued to struggle.

team in the old International Professional League in the first decade of the 1900s. In 1915, the Pittsburgh Yellow Jackets were founded and became a powerhouse in the United States Amateur Hockey Association during the mid-twenties, winning back-to-back championships in 1924 and 1925.

With the NHL wanting to expand further, the league granted a franchise to Pittsburgh for the 1925–26 season. The team would mostly be composed of players from the Yellow Jackets, and immediately there was skepticism of how well the team would do without full-fledged professionals.

The Pirates, named after the major league baseball team in the same city, would prove the doubters wrong. The team managed to sign star defenseman Lionel Conacher, who had previously played for the Yellow Jackets, for a staggering $7,500 per season. Player-coach Odie Cleghorn, himself an aging former star player, became the first coach to utilize line changes regularly. He would use three forward lines and change them every six to eight minutes. This new tactic allowed the Pirates to stay fresh, and they finished a surprising third in the league in their first season.

In addition to Conacher, many of the amateur Yellow Jackets proved to be able to more than hold their own against professional competition. Goaltender Roy Worters immediately became one of the league's top netminders, posting the second-best goals-against average (GAA) in the league at 1.90. Forwards Hib Milks, Duke McCurry, and Harold Darragh all posted double-digit goal totals that season as well.

While the team would miss the playoffs the following season, the Pirates would make the playoffs again in the 1927–28 season but would lose in the first round to the eventual Stanley Cup winners, the New York Rangers. That season would prove to be the team's last playoff appearance, and the team would struggle both on the ice and in the box office the next few seasons.

Which was the first U.S. club to compete in the NHL?

The Boston Bruins became the first U.S. entry to join the league in 1924. Two years later, three U.S. teams—New York Rangers, Chicago Black Hawks (later spelled Blackhawks), and Detroit Cougars—were admitted into the league.

Where was the first NHL game played outside of Canada held?

In December 1924, the Boston Bruins took on the Montreal Maroons in Boston. The American squad won 2–1.

Who were the New York Americans?

Along with the Pittsburgh Pirates, the NHL put another team in the United States for the 1925–26 season, in the glitz and glamour of New York City and Madison Square Garden.

The team would be nicknamed the Americans and was managed and coached by Tommy Gorman, who had won three Stanley Cups managing the Ottawa Senators earlier in the decade. The owner was "Big" Bill Dwyer, one of the most prominent players

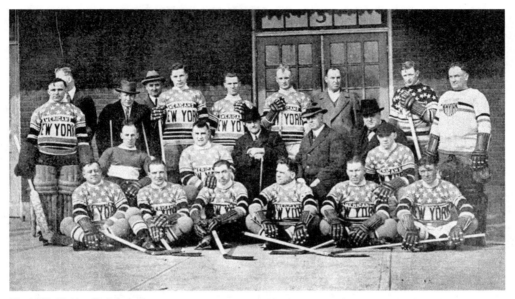

The 1925–26 New York Americans.

in New York's criminal underworld. He made his fortune in the bootlegging business and began to invest the money into legitimate outlets such as the Americans.

The battle for players with other pro leagues in the west was still going strong, so Gorman and Dwyer came up with a creative way to stock the Americans with players: they simply bought the contracts of the entire Hamilton Tigers roster, which had finished first in the league the previous season, for $75,000.

The franchise's first-ever home game, against the Canadiens, saw the Americans lose 3–1. However, the game was a sellout, with over 18,000 in attendance.

While the team was a disappointment on the ice, finishing only fifth, it was a humongous hit with the New Yorkers in the box office. So much so that the Garden management wanted to get a team of its own.

When did the Rangers, Blackhawks, and Red Wings begin?

The NHL continued its aggressive expansion into the 1926–27 season and awarded three new franchises to New York, Chicago, and Detroit. With the Western Canada Hockey League, the only other major pro league, on the brink of folding, there would be plenty of players available for these new teams.

After the financial success of the Americans in their inaugural season, Tex Rickard and the Madison Square Garden management wanted a team of their own and figured that the city could manage two teams. They would be granted a franchise, which would be called the Rangers. The team was assembled by Conn Smythe, but he had a falling-out with the Garden management and was dismissed before the team ever played a game.

Lester Patrick, cofounder of the old Pacific Coast Hockey Associations, would manage and coach the team for their first seasons.

The Chicago team was originally owned by a group led by former football star Huntington Hardwick, but it was sold after only one month to the city's coffee tycoon, Frederic McLaughlin. The team was named the Black Hawks, named after the army division that McLaughlin once served in. The team was composed of players from the WCHL's Portland Rosebuds, who Hardwick had purchased for $100,000 when he owned the team.

The NHL got five applications from five different groups for the Detroit franchise, and the league awarded the new team to Wesley Seybourn and John Townsend, who represented a large group of investors formed by sports promoter Charles Hughes. The team would be composed of players from the WCHL's Victoria Cougars, who the team purchased in similar fashion to Chicago. The Detroit franchise would be called the Cougars, just like the name of the team the players were leaving.

Where did the Chicago Blackhawks get their name and logo?

During World War I, Blackhawks owner Frederic McLaughlin served in a machine gun battalion nicknamed the Black Hawks. When he returned home, he named the team after his old service battalion, and his wife drew the famous Native American head logo.

Why did the Detroit Cougars change their name in 1930?

Detroit fans found "cougars" too difficult to say, so they became the Detroit Falcons in 1930. Two seasons later, they became the Red Wings.

ERA OF BIG ARENAS

What was the Montreal Forum?

The Montreal Forum was the longtime home of the Montreal Canadiens, as well as the home of the old Montreal Maroons.

Ever since the demise of the Montreal Wanderers, as well as the old Montreal Arena in a fire, the English community of the city was looking to re-establish a team for itself, as well as an arena for the team to play in. The idea for the arena was first conceived in 1923 by Sir Edward Beatty, the president of Canadian Pacific Railway.

The site chosen for the new rink was a roller-skating arena known as the Forum, and the original name was kept. It was also previously the site where hockey legends such as Frank and Lester Patrick, Art Ross, and Russell Bowie played outdoor ice hockey as youths. The original plans called for a seating capacity of 12,500 seats, but because of financial reasons they had to scale it back to just 9,300 seats. Construction began the next year, and by November 29, 1924, after just 159 days of construction, the arena hosted its first game.

The Montreal Forum as seen from Atwater Street. While the interior was demolished in 1998, the exterior still stands today.

The Forum was originally used only by the Maroons, but in 1926, the Canadiens moved in and became co-tenants. The building was home to 24 Stanley Cup championships, two by the Maroons and 22 by the Canadiens. In addition to the NHL, the Forum also hosted all other levels of hockey, ranging from the junior, amateur, and senior levels.

After the demise of the Maroons in 1938, the Canadiens continued to use the Forum until 1996. The Forum underwent two renovations, the first in 1949 and the second in 1968. By the time the Forum closed in 1996, the capacity had reached 17,959.

The Canadiens played their final game at the Forum on March 11, 1996, when they defeated the Dallas Stars 4–1. Following the game, many previous Montreal greats were presented to the crowd, including perhaps the most beloved Canadiens player of all time, Maurice Richard, who received a 16-minute standing ovation. A flaming torch was carried from the Montreal dressing room by Emile Bouchard and was passed to each of the former Montreal captains, including Jean Beliveau, Henri Richard, and Yvan Cournoyer, before it finally reached the Canadiens captain at the time, Pierre Turgeon.

The Forum was gutted and converted into an entertainment center called the Pepsi Forum. Center ice has been recreated in the center of the complex, surrounded by a small section of the grandstand. Outside the complex there is a large bronze Montreal Canadiens logo with 24 bronze Stanley Cup banners. The entire building now serves as a tribute to the Forum's storied history. It was declared a National Historic site of Canada in 1997.

Which world-famous arena is actually the fourth arena to bear the name?

Madison Square Garden is the fourth venue to bear the "MSG" name. The first venue existed from 1879 to 1890, and the second existed from 1890 to 1925. Both were located on Madison Square, on East Street and Madison Avenue. In 1925 a third Madison Square Garden opened in a new location, on 8th Avenue between 49th and 50th streets. This arena lasted until 1968. The fourth and final "version" of Madison Square Garden opened in 1968 after the Pennsylvania Railroad tore down the aboveground portion of Pennsylvania Station.

The first Madison Square Garden (top) existed from 1879 to 1890, and the second (shown at bottom in 1893) lasted from 1890 to 1925.

MSG has been home to the New York Rangers since Tex Rickard, builder of the third incarnation of the MSG, was awarded the franchise for the 1926–27 season. The Rangers continue to play at Madison Square Garden. Nowadays, it is often referred to as the "World's Most Famous Arena." It is also the home of the NBA's New York Knicks. It has hosted many events, including three Stanley Cup Finals, five NBA Championships, the Big East Basketball tournament, and multiple tennis, boxing, and wrestling matches. Beginning in January 2014, singer Billy Joel became the "fourth franchise" at Madison Square Garden when he began performing a monthly concert there.

Which arena served as home to the Detroit Red Wings up until 1979?

Olympia Stadium, sometimes referred to as "the Old Red Barn," served as home for the Red Wings from 1927 up until 1979. In 1926 several Detroit businessmen organized the Detroit Hockey Club and purchased the Victoria Cougars hockey team, along with a piece of land at the corner of Grand River Avenue and McGraw Street. This became the cornerstone for the building. The Cougars played their first game at Olympia Stadium on November 22, 1927. The Cougars' name would eventually be changed to the Red Wings in 1932 by new owner James E. Norris.

Like many arenas, Olympia hosted many other events. These events ranged from the NBA All-Star Game in 1959 to two Beatles concerts in 1966 to boxing matches. The arena was also home to the Detroit Pistons of the NBA from 1957 to 1961.

In 1975 the Wings seriously considered moving to the city of Pontiac, due to the decline of the neighborhood surrounding Olympia Stadium since the Detroit Riot of 1967.

In fact, there were two separate murders that took place in the shadows of the arena. The city of Detroit then offered the Red Wings a deal that gave them a riverfront arena in a different area of Detroit. The Red Wings accepted the deal and moved into the Joe Louis Arena in 1979. The Wings played their final game at Olympia Stadium on December 15, 1979. The arena was demolished in 1987, and the Michigan National Guard's Olympia Armory occupies the site. A historical marker is posted inside the armory to honor the Olympia Stadium.

What was Chicago Stadium?

Chicago Stadium was the longtime home of the Chicago Blackhawks. It was the team's home arena from 1929 until 1994.

The building was the idea of the famous Chicago sports promoter Paddy Harmon, who was interested in getting an NHL franchise for the city. After he lost out in the bidding for the franchise, he worked to get Chicago Stadium built as a way to gain at least partial control of the team.

The building was eventually completed on March 28, 1929, at a cost of $9.5 million. At the time of its opening, it was the pinnacle of luxury and size for sports arenas. Modeled after Detroit's Olympia Stadium, it had the largest capacity for an indoor arena up until that point and was the first arena to have an air-conditioning system. Chicago Stadium saved the franchise, which had struggled to make money in the cramped, run-down Chicago Coliseum.

Chicago Stadium, home of the Chicago Blackhawks, as it looked in 1930.

The arena earned the nickname "The Madhouse on Madison" due to the world's largest pipe organ that was played during hockey games. The dressing rooms at Chicago Stadium were placed underneath the seats, and the cramped corridor that led to the ice, with its twenty-two steps, became somewhat legendary. When the Blackhawks scored an empty net goal in Game 7 of the 1971 Stanley Cup semifinals, broadcaster Dan Kelly remarked that he could feel the broadcast booth shaking, illustrating how crazy it sometimes got there.

While it was originally conceived for hockey, Chicago Stadium was also used for other purposes. It hosted Democratic and Republican national conventions, was a concert venue that hosted the likes of Frank Sinatra and the Beatles, and was also home to the Chicago Bulls of the NBA beginning in 1967.

By the end of the 1994 season, the Blackhawks, as well as the Bulls, had moved into the United Center, and in front of a teary crowd of fans, the Chicago Stadium was demolished in 1995. There is a plaque in the pavement on the north side of Madison Avenue to commemorate where the mighty arena once stood.

Which arena outside of New York City was designed by Tex Rickard?

Boston Garden was designed by Tex Rickard, the same man who built the third rendition of New York City's Madison Square Garden. It opened in November of 1928, under the name "Boston Madison Square Garden," and was later shortened to Boston Garden.

Boston Garden is home to the Boston Bruins.

The Garden was host to the Boston Bruins of the NHL, as well as the Boston Celtics of the NBA.

Rickard wanted to expand his empire by building a series of seven "Madison Square Gardens" all across the states. However, due to high costs and Rickard's death, Boston Garden was the last of the series. Hockey debuted there on November 20, 1928, in a game between the Bruins and the Montreal Canadiens. The arena was originally designed for boxing matches, so that every seat could be close enough to easily see the boxing match, so because of this design, fans were much closer to the players during Bruins and Celtics games. The arena also had excellent acoustics. When a sold-out crowd was cheering and chanting, the impact was enormous. The arena did have several flaws, however. First, the rink was undersized, giving the Bruins an advantage over their opponents. Second, the Garden had no air conditioning, sometimes causing a layer of fog to appear on top of the ice during playoff games, which were played in the spring. The arena also suffered from occasional power outages.

The last game played at the Garden was on May 14, 1995. It was Game 5 of the Eastern Conference quarterfinal series between the Bruins and the New Jersey Devils, a series the Devils would win. It was demolished in 1997. The site where the arena once stood is now a parking lot for the new arena, the TD Garden. When the Bruins won the Stanley Cup in 2011, the rally started at the site where the Boston Garden once stood.

Which arena was sometimes referred to as "the Barn" and later "the Checkerdome"?

St. Louis Arena was an indoor arena that was host to the original St. Louis Eagles team and later the St. Louis Blues. The building stood from 1929 to 1999. The arena also hosted numerous conventions, concerts, political rallies, and other sporting events.

The structure was completed in 1929 and at the time was the second largest indoor entertainment space in the country, behind Madison Square Garden. The arena was not well maintained after the 1940s (the Eagles only lasted for one season, in 1934–35) and by the time the St. Louis Blues arrived in 1967, the arena had fallen into such poor condition that they were forced to do heavy renovations. In 1977 Ralston Purina purchased the Arena and the Blues. The building was renamed "the Checkerdome" after the company's checkerboard logo.

The Blues played their last home game at the Checkerdome in 1994 before moving into the Kiel Center, now known as the Scottrade Center. In 1999, despite the public being overwhelmingly in favor of saving it, the Checkerdome was demolished. A business/residential development now occupies the land.

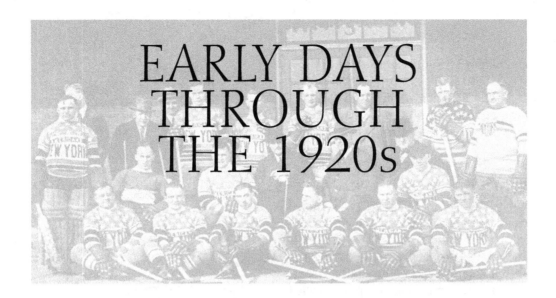

EARLY DAYS THROUGH THE 1920s

Which team, despite being the first in New York, struggled for much of their existence?

The New York Americans came into the league in 1925 as the third NHL expansion team and the second from the United States. Thomas Duggan and Bill Dwyer were awarded the franchise. Together they purchased the rights to the Hamilton Tigers, whose players had been suspended from the league after going on strike in an attempt to earn higher pay.

Success did not come easily to the Americans, despite having a roster that finished first the previous year. In their 17-year history, they never eclipsed the 20-win mark, and they made the playoffs just five times, making it past the first round only twice.

Their best season came in the 1928–29 campaign led by Roy Worters, who boasted an incredible 1.21 goals-against average and claimed the Hart Trophy. Despite Worters's laudable effort, the Americans continued to struggle, unable to make it out of the first round of the playoffs.

In the 1931–32 campaign, Worters's play started to decline. He was still able to lead the Americans to the playoffs once more before retiring after the 1936–37 season. For the 1937–38 season, the Americans signed veterans Ching Johnson and Hap Day, again making the playoffs only to be defeated by the Blackhawks in the second round. Despite making the playoffs the following two years, the Americans were forced to disband in 1942.

Which referee imposed a fine on a player in the middle of a game?

Cooper Smeaton (1890–1978) officiated his first professional hockey game in 1913 between the Montreal Canadiens and the New York Wanderers. He made an offsides call on Montreal tough guy Newsy Lalonde. Smeaton recalls, "When Lalonde heard the call, he wheeled around and came tearing back at me like he was going to knock my head off. Well there I was, just a rookie with a better-than-passing knowledge of the rulebook, and I knew I had the right to fine him. So I said, 'Two minutes and five dollars!'" In 1931, the NHL named him as the league's head referee. Smeaton held that position for six years before retiring.

Which NHL referee also doubled as a journalist?

Bobby Hewitson (1892–1969) was known by many as a voice on the "Hockey Night in Canada" radio broadcasts in the 1930s and 1940s. Between periods during the Toronto Maple Leafs home games, Hewitson appeared on a popular segment called "The Hot Stove League." He was also the sports editor of the *Toronto Telegram* daily newspaper. He started to call games when a friend of his gave him the idea. When Hewitson officiated collegiate and junior games, he used a bell because he didn't

Cooper Smeaton

own a whistle! In 1925, Hewitson officiated games in the NHL. Balancing referee duties with his job at the *Telegram*, Hewitson impressed the league president at the time, Frank Calder. When Hewitson was offered more money to work solely in the NHL, he denied it, saying, "The paper is my first love. Hockey comes after."

NEW YORK RANGERS

Who was the primary architect of the new but very successful New York Rangers franchise?

As soon as they stepped onto the ice in the 1926–27 season, the Rangers became an immediate hit in New York City. They quickly overtook their fellow housemates—the Americans—in the box office and on the ice, becoming known as "the classiest team in hockey."

The architect of these teams was Lester Patrick, who had taken over the club after Conn Smythe was fired before the team even played a game.

In their first season, the Blueshirts took the league by storm, finishing first in the American Division with a 25–13–6 record before losing in the semifinals to Boston. In the following season, the Rangers again were among the top teams in the league, finishing second in their division and winning the Stanley Cup.

From that point on, the Rangers continued to do well on the ice, as well as in the box office. They won two more Stanley Cups (1933 and 1940) before the United States entered World War II in December 1941.

Why did Red Dutton curse the New York Rangers?

In the early 1940s, Red Dutton, the coach and manager of the New York Americans, decided that he wanted to move the team to Brooklyn. While they changed their name and practiced at the Brooklyn Ice Palace, they continued to play at Madison Square Garden.

When World War II derailed the construction of Dutton's new arena, the franchise was forced to fold. After the conflict ended, Dutton sought to revive his team, but a group of owners led by the Rangers would not allow it. Dutton, angered by this, declared that the Rangers would never win the Stanley Cup as long as he was alive. He died in 1987, and the Blue Shirts did not win another Stanley Cup until 1994.

BOSTON BRUINS

After entering the NHL, how quickly did the Boston Bruins grow from a losing team to a winner?

The team only managed a 6–24–0 record (for last place) in its first season. However, plans were in place to develop a winner, and in the Bruins' third season—1926–27—they really improved. The club's formula was simple enough: if the other team can't score, they can't win. General manager Art Ross purchased several stars from the recently collapsed Western Hockey League, including the team's first superstar, a defenseman from Fort Qu'Appelle, Saskatchewan, named Eddie Shore.

The Bruins actually reached the Stanley Cup Finals that season, even though they finished only one game above .500, eventually losing to the Ottawa Senators. That was

---

What was unique about the Bruins' coach during the 1928–29 season?

The Boston Bruins have had some curious coaches over the decades, and one of the most unique was Cy Denneny. In the 1928–29 campaign, he spent his only season in Boston as a player-coach. The team started out slowly and lost their first game at Boston Garden.

Eventually, the Bruins launched a record-breaking 13-game unbeaten streak (11–0–2) and did not lose for the entire month of January. Scoring leader Harry Oliver had 17 goals and 23 points.

the first Cup Final to be between exclusively NHL teams.

The Bruins won their first Stanley Cup in the 1928–29 season. By that time, Shore—also known as the Edmonton Express (from his days as a member of the Edmonton Eskimos)–had become one of hockey's greatest stars and for years would be the backbone of Boston's hockey club.

Who was the difference-maker in the 1928–29 season for the Bruins, when they finally won their first Stanley Cup?

Cecil "Tiny" Thompson joined the Bruins just in time for the team to move to the newly built Boston Garden, where the team won its first Stanley Cup in 1929. However, Thompson was not as "tiny" as his nickname suggested. He measured 5'10" and weighed 160 pounds, which in those days was not considered small.

Cecil "Tiny" Thompson

The team also included stars such as the shutdown defensive pairing of Hall of Famer Shore and captain Lionel Hitchman. Other top players included Harry Oliver, Dit Clapper, and Dutch Gainor.

Thompson started a 10-year run between the pipes for Boston with a 1.15 goals-against average and then nearly halved that during the playoffs!

His GAA over a five-game sweep was 0.60. He went 3–0 against the Montreal Canadiens and 2–0 over the New York Rangers in the league's first all-American Stanley Cup Finals in 1929.

PITTSBURGH PIRATES

What was the first hockey franchise in Pittsburgh?

The Pittsburgh Pirates existed in the NHL from 1925–26 to 1929–30. The Pirates' lineage can be traced back to the Pittsburgh Yellow Jackets of the U.S. Amateur Hockey Association. The Jackets were eventually sold to attorney James F. Callahan.

In 1925, the NHL granted a franchise to Pittsburgh, and Callahan renamed his franchise the Pittsburgh Pirates after receiving permission from the owner of the Pittsburgh Pirates baseball team.

The Pirates played their inaugural season in 1925–26. They were led by team captain Lionel Conacher and goaltender Roy Worters. In their very first NHL game, they defeated the Boston Bruins 2–1. Two days later, the Pirates stunned the mighty Canadiens 1–0 in what would be the legendary Georges Vezina's final game. They lost their home opener, however, to the New York Americans 2–1 in overtime. In 36 games they posted an admirable record of 19–16–1, finishing third in the league.

Their first season, however, would arguably be their best. In their second season, they finished fourth and missed the playoffs. The next year they managed to earn a playoff spot but lost in the semifinals to the New York Rangers. This would be the last time the Pittsburgh Pirates would make the playoffs. Due to financial setbacks, Callahan was forced to sell the team, which was then relocated to Philadelphia—as the Quakers—for one season before permanently disbanding.

Which modern NHL player has followed in the footsteps of his ancestor, Lionel Conacher?

Cory Conacher is the most recent of a lineage that includes the likes of the legendary Lionel "the Big Train" Conacher and his younger brother Charlie, also known as "the Big Bomber." Cory played collegiate hockey at Canisius College, where he became the school's all-time leader in points (147), goals (62), and game-winning goals (12) in only 129 games.

Due to his small size (5'8"), Conacher went undrafted through his four years at Canisius. He would leave as one of the program's most decorated players, setting 12 records. He subsequently signed in 2010–11 to amateur tryouts with the Rochester Americans, Cincinnati Cyclones, and the Milwaukee Admirals. On October 6, 2011, Conacher signed a one-year contract with the Norfolk Admirals of the AHL (then affiliate of the Tampa Bay Lightning).

In the 2011–12 season, Conacher impressed the Tampa Bay Lightning brass in training camp and quickly established himself as a prolific scorer. While leading the Admirals in goals and points during their 28-game winning streak—a professional hockey record—Conacher signed a two-year, two-way contract with the Tampa Bay Lightning. He helped lead the Admirals to their first Calder Cup and was awarded the league MVP award.

Due to the lockout, Conacher was forced to start the 2012–13 season with the Lightning's new AHL affiliate, the Syracuse Crunch. After the lockout Conacher was asked to attend training camp for Tampa Bay and proceeded to make an immediate impact by scoring his first NHL goal on opening night in a 6–3 win over the Washington Capitals. He continued to produce and by the trade deadline, he was second in NHL rookie scoring with 24 points in 35 games. At the trade deadline, however, he was traded to the Ottawa Senators in exchange for goaltender Ben Bishop.

The trade ended up being one of the more one-sided deals of the season as Bishop shone in Tampa Bay and received mention as a Vezina candidate, while Conacher struggled to find his footing in Ottawa, sitting multiple games as a healthy scratch. This was the beginning of a slow decline for young Conacher, who found himself placed on waivers by the end of the season and claimed by Buffalo only to be released by the time of his free agency.

On July 1, 2014, Conacher signed with the New York Islanders as a free agent on a one-year contract but again found himself on waivers by December. He spent the next two seasons with the AHL affiliate in Bridgeport but was traded in March of 2015 to Vancouver for a spot on the Utica (AHL affiliate) squad. He had five goals for 23 points in 28 games with Bridgeport.

OTTAWA SENATORS

Which team was known as the Super Six throughout the 1920s?

The Ottawa Senators of the 1920s have been considered the first of the National Hockey League's powerhouses. Between 1920 and 1927, they finished in first place seven times and won four Stanley Cups. The team boasted Hall of Famers such as Frank Nighbor and Cy Denneny. They played with a defense-first policy and were so dominant that the NHL created a rule that forced defensemen to leave their own zone once the puck had left the zone.

In 1919, youngster Clint Benedict led the league in goals-against average, and Nighbor finished third in the league with 25 goals in 23 games. The Senators defeated Seattle in the Stanley Cup Finals and claimed their first Cup as a member of the NHL.

The following year Benedict, again, led the league in goals-against average, and Denneny came in second in goals with 34 tallies in 24 games. The Senators defeated Vancouver in five games to claim their second straight Stanley Cup.

Clint Benedict

In 1921–22, Frank Boucher and King Clancy joined the team. The Senators won the regular season title but fell to the Toronto St. Pats in the playoffs.

In 1922–23, Benedict, Nighbor, and young defenseman Lionel Hitchman led the team to another first-place finish and another Stanley Cup championship.

In 1924, the Senators' prospect pool was so deep they could afford to trade away Clint and Harry Broadbent in 1924 to make room for two other prospects, Alec Connell and Hooley Smith. All four of them would go on to become Hall of Famers.

In 1926 Benedict, along with Broadbent, led the Montreal Maroons to a Stanley Cup victory over the Senators. Connell and Smith, who replaced Benedict and Broadbent, paced the original Senators to their final Stanley Cup victory. The team disbanded several years later due to financial problems.

MONTREAL MAROONS

From the 1926–27 season to the 1934–35 season, how many times did the Montreal Maroons miss the playoffs?

Only once. After struggling through their freshman year in the league, finishing fifth out of six teams, the Montreal Maroons saw immediate success the following season.

The team, fortified by the addition of top players such as Nels "Old Poison" Stewart, Babe Siebert, and Bill Phillips, saw the team improve to a 20–11–5 record—good for second in the league. They would defeat the Pittsburgh Pirates in the opening round and then upset the favored Ottawa Senators in the next round to win the NHL playoffs. They squared off against the WCHL's Victoria Cougars for the Stanley Cup and defeated them three games to one.

This would be the start of what would be a very successful beginning for the team, both on and off the ice. Over this time, the team compiled a 186–167–59 record and captured another Stanley Cup in 1935.

The Maroons also had the legendary Clint Benedict in goal. He recorded four straight seasons with a GAA under 2.00. He also became famous for being the first goalie to wear a face mask in the NHL, wearing it for a short time in the 1929–30 season after a shot from the Canadiens' Howie Morenz broke his nose. The mask didn't work out too well, however: Benedict would break his nose again.

EARLY TITANS

Who was the first president of the National Hockey League?

Originally a newspaper man by trade, Frank Calder was named secretary of the old National Hockey Association. In 1917, when the National Hockey League was being organized in

41

Montreal, Calder moved over to the new circuit and was named the new league's first president. A non-player, Calder helped form the solvent, strong base that is today's NHL.

The league presented the Calder Trophy and later the Calder Memorial Trophy for Rookie-of-the-Year honors to commemorate the service of this avid hockey fan who remained the league's only president for 26 years. Calder, a member of the Hall of Fame, died on February 4, 1943, and was succeeded by Mervyn (Red) Dutton, who kept the post as interim president during the World War II years until Clarence Sutherland Campbell was picked as full-time president at the end of the war.

Which former player, coach, and manager became known as "the Silver Fox"?

No single individual contributed more to the improvement of professional hockey on every level—playing, coaching, managing, and operating—than Lester Patrick, dubbed "the Silver Fox" because of his shock of gray hair and his uncanny foxiness in dealing with opponents.

In 1924, at the age of forty-two, Lester coached and managed the Victoria Cougars to a Stanley Cup over the Montreal Canadiens three games to one. In the same year, NHL franchises were awarded to the Montreal Maroons and Boston Bruins and a year later to the Pittsburgh Pirates and the New York Americans.

Patrick realized he couldn't match the salaries the big-time eastern moguls were offering players. He knew that the time of the Pacific Coast League had ended, so he sold his entire roster to the new owners in the East and planned to retire and move to California.

After nineteen consecutive years managing and frequently playing hockey, Patrick was ready to take a vacation. Then, Conn Smythe walked out on the Rangers, and Lester was called. He took the first available train east, and the new era in hockey for New York City had begun. Patrick labored for thirteen seasons behind the Rangers bench, dominating the annual ballot for "coach of the year." In fact, starting in 1930, the year the award came into existence, Patrick was honored seven of the first eight years.

Without a doubt, Patrick's finest hour as a coach came during the 1928 Stanley Cup playoffs when the Rangers faced the powerhouse Montreal Maroons in the final round. The Maroons were highly favored in the series, and to make matters worse, Madison Square Garden was unavailable to the Blueshirts because the circus was in town. Each game of the best-of-five series was to be played in the unfriendly Montreal Forum.

The Maroons won the first game, 2–0, and all of Montreal was expecting a three-game sweep. Undaunted, the Rangers

Lester Patrick was nicknamed "The Silver Fox."

skated out to meet the Maroons in the second game. Early in the second period, with no tallies on the scoreboard, Nels Stewart, a dangerous Maroon forward, broke into the clear and unleashed a whizzing shot that caught the Rangers netminder, Lorne Chabot, squarely in the left eye.

With Chabot out of the game, surely now the Rangers were sunk. With no spare goaltender and the gloating Maroons refusing the Blueshirts the services of a by-standing netminder, all hope seemed to be lost. But in typical Patrick fashion, the 44-year-old Silver Fox stepped forward and strapped on the pads. In two periods of play, Patrick stopped 18 of 19 shots and helped the Rangers win the game, 2–1. Patrick's heroics in goal became an instant legend as the Rangers rallied to win their first Stanley Cup.

Who proposed twenty-two pieces of legislation in the NHL rule book?

Although Lester Patrick was the more famous member of Hockey's Royal Family, his brother Frank also made a name for himself and was influential in his own way. There are twenty-two pieces of legislation in the NHL rule book that Frank proposed, including the origination of the blue line.

Frank had been an excellent defenseman, starring with McGill University and later for the Renfrew Millionaires with his brother, Lester.

The Patricks moved west to Nelson, British Columbia, where they began their own league and built arenas for all the teams—how's that for starting from the ground up? They were so successful that they bagged the Stanley Cup in 1915, later selling their players to the NHL.

Frank, a Hockey Hall of Famer, later coached Boston and managed the Canadiens prior to his death in 1960.

Who was responsible for founding the Boston Bruins?

The Boston Bruins' franchise was conceived as a result of a Stanley Cup playoff in Montreal. After wealthy grocery merchant Charles Adams saw his first playoff series, the former counter boy solicited the help of prominent Canadian hockey player and leader Art Ross. With Adams backing and Ross handling hockey operations, the Bruins were born.

Two years later, Adams, desperately in need of strong players, purchased the entire Western Canada League from the Patrick family. He then followed this move by guaranteeing $500,000 to help build Boston Garden, which became home of the Bruins. Adams was inducted into the Hockey Hall of Fame in 1960, more than 10 years after his death.

Who was the first owner of the Chicago Blackhawks?

Major Frederic McLaughlin was an American businessman and soldier who served in World War I. McLaughlin graduated from Harvard and inherited his father's successful coffee business, McLaughlin's Manor House.

Which former legend and team owner has his name etched on the Stanley Cup eight times?

One of the most influential and colorful characters associated with the National Hockey League, Conn Smythe first gained notice in the months following the start of World War I in which he gallantly served. After returning to civilian life, Smythe played center and captained the University of Toronto's varsity hockey club while majoring in engineering. Smythe's team did the unprecedented when it won the Ontario Hockey Association's Junior Championship.

But Smythe would become world renowned for his stewardship of the Toronto Maple Leafs beginning in the late 1920s when he became the face of the club. Conn decided to build his team around a couple of young aces with rare promise. One of them was Hap Day, a forward-turned-blueliner, and Joe Primeau.

His deals—especially the one that brought colorful defenseman King Clancy to Toronto—usually had a touch of genius, and in 1932, the Maple Leafs won their first Stanley Cup for Smythe. His club was regarded as the "Gashouse Gang" of the NHL because of such robust characters as Day, Primeau, Clancy, Charlie Conacher, Red Horner, Baldy Cotton, and Busher Jackson.

When his Gashouse Gang sagged in the mid-thirties, Conn built a new empire around his gifted center, Syl Apps, and goalie, Turk Broda. In April 1942, they won the Stanley Cup in a seven-game series over Detroit in which the Maple Leafs fell behind three games to none—and then won four straight. This Cup Final feat was unprecedented in NHL history.

With Day behind the bench, the Leafs won the Stanley Cup in 1947, 1948, and 1949—a three-straight sweep that had never before been done. With Primeau as coach, Toronto won another title in 1951. Smythe's club, during his tenure, won eight total Stanley Cups. Eventually Smythe resigned as president and managing director of the Leafs and appointed his son, Stafford, to the position.

Conn Smythe was elected to the Hall of Fame in 1958, and the trophy presented to the most valuable player in the playoffs was named in his honor.

In May 1926, the NHL granted an expansion franchise to former football star Huntington Hardwick. On June 1, McLaughlin, with no experience in the hockey business, purchased the franchise from Hardwick. He decided to name the team the Black Hawks (the two-word spelling remained until 1986) after the nickname of his famed wartime Army unit.

As a hockey club owner, McLaughlin became notorious for his oddball schemes. A patriotic American, McLaughlin had as his goal to fill his roster with as many Americans as possible. For that reason, he was scorned by the league's Canadian owners, but by the 1937–38 season, the Major's Black Hawks roster was sprinkled with Americans. In fact the coach, Bill Stewart, also was one of Uncle Sam's own. Better still, the Stewart-led Chicago sextet captured the second Stanley Cup in Blackhawks history.

SHINING STARS

Which Montreal legend died after having a nervous breakdown, brought on by a severely broken leg?

What Bobby Orr, Wayne Gretzky, and, more recently, Sidney Crosby have meant to contemporary hockey fans, Howie Morenz was in the late 1920s and early 1930s THE number-one superstar. At his peak with the Montreal Canadiens, Morenz was admired for his speed and will to win. Born in Mitchell, Ontario, in 1902, the young Morenz was often pushed around and beaten by the older boys. But as Howie grew to manhood, he would become the star of the Stratford, Ontario, team, and he captured the attention of Canadiens owner Leo Dandurand. Dandurand confided with his aide, Cecil Hart, and both agreed it would be prudent to sign Morenz before the Maroons, Hamilton, Ottawa, or Toronto beat them to it.

Morenz was a superstar in his second year of big-league play. He finished second in scoring to Cecil "Babe" Dye of Toronto and was doing things with the puck that astonished even such skeptics as Conn Smythe, founder of the Maple Leafs empire. Many respected hockey observers claim that Morenz was singlehandedly responsible for the successful 1920s NHL expansion into the United States.

Morenz's scoring abilities began eroding in 1933–34 when he finished forty-eighth on the NHL scoring list. Even worse, Morenz was booed several times by his formerly loyal Montreal Forum supporters. He was thirty-three years old at the time and appeared at the end of the line.

Just prior to the 1934–35 season, Morenz was traded to the Chicago Black Hawks. Morenz scored only eight goals for the Hawks, and a season later, he was dealt to the New York Rangers, but he was a shadow of his former self, and New York's Lester Patrick was happy to return him to the Canadiens for the 1936–37 season. Reunited with old buddies Johnny Gagnon and Aurel Joliat, every so often he'd bring the Forum crowd to its feet with one of the exquisite Morenz rushes.

Howie Morenz

45

He was doing just that on the night of January 28, 1937, at the Forum, when a Chicago defenseman caught him with a body check, sending Morenz hurtling feet first into the end boards. It wasn't a normal spill, and Howie had lost all control as he skidded towards the boards. When his skate rammed into the wood, a snap could be heard around the rink. Morenz crumpled in excruciating pain and was rushed to the hospital with a badly broken leg.

Once in the hospital, the thirty-six-year-old Morenz began brooding about his fate. Instead of recuperating, he suffered a nervous breakdown and developed heart trouble. Perhaps too late, the hospital officials forbade all but Morenz's immediate family from visiting him. Then, early on March 8, 1937, Morenz was given a complete checkup. It deceptively appeared that he was rallying. A few hours later, Howie Morenz was dead.

Who won the most Hart Trophies out of any defenseman in NHL history?

Boston legend Eddie Shore has four Hart trophies—the most of any blueliner (1932–33, 1934–35, 1935–36, and 1937–38).

The old Pacific Coast Hockey League, directed by Frank and Lester Patrick, had run aground in 1925, and the Patricks were auctioning off some excellent players at reduced prices, including Shore, Harry Oliver, and Perk Galbraith. Charles Adams, the Bruins owner, had the money, and for $50,000 he purchased Shore, Duke Keats, and Frank Boucher in a seven-man package.

Nobody really knew it that summer, but the first Boston army had begun to form, and Eddie Shore was to be general. Until Shore came along, the Bruins lacked a definitive image. They were both amusing and pathetic, effervescent and fumbling, but if you tried to find an adjective that would adequately describe them, you wound up with nothing. Shore changed that!

Shore was brash beyond belief and just as mayhem oriented. In his second NHL season, Shore set a league penalty record with 166 minutes' worth of fouls.

Eddie Shore's boisterous antics did not win any hearts on opposing teams. Which particular rival squad is known to have taken it most personally?

Shore's continual clashes with the Montreal Maroons were legendary. Several of the

Eddie Shore

Which Bruins general manager is known for concocting some of the league's earliest public relations stunts?

In 1926, after finding a star in the exhilarating young Eddie Shore, general manager Art Ross rustled up one of the first PR ploys in history. While the Bs squad took the ice for the opening face-off, Shore was strangely missing in action. The crowd was abuzz with worry that they wouldn't get their money's worth with Shore nowhere to be seen.

Before long, the band would break into a chorus of "Hail to the Chief," and Shore would skate out in a matador's cloak trailed by a valet, who would then remove Eddie's cloak, allowing him to join his teammates at the dot.

Montreal players had decided that Shore was too liberal in his manhandling of them. With trip-hammer consistency, the Maroons clobbered Shore, racking up quite a few penalties.

After suffering a torn cheek and a slit chin from two separate slashes in the waning minutes of the game, Shore was felled by a clout in the mouth, losing several teeth in the process, and was knocked out cold. He had to be carried from the rink after lying unconscious on the ice for fourteen minutes.

In that one game, Shore accumulated a broken nose, three broken teeth, two black eyes, a slit cheek, a gashed chin, and a two-inch cut over his left eye. Not skipping a beat, he was a testament to toughness as he returned to action in the very next game.

Why did the Shore era come to an untimely end in 1939?

In 1939, Shore was nearing the end of his contract, and it was thought he might be done with the Boston franchise. The New York Americans indicated they would make a handsome offer for Shore, and Ross seemed interested when they suggested a $25,000 tab.

While Ross was mulling it over, Shore was doing some business of his own. He had purchased the Springfield Indians—one of the founding members of what is today's top-tier minor hockey league in North America, the American Hockey League.

Ross was livid when he heard of the news but unwillingly came to an agreement that Shore would play with the Bruins after December 15, 1939, in case of an emergency, but he would continue playing for and managing the Springfield sextet in the meantime. Shore played in three games and scored his final goal as a Bruin on December 5, 1939. By December 15, Shore was fed up with Ross and his chicanery. He revealed that he would no longer play for Boston because the club wouldn't permit him to fulfill his playing obligations in Springfield.

Ross finally traded Shore to the New York Americans, where he'd play one last season, thus ending the Shore era in Boston. In Springfield, he was known for his ruthless ownership and terrible treatment of his players.

He continued to own the team until 1976, and he later died of a lung infection in 1985. He was elected to the Hall of Fame in 1947 and became the second Boston Bruin to have his number retired. The AHL named its defenseman of the year award in his honor.

Which legendary goaltender played only 20 minutes of the 1925–26 season after being diagnosed with tuberculosis?

Georges Vezina, the "Chicoutimi Cucumber," was the acme of gentility on the ice. Few were aware of Vezina's philosophic nature. During the 1922–23 season, Vezina's body was being tortured by the early symptoms of tuberculosis. But there was no outward suggestion that Vezina was faltering.

In the 1923–24 season, Vezina led the Canadiens to the playoffs, leading the league in fewest goals-against (1.97) as the first netminder in NHL history to average fewer than two goals-against per game.

The Canadiens took the series over Ottawa and went on to defeat the Vancouver Maroons of the PCHA before reaching the Stanley Cup Finals for the first time in five years. Vezina then led the Canadiens to a two-game sweep over the Calgary Tigers (WCHL) in the best-of-three Cup Final. This was Montreal's first title as a member of the NHL and only second championship in the history of the club.

The next season fared slightly worse for wear; the Canadiens reached the Cup Final once again—if only by luck, as the regular season champion Hamilton Tigers were suspended after refusing to play without more pay.

Not for a lack of effort, Vezina still finished the regular season, leading the league with a new best of 1.81 goals-against average. But ultimately, the effort amounted to little as the Final saw Montreal fall to the Victoria Cougars.

At the start of the 1925–26 season, Vezina seemed ready to carry his team once again. This time, though, his disease would prove too much for him to handle. Just 20 minutes into the first game of the season, he collapsed on the ice.

It was the end of the trail for Vezina, and he knew it. At his request, he was taken back to his hometown of Chicoutimi, where doctors diagnosed him with an advanced stage of tuberculosis.

On March 24, 1926, Georges Vezina passed away. An enormous funeral, held in the old cathedral at Chicoutimi, saw play-

Georges Vezina

ers and fans from all parts of the country deliver their final tribute to the gallant goaltender.

A year later, the Canadiens' owners donated a trophy in his honor, which is now given to the top goaltender in the NHL every season. He was later inducted into the Hall of Fame, in 1945, as one of the original nine inductees.

Who was the shortest player to ever play in the NHL?

At 5'3", goaltender Roy "Shrimp" Worters played 12 NHL seasons for the Pittsburgh Pirates, Montreal Canadiens, and New York Americans. Over the course of his Hall of Fame career, Worters recorded 66 shutouts.

The Toronto native spent several years in amateur and senior hockey leagues prior to making the jump to the NHL. He starred in net for the Pittsburgh Yellow Jackets of the United States Amateur Hockey Association, leading them to championships in both seasons.

When the Yellow Jackets became the Pittsburgh Pirates, Worters continued to shine in net. He remained with the Pirates for three more years before being traded to the New York Americans.

During his first year with the Americans, he posted a staggering 1.15 goals-against average and became the first goaltender to win the Hart Trophy as league MVP. The Americans were a relatively weak team and would make the playoffs only once more during Worters' career. He would, however, win the Vezina Trophy in 1930–31 as the first NHL goaltender to record back-to-back shutouts.

Worters was forced to retire following the 1937 season due to hernia surgery. He died of cancer in 1957 and was posthumously inducted into the Hall of Fame in 1969.

Which famous line helped the New York Rangers win two Stanley Cups in the late '20s and early '30s?

The A Line, or Bread Line, was one of the most prolific scoring lines of the early NHL years. The line consisted of brothers Bill and Bun Cook and Frank Boucher. While playing on this line, Bill Cook went on to lead the team in scoring six times.

Many regard Bill Cook as the finest right winger of all time. Certainly, he ranks among the greatest—past or present—along with Gordie Howe and Bernie "Boom-Boom" Geoffrion. What set Bill Cook apart from the others, ironically, was his inseparability from brother Bun, who was often overshadowed by Bill's abilities, and linemate Frank Boucher.

When the Rangers won the Stanley Cup in 1928 and again in 1933, it was Bill Cook leading the way with Bun and Boucher at his side. Although he originally made his mark in Canadian pro hockey, Bill became part of the warp and woof of the New York sporting scene and remained a Ranger until his retirement after the 1936–37 season.

With Boucher as manager, Bill returned to New York to coach for a brief term from December 1951 through the 1952–53 season. He was named the first captain in Rangers history and scored the first goal in the franchise's storied history. He was inducted into the Hall of Fame in 1952 as the first Ranger to receive hockey's highest honor.

Which goalie died just months after becoming the first—and only—NHL goaltender to captain a Cup-winning team?

The Chicago Black Hawks' "Smiling Charlie" Gardiner usually wore a broad smile when he stepped between the pipes. At first this seemed the height of presumptuousness, since his goalkeeping was hardly flawless. But he worked diligently at his trade.

By 1929, Gardiner had improved so much that he finished second to the immortal George Hainsworth of the Montreal Canadiens in the race for the Vezina Trophy. He finally won it in 1932.

In 1932–33, the Hawks finished fourth and just out of the playoffs. The following year, they rallied and launched their most serious assault on first place. Gardiner's goaltending had reached new degrees of perfection. He allowed only 82 goals in 48 games and scored 10 shutouts.

Before the 1933–34 season, his fellow teammates unanimously elected the relentless goaltender to captaincy. However, unbeknownst to him and his doctors, Gardiner was suffering from a chronic tonsil infection that frequently left the ironically monikered "Smiling Charlie" cringing in crippling pain.

On December 23, 1932, Gardiner made his condition public but continued to play the very next night, starting in net at Toronto. Winning the Stanley Cup became an obsession for him, but while his mind was pushing forward, his body was hanging back.

In January, Gardiner was reported to have told Coach Tom Gorman, "I can't see … [there are] black spots before my eyes." Gorman told Gardiner not to worry—those were just pucks. He'd frequently be seen at every whistle leaning against his crossbar to keep from blacking out.

Relentless in his quest for the Cup, Gardiner posted a 1.63 goals-against average, including a 10-shutout performance in the regular season, leading the team into the playoffs.

Facing the fiery Detroit Red Wings, whose firepower included Ebbie Goodfellow, Larry Aurie, and Cooney Weiland, in a best-of-five series, the Black Hawks won the first game, 2–1 in double overtime at Detroit.

In the second game, also at Detroit's Olympia Stadium, the Hawks ran away with the game, this time with a 4–1 victory. When the teams returned to Chicago

"Smiling Charlie" Gardiner

for the third and what appeared to be the final game, Detroit would win the game by a score of 5–2, forcing a Game 4.

As he took his place in the crease for the final game, Gardiner's body looked visibly numb with fatigue. Before the team took the ice, Gardiner had pleaded with his teammates to put just one puck in—the rest he would take care of. Lo and behold, after three scoreless periods and a scoreless sudden-death overtime period, the game came down to one goal in double overtime.

When the referees finally whistled the team back to the ice for the final overtime frame, the Chicago players feared that Gardiner might collapse at any moment. Gardiner was beside himself with pain at this point, but he would fight as long as he could physically stand himself up on his skates.

Finally, at the ten-minute mark, the Hawks' tiny Harold "Mush" March moved the puck into Detroit territory and unleashed a shot at netminder Wilf Cude. Before the Detroit goalie could react, the puck sailed past him, the red light flashed, and the Chicago Black Hawks won their first Stanley Cup—and ended Gardiner's misery. Gardiner hurled his stick in the air and just barely made it back to the dressing room under a sea of thick back-pats from his stunned teammates.

Gardiner had managed a 6–1–1 playoff record, with two shutouts and a 1.33 goals-against average, leading Chicago to its first Stanley Cup in franchise history. During the Stanley Cup parade, Chicago defenseman Roger Jenkins carted "Smiling Charlie" around Chi-City, half-amused and half-brooding what many knew was impending.

Returning home ten days later, Gardiner's doctor strongly advised him to stay in bed and get some rest for his ailing body. But the stubbornly optimistic Gardiner refused and in June of 1934, irony once again showed its ugly humor as Gardiner collapsed on his way to a singing lesson. The baritone is said to have brought down the house with his low, intoxicating tone.

Ultimately, Charlie fell into a coma that he never awoke from. The 29-year-old had suffered a brain hemorrhage as a result of the tonsil infection. In 1945, Gardiner became one of the earliest members of the Hockey Hall of Fame. He is said to have been one of the best net-minders of his day. And had his abruptly ended seven-year career not been cut short, he could very well have been regarded as one of the best goaltenders in NHL history.

Who was considered one of the first "offensive defensemen"?

One of the first "offensive defensemen," Harry Cameron was a scoring legend in his own time during the formative years of the NHL. Cameron's personality was also described as quite offensive, as he's regarded as one of the league's first temperamental stars. His antics resulted in a heap of fines for Toronto management, eventually pushing the organization to the point of having to suspend their star blueliner.

But despite his run-ins with the establishment, Cameron was instrumental in bringing three Stanley Cups to Toronto during his 11-year career. In 1924, Cameron was al-

> ## Which player earned his nickname because he was not only a great goal scorer but also great with his fists?
>
> **R**ight winger Harry Broadbent rightfully deserved his nickname "Punch," because he packed plenty of it with his fists, as well as with his stick. In fact, Punch holds a scoring record that still stands. In 1922, a year that saw Broadbent lead all NHL scorers, Harry lit the red lamp in sixteen consecutive contests. This feat has never been duplicated, even in today's faster, higher-scoring games.
>
> A Hall of Famer, Broadbent played on four Stanley Cup-winning teams, three with the Ottawa Senators and one with the 1926 Montreal Maroons. Punch finished up his career in 1929 with the New York Americans.

lowed to leave Toronto and journey to Saskatoon, where he chipped in three more solid seasons before retiring.

Who was the Hall of Famer who played forward, goal, and also was an NHL referee?

James Ogilvie "Odie" Cleghorn played for the Canadiens from 1918 to 1925 and completed his NHL career with two more seasons as a Pittsburgh Pirate. But it wasn't until the 1930s, when Cleghorn first donned the zebra stripes, that he gained true notoriety.

In the 1938 Bruins–Leafs Quarterfinal, Cleghorn made history handing out the league's first misconduct penalty to none other than the rowdy Eddie Shore. The series was a short, two-game battle in which the total goal count in both matches would decide the winner. Boston won the opener at home with a score of 3–0 and rode that momentum into Game 2 at Toronto with a 1–0 lead by the end of the first frame.

All of that momentum came to a screeching halt with the first call of the game on the Bruins' Shore—a two-minute tripping penalty. The hungry Leafs came out swinging, notching two goals while a flustered Shore watched from the penalty box. In response, the Bruins' forecheck came back with crushing force. The Leafs, now trailing by only two goals in the series, grew increasingly frustrated with Boston's checking game, stonewalling Toronto at every turn, courtesy of Bruins forward Red Beattie.

Toronto defenseman King Clancy, tired of the pressure, slyly urged Charles Conacher to take care of the problem, with a wink and a nod. Immediately, an obedient Conacher flew into Beattie's flushed features elbow-first. Odie, the tolerant referee that he was, chose to overlook the foul.

Capitalizing on the leeway, not more than a few minutes later, Clancy this time caught Shore's skate with his stick and violently tripped the star backliner. Again, Odie chose to overlook the foul. Shore, clearly displeased with the no-call, made every attempt to plead his case, but Cleghorn was unbudging and proceeded with the puck-drop. Odie waved Shore to the face-off circle but the blueliner, in the midst of a full-fledged tantrum, refused to comply.

Cleghorn's patience wearing thin, the referee ordered him to the box for a two-minute penalty. Soon enough, the infamous Eddie Shore temper came undone. The moment that Odie turned to skate back to the face-off dot, the vindictive Bruin rebelliously drew back his stick and sent a point-blank shot straight at the official's rear.

Furious, Cleghorn threw precedent aside and sentenced Shore to a 10-minute stint in the sin bin—a league first. Unfortunately for Shore, this meant a 10-minute man-advantage for a team that thrived on the powerplay—the Leafs scored four goals in those 10 minutes and went on to win the game and series.

Which player was notorious for his extremely rough play throughout the 1920s?

Sprague Cleghorn, brother of Odie Cleghorn, is regarded by many as the toughest and dirtiest player in the history of the game. He was a product of a rough neighborhood, "where everything you got you had to fight for," said the late Bobby Hewitson, then curator of the Hockey Hall of Fame. And he played hockey the same way. You could say that Sprague was well fitted for it.

Cleghorn's rough-and-tumble style was no secret. By the end of his career, Cleghorn's short fuse took credit for at least 50 incidents in which a player had to leave the ice on a stretcher. Sprague had played three years for the Senators when Ottawa, fed up with his violent antics, released the defenseman to Hamilton. Without missing a beat, Montreal jumped at the chance to bring the homegrown star in, executing one of the league's first-ever trades.

Safe to say he was less than elated with the Ottawa management's lack of loyalty and made no effort to conceal his discontent. Over the rest of his career, his distaste for the Ottawa franchise resulted in multiple sanctions, suspensions, calls for expulsion, stints in the sin bin, and even some trouble with the law. Cleghorn was threatened with incarceration twice, and both were results of events that transpired against the Senators organization. The first of which came during a 1922 playoff matchup featuring a merciless brawl that left three of his former teammates, Cy Denneny, Frank Nighbor, and Eddie Gerard, with a glut of stitches and broken bones. Cleghorn rightly drew a match penalty and a $30 fine, calls by Ottawa management to expel him for good, and most notably, the ire of Ottawa police.

His second run-in with the law actually resulted in the rabble-rouser trading

Odie (left) and Sprague Cleghorn

53

in his hockey mitts for a pair of silver bracelets. In the closing period of a 1923 playoff game against his old pals from Ottawa, Cleghorn slashed Sens defenseman Lionel Hitchman in the dome and drew an assault charge from an Ottawa law enforcement that was more than happy to finally put the troublemaker in cuffs. Notwithstanding all of his borderline-deranged behavior, Cleghorn still managed to find a spot for himself in the Hockey Hall of Fame in 1958.

Which Denneny brother skated for five Stanley Cup teams?

After the Toronto Shamrocks caved in financially, the Denneny brothers were signed by the Toronto Arenas, where they skated together on a line centered by Duke Keats. This powder-keg line accounted for 66 goals during the 1916 season, rising to first in the league for scoring by a single line. The Arenas, on the other hand, finished dead last.

Happily, Cy was rescued when the Ottawa Senators pulled off the coup of the season by sending $750 and a player named Sammy Hebert to Toronto in return for Denneny's services. It took only one season for Cyril to establish himself as the top left winger on the powerful Senator squad—no one would unseat him for the next nine years.

Despite his small stature, Denneny was still sometimes cast into an enforcer's role to protect his smaller, mild-mannered linemates. The rugged Harry Broadbent was a tough cop on the beat as well, and when this duo paired together, they were gleefully referred to as "The Gold Dust Twins" by the Ottawa faithful.

Cy skated for five Stanley Cup teams in his long and illustrious career, four with the Senators and a fifth with the 1929 Bruins. He was a regular scoring machine, and although he only led the league once in total points, he never dropped below fourth in scoring for 10 consecutive years.

After retiring in 1929, Cy saw service as a referee and hockey coach. He became a member of the Hockey Hall of Fame in 1959, to which he responded—the class act that he was—with a heartfelt thank-you letter addressed to curator Bobby Hewitson.

Which Hall of Famer played professional baseball and football, in addition to hockey?

A winger with limitless potential, Cecil "Babe" Dye stood out from the rest of the young athletes who learned their trade in the renowned Jesse Ketchum School in Toronto. Shortly after the death of his father, Cecil's mother, Essie Dye, moved the family to Toronto while Babe was still a baby. Essie, a phenomenal athlete in her own right, vowed that her son would not lack athletic instruction, taking matters into her own hands. Her first order of business was to flood the backyard rink adjacent to their house and lace up the skates with Cecil. She taught her son everything there was to know from the art of puck handling to the science of a killer fastball.

Cecil began his professional hockey career in 1919 with the Toronto St. Patricks. The small-statured Dye, standing at 5'8" and clocking in at 150 pounds, wasn't exactly the picture of intimidation, and being slower on his skates, he was easy to underestimate—

that is, until he managed to get the puck on his tape. Dye soon came to be renowned for his beautiful stick-handling abilities and his hard-and-heavy shot. He then spent the next 11 years frequenting atop the NHL's scoring leader rankings, leading the league three times between 1920 and 1925. Although the multipurpose young athlete declared from the start his allegiance to hockey, foregoing a sizable offer from baseball's Connie Mack and the Philadelphia Athletics, Cecil certainly had no intention of resigning to the life of a one-trick pony. While he chose to spend his winters on ice, he still found a way to spend the warmer months out on the diamond.

Dye, aptly nicknamed "Babe" by his hockey teammates after the Great Bambino himself, spent his hockey off-seasons in the outfield for Baltimore, Buffalo, and Toronto in the International League. And just for good measure, he also spent time getting some football in the mix. He

Cecil "Babe" Dye

wrapped up the trifecta of Toronto professional athletics starting as halfback for the Toronto Argonauts (CFL). Babe was finally elected to the Hockey Hall of Fame in 1970, eight years after his death.

Who was the high-scoring center man who helped Seattle become the first American team to win the Stanley Cup in 1917?

Frank Foyston was a scoring machine. The center on the powerful Toronto team of the early NHA, Foyston, centering a line with wingers Alan Davidson and Jack Walker, helped catapult the Ontarians to the coveted Stanley Cup in 1914, Toronto's second year of operation.

Foyston labored for one more season with Toronto before jumping leagues to play for Seattle of the PCHA. Frank terrorized Pacific Coast goaltenders for the next nine years at Seattle, winning the league scoring title twice and directing his newly found sextet to the 1917 Stanley Cup.

Frank was a fixture at center for Seattle until 1925, when the Washington franchise dropped out of the league. Foyston signed with the Victoria club and adapted beautifully to his new surroundings, helping his new team to the Stanley Cup in his very first season there. Frank played one more season with Victoria before the entire western league collapsed under him. Skating in the twilight of his career, Foyston finished out his playing days with Detroit of the NHL. One of the great scorers of all time, Foyston is a member of the Hockey Hall of Fame.

Which Montreal goaltender measured only 5'6" but still won three straight Vezina trophies?

Montreal Canadiens goalie George Hainsworth was an English Canadian who measured only 5'6", compared to his tall, distinguished French predecessor, Georges Vezina. Furthermore, at thirty-three years of age, Hainsworth seemed to be approaching the end, rather than the beginning, of his major-league career.

Due to the less than impressive start to Hainsworth's career, Canadiens fans did not think Hainsworth was a worthy successor to Vezina. But Hainsworth played every one of the forty-four games on the Canadiens' schedule and finished the season with a goals-against average of 1.52, bettered only by Clint Benedict of the Maroons, who registered a 1.51 mark. Little by little, the Canadiens' fans began warming up to Hainsworth. He won the Vezina Trophy first in 1926–27, again in the 1927–28 season with a remarkable 1.09 goals-against average, and managed to improve on that in 1928–29, this time allowing only 43 goals in 44 games for a 0.98 mark.

Hainsworth seemed to improve with age. In 1928–29 he recorded 22 shutouts in 44 games and continued to excel for the Canadiens until the 1932–33 campaign. The entire Montreal team from Morenz to Hainsworth was in a slump that year. It hit its lowest point on February 21, 1933, when Les Canadiens visited Boston and were demolished 10–0. His boss, Leo Dandurand, was furious with Hainsworth, who had given up several "easy" goals and made up his mind to trade him at the earliest opportunity. One afternoon he picked up the telephone and called Conn Smythe, manager of the Maple Leafs. Within a few minutes, it had been agreed that Smythe would trade Toronto goalie Lorne Chabot for Hainsworth. Hainsworth lasted three full seasons in Toronto, during which the Leafs twice led the league, before returning briefly to Montreal in 1937, where he played several games before retiring.

Which Hall of Famer was nicknamed "The Western Wizard"?

George Hay was a high-scoring portsider on the original Regina Capitals team of the newly formed WCHL. Hay scored 22 goals in 25 games during the Caps' first season and was instrumental in their winning the league championship only to lose to Vancouver in their postseason playoff series.

Hay chipped in three more solid seasons with Regina and one more with Portland when the franchise was shifted before joining Chicago of the NHL in 1927. Traded to Detroit the following season, Hay continued scoring well until his retirement in 1933.

Who was the second player to have his number retired by a franchise and first for the Bruins?

Along with Eddie Shore, Lionel Hitchman gave the Boston Bruins one of the most fearsome defense combinations in National Hockey League history. The Toronto-born backliner broke into the majors with Ottawa in 1922–23 but was traded to Boston in 1924–25. He remained a Bruin until his retirement after the 1933–34 season. Defense-oriented to a fault, Hitchman scored more than ten points only once in his career—11 points in 1925–26—but more than compensated for that deficiency with his superb backline hitting, stick checking, and playmaking. On February 22, 1934, he became only the second player in North American sports history to have his number retired by a franchise, just 8 days after Toronto made Ace Bailey the first.

Who was the very first recipient of the Hart Trophy?

When old-timers get together to reminisce about the great two-way players of all time, Hall of Famer Frank "Dutch" Nighbor's name invariably pops up. Never a rough or dirty player, Dutch was a model of controlled, artistic hockey whether playing offense or back checking on defense.

Frank started his career with Toronto of the NHA and then spent two seasons with Vancouver of the PCHA, helping the Millionaires to the Stanley Cup in 1915.

But Dutch Nighbor is best remembered for his long and distinguished career with the Ottawa Senators. Nighbor spent thirteen years with the Senators, playing on four Stanley Cup winners and helping to earn his team the nickname of "the Super Six."

Frank was the very first recipient of the Hart Trophy, awarded annually to the league's most valuable player. He also was a two-time winner of the Lady Byng Trophy for combining sportsmanship and playing excellence.

Who starred in the 1927 playoffs for the Bruins and almost singlehandedly pulled off an upset of the mighty Senators?

Mild-mannered Harry Oliver was a veteran of sixteen professional hockey seasons, eleven Stanley Cup playoffs, and one Cup championship. He broke in with Calgary of the old WCHL and led them in scoring over his five-year stay there.

Oliver moved east in 1927 and was welcomed with open arms by the NHL's Boston

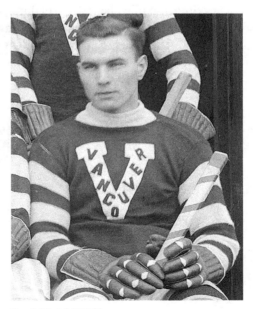

Frank "Dutch" Nighbor

57

Bruins. Harry responded nicely to the B's hospitality, leading them in scoring and right into the playoffs. Harry O was a star of the 1927 playoffs for the Beantowners, almost singlehandedly pulling off an upset over the strong Ottawa Senators in the Cup finals.

Oliver led the Bruins in scoring again during that championship season of 1929. Boston steamrollered to the Cup, flattening the New York Rangers, and Harry, once again, was outstanding in the finals.

Ollie spent five more seasons with Boston before being sold to the New York Americans in 1934. He skated with the Amerks for three campaigns before retiring in 1937. Harry Oliver is a member of the Hockey Hall of Fame.

Who was the first captain of the New York Rangers?

Known as "The Original Ranger," Bill Cook was named the first captain of the historic New York Rangers in their inaugural season in 1926–27. Cook had previously played in the WCHL (Western Canada Hockey League) for the Saskatoon Crescents, then the WHL (Western Hockey League) when the Crescents became the Sheiks prior to the league folding in 1926. The following year, it was expected Cook and his brother, Bun, would join the Montreal Maroons of the NHL, but while managers were waiting to speak with them, then Rangers manager Conn Smythe traveled to Winnipeg and offered the brothers a contract. Bill Cook was officially the first player to ever sign with the franchise and was named the captain shortly after.

What was the name given to the Montreal Maroons' high-scoring top line?

The Montreal Maroons' "Big S Line" was comprised of Babe Siebert, Nels Stewart, and Hooley Smith. While playing on the line, Stewart won two Hart Trophies. The line was one of the highest-scoring units in the league, as well as one of the most heavily penalized. In addition to the "Big S Line," the team was led on the back end by Mervyn "Red" Dutton, a tough but talented defenseman—an all-around effort that helped the Maroons to a Stanley Cup in 1926.

THE 1930s

WEATHERING THE DEPRESSION

What was the first NHL team in St. Louis?

The St. Louis Eagles were an NHL team that existed for only one season. The team was originally founded as the Ottawa Senators in 1883. Due to financial constraints, the Senators were forced to move to St. Louis. The team, however, continued to suffer from financial trouble due to high travel expenses. Having already asked permission from the NHL to suspend operation once in the past, in 1935 the team was forced to permanently halt operations and disperse their players among the remaining NHL teams.

When the St. Louis Eagles of the National Hockey League folded in 1935, the league bought the franchise and its players. It then held a draft. Which players went for the highest price?

Goalie Bill Beveridge and forwards Carl Voss and Glen Brydson were sold to the Montreal Canadiens, Detroit Red Wings, and the New York Rangers, respectively, for $4,000 each. The Montreal Maroons got Joe Lamb for $3,250, while Irvine Frew went to the Canadiens for $2,750.

Others went more cheaply. The New York Americans paid $2,000 for Peter Kelly. Bill Cowley went to the Boston Bruins for $2,250, and the Toronto Maple Leafs paid $500 for Gerald Shannon.

The prize catch turned out to be Cowley, who later became an All-Star center for Boston and one of the most adept passers the game has known. He eventually was voted into the Hockey Hall of Fame.

While the majority of the St. Louis Eagles proved no more than a footnote in NHL history, there were exceptions. Clifford Purpur, whose nickname was "Fido," had a long and illustrious career with the Black Hawks. Voss became a star with the Red Wings and later referee-in-chief of the NHL. He is also a member of the Hockey Hall of Fame.

Which city did the Philadelphia Quakers' franchise originally call home?

The Philadelphia Quakers were originally from Pittsburgh. The Pittsburgh Pirates only played 5 seasons, before they relocated to Philadelphia in 1930–31.

What caused the Philadelphia Quakers to fold?

When the Pirates relocated to Philadelphia and were renamed the Quakers, their woes continued. Not only did they continue to have financial issues, but their on-ice performance was equally as bad, if not worse. It took the team three games to score a single goal and another three games to get their first win. The Quakers ranked last in both offense and defense. They finished with an abysmal 4–36–4 record, the lowest winning percentage in NHL history until 1974–75, when the Washington Capitals broke it. At the end of the season, the Quakers announced that they would not field a team for the 1931–32 season. Philadelphia would remain without a team until the Flyers came into the league as an expansion franchise in 1967.

What ultimately led the to the end of the first NHL era in Ottawa?

By the 1929–30 season, the Senators were desperate for cash. In 1930–31, the team began to desperately sell players in an attempt to make ends meet. In 1931–32, the Senators asked the NHL for permission to suspend operations in order to rebuild their finances.

The Senators returned after sitting out for one season, but they finished with the worst record in the league. In 1933–34, rumors surfaced that the Senators might merge with the New York Americans. The Senators went on to finish last for the second year in a row. Following the season, the Senators announced that they would not return to Ottawa the following campaign. The franchise was moved to St. Louis. The once mighty Ottawa Senators were no more, and hockey would not return to Ottawa until the "new" Ottawa Senators entered the league in 1992–93.

Was there ever a referee that previously played in the NHL?

As a matter of fact, yes. Francis "King" Clancy played nine seasons for the Ottawa Senators and seven for the Toronto Maple Leafs. He is most remembered from a game against the Edmonton Eskimos in the 1923 Stanley Cup Finals, when Clancy became the first player in the NHL to play all six positions.

Goaltender Clint Benedict took a two-minute penalty, and in those days, goalies served the penalties themselves. For two minutes, Clancy stopped everything that came his way. He went on to play until the 1936–37 season.

After a brief coaching stint with the Montreal Maroons, he officiated NHL games for 11 seasons. His nickname came from his father, who played football, but Francis was also a King … on the ice. As a player, coach, and referee, the King was able to do it all.

Which franchise folded as a result of financial difficulties during the Great Depression?

Both Montreal franchises were experiencing a lot of financial difficulties during the Depression, but the Canadiens attracted more fans than the Maroons did. As a result, the Maroons finished last in the league in attendance for three straight years prior to their exit. The Maroons' financial troubles often forced them to trade away high-priced players, such as star winger Hooley Smith.

In 1938–39, the Maroons suspended operations. The owners wished to move the franchise to St. Louis. St. Louis had proved that it could support an NHL team when the Ottawa Senators had moved there in 1934–35. The franchise, however, only lasted one year in St. Louis, largely because of the high costs of traveling. It was because of this that the league did not give St. Louis another chance and allow the Maroons to relocate there.

The owners of the Maroons again attempted a sale of the franchise, this time to a group from Philadelphia led by Montreal Canadiens board member Len Peto. The deal would eventually fall through when Peto was unable to obtain a usable arena for the Maroons to play in. The league gave Peto until the end of the 1946–47 to find a suitable arena. When he failed, the Maroons were officially gone for good.

How did the end of Prohibition cause the New York Americans to struggle financially?

When he purchased the team, Bill Dwyer was the most celebrated Prohibition bootlegger in New York City. Understandably, due to his illegal activity, Dwyer got into trouble with various U.S. authorities. In 1933, when Prohibition ended, Dwyer faced larger problems, and his difficulties really began to develop a year later. He owed the government over $4,000,000 in back taxes on income earned. He was also preoccupied with all of the charges being brought up against him, not to mention the legal fees. His once immense fortune was suddenly being quickly depleted.

The Americans, in the meantime, were strapped for cash. They were never the strongest of New York's two franchises, but Dwyer was usually there to make up for any

---

Who was the first non-Canadian-born captain to win the Stanley Cup?

While the popular answer is the Stars' Derian Hatcher in 1999, he was just over 70 years too late. In 1926, the Montreal Maroons won the Stanley Cup with Scottish-born captain Dunc Munro.

times there was a shortage of cash. That wasn't the case during the 1934–35 season. In fact, several times, the Americans couldn't meet their team's payroll.

GROWTH OF THE MINORS

Which league was the precursor to the modern American Hockey League?

The International-American Hockey League was originally founded in 1936. It was formed from teams in the International Hockey League and Canadian-American Hockey League. Of the 13 teams from the league, eight banded together to form the IAHL. After just 11 games, the Buffalo Bison franchise folded, reducing the number to 7. The league operated until 1940, when the last remaining Canadian franchise dropped out. The league then changed its name to the American Hockey League. It is now recognized as the primary developmental league for the NHL.

What makes the Hershey Bears significant?

The Bears, who played their first game in the International-American Hockey League in 1938–39, are the oldest member of the AHL and the longest continually operating professional hockey franchise in North America outside of the NHL's Original Six.

The Bears have won the most championships in AHL history, capturing the Calder Cup 11 times, most recently in 2009–10, the second of back-to-back titles.

The team's beginnings can be traced to 1932–33, when they were known as the Hershey B'ars and played in the Tri-State League, which was reformed into the Eastern Amateur Hockey League in 1933–34. They changed their name to the Bears in 1936–37, two seasons before joining the IAHL.

What role did James Norris and the Chicago Shamrocks play in the demise of the American Hockey Association?

In 1930 the AHA approved the creation of a franchise in Chicago. The team, owned by James Norris Sr., became known as the Chicago Shamrocks. Norris decided to start the Shamrocks because he had tried to bring a second NHL franchise to Chicago but was blocked when Black Hawks owner Major McLaughlin refused to surrender his territorial rights. When the Shamrocks came into the league, they decided to rename the league the American Hockey League.

The logo of the Hershey Bears. The Bears are the oldest team in the AHL, making them the longest continually operating pro hockey team in North America outside the NHL's Original Six.

It was the aspiration of the team owners that they would be a superior league to the NHL. They refused to sign an agreement that would recognize the NHL's superior status, which would give the NHL the right to draft players from AHL clubs.

It was shaky finances that would ultimately be the undoing of the AHL. By January of 1932, two clubs, the Minneapolis Millers and the Buffalo Majors, had folded. Other teams were also struggling to meet their players' payrolls.

A proposed Stanley Cup challenge series between the two leagues ended up failing, and Norris, who had been one of the major backers for the league, left in the spring of 1932. Instead he applied for an NHL franchise in St. Louis, but he was denied due to travel costs. He was instead offered to purchase the bankrupt Detroit Falcons. There was one condition, however: his Chicago Shamrocks had to cease operations. This was the final blow to the AHL's grand ambitions to be a league that could compete with the NHL. The AHL went back to being known as the American Hockey Association, and in August of 1932, they signed an affiliation agreement with the NHL. They were eventually shut down in 1942.

Which west coast hockey minor league was Frank Patrick president of?

Frank Patrick was president of the Pacific Coast Hockey League. The league contained teams from the western United States and parts of western Canada. It existed in several incarnations.

The first period of the PCHL, which lasted from 1928 to 1931, contained four teams: the Portland Buckaroos, the Seattle Eskimos, the Vancouver Lions, and the Victoria Cubs, who became the Tacoma Tigers in the final year after the Cubs' arena burned down. The Patricks owned the franchises based out of Vancouver and Victoria. The Vancouver franchise won the championship all three years.

The second incarnation lasted from 1931 to 1941. From 1931 to 1936, there was technically no league called the PCHL. Teams from the first PCHL joined the Western Canada Hockey League or the North West Hockey League. In 1936, the Seattle, Portland, and Vancouver franchises, which were playing in the North West Hockey League, joined with a team from Oakland to reform the PCHL. The Oakland team would eventually relocate to Spokane. Due to World War II, the league disbanded in 1941.

Frank Patrick, shown here when he played for Vancouver; he later became president of the Pacific Coast Hockey League.

The third and final incarnation of the league happened in 1944, in large part due to Hall of Famer Al Leader, who managed the league. The league grew out of teams from the Southern California Hockey League and the Northwest International Hockey League. In 1948 the ten-team league voted to turn pro and was recognized as such by the NHL. In 1951, after the league decreased to six teams, it merged with the Western Canada Senior Hockey League, adding three new franchises. The next year the league became the Western Hockey League, which operated until 1974.

NOTABLE EPISODES

When did the president of the National Hockey League offer to decide the result of a playoff game by the toss of a coin?

Difficult as it is to imagine, NHL president Frank Calder actually attempted to settle a tie between the Toronto Maple Leafs and Boston Bruins by the flip of a coin.

It happened this way: On April 3, 1933, the Bruins and Maple Leafs finished regulation time of their decisive play playoff game tied at 0–0. They then battled their way through five 20-minute overtime periods without a result. At this point, Calder requested a conference with the team's respective managers, Conn Smythe of Toronto and Art Ross of Boston. "This game," said Calder, "has developed into an endurance marathon. It is now about 1:45 A.M. Your teams are dead tired, and so are your fans. You can, of course, continue playing until a goal is scored. But the winning team is scheduled to play against the Rangers in New York tomorrow night—no, it will be tonight—and if this game continues the winners will surely be in no condition to face the rested Rangers.

"So, if you want to toss a coin to decide this game, it will be alright with me. How about putting my proposal up to your players?"

Neither Smythe nor Ross, both extraordinarily combative types, were anxious to have the game settled anywhere but on the ice. However, in deference to the league president, they agreed to consult with their players. When Smythe entered the Toronto dressing room, he found his Maple Leafs stretched out flat on the floor rather than relaxing on their benches. They were utterly fatigued and seemingly in no condition to go on. But when Smythe revealed Calder's tie-breaking proposal, they rejected it out of hand.

"To hell with tossing a coin," said Harold Cotton of the defending champion Leafs. "We're the champs, and they've got to beat us on the ice."

The game resumed and was ultimately decided when little Ken Doraty of Toronto scored the game's only goal after two hours, 44 minutes, and 46 seconds of tense play.

How did Ace Bailey's career end?

On December 12, 1933, Bailey skated for the Toronto Maple Leafs against the Boston Bruins. The Bruins grew frustrated at the way the match was going. During the game the Leafs' King Clancy tripped Boston's Eddie Shore. Thinking that it was Ace Bailey who tripped him, Shore angrily pursued Bailey in an attempt to get even. Shore skated fiercely towards Bailey and struck him across the kidneys, sending him head over heels until he landed violently on his head.

Badly hurt, Bailey was rushed to the hospital, where the doctors claimed he had little hope of survival. The doctors performed two separate brain operations in order to save his life. He would eventually recover enough in order to live a normal life, but his hockey-playing days were over.

After a month, Shore was suspended by the NHL for 16 games. Later, a group of NHL All-Stars held a special All-Star Game benefit on Ace Bailey's behalf. At the game, Shore shook hands with Bailey and apologized for the hit.

Ace Bailey

In the 1936 Stanley Cup playoffs, what record did the Detroit Red Wings and the Montreal Maroons establish that has never been broken?

In the first game of the playoffs, the Detroit Red Wings and the Montreal Maroons went scoreless through regulation and ended up playing almost two full games of overtime. The game went until 16:30 of the sixth overtime, which was—and still is, to this day— the longest game in league history at 176 minutes and 30 seconds.

At 2:25 A.M. on Wednesday, March 25, 1936, at the Montreal Forum, Red Wings rookie Modere "Mud" Bruneteau picked up an errant pass from teammate Hec Kilrea. He then fired a low shot past the Maroons' goaltender, Lorne Chabot, nearly six hours after the game began.

Between periods, Red Wings staff had to massage players with rubbing alcohol and feed them teaspoons of sugar dipped in brandy to keep them going. Detroit goalie Normie Smith stopped 89 shots and Montreal goalie Chabot stopped 65 shots before Bruneteau iced the win for the Wings.

How did the Wings and fans celebrate the victory?

More than 9,000 fans at the Montreal Forum remained to witness the end of the marathon match. Some showered Bruneteau with dollar bills, and he brought the money into the locker room to share with his teammates. The bruising blueliner Wil-

When did a woman move into the goal judge's seat and press the red light button for the Rangers?

On March 28, 1938, the New York Rangers and the New York Americans confronted each other in the deciding game of the first round of the Stanley Cup series. With the score tied 2–2, the match went into sudden-death overtime, then a second and a third.

The tension became too much for one female Rangers fan who, at one point, rushed down to the goal judge's area following a scramble in front of the Americans' net and pushed the red light buzzer, signaling a goal. After order was restored and play resumed, the legitimate goal light was eventually lit by the Americans' Lorne Carr, ending the longest game ever played on Garden ice.

fred "Bucko" McDonald—who was runner-up for Rookie of the Year during the 1935–36 season—was also collecting some money. Before the game, a fan had offered Bucko $5 for every Maroon he knocked down. Bucko floored 37 Maroons that night, which gave him $185.

When did Montreal finally score a goal?

Goalie Normie Smith shut out the Maroons later on in Game 2 with a score of 3–0 and ran his Stanley Cup-record shutout streak to 248 minutes and 32 seconds before Montreal finally scored in Game 3. Smith finished the series with a GAA of 0.20 in a three-game sweep of the Maroons.

Which goalie was the first to be given the nickname "Mister Zero"?

For years the Bruins' manager, Art Ross, had received excellent service from goalie Tiny Thompson, and so it was no surprise when Tiny started the 1938–39 campaign in the Boston net. But Ross was unhappy, not so much about Thompson as about not having a young goalkeeper, Frank Brimsek, who was impressing scouts at nearby Providence in the International American League. Brimsek was that rare breed—a good American-born, American-developed player, who had learned the game in the cold wastes of Eveleth, Minnesota. Also, the Detroit Red Wings had revealed their willingness to spend $15,000, at the time a respectable sum, for Thompson.

Ross put one and one together. Thompson was aging; Brimsek was ready. Late in November 1938, the Bruins announced that their veteran goalie had been sold to Detroit. Brimsek would henceforth start in the Boston goal. Neither Thompson, his teammates, nor most of the Bruins fans could believe the news. After all, Tiny had won the Vezina Trophy four times and was still considered one of the finest goalies around even after playing ten years in the NHL.

Brimsek did nothing to enhance his image. He had an idiosyncrasy of wearing a pair of old, red hockey pants instead of the traditional gold, brown, and white Bruins outfit, and his footwork was less than sparkling.

However, the doubts about Brimsek's potential were eliminated within his first dozen games. In a stretch of three weeks, he recorded six shutouts in seven games, was immediately dubbed "Mister Zero," and went on to win both the Calder Trophy and Vezina Trophy.

SUPERSTARS OF THE 1930s

Which member of the Bruins was overshadowed by the play of the Kraut Line?

Overshadowed during most of his National Hockey League career by teammate Milt Schmidt, Bill Cowley nevertheless has been regarded as one of the classiest playmakers.

He entered the NHL during the 1934–35 season with the St. Louis Eagles but became a Bruin to stay the following year. He starred for the Boston sextet through the 1946–47 season. Smaller than Schmidt, Cowley relied on guile more than strength, emphasizing subtlety over Schmidt's accent on sock. Many critics believe that if Cowley had been blessed with line mates such as Woody Dumart and Bobby Bauer, who complemented Schmidt on the Kraut Line (a reference to the three players' German heritage), then Cowley would have been by far the most productive Bruin.

Over the course of his career, Cowley was named an All-Star five times and won the scoring title in 1941. During the 1944 season, Cowley averaged 1.97 points per game. Only two other players averaged more points per game in one season: Wayne Gretzky and Mario Lemieux. Cowley finished his career with 548 points in 549 games. Upon his induction into the Hall of Fame in 1968, he became the only member to have begun his career with the St. Louis Eagles.

Which Howe played for Detroit from the mid-thirties through the mid-forties?

Syd Howe played 17 seasons in the NHL for the Ottawa Senators, Philadelphia Quakers, Toronto Maple Leafs, St. Louis Eagles, and Detroit Red Wings. He played the majority of his career with the Red Wings.

Syd Howe

67

What was the first unofficial All-Star Game?

In 1934 the NHL decided to hold a benefit game for Ace Bailey, who the year before had his career ended due to a vicious check from Eddie Shore. The game saw the Maple Leafs battle against an All-Star Team made up of players from the other seven teams. The Leafs prevailed by a score of 7–3.

One of the highlights of the event occurred prior to the game when Bailey presented Shore with his All-Star jersey and afterward shook his hand, showing to all that he had forgiven Shore for the hit that ended his career. Bailey's number was retired by the Leafs at the game, making him the first NHL player to have his number retired by a team.

Howe joined the NHL with his hometown Senators, where he appeared in 12 games at the end of the 1929–30 season. After brief stints with the Quakers, Maple Leafs, and Eagles, Howe joined the Red Wings in 1934–35. While playing for Detroit, Howe was part of three Stanley Cup championship teams. In 1944 Howe scored six goals in a single game, second most all time to Joe Malone.

At the time of his retirement, Howe was the last active player who played for the Philadelphia Quakers and the original-era Ottawa Senators team. One year after his retirement, another Howe, named Gordie, joined the Red Wings and remained with the team until 1971, giving the Red Wings a star named Howe for 37 consecutive seasons. In 697 career games, Syd Howe recorded 528 points. He was inducted into the Hall of Fame in 1965.

Which colorful character was a defenseman, coach, and vice president for the Toronto Maple Leafs?

Some good old Irish luck intruded to help the Maple Leafs GM Conn Smythe obtain one of the most genuinely colorful characters hockey has known, Francis "King" Clancy. Frank developed an indefatigable spirit, which was embellished by his natural hockey talent. Despite his size, he joined the best amateur club in Ottawa.

When he was only 18, Clancy decided that he was ready for the NHL. So did Thomas Gorman, manager of the NHL's Ottawa Senators. When teammates realized what a surplus of gutsiness Clancy required to even dare to skate with the mighty Senators, they obliged by passing him the puck to see what he could do. When the practice concluded, Clancy received the equivalent of a standing ovation; veteran Senators patted him generously on the back and wished him well.

Gorman was one of the first to congratulate Clancy, but he remarked that his size was more suitable for the library than the hockey rink. He handed Clancy a contract as a substitute player. The two shook hands, and Clancy became a Senator substitute. After spending most of his rookie season on the bench, Clancy, only 147 pounds, eventually worked his way onto the First Team. As a member of the Ottawa club, Clancy won four Stanley Cups and appeared to be a fixture in the capital city. The Depression began and the Senators management needed money fast, and the only way to do that was to peddle a star to a wealthier club, and the most attractive star was King Clancy.

Thus, the Senator played right into Conn Smythe's hands. Conn was looking for a colorful superstar for his Maple Leafs team, and the moment he heard about Clancy's availability, he decided to get him. After betting on horse racing in order to get the money to acquire him, Smythe bought Clancy from Ottawa for $35,000 and threw in two extra players, Art Smith and Eric Pettinger, who were worth a total $15,000 on the NHL market. Clancy cost Smythe $50,000 but proved to be worth every penny of it. He later became an NHL referee and ultimately a vice president for the Maple Leafs.

Who has been afflicted by the "Curse of the King"?

During the 1920s, the Ottawa Senators won four Stanley Cups in seven seasons. They were anchored by Francis "King" Clancy, a defenseman known for being one of the toughest players around, despite his small stature. In 1930, however, the Senators traded Clancy to the Toronto Maple Leafs for $35,000 and two players. Within two seasons, the Leafs claimed the Stanley Cup.

It is said this trade spawned the "Curse of the King," as the modern-day Senators have neither won the Cup nor beaten the Maple Leafs in a playoff series since.

Which player starred on the Rangers' blue line for the first eleven years of the franchise's history and helped them win two Stanley Cups?

There have been few more colorful personalities in sports than Ivan Wilfred "Ching" Johnson, a bald defenseman who skated for the New York Rangers from their original NHL season, 1926–27, through the 1936–37 campaign. He ended his career a year later skating for the New York Americans.

A native of Winnipeg, Manitoba, Johnson was nicknamed "Ching" because he wore a wide grin on his face whenever he body checked an enemy to the ice—which was often—and when he smiled, his eyes gave him an Asian look.

Ivan Wilfred "Ching" Johnson

69

Johnson lost his original partner after three seasons when Taffy Abel was traded to the Chicago Black Hawks. But manager Lester Patrick obtained blocky French Canadian Leo Bourgeault, who became an outstanding defense mate for Ching. Of the three, only Johnson is in Hockey's Hall of Fame.

Following his retirement, he served as a linesman in the minors. One night, during a minor-league game in Washington, Ching forgot he wasn't a player anymore. While officiating, the ebullient Johnson watched a player get a breakaway and head toward the goal. Johnson the linesman became Johnson the erstwhile defenseman. Instead of remaining neutral, he darted across the ice and flattened the player. Asked later why he had made such a bizarre move, Ching smiled and said, "Just instinct, I guess."

Who centered Boston's "Dynamite Trio" in the late '20s and '30s?

"Cooney" Weiland centered "The Dynamite Trio," playing between Dit Clapper and Dutch Gainor when the Boston Bruins won their first Stanley Cup in 1929. He scored 43 times in 44 games that season. Weiland led the Hubmen to another title in 1939, then coached the Bruins to the Stanley Cup in 1940–41.

A winner of the Lester Patrick Trophy for "outstanding service to hockey in the United States," Weiland coached Harvard's Ivy League powerhouses from 1950 to 1971.

As a coach, Cooney always stressed defensive hockey. "Any championship team has to have a sound defense. They have to know when to play defense and how to check each man, keep his man under control."

Who was the first player to win the Calder Trophy?

There have been few more accomplished American-born players in the NHL than Carl Voss, who broke into the majors with the Maple Leafs in 1926–27 and played in 12 games. Two years later, he suited up in two more games before staying in the NHL for

---

Who was the NHL's first American-born and -trained goaltender?

Mike Karakas played six full seasons and parts of others for the Chicago Black Hawks. Karakas made his debut with Chicago in 1936 and won the Calder Trophy with a 1.85 goals-against average and overall record of 21–8. Two years later, he led the Black Hawks to the Stanley Cup championship, despite having a 14–25 record. Karakas played the final two games of the Stanley Cup Finals that year with a broken foot.

Throughout his career, Karakas had 28 regular season shutouts and another three in the playoffs. He played in all 48 games each of the six full seasons he played. Karakas was one of the original inductees to the United States Hockey Hall of Fame in 1973.

good but not without a lot of movement. His next game came with the Rangers (1932–33), but he was then immediately dealt to Detroit, then Ottawa (1933–34), St. Louis (1934–35), the Americans (1935–36), the Montreal Maroons (1936–37), and finally the Black Hawks (1937–38), where he gained most of his fame.

Coach (and major-league baseball umpire) Bill Stewart of the Black Hawks overruled club owner Major Frederic McLaughlin over Voss. The Major insisted Voss be cut from the squad as an obvious loser. Stewart was adamant. Voss would stay. He not only stayed but played a vital part in Chicago's most stirring hockey triumph, winning the Stanley Cup in 1938. In ten playoff games, Voss scored three big goals and two assists.

Yet, he left the majors after that season and gained renown later in life as referee-in-chief of the NHL under President Clarence Campbell. In that position, Voss was frequently criticized as a puppet of the club owners. He eventually retired and was replaced by Scotty Morrison.

Which goaltender won the Vezina Trophy four times while playing for the Bruins in the 1930s?

One of the National Hockey League's most accomplished goaltenders, Tiny Thompson won the Vezina Trophy four times in twelve NHL seasons. His rookie year, 1928–29, saw him produce an astonishing 1.18 goals-against average and twelve shutouts with the Boston Bruins. Boston also won the Stanley Cup that season. With Tiny in the nets, Boston finished first, winning the Prince of Wales Trophy in 1928–29, 1929–30, 1930–31, 1932–33, 1934–35, and 1937–38.

Thompson was prepared to continue in the Bruins' goal, but Boston had discovered sensational young Frankie Brimsek and decided to trade Tiny to the Detroit Red Wings. He later became the chief scout of western Canada for the Chicago Blackhawks, a position he held until his death in 1981. He is a member of the Hockey Hall of Fame. He is also the first goaltender in the NHL to record an assist by deliberately passing the puck with his stick to another player, who then scored. (Goalie Georges Vezina had recorded an assist previously when a puck bounced off his leg pad to a teammate, who then scored.)

Which player won the Hart Trophy his rookie season while leading his team to the Stanley Cup?

Nels Stewart, a strapping center, broke into the NHL with the Montreal Maroons in his typically dynamic fashion. During Nels's maiden season in 1925–26, he led the league in scoring and copped the Hart Trophy while leading the Maroons to the coveted Stanley Cup.

A big, rough player with a deadly accurate shot, Stewart was the pivot man for the Maroons' infamous "Big S Line" with Hooley Smith and Babe Siebert. As a unit, they were the roughest 'n' readiest forward line in the entire league. Stewart often would chew tobacco, produce juice and then spit it, blindingly, in the enemy goalie's eyes before shooting and scoring.

After seven seasons with the Maroons, Nels was sold to Boston, where he centered a line with Dit Clapper and Red Beattie. He continued his scoring heroics in Beantown, picking up his 200th career goal, as well as maintaining his bully-boy image. In 1935 he was suspended for fighting just before being peddled to the New York Americans.

Stewart played five years with the Americans, collecting his 300th career goal in 1938 and finally retiring from hockey in 1940.

Nels Stewart

Which player anchored Detroit's top line, leading them to become the first team to finish first and win the Stanley Cup in two straight seasons?

The Detroit Red Wings' first Stanley Cup championship in 1935–36 was accomplished in large part because of the work of Harry Lawrence (Larry) Aurie, dynamo of the Wings' first line, consisting of Aurie, Herbie Lewis, and Marty Barry. Aurie had been a member of the Red Wings sextet since 1927–28 and remained with the club through 1938–39.

Aurie, Barry, and Lewis sparked the Red Wings to first place again in 1936–37 and to another Stanley Cup triumph. Detroit thus became the first NHL team ever to finish first and win the Stanley Cup in two straight seasons. Aurie, however, had reached the end of his hockey rope, and the Red Wings sagged terribly in seasons to come.

Detroit manager Jack Adams always regretted not trading Aurie after the 1936–37 season. "Instead of standing pat," said Adams, "I should have traded. I'll never hesitate to bust up a champion team again."

Name the goaltender who came out of retirement to help his team with the Stanley Cup?

An excellent goaltender with Ottawa, then Detroit, Ottawa again, and finally the Montreal Maroons, Alec Connell played in the National Hockey League from 1924–25 through 1936–37. During the 1931–32 season, he had an unusual brush with death. Playing for Detroit, Connell tended goal at Madison Square Garden against the New York Americans. At that time, the Americans were owned by notorious Prohibition rum lord William "Big Bill" Dwyer, one of the richest bootleggers in the country. During the game, Connell engaged in a keen argument with the goal judge and tried to hit the judge with his large goalie stick. Unknown to Connell, the goal judge was a "hit man" for Dwyer. Members of the gang tried unsuccessfully to rub out Connell after the game, and only quick thinking by a cordon of police saved the goaltender's life.

Alex Connell came out of retirement to rejoin the Montreal Maroons in 1934. With Connell in between the pipes, the Maroons went on to win the Stanley Cup. Afterward, Connell retired again. Four years later the Maroons retired from the NHL.

Who served as left winger for the famed "Big S Line"?

Albert "Babe" Siebert broke into the professional hockey wars in 1925–26 with the Montreal Maroons. He was a high-scoring left winger during his rookie season and promptly helped the Maroons storm to the Stanley Cup.

Babe's thirst for body contact was instantly appreciated by Eddie Gerard, the Maroons' coach, and soon the strapping Siebert was shuttling back and forth from defense to the forward line. In 1930, Babe was moved up as a permanent portsider with the formation of the "Big S Line." Skating with Nels Stewart and Hooley Smith, this unholy trio was the scourge of the league, averaging well over 200 penalty minutes for the next three seasons.

Sold to the New York Rangers in 1932, Siebert was moved back to defense, where he was paired with the great Ching Johnson. This defensive duo decimated opposing wingers, and once again Siebert found himself on a Cup-winning squad.

The following season found Babe on the move again. This time he was off to Boston, where he was hastily pressed into service as a replacement for Eddie Shore. Shore had been suspended by the league following a brutal encounter with Ace Bailey. After Shore's reinstatement, he and Siebert formed one of the most feared blue line patrols in the entire league.

Babe was traded to the Montreal Canadiens in 1936–37, where he collected the Hart Trophy. Siebert played two more seasons with the Habs, captaining the 1938–39 squad.

He was named coach of the Frenchmen for the coming season, but that was never to be. Tragically, Babe Siebert died in a drowning mishap that very summer. During his fourteen-year career, he was a two-time Stanley Cup champion and was named an All-Star three times. He was selected to the Hall of Fame in 1964.

Albert "Babe" Siebert

73

Who scored the 1934 Stanley Cup-winning goal in double overtime to give Chicago its first Stanley Cup?

The Chicago Black Hawks' successes in their early NHL years can in large part be credited to Harold "Mush" March, who played exclusively for the Hawks from the 1928–29 season to his concluding year in the majors, 1944–45. March was at his best in the thirties, working on a line with Tommy Cook at center and Paul Thompson on the other wing.

On April 10, 1934, March scored the Stanley Cup-winning goal against Red Wings goalie Wilf Cude in double overtime to give the Windy City its first NHL championship club. Not surprisingly, March also was on the Hawks' second Stanley Cup championship squad in April 1938, scoring key goals in the fifth and final game of the series against the Toronto Maple Leafs. Although March never played on another Chicago Cup winner, he sparked the Hawks in the 1941 playoffs with two goals and three assists.

It has been said that one of big-league hockey's funniest sights was March, a smallish skater, hiding behind huge Taffy Abel, a Chicago defenseman, as Abel carried the puck into enemy territory. With March obscured, Abel would then drop his teammate the puck and allow Mush to shoot it between his opened legs.

Which former Hart Trophy winner and Montreal Canadiens star was nicknamed "The Little Giant"?

Aurel Joliat was a native of Ontario, having grown up in the New Edinburgh district of Ottawa. He learned his hockey on the frozen Rideau River along with Bill and Frank Boucher, who also were to achieve enormous fame in the NHL. In time Joliat graduated to a fast league in western Canada and arrived in a Canadiens uniform when manager Leo Dandurand decided to unload the aging Newsy Lalonde.

Aurel weighed 135 pounds at his heaviest, but his size never bothered him. It apparently motivated him to compensate with a vast repertoire of stickhandling maneuvers and pirouettes. "He transported the world of ballet to the hockey arena," said one admirer, to which Aurel replied, "A fellow *needs* finesse when he weighs only 135 pounds!"

Joliat teamed up with Howie Morenz in the 1923–24 season. The pair jelled perfectly right from the start, although Aurel was to prove that season that he could excel with or without Morenz at his side.

The Canadiens had gone up against the Calgary Tigers in the playoffs, and Morenz's shoulder was broken after he was hit by Red Dutton and Herb Gardiner. Joliat was a constant source of annoyance to his larger opponents. Once, after Aurel had thoroughly confounded Toronto's Babe Dye with a series of fakes, the distressed Dye skated over to Dandurand at the Canadiens' bench and said: "I'm tired of chasing that shadow of yours—that Frenchman, Joliat. Move him over to center, Leo, hold a mirror to each side of him—you'll have the fastest line in hockey."

At the time of his retirement, Joliat was third behind Morenz and Nels Stewart all-time for goals scored. He has since dropped out of the top 100. He does, however, remain ninth all time in goals for the Montreal Canadiens franchise. He was inducted into the Hall of Fame in 1947.

Who starred as left winger for the famed Kid Line?

Harvey "Busher" Jackson was the most tragic figure on Toronto's Kid Line of Charlie Conacher, Joe Primeau, and Jackson. Unlike his linemates, who acquired fortune after their retirement in the late thirties, Jackson encountered hard times

The "Kid Line," one of the most famous 1930s lines, included (left to right) Charlie Conacher, Joe Primeau, and Busher Jackson.

throughout his life. He was even given trouble by the Hall of Fame committee, which hesitated for years to nominate him allegedly because of his drinking problems.

A product of Frank Selke's Toronto Junior Marlboros, Jackson turned pro in 1929–30 with the Maple Leafs. According to Selke, Jackson was the "classiest" player he had ever seen. "He could pivot on a dime, stickhandle through an entire team without giving up the puck, and shoot like a bullet from either forehand or backhand. His backhand was the best I ever saw."

A typical Jackson play occurred on December 24, 1931, in a game against the Canadiens. The score was tied in sudden-death overtime as the clock ticked off the final seconds. Busher grabbed the puck, skated the length of the rink, and scored a split second before the gong sounded.

He was a major factor in the Leafs' first Stanley Cup triumph in 1932. Jackson remained with Toronto until 1938–39, when he was traded to the Americans. In 1941–42, the Amerks dealt him to Boston, where he finished his pro career in 1943–44. He was eventually elected to the Hockey Hall of Fame in 1971.

Which Hall of Fame player recorded 1,254 penalty minutes?

George Reginald "Red" Horner, who was signed by Conn Smythe in the fall of 1928, took basic training in hockey on the Toronto playgrounds, although he was born on his father's farm near Lynden, Ontario.

Toronto was playing the Pittsburgh Pirates, and the young Horner was starting on defense for the Maple Leafs. The game was less than a minute old when Frank Frederickson, the marvelous Icelandic-Canadian forward, moved the puck into the Toronto zone. Frederickson dropped his head one way and lurched the other way, leaving Horner immobilized like a statue. The shot went wide, and the puck skittered back to Pittsburgh territory, where Frederickson recaptured it and launched another attack.

Once again, Frederickson tested the rookie Horner. By then, Red had sized up his foe, and he dispatched Frederickson to the ice with an emphatic body check. The referee blew the whistle, and Red was sent to the penalty box. In his career, he would eventually serve 1,254 minutes worth of penalties, a record that went unbroken for years.

On the night of December 12, 1933, Horner was on the ice at Boston Garden when Eddie Shore of the Bruins knocked Ace Bailey of the Maple Leafs unconscious—and nearly killed Bailey—with a behind-the-back charge. Shore's seeming callousness infuriated Horner, who then hit Shore with a punch on the jaw. It was a right uppercut that stiffened the big defensive star like an axed steer and also resulted in a suspension for Horner.

Horner maintained such robust play through the thirties. In a playoff game against Chicago in April 1938, Red rapped Chicago forward Doc Romnes across the face with his stick. This time Red's attack was in vain. Chicago went on to win the Stanley Cup. Red continued playing through the 1939–40 season, when he finally retired. He was inducted into the Hall of Fame in 1965.

Who was considered to be one of the most exciting players of the 1930s and 1940s and had one of the hardest shots of its day?

There are those who insist today that Charlie Conacher was the most exciting player they had even seen and his shot was the hardest of its day, when slapshots were unheard of and a player beat a goaltender with a quick snap of his wrist.

Who was a defenseman for ten years, a coach for six, and NHL president for three?

Red Dutton, a great defenseman of the early NHL, broke into pro hockey with Calgary of the old WCHL. After five years with the Tigers, Dutton signed with the Montreal Maroons, where he spent four years gleefully bouncing opposing forwards off the boards.

In 1931, Red was traded to the New York Americans in exchange for the great Lionel Conacher. Red was one of the leading badmen of the day, but the Americans were basically a hapless bunch of skaters with no real leadership.

It was not until 1936, when Red became a player-manager of the Americans, that they began to approach respectability. Dutton's leadership got the Amerks into the playoffs, but he suffered a painful back injury and was forced to watch from the sidelines as the Toronto sextet bounced the Americans back to Broadway in the semifinal round.

After Dutton retired as a player, he served as manager for six more seasons. The Redhead remained very active on the pro hockey scene and was president of the NHL for three more years from 1943 to 1946. Dutton is a member of the Hockey Hall of Fame.

Charlie made his NHL debut on November 14, 1929, for the Toronto Maple Leafs at the Mutual Street Arena. Chicago's Black Hawks, with the redoubtable Charlie Gardiner in goal, were the opponents, and the fans filling the old Toronto ice palace were frankly skeptical of Conacher's ability to skate and shoot with the pros, especially since he never had basic hockey training in the minor leagues. The game was close, but Charlie was never out of place. At one point the puck came to him as he skated over the blue line. Conacher caught it on the blade of his stick and in the same motion flubbed the rubber in Gardiner's direction. Before the Chicago goalie could move, the red light flashed, and Conacher was a Leaf to stay.

At first, Smythe used Conacher on a line with Joe Primeau at center and Harold Cotton on left wing; but despite Conacher's instant success, Primeau still failed to click. Just before Christmas 1929, Smythe made the move that would alter hockey history. He pulled Cotton off the line and inserted Busher Jackson in his place at right wing. Hockey's first and most renowned Kid Line was born. Success was a dramatic volcanic eruption. Toronto defeated the Black Hawks, the Canadiens, and the Maroons right after Christmas and went undefeated until January 23 of the New Year. Charlie went on to become one of the most dynamic of NHL forwards. He later took a turn at coaching the Chicago Black Hawks with little success and was inducted into the Hall of Fame in 1961.

Which Hall of Famer played both right wing and defense for 20 consecutive seasons with the Bruins?

Dit Clapper, a tower of strength whether playing right wing or defense, labored for the Boston Bruins for twenty consecutive seasons.

Clapper's most memorable season as a forward came when he, Cooney Weiland, and Dutch Gainor combined to form the feared Dynamite Line. This trio swept the Beantowners to the 1929 Stanley Cup. With Dit's aid, the Bruins lost only five games in the entire 1930 season, but they were defeated in the playoffs by the Montreal Canadiens.

In 1939, after ten years as one of the premier forwards in the league, Clapper made the switch to defense. Paired with the legendary Eddie Shore, Dit made First Team All-Star, and the Bruins again won the Stanley Cup.

Dit Clapper's jersey is on display at the International Hockey Hall of Fame museum in Kingston, Ontario, Canada.

Clapper saw double duty as a player-coach during his last three years with the Bruins until his retirement as a player in 1947. He continued on as coach of the Bostonians for a few more seasons and was elected to the Hall of Fame.

Both Howie Morenz and Aurel Joliat are in Hockey's Hall of Fame, but the right wing on that famed Canadiens line is not. Who is he and what was his nickname?

Johnny Gagnon, "The Black Cat of Chicoutimi." Although Bill Boucher and Art Gagne had previously played alongside Morenz and Joliat, it was Gagnon who made the line complete when he came up to the Canadiens in 1930. As a rookie, Gagnon scored six of the line's seven goals in the playoffs as Montreal won the Stanley Cup.

That line—Gagnon in particular—proved that there was room for good little men in hockey. That Black Cat stood only 5'5" and weighed a compact 140 pounds.

THE 1940s

HOCKEY DURING WORLD WAR II

Which team lost its top goalie, top defensive pair, and top forward line and subsequently fell from first to last place in one year?

Every team was feeling the effects of World War II, none more than the New York Rangers. After finishing first in 1941–42 and reaching the semifinals in the Stanley Cup playoffs, the Rangers experienced a huge collapse.

In 1942 their goaltender, Jim Henry, top defensive pair of Art Coulter and Muzz Patrick, and their top line tandem of Alex Shibicky and the Colville brothers, Neil and Mac, all departed the team. The biggest loss was Henry.

The Rangers tried to use four different goalies to replace Henry. Collectively, the four goalies allowed 253 goals, more than five per game.

Head Coach Frank Boucher used 32 skaters, some of whom played for less than ten games.

They went five years without making the playoffs. During those years, they averaged just 11 wins. In 1947 they squeaked into the fourth and final playoff spot but lost in the semifinals.

While "The Great Darkness" was a time of political corruption in Quebec, what did that term mean for a Quebec hockey fan?

"The Great Darkness" was a time in Quebec (1936–39 and 1944–59) ruled by Premier Maurice Duplessis and his Union Nationale government, which suppressed modernization in the province. However, for the hockey fans of Quebec, "The Great Darkness" was the period between 1931–44, when the Montreal Canadiens were an embarrassing franchise.

Frederick Murray "Muzz" Patrick

The Habs of that era were so terrible, they almost moved to Cleveland! That's why the Canadiens team that won the Stanley Cup in 1943–44 is so revered, and had that group not emerged as a hockey powerhouse just as Canada was coming out of the Depression, there's a chance the Habs dynasty that followed in the 1950s may never have happened.

Which two main players led to the formation of the dynamic 1943–44 Montreal Canadiens?

A variety of elements led to the formation of the Habs that season, including the emergence of Maurice "Rocket" Richard, who was the scoring force in the NHL. Bill Durnan also claimed his spot in the Montreal net, and he later went on to win six Vezina Trophies in his seven-season career.

How did a founding member of the NHL help the 1943–44 Habs' success?

Tommy Gorman, one of the founding members of the NHL, was hired as GM of the Canadiens in 1940. He already had five Stanley Cups under his belt, with three different teams. Gorman rebuilt the franchise along with coach Dick Irvin and brought the Habs back to being contenders.

How many regular season home games did the 1943–44 Habs lose?

Zero.

How did many of the 1943–44 Canadiens players avoid going to war during World War II?

Len Peto, executive and director for Montreal, was also an executive with Canadair, which supplied the Royal Canadian Air Force with parts and aircraft and was able to negotiate his way around the conscription laws. He was able to keep many of the Habs players among those with "Home Service Only" status during World War II. So, while most teams were hit by the war, the Habs were generally unaffected, aside from losing defenseman Kenny Reardon, who returned to play for the Habs after the war ended.

Were Rocket Richard and Elmer Lach able to serve in WWII?

No. They both tried to volunteer for the war effort but were turned down. Richard even tried to enlist a second time and was turned down.

Before the 1943–44 season when the Habs won the Stanley Cup, why was Maurice Richard almost traded away from Montreal?

The 1943–44 season was Richard's sophomore season, but his rookie year was not good. He had suffered a plethora of injuries, including a broken leg, and had scored just five goals and 11 points in 16 games. Habs GM Tommy Gorman began to wonder if Richard could handle the rigors of playing in the big league and seriously considered trading his rights.

Coach Dick Irvin begged Gorman not to trade Richard and to give him another opportunity to live up to his potential. In 1943–44, Richard posted 32 goals and 22 assists in 46 games and then in the playoffs Richard scored 12 goals in just nine games, which included a five-goal game in Game 2 of the first round against the Toronto Maple Leafs.

The next season, the Rocket scored his history-making 50 goals in 50 games.

Which Montreal Canadien waited until 10 minutes before the first game of the season to sign with the Habs?

Goalie Bill Durnan, who was a 27-year-old amateur and eschewed the NHL and every-

Joseph-Henri-Maurice "Rocket" Richard

81

> ### What historic event took place during the final game of the 1944 Stanley Cup Finals between the Montreal Canadiens and the Chicago Blackhawks?
>
> In the final game between the Habs and the Blackhawks, the first-ever penalty shot awarded in a Cup final took place. Durnan stopped Chicago's Virgil Johnson's shot.

thing it stood for after a bad experience during a tryout with the Toronto Maple Leafs. He was already a star with the Kirkland Lake Blue Devils and the Montreal Royals, and he prepared to play out his career as an amateur.

However, the Montreal Canadiens sought him. He didn't sign his contract with the Habs until 10 minutes before his first game. Nonetheless, he ended up in the Hall of Fame with six Vezina Trophies and six First Team All-Star selections in his seven-season career.

What was so unique about Bill Durnan's style of play?

Durnan was ambidextrous, and there were instances when he would switch his stick from one glove to the other! Former NHL referee Bill Chadwick said, "It doesn't matter what side he's on, you've always got that big glove staring you in the face."

Chadwick believed Durnan was the best goalie he had ever seen.

Despite World War II, who were some players that were able to help the Detroit Red Wings win their third Stanley Cup in 1942–43?

Sid Abel, Johnny Mowers, Mud Bruneteau, Syd Howe, Carl Liscombe, and Joe Carveth, to name just a few.

That season was Mowers's third as the Wings' goaltender. He finished the regular season with a league-best 25 wins, six shutouts, and a 2.47 GAA on his way to the Vezina Trophy.

In the playoffs, Mowers won eight of 10 games with a 1.94 GAA, and he shut out the Boston Bruins in consecutive games to complete a sweep in the Stanley Cup Finals.

Howe had been purchased from the St. Louis Eagles nine years prior to this season. During this season, he was a consistent scorer and finished first among all Wings players with 55 points.

How did WWII affect the 1942–43 Stanley Cup champion Red Wings?

After the 1942–43 season, Johnny Mowers decided to enlist in the Royal Canadian Air Force and serve in WWII. When he did return to the Wings, he retired from the NHL a year later.

The 1943–44 season saw many offensive players starring in the NHL since many of the league's defensive players were serving in World War II. Sid Abel and Jack Stewart also served in the Royal Canadian Air Force in 1943–44 and 1944–45.

Which team during the 1930s made it to the Stanley Cup Finals six times in eight years but lost each time and then won the Cup six times in ten years during the 1940s?

During the 1930s and 1940s, the Toronto Maple Leafs were one of the best teams in the NHL. During the 1930s, the Leafs were led by Hall of Famers Charlie Conacher, Red Horner, and goaltender George Hainsworth. In 1932–33, 1934–35, 1935–36, 1937–38, 1938–39, and 1939–40, the Leafs made it all the way to the Stanley Cup Finals but fell each time.

After the Leafs' loss to the hated Rangers in 1940, Conn Smythe allowed Dick Irvin to leave and coach the Montreal Canadiens. He then brought in former Toronto Maple Leafs defenseman Hap Day to be head coach. Led by Day, captain Syl Apps Sr., goaltender Turk Broda, and later Ted Kennedy, the Leafs went on to win the Stanley Cup in 1941–42, 1944–45, 1946–47, 1947–48, 1948–49, and finally again in 1950–51.

Which team won the Stanley Cup in 1941 after losing just eight regular season games?

In 1940 the Boston Bruins traded away defenseman Eddie Shore and in 1941 won their third Stanley Cup. That season they lost only eight regular season games and tied 13. They defeated the Toronto Maple Leafs in a thrilling seven-game series to reach the Stanley Cup Finals and swept the Detroit Red Wings to win the Cup.

They were led by Bill Cowley, who finished tops in the league in scoring with 62 points. Roy Conacher and Milt Schmidt each had 38 points and Eddie Wiseman and Bobby Bauer contributed 40 points and 39 point respectively. Captain Dit Clapper led all Boston blueliners with 26 points and Frank Brimsek was again outstanding in net winning 27 games and posting a 2.01 GAA.

Which team won its first Cup in 1934 and again in 1938, despite a 14–25–9 regular season record?

After the Black Hawks finished last in the NHL in 1932–33, Tommy Gorman returned as head coach. That season the team scored a league low 88 goals but also allowed a league best 83 goals, in large part thanks to its team captain, goaltender Charlie Gardiner. The Black Hawks would finish 20–17–11, second in their division.

In the playoffs, the Black Hawks defeated the Montreal Canadiens, Montreal Maroons, and the Red Wings to win their first-ever Stanley Cup. Hero Charlie Gardiner would pass away that off-season due to complications from brain surgery. They would also lose coach Tommy Gorman, who went on to coach the Canadiens.

83

In 1937–38 the Hawks were entering their 12th season in the NHL and were coming off a terrible season. After replacing head coach Clem Loughlin with Bill Stewart, the Hawks continued to struggle through the season. They finished with a 14–25–9 record and somehow made the playoffs, beating out the Red Wings for 3rd place in the American Division by just two points.

The Black Hawks stunned the Canadiens in the first round in three games and then shocked the New York Americans, who finished with 12 more points than the Black Hawks. They would move on to face the Toronto Maple Leafs in the finals. Using three different goalies, most notably Mike Karakas, the Black Hawks defeated the Leafs three games to one and earned their second Stanley Cup.

WARTIME CHARACTERS

How did Steve Buzinski find his way to the NHL?

During World War II, the New York Rangers' starting goalie, "Sugar" Jim Henry, was drafted into the service. After his intended replacement was assigned to a wartime manufacturing job, general manager Lester Patrick invited several players to try out for the job. Buzinski, who had been playing senior hockey in western Canada, was one of them and won the starting spot.

What did Buzinski infamously say before giving up ten goals in one game?

During a game against the Montreal Canadiens in 1942, Buzinski snagged the first shot of the game with his glove; when defenseman Ott Heller skated by, the goalie remarked that catching the puck was "like picking apples off a tree."

After saying that, he allowed 10 goals as the Habs topped the Blueshirts 10–4.

How did Buzinski inadvertently find his way into the history books?

While he did not fare very well in the net, Buzinski did help shape history on two occasions during the 1942 season. During the 10–4 loss to the Canadiens, he gave up Maurice "Rocket" Richard's first NHL goal; Richard, of course, would go on to be one of hockey's greatest offensive players.

Buzinski also was in net when the Red Wings' Carl Liscombe recorded a then-record seven points in one game.

How many teams did Frank McCool play on before reaching the NHL?

McCool's career started with his hometown Calgary Broncos in the Alberta Senior Hockey League in 1936. A year later, he moved up to the Calgary Canadiens, who claimed the Memorial Cup. He then played hockey at Gonzaga University before enlisting in the Canadian Army, where he continued to play for the Calgary Currie Army squad before

> ## What unflattering nickname did Buzinski earn during his time with the Rangers?
>
> **D**ue to his generally ineffective play, Buzinski picked up the moniker "the puck goes in-ski." The goalie himself, though, claimed to have no idea where the nickname originated.

being deployed. At the start of the 1944–45 season, he reached the NHL, signing a contract with the Toronto Maple Leafs.

Did McCool find success at the highest level of hockey?

Despite his long road to the NHL, McCool immediately fit in with the Leafs. Not only was he their starting goalie for the 1944–45 season, but he also recorded 24 wins on the way to a Stanley Cup title and a Calder Trophy.

What records did McCool set during the 1945 playoffs?

McCool recorded three consecutive shutouts during the playoffs, although the record has since been tied by Patrick Lalime, Brent Johnson, and Jean-Sebastien Giguere. He also set a record for the fewest goals allowed in a Stanley Cup Finals with nine, but that record was broken by Tim Thomas, who allowed only eight in 2011.

How long did McCool's NHL career last?

While he played very well in his first season in Toronto, McCool struggled with ulcers. He only played 22 games during the next season and was forced to retire after two seasons with the Maple Leafs.

Who exactly were the Coast Guard Cutters?

The Cutters were a team based out of Baltimore and organized among men enlisted in the United States Coast Guard during World War II. While the team played in the Eastern Amateur Hockey League, they had more than their share of professional stars. In fact, Commander C. R. MacLean would try to persuade any hockey players who had a choice of service to choose the Coast Guard so they could join his team.

What was it like to face the Cutters in a game?

In addition to their skill on the ice, facing the Cutters was a spectacle in itself. They wore red, white, and blue sweaters with stars on the arms and crossed anchors on the chest and were constantly accompanied by a 30-piece marching band.

What unexpected consequence did MacLean's recruiting efforts have?

Because so many stars joined the Coast Guard to play hockey, MacLean had to split the squad into two different teams when they weren't playing league matches. The skaters would be divided into the Clippers and the Cutters and play intense intrasquad games, which George Taylor of the *Baltimore News-Post* called "more exciting than the Stanley Cup playoffs."

How did a Canadian end up playing for the United States Coast Guard team?

Art Coulter, who was the captain of the New York Rangers before WWII, was born in Manitoba and consequently held Canadian citizenship. Since he was making a career in America, he wanted to claim citizenship and did so once the war broke out. As a newly naturalized citizen, he was able to serve in the military and found his way to the Cutters.

Art Coulter

Who was the toughest opponent the Cutters ever faced?

Despite their amateur status, the Cutters faced off against the Stanley Cup champion Detroit Red Wings in January of 1944. The Cutters played the Wings tightly and only trailed by one goal during the third period but went on to lose 8–3. Manny Cotlow, a Coast Guard defenseman, explained that the Red Wings were not overly intimidating but simply played smarter than the servicemen.

Why did a riot break out when the Philadelphia Falcons hosted the Cutters?

During the game, Philadelphia's Marty Madore and the Cutters' Manny Cotlow got into a fight on the ice and another in the penalty box. Several Philadelphia fans intervened, hoping to give Madore the advantage; several players from the Cutters rushed over to aid Cotlow. Before anyone knew what was happening, a full-scale brawl broke out, and the police riot squad had to be called to the arena.

What caused the end of the Coast Guard Cutters?

Soon after their start, the Cutters faced some criticism for allowing star players to stay at home to play while average citizens were sent abroad to face combat. Their end was also signaled when, during a game at Madison Square Garden against the New York Rovers, a public address announcement was made stating that Joe Kucler, who was the club's leading scorer, would have to report for active duty after the game. The club was officially disbanded in 1944.

What record did Guidolin set when he was forced into NHL action?

During the 1942 season, the Boston Bruins were desperate to fill the holes in their lineup caused by military service. They signed Armand "Bep" Guidolin, who had recently won the Memorial Cup with the Oshawa Generals; he made his debut at 16 years, 11 months old, which, at the time, made him the youngest player to skate in the NHL.

What cause was Guidolin involved with towards the end of his playing career?

Guidolin was an early supporter of the formation of a players' union, even though the NHL Players' Association was formed after his time in the league was over.

Which all-time great did Guidolin coach in junior hockey?

In 1965, Guidolin took over the Oshawa Generals; at the time, they had a hotshot defenseman by the name of Bobby Orr.

How many teams did Guidolin lead from behind the bench?

After his career as a player, Guidolin became the coach of the Ontario Hockey Association's Belleville McFarlands and led them to the 1958 Allan Cup and 1959 World Championship. In 1965, he took over the Oshawa Generals before moving to the London Knights.

In 1972, he made the leap to the NHL, where he coached the Bruins for a season and a half; he then moved on to the Kansas City Scouts. His coaching career ended after 63 games behind the Edmonton Oilers' bench during the 1976–77 WHA season.

What nickname did Harry Lumley pick up as a young player?

While it was not the toughest nickname around, Lumley came to be known as "Apple Cheeks" for his rosy complexion, especially while he was playing.

How did the Owen Sound Orphans, one of Lumley's Senior League teams, get their name?

At the time, most minor-league clubs had a sponsor, but Owen Sound could not find one. Consequently, they took up the mantle as the Orphans.

Where did Armand Guidolin get his nickname "Bep" from?

Guidolin picked up the nickname "Bep" at an early age. He was the youngest child in the family and his mother, who spoke mainly Italian, pronounced "baby" as "beppy." Over time, that became condensed to "Bep."

What was unusual about Lumley's NHL debut?

After his time in juniors, Lumley played for the Indianapolis Capitals, the AHL affiliate of the Detroit Red Wings. He made his NHL debut for the New York Rangers in 1943, though; the Blueshirts needed an emergency goalie and worked out a one-game loan for Lumley. He was only 17 at the time, making him the youngest goalie to ever appear in the NHL.

How did Lumley respond to being traded twice in two seasons?

Early in the 1950–51 season, the Red Wings shipped Lumley to the Chicago Blackhawks; he suffered back-to-back 40-loss seasons and was traded to the Toronto Maple Leafs. His fortunes changed north of the border, though.

In the 1953–54 season, he was named a First Team All-Star and earned the Vezina Trophy with a masterful 1.86 GAA. He also set a league record with 13 shutouts, which stood until Tony Esposito posted 15 in 1969–70.

What technological advance did Lumley bring to goaltending?

Lumley's pads had an indentation below his knees; this would help the puck fall softly to the ice rather than bouncing back out for a dangerous rebound.

What advice would Lumley give to young players after his retirement?

While it was the way he earned his living, Lumley would urge children to play a position other than goalie. He would tell them that it did not take any intelligence to stop pucks.

What two events led to Theodore Kennedy's love affair with hockey?

Just before he was born, Kennedy's father was killed in a hunting accident. His mother began selling candy at the local hockey arena to earn extra money, so "Teeder" grew up around the game. Later, when he was seven years old, a family friend took Kennedy to see the Toronto Maple Leafs play in Games 1 and 2 of the 1932 Stanley Cup Finals. Charlie Conacher became his hero, and Kennedy was hooked.

Where did Kennedy get the nickname "Teeder"?

Growing up, neighborhood friends struggled to pronounce Theodore and began calling him "Teeder." The nickname stuck, and it began appearing in print as Kennedy achieved success.

How did Kennedy find out the Toronto Maple Leafs were interested in him?

At home in Port Colborne, Ontario, Kennedy was called to the principal's office during his Latin class. While he thought he was in trouble, he simply had a phone call from Nels Stewart, who was a former NHL star and his coach on the local senior league team. Stewart told him that the Leafs' general manager, Frank Selke, was interested in Kennedy, and Teeder got on the train to Toronto immediately.

What advice did Kennedy receive before his first NHL game?

Before his debut, the Leafs' coach Hap Day told Kennedy to "stay with your check and keep him from scoring." Kennedy not only did that, but he picked up an assist as his line scored three goals in a 5–5 tie.

What incident with Gordie Howe was Kennedy involved in?

In Game 1 of a 1950 playoff series between Toronto and Detroit, Gordie Howe attempted to check Kennedy; Teeder dodged the hit, and Howe, unable to stop, slammed into the boards, sustaining serious injuries. The Red Wings claimed Kennedy had butt-ended Howe, although no penalty was called on the play. NHL president Clarence Campbell was at the game and stated that Kennedy had done nothing wrong; Howe also said, "Ted is too good of a player to deliberately injure another player."

Who did Kennedy get to meet before a game in 1951?

In October 1951, the Maple Leafs and Blackhawks played an afternoon exhibition game before their league game that evening. Princess Elizabeth, who would become Queen Elizabeth II, was in attendance and Kennedy, the Leafs' captain, got to meet her.

Why did Frank Selke think Kennedy never made an All-Star Team?

Despite putting up impressive statistics and claiming five Stanley Cups and a Hart Trophy, Kennedy was never a First Team All-Star. Selke claimed that Teeder lacked the "color" to be tapped for such an individualistic honor.

How long did it take Gus Bodnar to make an impact at the NHL level?

Bodnar joined the Toronto Maple Leafs in October 1943 after leading the Thunder Bay Junior A Hockey League in points the previous season. Eager to show he could play at the highest level, he scored his first NHL goal 15 seconds into the game, setting the record for the fastest first goal in league history.

Why did Kennedy turn down his first NHL contract?

When Teeder was 16 years old, he was invited to train with the Montreal Royals, who were affiliated with the Canadiens. Kennedy took the train to Montreal, but no one from the organization was there to meet him at the station; he also felt that management did not care about his request to stay closer to Lower Canada College, where he was studying. Before long, he was fed up with the experience and feeling homesick, so he returned home. When the season ended, the Canadiens offered him a contract, but Kennedy declined, remembering his unpleasant experience.

Was Bodnar's hot start with Toronto a fluke?

Bodnar's first season with the Leafs actually proved to be his best professional season. He recorded 62 points (22 goals, 40 assists) and won the 1943–44 Calder Trophy.

What other record did Bodnar set during his time as a pro?

In March 1952, Bodnar broke the record for the fastest three assists in league history. His teammate Bill Mosienko scored a record-setting hat trick in 21 seconds and Bodnar assisted on all three goals.

What awards did Bodnar claim after he retired from the NHL?

While his skating days ended in 1955, Bodnar stayed close to the game by coaching. In 1966–67, he lifted the Memorial Cup as the head coach of the Toronto Marlboros. He then spent time behind the bench of the WHL's Salt Lake Golden Eagles before returning to Ontario, where he was named 1972 OHA Coach of the Year for his work behind the Oshawa Generals bench.

In 1943 what became the first line to feature three brothers?

In 1943, while playing for the Chicago Black Hawks, Doug Bentley played left wing on a line with his brothers Max and Reginald. The three only lasted as a line for 11 games, as Reginald's NHL career lasted that long.

While playing together, both Doug and Max had breakout seasons. Doug posted 33 goals and 73 points, while Max netted 26 goals and 70 points.

Both Doug and Max are in the Hockey Hall of Fame.

POST–WORLD WAR II

Which player helped lead the Rangers to the Stanley Cup in 1940 and coached them to the final in 1950?

Lynn Patrick played ten seasons with the New York Rangers. In 1940, along with linemates Bryan Hextall and Phil Watson, he helped lead the Rangers to the Stanley Cup championship with 28 regular season points and four in the postseason.

In 1946–47 Patrick was named head coach of the Rangers' American Hockey League affiliate, the New Haven Ramblers. He appeared in 16 games as a utility player for the Ramblers. He remained with the club for two more seasons before he was promoted to head coach of the Rangers. In his first season with the Rangers, 1948–49, they did not make the playoffs. In his second season, they finished fourth in the division and made it all the way to the Stanley Cup Finals before falling to the mighty Detroit Red Wings.

Lynn Patrick in a 1939 photo.

How did a brawl between the Rangers and Canadiens break out in New York's Madison Square Garden in March of 1947?

The battle originally started when Rangers winger Bryan Hextall injured Canadiens defenseman Ken Reardon with a vicious body check. As Reardon was making his way off the ice, with blood pouring from his mouth, some of the Rangers rose from their seats on the bench to get a better glimpse of Reardon skating off the ice. The Canadiens thought the Rangers were going to jump Reardon and retaliated. The Canadiens, however, ended up fighting the Rangers fans, and the Rangers had to come to their aid. At one point there were over fifteen players fighting at once.

Maurice Richard broke his stick over Bill Juzda's head, and the two began to wrestle on the ground. Emile Bouchard grabbed Hextall's stick and dropped him to the ground with a punch. Bill Moe picked up his stick and snapped it over Bouchard's head, who did not even seem to notice. Moe then faced off with Bill Durnan. Hal Laycoe and Leo Lamoureaux exchanged punches until they collapsed into an embrace from exhaustion. The biggest punch of the brawl was said to have come from Joe Cooper of the Rangers, who ducked an upper cup from Murph Chamberlain and then punched Chamberlain so ferociously he flew back over the sideboards and into the front-row seat.

After 25 minutes there were only three penalties given out. Richard, Juzda, and Chamberlain each received 10-minute misconduct penalties.

When was the first official NHL All-Star game and how has it evolved over the years?

The first official NHL All-Star game was played on October 13, 1947, at Maple Leaf Gardens. The format of the game, which remained the same until the late 1960s, was for the reigning Stanley Cup champions to play against a selection of players from the five other teams.

91

When the NHL was divided into four divisions in 1974–75, the All-Star contest featured the Wales Conference stars versus the Campbell Conference stars.

In the 1990s the NHL Skills Competition was introduced, as well as the Heroes of Hockey game. The Heroes of Hockey game featured NHL alumni, and the Skills Competition allowed players to compete against each other in a series of events that allowed them to showcase their talents. The events included accuracy shooting, fastest skater, hardest shot, and an elimination shootout. Players today often like to get very creative in the shootout competition.

In 2011 the NHL developed the idea of doing a "fantasy draft" to decide the teams. The players that were chosen as All-Stars selected two captains. Each captain would then draft their own team by picking one player at a time.

There were three slightly different renditions of the famous "Production Line." What were they, and who was the only player that was on all three?

The original "Production Line" consisted of wingers Gordie Howe and Ted Lindsay and center Sid Abel. The trio helped the Detroit Red Wings become one of the best American teams in the NHL. In 1947–48, the trio was tops on the team in scoring, and in 1950 Lindsay won the scoring crown with the other two finishing right behind him in the scoring race. The feat has not been repeated since.

The next year, Gordie Howe won his first of four consecutive Art Ross trophies. He would continue to produce, finishing in the top five in scoring for the next 20 seasons.

After the 1951–52 season, Sid Abel was traded to the Black Hawks in order to make room for the extremely talented, and younger, Alex Delvecchio. The third and final rendition of the legendary line played together in the late 1960s. When Ted Lindsay retired, Frank Mahovlich replaced Lindsay at the wing. Howe was the only player to be on all three iterations of the Production Line.

THE FIRST DYNASTY

Which former Toronto Maple Leafs legend was also an Olympic pole vaulter?

The six-foot-tall Syl Apps Sr. won the gold medal at the 1934 British Empire Games in the pole vault and two years later finished sixth in the Olympic games.

Apps attended McMaster University, where he was recruited by Conn Smythe to play for the Toronto Maple Leafs. The center won the Calder Trophy in 1937. He served as the Maple Leafs' captain during the first NHL All-Star game in 1939. He won his first Stanley Cup in 1942.

While he was in the prime of his career, he joined the Canadian armed forces and served in World War II. After serving two years, he returned to captain the Leafs to two more Stanley Cups. After spending ten seasons in the NHL, all with the Leafs, Apps retired at the age of 33. He would go on to serve as a member of the Provincial Parliament in Ontario.

Which player became known as the "Dipsy Doodle Dandy from Delisle"?

Max Bentley is regarded by some purists as the most exciting—if not the best—center who ever lived. Max won the scoring championship in 1946 and 1947 while playing alongside his brother Doug and Bill Mosienko with the Chicago Black Hawks. He then went on to be the focal point of one of the biggest trades in NHL history when he was sent to Toronto.

Syl Apps Sr.

After a bit of an adjustment period with the Leafs, he got going, and there was no stopping him. Max went on to lead the Leafs to three straight Stanley Cup championships.

Age began to catch up with Bentley, and his play began to decline. In the summer of 1953, Frank Boucher was able to persuade both Max and Doug Bentley to join the Rangers. In their first game on the same team again, Max and Doug played on a line with Edgar Laprade, whose unique stickhandling and skating talents melded perfectly with the Bentleys, and the Rangers routed the Bruins, 8–3.

Max was a hypochondriac of the first order, important ammunition for enemy skaters during the homestretch of the 1953–54 season. During one game, Cal Gardner told Max that he didn't look well and should see a doctor immediately. He played a poor game; the Bruins won and gained a playoff berth while the Rangers finished fifth.

Max and Doug returned to Delisle, Saskatchewan, this time to stay. Doug died of cancer in 1972 while Max continued to operate the family wheat farm and tell stories about the great days of long ago.

Who played left wing for Toronto on one of the strongest, but also least publicized, lines in NHL history?

One of the strongest—and least publicized—lines in NHL history comprised Toronto's Syl Apps Sr. (center), Bill Ezinicki (right wing), and the least known forward of the trio, left winger Harry Watson. A onetime Brooklyn American, Watson skated powerfully, shot hard and true, and, unknown to most, was one of the kindest yet toughest forwards ever to patrol the majors.

Watson, Apps, and Ezinicki powered the Leafs to Stanley Cups in 1947 and 1948.

Every NHL skater respected Watson's fighting ability, although he frequently was a candidate for the Lady Byng Trophy for sportsmanlike play. Once, during a Leafs–Red Wings Pier Six brawl, Watson found himself confronted by defenseman Bill Quackenbush, also a Byng candidate. While everyone else was pushing and shoving, Quackenbush grabbed Watson by the shoulder. "Shall we waltz?" he asked, grinning. "No," Watson grinned back, "let's get in the middle and start shoving a bit. I think they're going to take pictures!"

Who played left wing with Max Bentley on the Chicago Black Hawks?

It is amazing how alike the Bentley brothers were on the ice. Max, a center for his 12-year career, finished with 544 points, while, Doug, a left wing and center who often teamed with his sibling on the same line in Chicago and with the Rangers, totaled 543.

After three failures in attempts to make NHL squads, Doug finally made it to the big leagues with the Black Hawks. He teamed with Max in 1942–43, and both reached stardom.

Doug led the NHL in scoring with 73 points that year. The next season he scored the most goals, 38, and was second in league scoring. He then joined his younger brother in the army and missed the 1944–45 campaign.

The brother act was broken up in 1947 when Max was dealt to Toronto.

Although Doug thought he might have some good years left in him, he was wrong. He had four seasons left as an NHLer and then retired in 1951 to coach Saskatoon of the Western League.

Doug was coaxed out of retirement to help the Rangers and joined brother Max in a drive towards a playoff spot in 1954. In his first game with the Rangers and after two years in retirement, Doug registered a goal and three assists. Max had two goals and a pair of setups, but the Rangers fell short in their playoff bid.

Doug went back to coaching Saskatoon the next year. Max joined him there in 1954. Doug made another brief comeback in 1962 with the Los Angeles Blades of the WHL.

Milt Schmidt

Who was Milt Schmidt?

Milt Schmidt is best known as the center of the famed "Kraut Line" of the Boston Bruins in the thirties. Schmidt played the pivot for Woody Dumart and Bobby Bauer and was a prime force in the Bruins' Stanley Cup championships of 1939 and 1941.

94

In 1940 Schmidt won the Art Ross Trophy and became the policeman of the Bruins' forward corps.

Although Schmidt's career began with a broken jaw, keeping him out for four weeks in 1937–38, and a painful ankle injury, keeping him on the sidelines again for the 1938–39 season, he recovered to lead the Bruins in playoff scoring in the 1939 postseason.

In 1955 Schmidt resigned from active duty and was given the coaching reins of a struggling Boston hockey club. He stayed on until 1962–63, when Phil Watson was called in to take charge. But Watson could not rejuvenate the Bruins, and Schmidt again took over in the middle of the 1962–63 season.

He stayed atop the Bruins organization as general manager from 1966 until 1973 and saw his club win two Stanley Cups with help from trades that he masterminded.

Perhaps the greatest coup of Schmidt's managerial career was engineering the famous—or infamous—trade between the Bruins and Black Hawks in which Chicago received goalie Jack Norris, defenseman Gilles Marotte, and center Pit Martin in return for forwards Ken Hodge, Fred Stanfield, and Phil Esposito. Hodge, Stanfield, and Esposito formed the backbone of the feared Bruins power play that enabled them to walk away with the Stanley Cup in 1970 and again in 1972.

When the NHL expanded in 1974 to 18 teams, Schmidt accepted the position of general manager of the expansion Washington Capitals. Beset by lack of talent due mostly to the slim packaging in the expansion draft, the Caps finished with the worst record in league history, leaving Schmidt the unenviable task of trying to build a contenting hockey club from the ashes of disaster. Furthermore, in his first season, Schmidt exhausted three coaches—Jimmy Anderson, Red Sullivan, and, finally, himself.

He was elected to the Hall of Fame in 1961 after registering 575 career points in 776 games.

In 1950, who became, at that time, only the second goalie to win the Hart Trophy?

A classic example of a superb goaltender yoked to a mediocre hockey club was the New York Rangers' Charlie Rayner. "Bonnie Prince Charlie," a bushy-browed, acrobatic netminder, broke into the professional ice wars with the old New York Americans before donning the red, white, and blue Rangers sweater in 1945.

Laboring for a Rangers team that never finished higher than fourth place, Charlie almost singlehandedly guided the Rangers to the final round of the 1950 playoffs only to see the Blueshirts fall to the mighty Detroit Red Wings in the final game—a heart-stopping, double-overtime affair.

Chuck was the overwhelming favorite choice for the 1950 Hart Trophy, and it was the first time since 1929 that honor was bestowed upon a backstop.

A courageous netminder who constantly played with a painful assortment of injuries that would have kept lesser men on the sidelines, Rayner was in such agony near the end of his career that he had to be lifted off the ice by his teammates and propped up against the goal cage after making a save. In 1953 Rayner lost his starting job to Gump Worsley and then retired later that year. He was inducted into the Hall of Fame in 1973.

Which player, after having a grenade blow up in his face, was told he would never play again but went on to win the Calder Trophy?

When Conn Smythe returned to Toronto after serving in Europe during World War II and began rebuilding the Maple Leafs, he emphasized a policy of hard-nosed hockey. Smythe went about his business of finding youngsters who fulfilled his requirements. One of these kids was Howie Meeker, a fighter of the Smythe mold.

During World War II, a grenade blew up in his face, and doctors said he'd never play hockey again. But there he was, a rookie on the 1946–47 Leafs. Meeker was fast, tough, and he loved to fight with Gordie Howe of Detroit and Tony Leswick of the Rangers. In April 1947 Meeker was voted as Rookie of the Year.

Meeker was part of the famed, second-generation "Kid Line," along with Vic Lynn and Teeder Kennedy. Lynn was not an especially heavy scorer, but he was big and rough, and he hit hard. Kennedy couldn't skate very well, but he seemed to have the puck all the time. As a unit they meshed perfectly, and they reached their collective peak early on in the 1947–48 season. Complemented by two other strong lines, the Kid Line steered the Leafs to another Stanley Cup win in 1948 and still another in 1949.

Toronto missed in 1950, but in 1951 the Leafs reached the Cup finals against the Montreal Canadiens. With Toronto leading the series three games to one and the fifth game in sudden-death overtime, Meeker helped create the Cup-winning goal by teammate Bill Barilko. Howie outsped several pursuing Montreal players early in the overtime, captured the puck, and set up teammate Harry Watson who, in turn, got the puck to Barilko, who shot the rubber over goalie Gerry McNeil.

The quality of Meeker's play ebbed after that grand moment, and he retired after playing only five games for the Leafs in 1953–54. Meeker was named coach of the Leafs in 1956–57 and by season's end gave way to Billy Reay. He would go on to become the general manager for the Leafs until Stafford Smythe fired him.

Later, he became a popular television "color" commentator and was inducted into the Hall of Fame as a broadcaster in 1998.

Which player became known as "Wild Bill"?

"Wild Bill" Ezinicki had sinewy arms and a body that bulged from daily weight-lifting. A right winger for the grand Toronto Cup winners (1947–48, 1948–49), he had a passion for free-skating that was outdone only by his passion for body checking.

Once Wild Bill had four teeth knocked out in a key homestretch game, but despite the pain and nervous shock, he returned to score the winning goal. He collided with opponents—usually bigger opponents—from any direction. Sometimes he waited for an opponent to speed in his path and then he would bend forward, swing his hips, and send his foe flying over him. If Ezzie got the worst of a fracas—which did not happen often—he could still get consolation from his insurance policy; the policy paid him $5 for every stitch resulting from a hockey injury.

Ezinicki was adored in Toronto and despised everywhere else. The Red Wings charged him with deliberately injuring goal-scorer Harry Lumley. *Boston Globe* writer Herb Ralby once said, "Toronto has the leading candidate for the most hated opponent in Ezinicki."

On November 8, 1947, Ezinicki crumpled Rangers center Edgar Laprade to the ice with a body check. Laprade suffered a concussion, and Rangers coach Frank Boucher protested to Clarence Campbell, the league president.

Eleven days after the incident, Campbell completed his investigation and said, "Reports of the officials show that the check by Ezinicki was perfectly legal and not a charge. The injury to Laprade was not caused by Ezinicki's stick, but by Laprade striking the ice as he fell."

Which Montreal goaltender won the Vezina Trophy from 1944 through 1947?

That would be Bill Durnan. His approach to goaltending suggested Georges Vezina. Like Vezina, Durnan played without a pair of skates until his teens, when a friend "borrowed" his father's unused blades and urged Bill to wear them. Durnan protested that it made little sense wearing the blades even if he was playing goal because he really couldn't skate. In time he made it to Montreal.

"We weren't impressed with Durnan at first," said Canadiens manager Tommy Gorman, "but he seemed to get better with every game. As goaltenders go he was big and hefty, but nimble as a cat."

Les Canadiens assumed that Durnan would fit right into the lineup for the 1943–44 season, especially when they learned that Paul Bibeault received his call to the Canadian army. Gorman invited Bill to the Canadiens' training camp at Saint-Hyacinthe, Quebec, and the elderly "rookie" quickly impressed Irvin with his ability to glove shots.

"Sign him up," Coach Dick Irvin urged, "and we'll open the season with Durnan in the nets."

They did, and Les Habitants were off and running to one of the most extraordinary seasons that any team ever enjoyed in the NHL (38 wins and only 5 losses). Durnan, in turn, developed into one of the NHL's finest goaltenders. He would star in net for six more seasons for the Canadiens and was an All-Star in six of his seven seasons. He won the Vezina Trophy six times and was inducted into the Hall of Fame in 1964.

Which player was known for scoring what became known as "garbage goals"?

One of the best NHL scorers was Gordie Drillon, a 6'2", 178-pound right winger from Moncton, New Brunswick. Hefty and handsome, Drillon alarmed the Leafs' general manager Conn Smythe in one way: He seemed disinclined to fight, and that left Conn wondering whether Gordie could fill Charlie Conacher's skates.

In his rookie year, 1936–37, Drillon scored 16 goals and 17 assists for 33 points in 41 games. A season later, he established himself as a first-rate forward with 26 goals and 26 assists for 52 points. He led the league in goals and points.

Unfortunately, Drillon had two raps against him: He was following the beloved Conacher, and he had a habit of scoring the kinds of goals that lacked spectator appeal. The public considered Drillon more lucky than skillful and tended to label his efforts as "garbage goals." Those who followed Drillon and studied his craft soon realized that there was a subtle secret to Gordie's goal scoring. Drillon would park himself in front of the net, angle his stick, and allow passes to ricochet off the stick blade and into the cage before the goalie could move. This skill was accomplished after many weeks of practice with his goaltender.

Once, Drillon was severely withered by veteran players on the New York Americans, who happened to steal a look at Drillon in a private workout with Turk Broda and a teammate. Red Dutton, GM and coach of the Americans, drifted by and heard the carping. He admonished his athletes that they'd do better to study Drillon than to scorn him. That night Gordie scored two of his "garbage goals," the Maple Leafs won, and Dutton lost not only the game, but a hat he had thrown on the ice in utter disgust after his players had allowed Gordie's second goal.

Drillon was named to the Hall of Fame in 1975.

Which goaltender appeared to be the opposite of the typical NHL goaltender?

Any similarity between Walter "Turk" Broda and a standard big-league goaltender was a mirage. Pudgy and slow on his feet, Broda seemed to be the antithesis of a goaltender.

Although his skating was poor, Broda earned a spot on the school team by default. Luckily, his principal noticed that Turk betrayed an unusual enthusiasm. The principal began working privately with his student, teaching him the finer points of goaltending, until Broda's game began to improve. He soon caught on with a local club, the Brandon North Stars, and played goal for them in a one-game playoff with the Elmwood Millionaires; unfortunately, Broda's club lost 11–1.

One spring the Red Wings were on an exhibition tour of western Canada. One of their stops was Winnipeg, and it was there that Broda made his presence known. He discovered that Detroit GM Jack Adams was staying at a downtown hotel. Turk

Davey Kerr

found out the room number of Adams, and when he met him he asked if he could meet some of the Red Wings players. Impressed with Broda's enthusiasm, Adams offered Broda a ticket to the game. Minutes after the game ended, Adams invited Broda to the Red Wings training camp the following fall.

After spending much of his time in the minors for the Red Wings, Conn Smythe bought his contract from the Detroit organization. Leafs fans wondered who Broda was, but they soon found out. Turk finished his critical rookie year as a Maple Leaf with a 2.32 GAA, fifth best in the eight-team league, but so close to pacesetters Davey Kerr, Normie Smith, Wilf Cude, and Tiny Thompson that he proved that he belonged with the best, at least for the moment.

The Maple Leafs' accent-on-offense style of play made it enormously difficult for Broda to win the Vezina Trophy, but carefree Turk didn't seem to mind. "Sure those goal hungry forwards can make life tough for me," he said, "but I don't mind as long as Mr. Smythe and fans don't expect me to lead the league in shutouts."

Broda won the Vezina in 1941 and 1948, helped the Leafs to six Stanley Cups, and eventually earned shiny immortality in the Hall of Fame.

Which defenseman was considered to be too awkward to make it big in the NHL but went on to become an important player for the Montreal Canadiens?

A tall French-Canadian defenseman, Emile "Butch" Bouchard learned his hockey on the sidewalks of Montreal not far from the Forum during the early thirties. At first, Bouchard was considered too awkward to be an effective hockey player. His long arms and legs suggested an octopus trying to maneuver on the ice, and when young Butch tried out for the team at Academie Roussin, he literally fell on his face.

The Bouchard family moved, and Butch enrolled at St. Francis Xavier School, where he easily won a berth on the team. His style continued to improve, and before long, Paul Stuart, a Montreal sports commentator, invited Bouchard to join his amateur team. In time, Bouchard was signed to play for the Verdun Maple Leafs, along with another promising young man named Joseph Henri Maurice Richard.

After graduating, Bouchard was spotted by Montreal Canadiens coach Dick Irvin and assigned him to Providence of the American Hockey League. After a season there, he was signed to a Canadiens contract, despite underwhelming enthusiasm from the front office.

He became a mainstay of the Canadiens and ultimately achieved Hall of Fame status.

Which player was nicknamed "the Old Lamplighter"?

A hard-nosed left wing who scored enough goals to be nicknamed "the Old Lamplighter," Hector "Toe" Blake remained a Montreal hockey player for his entire NHL career, suiting up for the Maroons his rookie year and then finishing his career as a Canadien.

Blake played hard and talked loud, something that didn't endear him to referees around the NHL. That's why to this day it remains a mystery how Blake won the Lady Byng Trophy in the 1945–46 season. But Toe had been a trophy winner long before that.

While the Canadiens finished sixth in 1938–39, Blake led the league in scoring. His awards included the Hart Trophy and an All-Star nomination. The Canadiens were improving, with Blake leading the way, but they didn't reach maturity as a championship club until the 1943–44 season, when head coach Dick Irvin inserted the young and fiery Maurice "Rocket" Richard on the right wing on the line with Blake and Elmer Lach.

The trio, which was named the Punch Line, finished 1-2-3 in scoring on the team, and the Canadiens finished first and won the Stanley Cup. The Punch Line became one of the classiest units in the league annals and helped the Canadiens to another Stanley Cup.

When Irvin resigned as coach, Blake took over and piloted Les Canadiens to a first-place finish nine times and was regarded by many as the finest all-around coach the NHL had ever seen. But with each triumph, Blake became more and more irritable, more difficult on his players, and perhaps most importantly, on himself. After the Canadiens finished first in the NHL East division and won the 1968 Stanley Cup, Blake finally gave in to his better judgment and retired. He was inducted into the Hall of Fame in 1966.

Which team was the first to come back from being down 3–0 in a series?

During the 1941–42 playoffs, the Toronto Maple Leafs made their way to the Stanley Cup Finals against the Detroit Red Wings by beating the Rangers, who were in first place.

Though the Maple Leafs were heavily favored to win, they quickly found themselves down 3–0 in the series. Leafs coach Hap Day then made a bold decision in an attempt to spark the Leafs' comeback. He benched veterans Gordie Drillon and Bucko McDonald and replaced them with rookies. This move seemed to light a fire as his team went out and fought off elimination in Game 4 by winning 4–3.

After Detroit's coach, Jack Adams, was suspended indefinitely for rushing the ice after Game 4 and assaulting the referee, Toronto dominated Game 5 and won by a score of 9–3. The Leafs went on to shut out the Red Wings 3–0 in Game 6, setting up a Game 7 in Toronto.

In Game 7, Detroit opened up with the early advantage and tightened up their defense in an effort to preserve the lead. It would not prove effective, as Toronto scored three unanswered goals and completed one of the greatest comebacks in hockey history.

Which all-time great Detroit Red Wings player began his career in 1947?

Gordie Howe got his first taste of professional hockey at the age of 15. He caught the eye of Detroit Red Wings scout Fred Pinckney, signed with the team, and was assigned to their junior squad. Howie made his NHL debut in 1947 and first wore the number 17. It was not until Roy Conacher left the team that he donned his legendary number 9 jersey.

How did Clarence Campbell become president of the NHL?

Prior to his death, Frank Calder was grooming Campbell to be his successor, but when World War II broke out, Campbell enlisted in the Canadian Forces. However, when Calder died, Campbell was still overseas. Red Dutton was therefore selected as the in-

> ## What happened to Frank Calder that caused Marv Dutton to be named president of the NHL?
>
> In January of 1943, Frank Calder was presiding over a meeting of the NHL board of governors in Toronto when he suffered a heart attack. After about a week, Calder seemed to feel better enough to travel. When he returned home to Montreal, he checked himself into a hospital, where soon after he suffered another heart attack, this time fatal. Merv "Red" Dutton was asked to serve as president following Calder's death, and he held the position until 1946.

terim president of the NHL. Dutton, however, did not want the job, and upon Campbell's return, he resigned the position, and Campbell accepted it.

What action is Campbell best remembered for as president?

Campbell is perhaps best remembered for suspending Montreal star Maurice "Rocket" Richard for the remaining three games of the 1955 regular season, as well as the entirety of the playoffs. The suspension was a result of an on-ice incident in which Richard punched a referee in the face. The decision was incredibly unpopular among Montreal fans and ended up causing a riot at a game Campbell was attending several days later.

Who was nicknamed "Tough Tony"?

In 1946 it was clear to Frank Boucher, who had taken over the helm of the Rangers, that new blood was needed to replace the pre-war heroes, who had lost their spark and their style upon their return. One of the first of the "finds" was a small, bulldog-type forward named Tony Leswick. Within two years "Tough Tony," as he was known on Broadway, became the team's leading scorer. The turnabout for the Rangers from chronic losers to consistent winners didn't happen overnight, but Leswick went a long way towards pumping the blood into the post-war team. He not only led the Rangers in scoring during the 1946–47 campaign but was just as useful as the supreme needler of the opposition and "shadow" of its leading scorers.

To assess the influence Leswick had on the Rangers, look no further than the defense he played against Rocket Richard, then the most feared scorer in the NHL. During one episode at the Montreal Forum, Tough Tony needled the Rocket, and Richard swung his stick at Leswick. The referee sent Richard to the penalty box with a two-minute minor. Leswick didn't stop there and pestered the Rocket throughout the match. With just a minute remaining, Richard blew up again, and again the referee sent him to the penalty box.

At game's end, Richard bolted from the penalty box and charged Leswick, whereupon the two of them brawled for several minutes while teammates and officials attempted to separate the pair. The Richard–Leswick feud continued for several years.

Which famous hockey magazine was founded in 1947?

In 1947 journalists Ken McKenzie and Will Cote founded *The Hockey News* magazine. Since then it has become the most recognized hockey publication in North America. The magazine publishes 34 regular issues and several other special magazines per year. The magazine is also available online.

Which famous line finished 1-2-3 in scoring for the 1939–40 season?

The Boston Bruins' Sauerkraut Line, or simply Kraut Line, was comprised of center Milt Schmidt, left winger Woody Dumart, and right winger Bobby Bauer, all of whom are Hall of Famers. The line was so attached that they in fact lived together in a single room in Brookline, Massachusetts.

Ken McKenzie (left) with Stan Fischler

Together, they became so accomplished that they finished 1-2-3 in scoring for the 1939–40 season. Schmidt led the group with 22 goals and 30 assists. The Kraut Line helped the Boston Bruins capture the Stanley Cup in the 1938–39 and 1940–41 seasons. In their seven seasons together, they notched 781 points.

Who centered Montreal's famed "Punch Line"?

Elmer Lach, the center on the Montreal Canadiens' fabled Punch Line, broke in with the Habs in 1940–41, promptly helping the Frenchmen squeeze into the Stanley Cup playoffs. The following season, the infamous Lach injury jinx that was to earn him the handle of "Elmer the Unlucky" began to surface. In the opening game of the 1941–42 season, Lach crashed into the boards, breaking his arm in two places. He was sidelined for the entire season, but it was only the first in a long line of painful injuries for the big guy.

After his year of convalescence, Lach was elevated to first-line status, where the aggressive forward took a regular shift, skated on the power play, and killed penalties as well.

In 1943–44, the legendary Rocket Richard joined the Habs' forward line, with Lach and Toe Blake completing the Punch Line. With that kind of firepower behind them, the Canadiens steamrolled to their first Stanley Cup in thirteen years.

In all, Lach labored for thirteen seasons wearing the *bleu, blanc, et rouge*—a stretch that saw the Frenchmen win three Stanley Cups and finish first in the league four consecutive times. Lach finished his career in 1954, having scored 215 goals and 623 points and gaining an endless number of stitches for the Canadiens. He was inducted into the Hall of Fame in 1966.

Did the NHL ever employ a blind referee?

Well, sort of. Bill Chadwick was a hockey player until an accident left him with only one good eye. According to Chadwick, it helped him, as he recalls, "You see, because I was using only one eye, that fact was always on my mind and it made me work harder than the other fellows."

In 1945, he called the seventh game of the Stanley Cup Finals between the Toronto Maple Leafs and the Detroit Red Wings. With the game tied at one, he called a cross-checking penalty on Syd Howe of Detroit. Toronto scored on the power play to win the game and the Cup, causing Red Wings owner Bruce Norris to have a disdain for the one-eyed ref. Chadwick, also known as "The Big Whistle," was recognized as one of the league's best officials. Known as the pioneer of hand signals that are still used today, he continued to officiate until his retirement in 1955 and was inducted into the Hockey Hall of Fame in 1964.

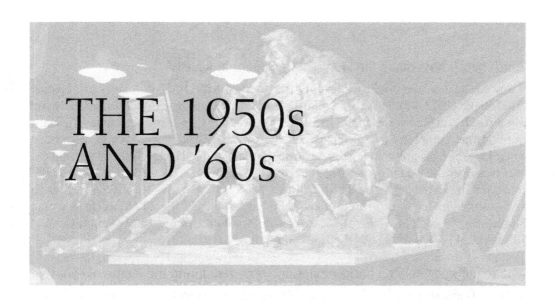

THE 1950s AND '60s

FROM BUMBLING TO A BREAKOUT DECADE

Who began the tradition of players skating around the ice with the Stanley Cup?

When the Detroit Red Wings won the Stanley Cup in 1950, Ted Lindsay lifted the Cup and skated around the ice with it out of respect to the local fans.

What was notable about Red Kelly's eight Stanley Cups?

Red Kelly is the only player in NHL history to have played on eight Stanley Cup-winning teams without having ever played for the Montreal Canadiens. Kelly made his name as a defenseman for the Detroit Red Wings, where he won four Stanley Cups. Towards the end of his career, however, Kelly was traded to the Toronto Maple Leafs, where head coach Punch Imlach converted him to a center. The change reinvigorated Kelly, and he won four more Cups during his eight seasons with the Maple Leafs.

How did Maurice Richard begin the Canadiens' 1950s dynasty?

Late during the 1954–55 season, Maurice Richard was suspended for the remainder of the year after he punched a linesman. His punishment sparked a riot by fans in Montreal, who felt their star was being unfairly treated. Richard was often targeted on the ice through violence and responded to a hit to the head from Boston's Hal Laycoe with a vicious slash of his own. When linesman Cliff Thompson tried to intervene, Richard hit him too. Richard spoke to the city via radio in an attempt to calm the tensions. In addition to asking the city to peacefully support the Habs, he promised that he would return the next season by helping the team win the Stanley Cup. True to his word, Richard and the Canadiens delivered, as they would go on to win an unprecedented five cups in five years.

Which bench boss made the Montreal Canadiens a dynasty?

If any coach deserves credit for leading the greatest team in NHL history, it's Hector "Toe" Blake (1912–95). He was previously a part of the famous "Punch Line" featuring Elmer Lach and Maurice Richard. In 1944, he scored the Cup-winning goal for the Habs in overtime, completing a sweep against the Chicago Blackhawks. His career ended when he broke his ankle in a game against the Rangers in 1948. While his playing career was over, he was only getting started. In 1955, Blake replaced Dick Irvin as the coach for the Canadiens. The Victoria Mines, Nova Scotia, native was fluent in French and was able to keep his former linemate Richard in check. It paid off, as Blake won a Stanley Cup in each of his first five seasons and went on to win a total of eight Cups in 13 seasons. His 500 wins with the Habs is the most in team history.

What equipment-related hockey milestone occurred during the Montreal dynasty?

In 1959, Canadiens goaltender Jacques Plante was struck in the face with a puck during a game at Madison Square Garden. In order to return to the game, he wore his practice face mask against the urging of coach Toe Blake and general manager Frank Selke. Plante would win 18 straight games wearing the mask, and the tradition of wearing a goalie mask as a part of regular hockey attire was born.

At the time of his retirement following the 1959–60 season, which player was the all-time leader in goals?

Maurice Richard, who played his entire 18-year NHL career with the Montreal Canadiens, retired from hockey in 1960. At the time of his retirement, Richard was the all-time leader in goals scored, although his total has since been surpassed. He was the first player to score 50 goals in a single season and the first player to reach 500 career goals. The NHL waived the minimum five-year wait and inducted Richard into the Hall of Fame the next year.

Who was the first black player to appear in the NHL?

In January 1958, the Boston Bruins called up Willie O'Ree from their farm affiliate, the Quebec Aces. While he only played two games in Boston, he appeared 43 times for the Bruins in the 1960–61 season. He was the first African-Canadian to make it to the NHL.

SUPERSTARS OF THE 1950S

Which goaltender took over for Toronto legend Turk Broda due to his weight issues late in his career?

A case could be made for Al Rollins as the most underrated goalie in NHL history. As understudy for Toronto's legendary Turk Broda in 1949–50, Rollins consistently played

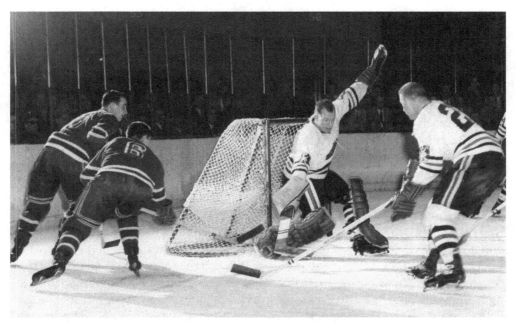

Al Rollins

well but was always overshadowed by his more colorful teammate. During the 1950–51 season, however, Broda had a "Battle of the Bulge" episode with Leafs owner Conn Smythe regarding issues with his weight. Broda was benched, while Rollins played forty games for the Leafs. Rollins won the Vezina Trophy thanks to an impeccable 1.75 goals-against average. His numbers were even better in the playoffs, as he had only six goals allowed in four games while helping the Leafs win the Stanley Cup.

Rollins played one more season in Toronto before he was traded to Chicago before the 1952–53 campaign. Rollins would have several successful years in Chicago, including a 1953–54 campaign that saw him earn the Hart Trophy as the league's Most Valuable Player.

Which NHL Hall of Fame defenseman played for six Stanley Cup Montreal teams but was often overshadowed by Doug Harvey?

When defenseman Tom Johnson was inducted into the Hall of Fame in June of 1970, veteran Hall of Famer Eddie Shore reportedly was so upset that he demanded to buy *back* his own acceptance.

Actually, Johnson was an unobtrusive, effective defenseman who skated for six Stanley Cup wins with the Montreal Canadiens in 15 NHL years. Throughout his career, Johnson was overshadowed by the more capable Doug Harvey. Notorious as a dangerous man with his stick, Johnson was lowly regarded as a fighter and once was indicted,   107 along with several other players, by the Rangers' Andy Bathgate in an article in *True* magazine as a "spearer."

After his playing career, Johnson became an administrator with the Boston Bruins, coaching the Hub sextet in 1970–71 and 1971–72. "People said," Johnson once remarked, "I showed no emotion on my face, although that's not quite true. I showed plenty when we won the Stanley Cup at Boston in 1972." A year later Johnson was replaced as coach—supposedly because he was too relaxed with the players—by Armand "Bep" Guidolin and given a front office position.

Which legend was named an NHL All Star for a record 23 times and was the oldest player to ever play in an NHL game?

It was a measure of Gordie Howe's dominant position in hockey when he finally retired from the NHL prior to the 1971–72 season. He had played in 1,687 regular season games, scored 786 goals, 1,023 assists, and 1,809 points, while receiving 1,643 minutes in penalties—each, at the time, being a league record. Between the years of 1946 and 1971, Howe won the Hart Trophy as the most valuable player six times and the Art Ross Trophy as leading scorer six times. His artistry, versatility, and durability, as well as the fact that he successfully spanned three distinct hockey eras, places him at the apex of hockey achievements.

When Howe was a young teenager, he was invited to the Detroit Red Wings' camp and was signed to a contract by their coach Jack Adams. After signing, Howe was assigned to the Wings' junior farm team in Galt, Ontario. He was unable to play for a year due to the maximum number of players having been already signed, so he worked out with the team and played in exhibitions. The next year found him playing with the Omaha Knights of the junior United States Hockey League before he joined the Red Wings in 1946. In his first three years in the NHL, he scored 7, 16, and 12 goals. He finally broke through in the 1949 playoffs, when he was the high scorer with 8 goals and 11 points.

Howe reached the top of the league in the 1950–51 season, when he led the NHL in scoring with 86 points (43 goals, 43 assists). He followed that up with more league-leading efforts: in 1951–52 he netted 86 points (47 goals, 39 assists); in 1952–53 he scored a then-record 95 points (49 goals, 46 assists); and in 1953–54 he added 81 points (33 goals, 48 assists). No other player had ever led the league in scoring for more than two years in a row. Gordie again was at the top of the scoring list in 1956–57 (44 goals, 45 assists) and continued to dominate the game through the late fifties and early sixties. He was forced into retirement in 1971 due to a chronic wrist problem.

In the 1973–74 season, Howe returned to the ice at the age of 45 alongside his sons, Marty and Mark, as the trio signed with the Houston Aeros in the newly formed World Hockey Association (WHA). The Howes led Houston to consecutive WHA titles.

After the WHA folded prior to the 1979–80 season, Howe signed on for one more year in the NHL with the Hartford Whalers at the age of 51. He was inducted into the Hall of Fame in 1972, had his #9 retired by the Red Wings, and is considered one of the greatest players of all time.

108

Doug Harvey (left, obviously) and Gordie Howe (right)

Which player won the Norris Trophy seven times, the second most ever?

Defenseman Doug Harvey was so laconic in style, so calmly sure of himself, that he executed plays of extreme complication with consummate ease. Lacking the flamboyance of an Eddie Shore, who starred in the pre–World War II years, or other Hall of Fame defensemen, Harvey was slow to receive the acclaim he deserved.

Although Harvey was not known as an excessively dirty player, he was occasionally moved to violence when he was suitably provoked. Once, during a game with the Rangers in New York, Harvey planted the pointed blade of his stick in Red Sullivan's gut and sent the Rangers center to the hospital with a ruptured spleen. For a time, Sullivan's condition was so grave he was given the last rites of the Catholic Church. Fortunately, he recovered completely and returned to play out his career in the NHL.

Harvey was a superb rusher but lacked the blazing shot that characterized Bobby Orr. There is little doubt that Orr was better offensively but not as much as statistics would suggest. "Harvey," wrote author Josh Greenfield, "could inaugurate a play from farther back and carry it farther than any other defenseman." He was a consummate craftsman, perhaps unmatched among defensemen of his time for union of style, wisdom, and strength. He won the James Norris Memorial Trophy as the best defenseman in the game seven times; only Orr won the award more with eight Norris Trophies.

109

It appeared that Harvey's NHL career had ended after his 1963–64 campaign with the Rangers, but he returned to the majors in 1966–67 with the Detroit Red Wings. Again he seemed to be through, but in the 1968 playoffs the St. Louis Blues inserted Doug into their lineup for the playoffs against Philadelphia, and he helped the Blues oust the favored Flyers. He played the entire 1968–69 season for St. Louis and was quite capable but ultimately ended his playing career at the end of the year. Harvey remained a factor in hockey and was inducted into the Hall of Fame. When the WHA was organized, he was named an assistant manager of the Houston Aeros, where he helped negotiate the signings of Gordie Howe and his sons, Mark and Marty.

Which player is credited with perfecting the slapshot?

Nicknamed "Boom-Boom" because of the reverberation of his stick hitting the puck and the puck hitting the end boards (although it often went directly into the net), Bernie Geoffrion had many of the incendiary qualities of Maurice "Rocket" Richard.

He began delighting teammates late in the 1950–51 season after scoring 103 goals in 57 Montreal junior-league games. Geoffrion realized that the Calder Trophy for Rookie of the Year was given to players who had skated in twenty or more games. By waiting until there were fewer than twenty games in the 1950–51 schedule, he thus became eligible to win it the following season.

During the 1954–55 season, Geoffrion became the center of controversy in the last week of the schedule when teammate Maurice Richard was suspended for the remainder of the season. Richard was leading the league in scoring at the time and appeared certain to win his first points title. But once the Rocket was suspended, Geoffrion moved ahead of him and won his first scoring championship. As a result of the triumph over the fan-favorite Richard, Geoffrion was vilified for several years by his hometown fans. However, he continued to play superbly and won the scoring championship and Hart Trophy in 1960–61.

When he finally retired at the conclusion of the 1967–68 season, Geoffrion had scored 393 career goals, placing him behind only a handful of players including Gordie Howe, Richard, Bobby Hull, and Jean Beliveau. He is the second man—after Richard—to score 50 goals in one season, accomplishing the feat in 1960–61. On August 24, 1972, Geoffrion reached another milestone when he was inducted into the Hall of Fame. He was named coach of the newly organized Atlanta Flames of the NHL prior to the 1972–73 season and led them to the playoffs in 1973–74, their second full year in the league. He was diagnosed with stomach cancer and died on March 11, 2006, the same day his number 5 jersey was retired by the Canadiens.

Who served as an integral part of the "Pony Line" in Chicago along with the Bentley brothers?

Bill Mosienko was an integral part of Chicago's renowned "Pony Line" with Max and Doug Bentley. A speedy winger, Mosienko carved his niche on March 23, 1952, when he scored a record three goals in 21 seconds against the Rangers at Madison Square Garden.

Mosienko's lightning-like moves were evident before and after that memorable game. He came to the Blackhawks during training camp for the 1940–41 season, a 19-year-old who appeared too fragile for the NHL. At first Mosienko was farmed out to Providence and then Kansas City, but eventually he returned to Chicago, where he was put on a line with the Bentleys. Dubbed the "Pony Line" because of the small, coltish moves of the three skaters, the unit ultimately became one of the most exciting in Chicago history. Mosienko remained a Blackhawk from 1941–42 until his retirement following the 1954–55 season. He never played on a Stanley Cup-winning or first-place team, but he scored 258 goals and 282 assists for 540 points in 711 NHL games. And it is likely that his three goals in 21 seconds will remain a record never to be equaled in the NHL.

Bill Mosienko

Who beat out Jean Beliveau for the Calder Trophy in 1954?

When the majestic, 6'2", 192-pound Jean Beliveau joined the Montreal Canadiens, the man picked to fill his skates in the Quebec Junior Hockey League was scrawny Camille "the Eel" Henry, a 5'10", 140-pound weakling with an extraordinary puck sense. What Beliveau had in size, Henry had in brains. There never was a craftier forward who could thread the needle with a pick and stick if need be.

Inevitably, Henry reached the NHL and was an instant hit. However, his club, the New York Rangers, employed Henry mostly in power-play situations during his rookie year. The Eel not only scored 24

A 1944 photo of Camille Henry

goals but also won the Calder Trophy as Rookie of the Year in 1954. Perhaps more amazing was the night Camille scored four goals in one game against Detroit goalie Terry Sawchuk, then believed the best in the game at his position.

Almost overnight, Henry became one of the most popular hockey players ever to skate in New York. After being traded to the Providence Reds of the American Hockey League during the next season, Henry returned to the Rangers in 1956 and starred for the team until 1964–65. It was at this point that New York dealt him to Chicago in a trade that caused considerable protest. However, Camille returned to New York again for the 1967–68 season. He spent the next two years, his last as a player, in St. Louis and then turned to coaching, where he led the New York Raiders of the World Hockey Association.

EXPANSION IN THE 1960s

Which six teams entered the NHL in 1967 as part of the great expansion?

They were the California Seals, Los Angeles Kings, Minnesota North Stars, Philadelphia Flyers, Pittsburgh Penguins, and St. Louis Blues. All of them operated in the NHL's West Division. Midway through the season, the California Seals changed their name to the Oakland Seals.

The first selection in the 1967 expansion draft was a goalie. Who was he?

Terry Sawchuk, who was picked by the Los Angeles Kings.

Who was the winningest coach in the NHL?

That would be Peterborough native Scotty Bowman. His playing career was cut short when he suffered a fractured skull when slashed in the head during a minor-league hockey game. He started as a coach for the Ottawa Junior Canadiens and won a Memorial Cup with them in 1958. He also ran the bench for the Peterborough Petes before entering the NHL in 1967. Thanks to the expansion, Bowman became an assistant coach for the St. Louis Blues, working under head coach Lynn Patrick. A slow start prompted a resignation from Patrick, and Bowman took the reins from there. In the Blues' first three years of existence, they reached the Stanley Cup Finals. While the Blues lost in all three Finals, Bowman would go on to win nine Stanley Cups with the Canadiens, Penguins, and Red Wings. He called it a career after Detroit's run to the Cup in the 2001–02 campaign, finishing with a league best of 1,244 wins.

Who is known as the Babe Ruth of St. Louis hockey?

When Red Berenson, the scholarly center with the educated stick, was traded by the New York Rangers to the St. Louis Blues in November 1967, the deal was largely ignored. But when Berenson was dealt from St. Louis to the Detroit Red Wings early in February 1971, the news resounded with the impact of a thunderclap. In less than four years, the anonymous redhead from Regina, Saskatchewan, emerged as the Babe Ruth of St. Louis hockey, the man who put the Blues on the ice map and into the Stanley Cup Finals. Then, without warning, he was traded away by the very team that coveted him so dearly. It was the shot heard 'round the hockey world. The precise reasons for the trade may never be known, but its repercussions lasted for years.

Red found himself a home in Detroit in more ways than one. He had B.A. and M.A. degrees from the University of Michigan and, of course, played much of his college hockey in that area. When Berenson was named an All-American at Michigan, the late Jack Adams, Detroit's vitriolic manager, attempted to lure him to Detroit. However, the Montreal Canadiens owned Red's rights at the time and had no intention of parting with him.

Red Berenson was the Babe Ruth of St. Louis hockey; he also played for the Red Wings, Rangers, and Canadiens.

Berenson's hockey smarts weren't always appreciated. Montreal's Toe Blake underplayed Berenson, and he insisted he never got a good chance to prove himself. Red hardly saw more ice time when he was traded to the Rangers. At first it seemed like he would thrive in his new home, but an injury sidelined him, and his place was taken by Orland Kurtenbach. Every time Berenson made a comeback, he'd suffer another injury, and the word unfairly made the rounds that he was brittle.

Red was traded to St. Louis by the Rangers in 1967, where he became an instant star. But by the 1970–71 season, Berenson had worn out his welcome with St. Louis and their owners, the Salomon family, likely because of his deep involvement in the burgeoning players' association. He was traded to Detroit with Tim Ecclestone. Since his playing career came to a close in 1978, Berenson set down a new career path. He coached the Blues for parts of three seasons in the early '80s before settling in at his alma mater, where he has been the head coach of Michigan's hockey team since 1984.

Besides the cities that were chosen for expansion, how many locations bid for a team?

In addition to the six cities that were awarded expansion teams in 1967, Baltimore, Buffalo, and Vancouver also made official bids. Cleveland and Louisville also contacted the league but did not make a formal pitch.

What were the main concerns that expansion caused for fans?

Besides the obvious complaint of the loss of tradition, some fans thought that the NHL was expanding too fast. They favored a more gradual expansion model, similar to that of major-league baseball, adding a pair of teams at a time. They felt that one large expansion, instead of three smaller ones, was setting the NHL up for a collapse.

How were the playoffs organized with six new teams?

To ensure that the new franchises had a shot to make the postseason, the NHL placed all of them in the West Division. When the playoffs came, the top four teams from each division qualified. In 1967–68, these teams were Montreal, New York, Boston, Chicago, Philadelphia, Los Angeles, St. Louis, and Minnesota.

Was there any competitive balance in the playoffs?

While the divisional games were even, the Original Six teams had a clear advantage over the new franchises. When the playoffs began, three of the Eastern conference teams had better records than the best Western conference team. In the 1968 Stanley Cup Finals, the Montreal Canadiens swept the St. Louis Blues with little difficulty.

Which expansion player won the Conn Smythe Award in the 1968 Stanley Cup Finals?

Despite being swept, Blues goalie Glenn Hall earned the Conn Smythe Award for his efforts. In Game 3, which St. Louis lost 4–3 in overtime, Hall made 42 saves; the Blues were outshot 46–15. That performance prompted Red Burnett, the era's premier hockey writer, to observe that "a number of Hall's saves were seemingly impossible. Experts walked out of the Forum convinced no other goaltender had performed so brilliantly in a losing cause."

Glenn Hall

Which National League Hockey club reached the Stanley Cup Finals three times but never won any of the 12 games?

The St. Louis Blues reached the Stanley Cup Finals in 1968, 1969, and 1970. In '68 and '69, they were swept by the mighty Montreal Canadiens, and in 1970 they were swept by the Boston Bruins.

SUCCESSES AND FAILURES

In the 25 years of the Original Six era, who was the only team besides Montreal, Detroit, and Toronto to win the Cup?

In the late 1950s, the Chicago Blackhawks struck gold when they picked up three young prospects. Forwards Bobby Hull and Stan Mikita, along with defenseman Pierre Pilote, would star for the Blackhawks for more than a decade. They also obtained star goaltender Glenn Hall and veteran forward Ted Lindsay, who was coming off the best year of his career, from Detroit.

After two first-round playoff exits to the Montreal Canadiens in 1959 and 1960, they were finally able to break through and defeat the Habs in the semifinals in 1961. The Blackhawks would then go on to win the Stanley Cup, defeating the Detroit Red Wings for their third championship in team history.

When did Bobby Orr arrive in Boston?

Following World War II, the Boston Bruins often made the playoffs but suffered droughts in the early and mid-60s. By that time, the Beantowners had acquired the rights to a gifted, young defenseman named Bobby Orr. After years of Orr fanfare in the Boston media, Bobby finally signed on with the Bruins for the 1966–67 season.

As a kid growing up through the youth ranks, Orr always had been a prodigy. Major-league scouts had touted him as a thoroughly unique skater and stick handler before he had ever reached high school age in his native Parry Sound, a summer fishing resort town some three hours north of Toronto. Orr was discovered by hockey professionals as a 12-year-

Ted Lindsay's Blackhawks trading card.

115

A 2010 photo of Bobby Orr at the NHL Winter Classic.

old playing in a midget hockey game in the Ontario town of Gananoque. At that time a professional team could gain control of a twelve-year-old simply by putting his name on a protected list. It was already clear that Bobby Orr was the most remarkable young player to come along since Gordie Howe.

The Bruins noticed him at the Bantam level and secured his rights. By the time he was 14, he was already playing junior hockey for the Oshawa Generals, and eventually he set several junior scoring records for a defenseman.

At the time, the Bruins were in last place. In order to soothe their disappointed fans, Boston officials began promoting Bobby. When he comes up, they said, the Bruins would be great again. He finally arrived at the Boston training camp in the autumn of 1966 when he was barely seventeen. "I was scared stiff," said Bobby. "I don't know whether I could play in the NHL. And I was alone." Orr entered the NHL as an 18-year-old rookie, along with an unprecedented contract negotiated by his agent, Alan Eagleson. At the time, the maximum a rookie could make was $8,000 per season. Eagleson managed to secure a starting salary of $25,000 for Orr.

Orr proved his worth immediately. Playing in the rougher pro ranks, he quickly adapted and became one of the league's best offensive defensemen, finishing with 41 points in 61 games. "People are crazy if they want to fight him," Bruins coach Harry Sinden said. "He's got about the fastest hands in hockey." Orr was an easy choice for the Calder Trophy as Rookie of the Year and is widely considered to be one of the greatest players in NHL history.

Orr's assets included incredible skating ability combined with natural hockey savvy and the talent to shoot the puck harder and with greater accuracy than most forwards. Combined with center Phil Esposito, Orr helped the Bruins to Stanley Cups in 1970 and 1972. One of the precious few talents who could fill opposition arenas with his mere presence, Bobby developed what was known as "The Orr Effect." Unfortunately, knee injuries plagued him throughout his career; after two NHL seasons, he underwent two operations. The second operation was completed before the 1968–69 season, and there was serious concern in Boston that Orr might never be fit to skate normally again. When he arrived in training camp, the knee bothered him so much that he was ordered off the ice. In time, however, he returned, and with each week, the knee grew stronger and stronger. It was so strong in the 1969–70 season that Orr was able to play the entire seventy-six-game schedule, as well as the lengthy playoffs, without missing a game.

Although Orr continued to dominate the NHL scene through the 1974–75 season because of his offensive contributions, his weakness defensively and in the area of public relations became dramatized. Despite Orr and his scoring teammate, Phil Esposito, the Bruins were unable to overtake the Buffalo Sabres in the regular season race for first in the NHL Adams Division. And in the playoffs, a weaker Chicago Black Hawks club wiped out the Bruins in the opening round. Orr himself admitted that his much operated-upon knees had braked his skating ability, and there was considerable question just how long he could last as the dominant athlete in big-league hockey. After a brief stint with the Chicago Blackhawks, Orr retired as a player in 1978. Orr led the National Hockey league in scoring twice (1970, 1975). He won the Hart Trophy as the NHL's Most Valuable Player three years in a row (1970, 1971, 1972) and won the James Norris (best defenseman) Trophy a record eight years in a row from 1968 through 1975. He won the Calder Trophy as Rookie of the Year and was a First Team All-Star defenseman eight consecutive times. He finished his career with 915 points in 657 games, and in 1979 he had his number 4 retired by the Bruins and was elected into the Hall of Fame.

What player's tragic death resulted in the NHL naming an award in his honor?

In 1963 Bill Masterton scored 82 points for the Cleveland Barons of the American League. However, he decided to quit pro hockey when none of the NHL teams had any interest in his services. He would go on to attend the University of Denver and get his Master's degree in finance. When the Minnesota North Stars came into the league, they invited him to training camp, and he battled his way onto the team. In 1968, in a game against the Oakland Seals, Masterton was hit hard by two defensemen and flipped backwards, hitting his head on the ice. He would never regain consciousness. For 30 hours, doctors managed to keep him alive, but the massive internal brain injury was too severe. He died on January 15, 1968. Following his death, the NHL Writers Association created the Bill Masterton Memorial Trophy. Since then, it has been given annually to the player who best demonstrates Masterton's qualities of perseverance, sportsmanship, and dedication to hockey.

Which player has his name on the Stanley Cup a record seventeen times?

A day after the Montreal Canadiens clinched first place in the National Hockey League in March 1968, Sid Abel, general manager-coach of the Detroit Red Wings, made it quite clear how important captain Jean Beliveau was to the Canadiens. "If Beliveau stays healthy," Abel predicted, "the Canadiens are a cinch to win the Stanley Cup, too." Two months later, Abel's forecast was realized. The Flying Frenchmen of Montreal defeated the Boston Bruins in four straight games; the Chicago Black Hawks in five; and finally the St. Louis Blues in four. Beliveau, known in the French-speaking province of Quebec as *"Les Gros Bill"* (Big Bill), as always, led the team to victory.

117

A typical Beliveau team-first gesture, which endeared him to his colleagues, occurred late in December 1967, when the Canadiens were playing Punch Imlach's Leafs at Maple Leafs Gardens in Toronto. The Leafs were carefully guarding a 2–1 lead with less than three minutes remaining in the game when Beliveau tied the score after teammate John Ferguson had relayed the puck to Claude Provost who, in turn, passed to Beliveau. Instead of accepting congratulations for his effort, Beliveau lamented the fact that Ferguson was not given an assist for the play.

As a captain, Beliveau was surprisingly diffident. He rarely, if ever, shouted to his teammates on the bench, and he was hardly the rah-rah type in the dressing room. Yet, somehow, he managed to inspire grand efforts from the men who wore the red, white, and blue uniforms of the Canadiens. More than anything, it seemed to come from Beliveau's quiet charisma, inspired by how he acted more than what he said. "It's hard to put into words how we felt about Jean," former teammate Ralph Backstrom once explained. "It's just that … well, we were so damned proud to have him as our captain."

Beliveau retired from the ice in 1971, and his jersey number, 4, was retired with him. He won 10 Stanley Cups as a player, as well as another seven as a member of the Montreal front office. He currently sits second all time in points for the franchise and is tied with Saku Koivu for longest tenured captain in team history.

Which Hall of Fame goalie first played for the Rangers but later starred for the Montreal Canadiens?

Gump Worsley was one of the most colorful, cantankerous, and stubborn characters in modern-day hockey. The nomadic netminder saw duty with ten clubs in five different leagues over his 24-year professional career, leaving a hilarious trail of Worsley anecdotes wherever he parked his pudgy frame.

Originally the property of the New York Rangers, Gump came up to the NHL with the 1952 Broadway team. Worsley was the diamond in the rough on this conglomeration of underachievers. His fearless performances while facing as many as fifty shots per game earned him the Calder Trophy as the NHL's Rookie of the Year. Worsley's comic-strip form became a fixture for New York's hockey community until the summer of 1963. At the annual league

Gump Worsley

meetings in Montreal, Worsley was traded to the Montreal Canadiens. Gump was thirty-four years old when he was traded to the Habs, and although few knew it at the time, Worsley was about to be reborn.

Gump was a Canadiens fixture for the next four seasons, steering them to three more Stanley Cups and twice winning the coveted Vezina Trophy, awarded annually to the league's top netminder. Midway through the 1969–70 season, Worsley then almost forty years old, was sold to the expansionist Minnesota North Stars. Teamed with another veteran, Cesare Maniago, this Mutt & Jeff pair of backstops proved they still had some good games left as they steered the Stars into the next five consecutive seasons.

After the 1972–73 season had ended, Gump, for the umpteenth time, announced his retirement from pro hockey. He returned to his home to watch the Stanley Cup Finals before settling down to a life of leisure. The final round that year pitted his Montreal Canadiens against the powerful Chicago Black Hawks. The series was being billed as a "battle of the goaltenders" as Hab Ken Dryden and Hawk Tony Esposito reigned as the league's top two stoppers. When the smoke cleared after the highest-scoring slugfest of a final round in recent history, Gump showed that his retirement age had not mellowed him one bit. "If those two guys are supposed to be the best," he observed acidly, "then I know I can play at least one more year." He did just that at the age of forty-five, playing one more season with Minnesota before hanging up his goalie pads for good.

Which Hall of Famer's career almost ended at the age of 23 due to chronic lower spinal deterioration that required spinal fusion surgery?

Jean Ratelle, the gifted young New York Rangers center, felt the shock waves near the end of the 1965–66 season. The end of a bright career loomed for the French-Canadian ace. He was taken to a doctor, who diagnosed him with chronic lower spinal deterioration and prescribed delicate spinal fusion surgery. It was a tricky operation, involving bone grafts. Normally, the chances of complete recovery for a hockey player who bounced around the ice as if he were caught in a crazed pinball machine are not bright.

There seemed no way that Jean could repeat his performance of a season earlier when he had scored 21 goals, and the Rangers' new coach, Emile Francis, was predicting stardom for the lanky kid from Lac St. Jean, Quebec. In his last year of junior hockey, Ratelle had been called to the big club for a three-game tryout. He impressed Madison Square Garden critics by scoring two goals in three games. In 1961–62, a season later, Ratelle started the year with the Rangers, but after playing a few games rather dismally, he was demoted to Kitchener of the old Eastern Pro League. When the next Rangers training camp opened, Ratelle returned and flopped for the second year in a row. He was then dispatched to Baltimore, where he enjoyed a good season. He believed he was now ready to stick with the Rangers, but manager Muzz Patrick offered him a bush-league salary, so Ratelle returned to Montreal. Patrick, however, was soon dismissed, being replaced by Emile Francis, who persuaded Ratelle to return.

119

In 1965–66 Ratelle had a good year, scoring 21 goals until his back pains demolished his joy. The spinal fusion operation was followed by a black cloud of fear. Jean was plagued with doubts as he journeyed to Kitchener, Ontario, for the Rangers training camp in September 1966. Could he make a comeback? Hampered by injuries, Ratelle had hit the bottom of the trough. Some Ratelle-watchers believed the trouble was in the coaching. When Francis fired his coach and took over the duties in 1966–67, he immediately inserted Ratelle on a line with Vic Hadfield and Jean's boyhood chum, Rod Gilbert. The gears meshed neatly, and the Rangers made the playoffs for the first time in five years. The Ratelle–Hadfield–Gilbert trio—later to be nicknamed the GAG Line— emerged as the Rangers' most consistent unit. Ratelle scored 28 goals and finally seemed ready to fulfill his promise. Employing a crisp wrist shot, Jean embarked on a string of three consecutive 32-goal seasons. He was the club's leading scorer throughout those campaigns and commanded the respect of teammates and opponents alike as a quiet, efficient centerman. His forte was not power but grace. His skates glided lyrically across the glistening ice surface as he put beautiful syncopated passes right smack on the sticks of his wings, setting them up for perfect scores. But, somehow, the hockey world would fail to take notice of Ratelle until the 1971–72 season.

In February of 1972, Ratelle became the first member of the Rangers to reach the 100-point mark in a single season. He finished the season third in the league behind Phil Esposito and Bobby Orr. Ratelle was eventually sent to the Bruins as part of a deal that sent Esposito to New York. Ratelle finished his career with 1,267 points in 1,281 career games. He was elected to the Hockey Hall of Fame in 1985.

Which Hall of Famer was nicknamed "Snowshoes" due to his slow, plodding skating style?

Mocked for his languid play in New York and Chicago, Allan Stanley later was revered in Boston and Toronto, where he crystallized into one of the most accomplished defensive de-

fensemen in the National Hockey League from 1956 through 1967. Stanley originally climbed to the NHL via the Providence Reds of the American League. The Rangers spent what then was regarded as a staggering amount ($80,000) for the husky defensemen, who made his NHL debut in 1948–49. Harsh Madison Square Garden fans took a dislike to his non-belligerent tortoise-like movements and ironically dubbed him "Sonja" as in Sonja Henie, an internationally famous ice skater. Stanley's manager, Frank Boucher, appreciated his defenseman's play but ultimately responded to the fans' criticism by trading Stanley to

Vic Hadfield

Chicago in November 1954. Allan was less than successful in the Windy City and was traded to Boston in 1956–57. There, Stanley flourished for two years but was dealt to Toronto in 1958–59 and played on four Stanley Cup championship teams under manager-coach Punch Imlach. His last NHL season was spent with the Philadelphia Flyers.

Who was recognized as one of the hardest, cleanest body checkers in the game?

Among the hockey pros, Bob Baun was recognized as one of the hardest and cleanest body checkers in the game. Players respected Baun for his respect of the rule book. Billy Harris, Baun's teammate in Toronto and later Oakland (Seals), once put it this way: "His duels with Bobby Hull are legend now. And the respect they showed each other was evident every time they collided. You seldom saw an elbow or a raised stick. Just a brutal test of strength between two fine athletes."

Sometimes, Baun got caught in his own obstacles, as he did in March 1961 in New York. Camille Henry of the Rangers ran into Baun, and in the entanglement, Henry's skate sliced through the skin of Baun's neck. It appeared to be a routine injury, and Bobby returned in the third period. But seconds after he boarded the team bus following the game, he began to gasp desperately. He attempted to yell for help but couldn't squeeze out a sound. Neck muscles cut by the skate had started to hemorrhage. Bobby gagged as his tongue slipped down his throat. Fortunately, teammate Tim Horton found him and got him to the hospital quickly.

Among all his notable achievements, Baun's most stirring heroics came in the 1964 Cup finale. The Leafs trailed Detroit in games, 3–2, and were clinging to a 3–3 tie in the sixth game. With ten minutes remaining, Baun threw his leg in front of a Gordie Howe shot. The rocklike, rubber disk cracked a bone in Baun's ankle, and he had to be carried from the ice. The period ended with the score still tied. As the players left the ice to prepare for a sudden-death overtime, the team doctor stuck a needle in Baun's foot, pressed the painkiller into his veins, then swathed the ankle with bulging bandages.

With the series tied, 3–3, the Leafs ordered Baun to a doctor for X-rays of his broken ankle, but he refused. "If there was anything wrong, I didn't want to know the details," Baun remarked. Riddled with painkillers, Baun took a regular turn throughout the final game. Toronto won, 4–0, although his inconsistency prevented him from being named a First Team All-Star. With or without All-Star recognition, Bobby more than made his presence felt in the NHL.

Which legendary Red Wing was nicknamed "Fats"?

"He's not the brawniest hockey player I ever saw—but he is one of the brainiest." Those were veteran Red Wings trainer Ross "Lefty" Wilson's words in describing his longtime teammate, friend, and now boss as he presented Alexander Peter Delvecchio the Lester Patrick Award in New York on March 18, 1974.

A statue of Alex Delvecchio was installed in the Joe Louis Arena in Detroit.

No one was better qualified to assess the talents of the former Red Wing than the irresistible Mr. Wilson, who watched Alex through twenty-two seasons as a player with the red and white machine.

Then, in the 1973–74 season, Lefty and all hockey watched as the likeable and well-respected "Fats" moved from the role of team captain and highest active-scoring player (Detroit and NHL total: 1,549 games played; 465 goals; 825 assists; 1,281 points; and 383 penalty minutes) to coach and general manager of the team he skated for for so long and so well.

Taking over as coach on November 7, 1973, Delvecchio quietly replaced turmoil and uncertainty with harmony and new spirit. The change was so evident that owner Bruce A. Norris tapped the former number 10 to be number one in shaping the future of the Red Wings. On May 21, 1974, Alex Delvecchio became general manager and coach with full authority in every phase of the club's operation. In June 1975, he gave up the coaching reigns to Doug Barkley and concentrated on managing. He is currently third in points and goals in Red Wings history, and his number 10 was retired in 1991. He was inducted into the Hall of Fame in 1977.

Which goaltender was the second player in Rangers history to have his number retired?

On May 17, 1965, Eddie Giacomin was signed by the New York Rangers. He was hardly impressive in 36 games as a rookie, and Rangers management sent him to the minors for more seasoning.

In 1966 the Rangers' brass staked everything they had on Giacomin. The team had finished out of the playoffs for the previous five years, and weak goaltending and poor defense were big factors. General manager and coach Emile Francis was impressed with Giacomin, despite his poor rookie showing. Giacomin got the starting job and finished the season with a 2.61 average and a league-leading total of nine shutouts. The Rangers made the playoffs, and Giacomin was given a berth as a First Team All-Star.

When Giacomin returned to the Rangers' training camp in Kitchener, Ontario, the following season, he learned that he would be sharing the goaltending chores with Gilles Villemure, a veteran of seven minor-league seasons and a few stints with the Rangers. Giacomin disapproved of the two-goalie system. He insisted that he needed the extra work to stay at his sharpest. He vehemently denied charges that he was tired at season's end and that he had failed in the playoffs. He had no choice, however, except to abide by Francis's decision. After eleven years of being the intrepid, barefaced goalie, Giacomin also decided to wear a face mask. The two-goalie system worked, and by the end of the 1970–71 campaign, Giacomin had captured the coveted Vezina Trophy along with Villemure. Eddie Giacomin finished with a goals-against average of 2.15, the best of his professional career.

Giacomin retired in 1978, and his number 1 jersey was retired by the Rangers in 1989. He was elected to the Hall of Fame in 1987.

Which goalie appeared in 552 consecutive games?

Glenn "Mr. Goalie" Hall, one of the greatest professional netminders of all time, managed to appear in an amazing 552 consecutive contests (including playoffs) without missing a single game. Yet, Hall was so fearful of his hazardous occupation, he would often get violently ill before games.

Over his 18-year, big-league career, Hall labored for three NHL clubs—the Detroit Red Wings, Chicago Black Hawks, and St. Louis Blues. He was named First Team All-Star goalie seven times and had his name inscribed on the Vezina Trophy as the league's top goaltender three times.

Despite taking scores of painful stitches in his face, Hall did not don a goalie mask until the twilight of his career, claiming it restricted his vision when the puck was at his feet. One night, during the 1957 Stanley Cup playoffs, a screened shot suddenly flashed out of a tangle of bodies and smashed into Hall's maskless face. The game was delayed for a half hour while Hall took 23 stitches in his mouth before returning to finish the game.

Hall was inducted into the Hall of Fame in June of 1975.

Who coached and managed the powerhouse Toronto Maple Leafs of the sixties?

One of the most successful and cantankerous coaches in major-league hockey history is George "Punch" Imlach. Imlach's tough-as-nails approach to the game won four Stanley Cups with the powerhouse Leafs teams of the sixties. Only three other NHL coaches, Scotty Bowman, Toe Blake, and Hap Day, have accounted for more silverware than that.

George "Punch" Imlach

Before his days as coach of the Leafs, Punch spent eleven years with the minor-league Quebec Aces as a player, coach, and general manager, and eventually, part owner. Then Imlach joined the Boston Bruins organization as manager and coach of the Bruins' Springfield Indians of the AHL.

In 1958, Imlach was hired by the Maple Leafs to be one of two assistant general managers. They did not, however, have a general manager at the time, so Imlach reported to a seven-member committee led by Stafford Smythe, son of Conn Smythe. In November of that year, Imlach was promoted to general manager and eventually named himself as head coach. He went on to become one of the most successful coaches in Maple Leafs history. He brought the franchise their last Stanley Cup in 1966–67.

After his dominant run with the Leafs, Imlach was named coach and general manager of the Buffalo Sabres in 1970 and built the team into a powerhouse in two seasons. However, Imlach was forced to step aside from the coaching duties due to a massive heart attack during the 1971–72 season. This health scare didn't stop Imlach completely, though. As one writer observed following a gallbladder operation that Imlach underwent in 1972, "in Imlach's case, they probably removed the bladder and left the gall."

Which forward was originally destined for success with Montreal but was donated to the Black Hawks and eventually led them to a Stanley Cup championship?

A tall, awkward-looking forward, Ed Litzenberger seemed to be destined for a long career with the Montreal Canadiens when he reached the NHL in 1954–55. But the Black Hawks' franchise was close to folding at the time, and the league of governors agreed to help Chicago whenever possible. The Canadiens, therefore, donated Litzenberger to the Black Hawks, and Ed became a star in the Windy City. In 1961 he helped lead Chicago to the Stanley Cup. After being dealt to the Maple Leafs in 1962, Ed guided the Leafs in three straight Cup victories in 1962, 1963, and 1964. He left the NHL after the 1964 win.

Which Hall of Famer was able to weather two nervous breakdowns during his quest for superstardom in the NHL?

Perhaps the most misunderstood man in professional hockey is Frank Mahovlich, the one-time skating behemoth of the NHL. The "Big M" reached high and low points in his career with the Toronto Maple Leafs before being freed to join the Detroit Red Wings and later the Montreal Canadiens. As a young dashing left winger with the Maple Leafs, Frank achieved a high-water mark during the 1960–61 season, when he scored 48 goals and almost matched Rocket Richard's record of 50 goals.

After a falling out with Toronto manager Punch Imlach, Mahovlich was dealt to Detroit in 1968. Those who knew Frank best were convinced that the change of scenery would improve his game. "Detroit," said Frank's brother Peter, "is a different hockey city. Frank will be treated differently by the Red Wings." He was, and the results on the ice were visible immediately. Within a month, Frank scored seven goals and closed the season with the clear suggestion that better things were to come. Detroit coach Bill Gadsby said he would be delighted if Frank scored 35 goals in his first full season with Detroit. Mahovlich obliged with 49 goals, the most he had ever scored in twelve NHL seasons. It was the most goals for a Red Wings player since Gordie Howe scored the same number in the 1952–53 season.

Skating on a line with Howe and Alex Delvecchio, Mahovlich was a new man. With 118 goals, the line broke the record of 105 set in 1943–44 by the famed Montreal Punch Line (Rocket Richard, Toe Blake, and Elmer Lach). The line's point total of 264 smashed the 223-point mark set in 1956–57 by the Detroit Production Line (Gordie Howe, Ted Lindsay, and Norm Ullman). In the 1969–70 season, Frank scored 38 goals and 70 points and was a prime catalyst in pushing the Red Wings into a playoff berth for the first time in four years.

Mahovlich's play began to decline in 1971, and he was traded to Montreal. In his first full year with the Canadiens, he scored 96 points in 76 games and followed that with 93 points in 78 contests during the 1972–73 campaign. Once again he was a tower of power as Montreal marched to the Prince of Wales Trophy and the Stanley Cup in 1973. He surpassed the 500-goal mark during the 1972–73 season, and by the end of the year he had a then record of 502 career goals. In his final season, Mahovlich scored 31 goals and 49 assists to lift his NHL all-time totals to 1,182 games played, 533 goals, 570 assists, and 1,103 points. He jumped from the Canadiens to the World Hockey Associations' Toronto Toros during the off season and was named team captain. In his first WHA game, he scored a hat trick and led the Toros to a second-place finish in the league's Canadian Division. Mahovlich won six Stanley Cups throughout his career and was inducted into the Hall of Fame in 1981.

Which Norris Trophy-winning defenseman starred on the Black Hawks' blue line in the late fifties and sixties?

When the Chicago Black Hawks began their ascent from the depths of the NHL in the fifties to respectability in the sixties, smallish defenseman Pierre Pilote played a large role, although teammates Bobby Hull, Stan Mikita, and Glenn Hall received most of the credit.

Pilote was effective defensively and offensively; he could hit and hurt, and he could skate well and score. Before retiring after the 1968–69 season, Pilote amassed 80 goals and 418 assists for 498 points in 890 games.

Pierre's credentials include First All-Star Team (five times), Second All-Star Team (three times), Norris Trophy (three), as well as the captaincy of the Black Hawks when they won the Stanley Cup in April 1961.

During Pilote's later years, a bit of friction developed between the captain and outspoken stars such as Mikita. One of Pierre's dilemmas was that, as captain, he frequently had to deal with management and was unfairly labeled by some teammates as "a company man." Despite this, he persevered through an excellent career that culminated in June 1975, when he was elected to the Hall of Fame.

Pierre Pilote

Which player, after a mediocre NHL career, went on to become one of the greatest collegiate coaches of all time?

Murray Armstrong was an NHL forward who broke into the league with the Toronto Maple Leafs in 1938–39 before being traded to the New York Americans a year later. In 1943–44, after the Amerks folded, Armstrong became a Red Wing and stayed with the Detroiters until his NHL career ended in 1946. After he left the NHL, Murray became the head hockey coach at Denver University which, in turn, became one of the most successful collegiate hockey empires. Big-leaguers such as Black Hawks Keith Magnuson and Cliff Koroll were among the more successful Denver products. A winner of the NCAA Coach of the Year Award, Armstrong remained a controversial figure in American collegiate hockey because of his use of Canadian-born skaters as opposed to homebred stickhandlers. He led the team to five NCAA championships in 1958, 1960, 1961, 1968, and 1969. He retired to Florida and remained there until his death in 2010.

Murray Armstrong

Which Calder Trophy winner played third line center for six Stanley Cup-winning teams?

The hockey history of Ralph Backstrom reads like a proverbial good news–bad news story. Fortunate to become a part of the mighty Montreal Canadiens organization in 1958–59, when he won the Calder Memorial Trophy as Rookie of the Year, Backstrom was also unfortunate enough to play third-string center behind two of the game's finest, Jean Beliveau and Henri Richard. Despite this, he was still a key member of six Stanley Cup winners in Montreal.

After playing third fiddle for twelve seasons, Backstrom decided to retire in 1970 but was talked into returning, whereupon he was promptly traded to the Los Angeles Kings for Gord Labossiere and Ray Fortin. Switched to left wing, which he played in juniors, Ralph would become a favorite with the Los Angeles fans in 1972.

In February 1973, Backstrom was traded to the Chicago Black Hawks for young blood in the guise of Dan Maloney. Disgruntled with a return to the background behind the likes of Stan Mikita, he signed with the Chicago Cougars of the WHA in August 1973. He enjoyed success in the WHA, where he was named Most Sportsmanlike Player, 1974 All-Star, team leader in goals and points, and star of the 1974 WHA Canada–Russia series.

A symbol of Backstrom's hard-earned success was a letter he received from one of hockey's legends, Conn Smythe: "I have never believed in the statement that it doesn't matter whether you win or lose, but how you play the games. However, with your example in the Russian series, I have to say that it has some merit."

Whose slapshot was it that inspired Jacques Plante to don a face mask permanently?

Andy Bathgate at first appeared too much the pacifist for the NHL jungle. But he put up his dukes when necessary, licking such notorious cops as Howie Young, then of the Red Wings, and Vic Stasiuk of the Bruins. By 1954–55 Andy was in the NHL to stay and soon was being favorably compared with the greatest New York Rangers right wing ever, Bill Cook.

While it has never been firmly established who invented the slaphot—Bernie Geoffrion and Bobby Hull often are mentioned—Bathgate was among the earlier practitioners. It was Andy's shot at Madison Square Garden in November 1959 that smashed Montreal goalie Jacques Plante's face and inspired Plante to don a face mask permanently, thus ushering in the era of the goalie mask. Bathgate also was among the first to develop a curved "banana" blade.

By the end of the 1961–62 season during which Andy scored 84 points in 70 games, he had become the most popular Ranger and team captain and seemingly a permanent fixture on Broadway. He also was prime trade bait, and in February 1964, he was dealt to Toronto.

As a result of the trade, the Leafs won the 1964 Stanley Cup. Bathgate scored five important playoff goals and said getting traded to the Leafs was the biggest break in his life. But just a season later, Bathgate had a falling out with manager-coach Punch Imlach.

Imlach unloaded Bathgate to the Detroit Red Wings in 1965–66. His play declined sharply, and in 1967–68 he was dealt to the expansion Pittsburgh Penguins. He returned to form in Pittsburgh but appeared more and more disenchanted and departed the NHL in 1968. Andy played in Switzerland before returning to Canada to become coach of the Vancouver Blazers of the World Hockey Association in 1974. An eye injury suffered in a home accident in 1973 limited vision by 80 percent in Andy's right eye. Despite the impaired vision, Bathgate returned temporarily to active play in December with the Blazers before retiring for good after 11 games played.

Which NHL tough guy was involved in a baseball-like incident?

Philadelphia Flyers rough-and-tough defenseman Larry Zeidel was known for swinging his stick at his opponents. None was more famous than in 1968, when he squared off against Eddie Shack of the Boston Bruins at Maple Leaf Gardens in Toronto. The game was held there as a home game for the Flyers, as the roof to the Spectrum had blown off. Rumors swirled that Shack had made off-color remarks about Zeidel's Jewish heritage, which led the two to engage in the stick antics. It was also not the first time Zeidel was guilty of using his stick as a weapon. Both players were suspended, Zeidel for four games and Shack for three.

Ted Green (far right) played for the Boston Bruins.

What Canadiens enforcer made a splash just a dozen seconds into his first NHL game?

John Ferguson was originally tasked with the protection of team captain Jean Beliveau from the aggressors on the other team. A mere twelve seconds into his first NHL match, Ferguson dropped the gloves with Boston's Ted Green, and he won. But Ferguson was not only adept at racking up the penalty minutes, he also used his scoring touch to score the Stanley Cup-winning goal in 1969 to go along with his 29 goals and plus-30 rating in the regular season that year. He found his way onto two All-Star teams, as well as four more Cups with the Habs.

THE 1970s

NHL VS. WHA

Who founded the World Hockey Association in 1972?

Sports entrepreneurs Gary L. Davidson and Dennis Murphy were the founders of the World Hockey Association in 1972. Davidson was no newcomer to the professional sports rivalry, having been instrumental in the formation of the American Basketball Association in 1967.

"It's been conclusively proved by the players themselves that there is room in hockey for a second major league," declared Davidson, explaining the philosophy for the birth of the WHA. "That those players had the courage to follow the leadership of the WHA's equally courageous owners is ample testimony to our credibility."

Davidson was the creator of the non-reserve clause in the standard player contract of the league, something unique in professional sports. This, plus the innovations in the new league's rules, gave the Southern Californian cause for optimism concerning the future of the WHA, which had gotten off to a somewhat rocky start.

"You measure an enterprise by its growth," stated Davidson. "WHA franchises rose in value from $25,000 to $2 million within 18 months."

Davidson's active involvement with the league consisted mostly of assembling the financial package needed to put a league in business. He slackened off in his private law practice to put more energy in the league.

Davidson retired as president of the WHA in 1974, succeeded as WHA president by his crony, Dennis Murphy.

How much of a threat was this new major league to the NHL?

In 1972 the WHA began combing NHL rosters, looking to sign players for the new 12-team league. With each week, more and more NHL aces either threatened to, or actually   131 did, jump to the new league. The biggest player move occurred when Chicago Black Hawks scoring leader Bobby Hull signed a ten-year, $2.74 million contract with the Winnipeg Jets. Other stars going to the WHA included Gordie Howe and eventually a young 17-year-old prodigy named Wayne Gretzky.

Bobby Hull as a Blackhawk, c. 1964.

What initial successes did the WHA have?

Like most other upstart leagues, the WHA paid more than the NHL and poached several stars. They included the likes of Bernie Parent, Gerry Cheevers, Derek Sanderson, and J. C. Tremblay. The WHA's biggest star, however, was Bobby Hull; after joking he would only go to the rival league for a million dollars, the Winnipeg Jets signed him to a 10-year, $2.7 million contract.

Where else did the WHA get its players from?

Desperate to increase its talent base, the WHA began to sign European players. While the NHL had previously ignored most players from across the Atlantic, the WHA was able to sign the likes of Swedes Anders Hedberg and Ulf Nilsson.

What difficulties did the young league face during its initial season?

For all of its newfound star power, the WHA still struggled financially. Before the season even began, two franchises, the Dayton Arrows and the San Francisco Sharks, were forced to relocate; they became the Houston Aeros and the Quebec Nordiques respectively. Two additional franchises, the Calgary Broncos and the Miami Screaming Eagles, folded before they ever played a game. The Philadelphia Blazers and Cleveland Crusaders replaced them.

Why did the New York Raiders struggle to find a suitable arena?

When the WHA came into being, the league planned for its flagship team to call the Nassau Coliseum home. Nassau County, however, did not think the league was professional enough to occupy the brand-new arena and refused to make a deal; it instead hired William Shea to lobby the NHL for a franchise, which would be granted and become the Islanders. The Raiders then were forced to rent the ice at Madison Square Garden, which proved to be incredibly expensive and inconvenient. The team's owners defaulted, and the Raiders were taken over by the WHA; they were renamed the Golden Blades and sold to a new owner, but the league was forced to take control of the team again during the next season. The WHA then moved the club to Cherry Hill, New Jersey. They were renamed the Jersey Knights and played in an arena where the ice sloped upwards and the boards were topped with chain-link fence instead of plexiglass.

Which WHA teams made it to the NHL?

Out of the 16 WHA teams, four made it to the NHL: the Edmonton Oilers, the Hartford Whalers, the Quebec Nordiques, and the Winnipeg Jets. Of those four, only the Oilers remain in their original city, with the others moving to Raleigh, North Carolina; Denver, Colorado; and Glendale, Arizona, respectively.

How many WHA expansion teams went on to win the Stanley Cup?

The only WHA organization that has lifted Lord Stanley's chalice is the Edmonton Oilers, who won the title five times. The Carolina Hurricanes and Colorado Avalanche are also descendants of old WHA franchises, the Hartford Whalers and Quebec Nordiques respectively.

Which future NHL stars got their start in the WHA?

Given that the WHA was more willing to give talented young players a shot at professional hockey, several stars got their first taste of the big time there. Some of them included Wayne Gretzky, Mark Messier, Mark Howe, Rod Langway, and Mike Gartner.

Which owners were the driving forces behind the NHL–WHA merger? Who opposed the move?

In 1973, Bill Jennings and Ed Snider, the owners of the Rangers and the Flyers, respectively, approached the league about the possibility of a complete merger. Paul Mooney, the owner of the Bruins, Bill Wirtz, the owner of the Black Hawks, and Harold Ballard, the owner of the Maple Leafs, were against the move, as they had lost several players to the rival league.

Which famous players took sides in the dispute?

Bobby Hull, who had left the NHL for Winnipeg, was a massive supporter of the merger. Gordie Howe, on the other hand, believed that the WHA could survive on its own.

What happened to the remaining WHA franchises that were not part of the merger?

The other two remaining teams, the Cincinnati Stingers and Birmingham Bulls, were each given $1.5 million in compensation. The Stingers ceased operations almost immediately after the merger. The Bulls, on the other hand, played a few more years in the Central Hockey League before disbanding in 1981.

How did NHL president Clarence Campbell feel about the possibility of a merger?

In regards to the prospect of a merger, Campbell famously said, "They're our rivals. They were people that did their best to destroy us. Why would we salvage them now? To hell with them."

Who finally made the move towards unification?

John Ziegler, who succeeded Campbell as president in 1977, was more receptive to the prospect of a merger. It took several more years for the merger to become a reality, though; many of the WHA's teams began to fold, placing more pressure on the rival league to agree to the NHL's concessions.

What happened at the Key Largo Board of Governors meeting?

With the prospect of a merger on the table, five teams voted against the merger. They were the Canadiens, Canucks, Maple Leafs, Bruins, and Kings. Boston and Montreal opposed the move on territorial grounds; they did not want to share an audience with the Hartford Whalers and Quebec Nordiques, respectively. Los Angeles and Vancouver did not want to see more teams added on the East Coast, while all three Canadian teams did not want to see their television revenue further divided. Lastly, Maple Leafs owner Harold Ballard still held a grudge against the WHA for poaching some of the NHL's stars.

Which WHA team was originally located in Dayton, Ohio?

The Dayton Arrows franchise did not last more than a year in Dayton. They were plagued by a lack of a proper arena and a lack of fan interest. The Dayton Arrows were forced to move to Houston, where they were renamed the Aeros. The Aeros went on to become one of the more successful teams in the WHA. They won the regular season title and division championship four times each and boasted players such as Gordie Howe and his sons Mark and Marty. Led by the Howes, they won two straight Avco Cups in 1974 and 1975.

When the NHL merged with the WHA in 1977, the Aeros applied for entry into the NHL. In a last-ditch effort to save his franchise, owner Kenneth Schnitzer proposed to move to the NHL as an expansion team independent of the merger or be allowed to purchase a current NHL club and relocate it to Houston. Both plans failed, and the Aeros folded in 1978.

> ### Where did the Howe brothers live
> ### when they signed for the Houston Aeros of the WHA?
>
> **D**espite getting hefty contracts, the boys chose to live at home with their parents. They paid Mom and Dad $30 a week in rent.

How many Gordie Howe hat tricks did Gordie Howe himself have?

Despite them forever bearing his name, Mr. Hockey only recorded one Gordie Howe hat trick. That came in December 1955, when the Detroit Red Wings faced the Boston Bruins. A Gordie Howe hat trick is when a player scores a goal, receives an assist, and gets in a fight in the same game.

Where did Marty and Mark Howe learn to skate?

Their father taught them to skate on the ice of Detroit's Olympia Stadium. Such are the perks when your father is known as Mr. Hockey.

Which team did former legendary college hockey coach Jack Kelley coach?

Jack Kelley, former Boston University head coach, led the New England Whalers for three seasons. Kelley coached the Whalers to the best overall record in the WHA in 1972–73 and led them to a victory over the Winnipeg Jets to win the inaugural Avco World Trophy. Kelley resigned, however, after the Whalers' first season in Hartford. The championship that Kelley led them to was their only one in the WHA and under the name Whalers.

WHA CUP

What was the trophy given to the champion of the WHA, and what was it named for?

The Avco World Trophy, or simply the Avco Cup, was awarded from 1973 to 1979 to the champion of the World Hockey Association. The Avco Corporation, a defense contractor that wanted to advertise its consumer finance division, purchased the naming rights to the trophy. The trophy was often mocked, as many people considered it to have not nearly the value of the Stanley Cup, the rival NHL's championship trophy.

In order to win the trophy, like in the NHL, a team would play a best-of-seven series. Four of the seven times the trophy was awarded, the championship series ended in a sweep. The trophy was retired when the WHA folded and sits on display in the Hockey Hall of Fame.

Which team won the most WHA championships?

In 1972 the Winnipeg Jets signed their first major acquisition, NHL star Bobby Hull. A top line of Hull and Swedish stars Anders Hedberg and Ulf Nilsson led the Jets offen-

135

sively, and team captain Lars-Erik Sjoberg, who won several accolades as the WHA's top defenseman, led their blue line. The team also had other non-European players, such as Peter Sullivan and goaltender Joe Daley. Led by this core group of players, the Jets were the best and most successful team in the WHA's short-lived history. They won three championships, the most of any team, and defeated Wayne Gretzky's Oilers in the final Avco Cup championship series in 1979.

THE FLYING FRENCHMEN

How many Stanley Cups did Montreal win in the 1970s?

The Montreal Canadiens won the Cup a total of six times in the 1970s. They won it in 1970–71, 1972–73, and then four straight from 1975–76 to 1978–79. These six Cups continued Montreal's history of incredible success, giving them 22 total Cups. They have since won two more. For much of the 1970s, legendary coach Scotty Bowman manned the bench for the *rouge blanc et bleu*.

Which Hall of Famer holds the Montreal Canadiens record for most seasons and games played?

Henri and Maurice Richard began drifting apart as Henri, the kid brother, came into his own around the NHL. If the Rocket was the home-run hitter, the Pocket Rocket, as the younger Richard was known, was more the base stealer and opposite-field hitter on the Montreal Canadiens.

The Pocket Rocket was an essential cog in Frank Selke's rebuilding plan, and he was an asset to Sam Pollock's first years as Montreal's general manager as well. Les Canadiens finished first in 1965–66, breezed past Toronto in the first round of the playoffs with four straight wins, and appeared capable of disposing of the Detroit Red Wings at will in the Cup finals, especially since the series opened with two games at the Montreal Forum. But Detroit's hot hand, goalie Roger Crozier, was sizzling, and the Red Wings upset Les Canadiens in the first two games. They became favorites as the series shifted to the Detroit Olympia. But the Habs didn't lose again. The Cup-winning goal was scored by the Pocket Rocket in sudden-death overtime as he slid feet first toward the net. Crozier appeared to have the puck in hand, but both the puck and the Pocket got past him. Richard crashed into the end boards, and the puck slid into the goal.

Henri Richard, as a player, won more Stanley Cups (11) than any other player in NHL history. He was named captain of the Canadiens in 1971 and continued to wear the "C" until his retirement in 1975. The Canadiens retired his number 16 in 1975, and in 1979 he was elected to the NHL Hall of Fame. He finished his illustrious career with 1,046 points (81 more than his brother Maurice) in 1,256 games played.

Who served as captain for Montreal's four straight Cups?

Yvan Cournoyer. While playing for the Canadiens from 1963 to 1979, Cournoyer won the Stanley Cup 10 times. He served as team captain from 1975 to 1979.

The Canadiens won the Stanley Cup in 1976, but no member of the Canadiens won the Conn Smythe Trophy. Who did win it?

Reggie Leach of the Philadelphia Flyers was awarded the Conn Smythe for his performance in the playoffs that year. In the playoffs, he set an NHL record with 19 goals in 16 games. He added another 5 assists for 24 total points.

Who became the first defenseman to win the Conn Smythe Trophy?

One of the Canadiens' brightest prospects, Serge Savard, had to fight his way through a number of crippling injuries, which might have ended careers of other athletes.

As an example, Savard missed most of 1965–66 with the Montreal Junior Canadiens due to torn ligaments in his right knee. After a brilliant rookie season in 1968–69, when he was the recipient of the Conn Smythe Trophy for the most valuable player in the Stanley Cup playoffs, Savard missed the final weeks of the following season with a fractured leg. That injury caused him to sit out parts of the next two years as well, as he refractured the leg, and complications set in.

In 1972–73, Serge finally became healthy and reestablished himself as an integral part of the Habs' defense corps. Savard was part of eight Stanley Cup teams in 1968, 1969, 1971, 1973, 1976, 1977, 1978, and 1979, and in 1979, he won the Bill Masterton Trophy. The "Savardian Spin-o-rama," often thought to be named after Denis Savard, was in fact named after Serge Savard (the two are distant relatives). As a defenseman, Serge registered 439 points in 1,040 games. He was elected to the Hall of Fame in 1986.

Which player scored the tying goal against the Chicago Black Hawks in the 1971 finals and eventually led the Canadiens to their 16th Stanley Cup?

Speedy Jacques Lemaire at first did not really fulfill the expectations the Montreal Canadiens had for him, despite scoring 44 goals in 1972–73. Jacques was known for his potent slapshot, which he was not afraid to use, whether from 60 feet or 6 feet.

Which modern-day record did the Canadiens break in the 1976–77 season?

During the 1976–77 season, the Montreal Canadiens lost only 8 games throughout the course of the 80-game season.

It was Jacques's 80-footer, which sailed by Chicago goalie Tony Esposito, that tied the seventh game of the 1971 Stanley Cup Finals, and the Canadiens went on to win their 16th Stanley Cup. Jacques picked up 9 goals and 10 assists in the playoffs.

Jacques was hot again in 1974–75, tallying 36 goals and 56 assists for 92 regular season points. He won eight Stanley Cups with the Canadiens and is one of only six NHL players to score two Stanley Cup-winning goals. In 853 games played, he notched 835 points. He was inducted into the Hall of Fame in 1984.

He went on to coach the Canadiens for two years, the Devils for five years, the Minnesota Wild for eight years, returning to the Devils for another two years before finally retiring from coaching in 2011. In 1994–95, he led the Devils to the Stanley Cup.

Yvan Cournoyer is shown here coaching alumni of the Montreal Canadiens at the 2008 Legends Classic in Toronto.

Which Montreal great was nicknamed the "Roadrunner"?

Montreal's Canadiens are known as "the Flying Frenchmen," and nobody wearing the *bleu, blanc, et rouge* (blue, white, and red) uniform flew faster than Yvan Cournoyer, the compact right wing. Shooting and skating had been Cournoyer's main interest in life ever since he was a kid in the French-speaking town of Drummondville, Quebec. When he was 14, his family moved to Montreal, and he quickly climbed hockey's sand-lot ladder.

NHL scouts had heard good things about the little kid with the big part in his hair, but they really took notice after the final game of a Lachine–Verdun series. Yvan's club was trailing by one goal with less than a minute remaining when he captured the puck behind his own net. Bobbing and weaving, he skated around the opposition and shot the puck past the Verdun goalie. Then he scored the winning goal in sudden-death overtime.

The Canadiens were scanning the junior hockey horizon for future heirs to Henri Richard and Jean Beliveau, the reigning French-Canadian scoring titans. They called up Yvan for a five-game tryout in the 1963–64 season, and he scored in his first game. He went on to have a very successful career with the Canadiens. In 15 seasons he scored 428 goals and 863 points. He is also second all time to Henri Richard for most Stanley Cups with 10. He was nicknamed "Roadrunner" due to his small size and blazing speed. He was inducted into the Hall of Fame in 1982.

Who was the first player in NHL history to score 50 goals and 100 points in six straight seasons?

Until the 1974–75 campaign, when he was among the league leaders in scoring, Guy Lafleur hadn't really caught fire in the NHL, playing both right wing and center, "point" on the power plays, and killing penalties. Then Guy began to earn his *tri couleurs*. No one had ever doubted his skating ability, shooting, or stickhandling, but he was far from aggressive. Perhaps when Lafleur shed his helmet, people began to realize a change was in the works. Lafleur went on to become a full-fledged Canadiens star, the dream of any Quebecois boy.

Between 1971 and 1991, Lafleur played for the Canadiens, New York Rangers, and Quebec Nordiques in an NHL career that spanned 17 seasons, and he was part of five Stanley Cup championship teams. Lafleur is currently first all time in points, second in goals, and first in assists for the Montreal franchise. He is also tied for the Montreal franchise record with Steve Shutt for most goals in a single season with 60 in 1977–78. Lafleur was inducted into the Hall of Fame in 1988 and is one of only three players to return to the NHL after already being inducted into the Hall of Fame. In his distinguished career, he won three Art Ross Trophies (1976, 1977, 1978), two Hart Trophies (1977, 1978), and one Conn Smythe Trophy (1977). He became the sixth player to have his number retired by the Canadiens.

ARRIVALS AND DEPARTURES

Which two players were parts of major trades in the 1970s?

Marcel Dionne was drafted second overall by the Detroit Red Wings in 1971. In his first four NHL seasons with the Red Wings, Dionne developed into an NHL star, but his team failed to make the playoffs. In 1975, Dionne was traded to the Los Angeles Kings in what was the richest trade in NHL history at the time. The dynamic forward quickly became L.A.'s franchise player, centering the famous "Triple Crown Line" with Charlie Simmer and Dave Taylor. Dionne scored 50 or more goals in six out of twelve seasons with the Kings.

During the 1975–76 season, Boston Bruins superstar Phil Esposito was involved in a blockbuster trade that sent him and Carol Vadnais to the New York Rangers in exchange for superstar defensemen Brad Park, Joe Zanussi, and Jean Ratelle. When Esposito got the news of the trade, he wept and told coach Don Cherry, "If you tell me I'm traded to New York, I'll jump out that window."

Who in 1971–72 recorded a then-record 77 points his rookie year?

Marcel Dionne of the Detroit Red Wings, a developing superstar, had been almost as confused as his beleaguered team in recent seasons. The Detroiters suffered with six coaches in a half-dozen years while searching in vain for a playoff combination. It isn't

A retired Marcel Dionne makes an appearance during the 2008 Gordie Howe Night at the Pacific Coliseum in Vancouver, British Columbia.

that Dionne played bad hockey. In 1973–74, his 78 points (24 goals and 54 assists) led the team. In 1971–72, his 77 points as a rookie set a mark for National Hockey League freshmen (Teemu Selanne currently holds the record with 132), and the next season he upped the total to 90, with 40 goals and 50 assists.

Dionne's dilemma began midway through the 1972–73 campaign when Johnny Wilson was the Red Wings coach. A dispute surfaced between Marcel and the team's general manager, Ned Harkness, which led to them having a falling out. The boiling point was reached when Harkness accused the 5'8", 175-pound Dionne of not giving "the old 100 percent" in practice.

But Wilson soon was fired by Harkness, and into the maelstrom stepped Ted Garvin, a tough, "old school" coach who strictly policed facial hair and shaggy heads and ran his practices with heavy emphasis on fundamentals. Only days after Garvin took over, a major clash erupted between Garvin and Dionne. Before November 1973 was gone, so was Garvin, fired by Harkness—after only 11 games—and replaced by the easygoing Alex Delvecchio. Even with Delvecchio piloting the club, Dionne was in trouble. General Manager Harkness felt that Dionne symbolized the pampered, young hockey player. Harkness was given his walking papers, and into the breach stepped Delvecchio, a sophisticated, laissez faire operator who became both head coach and general manager.

In a dramatic departure from Garvin's rigid authoritarianism, Delvecchio took a soft-sell attitude toward skaters. In 1974–75, Dionne responded with 47 goals and 74 assists for 121 points. Still unhappy, Marcel was traded in June of 1975 and was obtained by the Los Angeles Kings. Dionne would play for the Kings for twelve seasons and with the Rangers for three. Over the course of his illustrious career, Dionne scored 731 goals and registered 1,771 points. He is currently 5th all time in points and 4th in goals. He is the all-time points leader for the Los Angeles Kings, and his number 16 was retired by the team in 1990. He was inducted into the Hall of Fame in 1992.

Which two teams entered the NHL in 1970?

The NHL expanded to 14 teams in 1970, when the Buffalo Sabres and Vancouver Canucks were welcomed to the league.

Which NHL franchises folded or were forced to relocate in the 1970s?

The Cleveland Barons were the only NHL club that flat-out folded in the 1970s. Several others were forced to relocate. The Kansas City Scouts, who came into the league in 1974, relocated to Colorado in 1976 and were renamed the Rockies. After six years in Colorado, the Rockies relocated to New Jersey and were renamed the Devils.

In 1972–73, a franchise was born in Atlanta. What was it called?

The Atlanta Flames franchise was born in 1972–73 with Bill Putnam serving as team president. He chose Cliff Fletcher as his GM and Boom-Boom Geoffrion as coach. Atlanta's goaltending was superior with Dan Bouchard and Phil Myre. The Flames finished 7th in the division and way out of the playoffs. The following season, they finished fourth 4th and squeaked into the playoffs, but they were swept by the Flyers. The Flames made the playoffs five of the next six seasons but only won two playoff games total. They were led by youngsters Tom Lysiak and Eric Vail, as well as veteran goaltender Phil Myre. The Flames moved to Calgary in 1980–81 and won their first Stanley Cup in 1989.

In 1974 the NHL added two new expansion teams. Which teams were they?

In 1974 the NHL added the Kansas City Scouts and the Washington Capitals. The Kansas City club lasted only two seasons before moving to Denver.

LIGHTING THE LAMP

How did future Hall of Famer Bobby Hull do when he jumped to the WHA?

When Bobby Hull executed his sensational leap from the National Hockey League's Chicago Black Hawks to the Winnipeg Jets of the World Hockey Association (WHA) in the summer of 1972, several hasty predictions were made. Some experts were confident that the Golden Jet could score more than 100 goals against WHA goaltenders. Then, there were those who believed that Hull's presence would guarantee nothing but standing-room crowds at the Winnipeg Arena.

Hardly any of those events took place. For two straight years, Hull missed the WHA scoring title, never nearing the 100-goal mark. True, the Jets finished first in their inaugural season, but they were far off the mark in the 1973–74 season, and attendance was conspicuously disappointing. Hull's defection from the National Hockey League was the major reason for the WHA's ability to become the game's second major hockey league overnight.

While playing 15 seasons for the Black Hawks, the Golden Jet led the NHL in goal scoring seven times and was a three-time points leader. He was named to the All-Star

141

team in 12 out of 15 seasons, and he won just about every available award. At the age of thirty-four, when he put on the Winnipeg Jets uniform for the first time, Hull had done just about everything that had been asked of him, but now he was facing the biggest challenge of his life.

The Jet scored 51 goals and 52 assists in 63 games to finish in a three-way tie for fourth place in the WHA scoring race. Bobby's point total was amazing considering that he frequently was skating at less than top speed. In 1975 Hull scored a record-breaking 77 goals but missed the WHA scoring title by five points to Andre Lacroix. Hull retired after the 1980 season and was inducted into the Hall of Fame in 1983.

Who could be described as the heart and soul of Chicago hockey?

Stan Mikita, the shifty Black Hawks center, is precisely that man. More than any National Hockey League club, the Black Hawks were decimated by World Hockey Association raids. First, the Golden Jet, Bobby Hull, jumped to Winnipeg. Then in 1973 the Black Hawks lost first-string defenseman Pat Stapleton and reliable center Ralph Backstrom to the Chicago Cougars. They were quality players that a team could ill afford to lose, unless it possessed a very strong backbone. That's where Stan Mikita came in. His combined excellence as a leader and an artistic scorer enabled coach Billy Reay's team to weather the storm.

Chicago finished first in the West Division in 1972–73, following Hull's exit, and Stan scored 27 goals and 56 assists for 83 points. His guidance for the younger players enabled the Black Hawks to reach the Stanley Cup Finals before the Montreal Canadiens eliminated them in six games. The Black Hawks had more trouble in 1973–74 with the loss of Stapleton and Backstrom along with the Philadelphia Flyers coming on strong. Chicago, nevertheless, finished a strong second, while Mikita led the team in scoring with 30 goals and 50 assists for 80 points.

If hockey doctorates were awarded, Stan would be first in line, judging by his cerebral play. "He automatically makes the right play," said Black Hawks manager Tommy Ivan, "and is already thinking about where the next one will develop, and heads in that direction." For vintage Mikita, one merely has to flash back to the 1974 semifinal round between Chicago and the Boston Bruins. With the series tied one game apiece, the Black Hawks rallied from a 3–1 deficit at home to pull within a goal of the Bruins with a minute to play in Game 3. Reay then yanked goalie Tony Esposito in favor of a sixth attacker. Chicago won control of the puck as defenseman Phil Russell led the Black Hawks' attack against Bruins goalie Gilles Gilbert. Russell barely missed a tip-in shot as Gilbert sprawled to make the save. Meanwhile, Mikita moved toward the action. He shot the rebound off the goalie's backside and into the net to tie the game at three. Chicago went on to win the game on a Jim Pappin goal in sudden-death overtime.

The Black Hawks didn't win the Cup, but they gave Boston a good run, and Mikita distinguished himself without Hull, Stapleton, or Backstrom at his side. He remained in Chicago until he retired in 1980. He is the Black Hawks' all-time leader in points and games played. In 1,394 games, he registered 1,467 points. He was the first Black Hawk to have his jersey retired and was inducted into the Hall of Fame in 1983.

Which Hall of Famer played for sixteen years as a defenseman and immediately became the coach of the Los Angeles Kings upon retiring?

Bob Pulford, a classy, two-way defenseman, labored for sixteen seasons in the National Hockey League for the Toronto Maple Leafs and later the Los Angeles Kings. Never a flamboyant player in the "superstar" category, Pulford quietly and efficiently got the job done, taking a regular shift, skating on the power play, and killing penalties.

Pulford finished his active-player career in 1972, retiring as the Kings' captain and stepping right into their coaching post. Under Bob's coaching, the Beverly Hills squad turned into one of the finest defensive units and serious playoff contenders. He won the Jack Adams Award in 1975 and led the King to their first playoff appearance in five years in 1974. He was, however, never able to lead the Kings past the second round of the playoffs. After five years with the Kings, he moved on and became coach and general manager of the Chicago Blackhawks. He was eventually promoted to senior vice president and took over the general manager duties again for three stints: 1992–97, 1999–2000, and 2003–05. He was inducted into the Hall of Fame in 1991.

Who is the only coach, besides Scotty Bowman, to win both the East and West Conference Trophies?

In the fall of 1974, Billy Reay became the longest tenured coach in the NHL and the only one, besides Scotty Bowman, to have won both the Prince of Wales Trophy (East Conference champions) and the Clarence Campbell Bowl (West Conference champions). Reay took over the bench of the Chicago Black Hawks in 1963, two years after they won their last Stanley Cup. His single greatest burden was the fact that he was unable to bring the ultimate glory back to Chicago Stadium.

Reay was a quiet man who did not enjoy a pleasant relationship with the press. In fact, his press conferences gained some notoriety for becoming sparring matches with writers.

He coached the Black Hawks for 14 years and three times led them to the Stanley Cup Finals. He was later fired during the 1976–77 season.

Which six-time All-Star along with Bobby Orr was part of the Bruins' dominant run in the early 1970s?

There are some critics who unequivocally believe that Phil Esposito is the finest center ever to skate in the National Hockey League. They point to the indisputable fact that he regularly led the NHL in scoring, that he was consistently voted to the First All-Star Team, and that the Boston Bruins' renaissance directly coincided with his arrival in Beantown at the start of the 1967–68 season. For further emphasis, the Esposito Marching and Chowder Society is quick to point out that Phil was chief architect of Team

Phil Esposito

Canada's pulsating four-games-to-three (with one tie) victory over the Soviet National Team in September 1972.

Because he worked with two burly and gifted wingmen, Ken Hodge and Wayne Cashman, Esposito was virtually unstoppable in his favorite camping ground outside the face-off circle, about 15 feet from the net. One scouting report on Esposito analyzed him this way: "Esposito combines reach, strength, intelligence, and competitiveness to the degree that the only way he can be countered is with superbly coordinated defensive play." As a result Esposito was the surest bet among active players with a chance of surpassing Gordie Howe's all-time record of 786 NHL goals. This proved that Phil could score equally well in the NHL as he could against the Europeans. In fact, he was the one member of Team Canada in 1972 who could not be handled by the Soviet defense.

As luck would have it, nearly all of Esposito's goals were forgotten when the Philadelphia Flyers knocked off the Bruins in six games in May 1974 to become the first expansion team to win the Stanley Cup. Unlike most opponents, the rambunctious Flyers completely manacled Esposito, who was topped in every department—especially face-offs—by the tenacious Bobby Clarke. Even more grating were the words of Bruins coach Bep Guidolin, who singled out Esposito and other Boston skaters for lack of effort. "Determination and second effort is what beat us," said Guidolin. "Our big players should have worked harder and put out more. Too much money is being paid to some individuals."

Esposito would go on to star for the Bruins for two more seasons. In nine seasons with the Bruins, Esposito scored 60 or more goals four times and scored fewer than 35 goals only once, a season in which he played only 12 games. He would also play for the Rangers for six seasons and again scored at least 30 goals in four of those six years. He finished his career with 717 goals, one of only five players to score 700 or more goals in NHL history. He was a two-time Stanley Cup champion, five-time Art Ross Trophy recipient, two-time Hart Trophy winner, and he was elected to the Hall of Fame in 1984. His number 7 was retired by the Bruins in 1987.

Which former New York Ranger great almost had his career end before it began?

Rod Gilbert's career almost ended before it even began. Playing for the Guelph Royals in the Ontario Hockey Association, he skidded on an ice-cream container top thrown to the ice by a fan and injured his back. Days later an opponent leveled him with a strong check, and Gilbert fell to the ice, his back broken. The first operation on his spine was a near disaster; his left leg began to hemorrhage, and amputation was seriously considered. During the summer of 1965, the bone grafts in his back weakened, and another operation was needed. Rod's career was in jeopardy; he played 34 games in a restrictive brace and then submitted to another operation. Happily, Rod's story has been uphill ever since.

In 1971–72 he scored 43 goals, finished fifth in the NHL in the scoring race, and was named right wing on the first All-Star team. He was the first Ranger in eight years to get a first-team nomination. In 1974 Gilbert passed Andy Bathgate as the Rangers' all-time leading scorer, and this milestone was celebrated by a five-minute, deafening standing ovation. He remains the Rangers' all-time scorer to date. In 1971–72 he was paired with Jean Ratelle and Vic Hadfield, forming the legendary GAG (goal-a-game) line that amassed 139 goals and 312 points.

In 1973–74 Gilbert scored 36 goals and 77 points despite the Rangers' problems. He showed his deep competitive spirit as he helped the Rangers in their upward spiral from sixth to third place. Rod's dramatic overtime goal in the semifinal playoff round against the Philadelphia Flyers was one of the most spectacular plays ever. Rod again topped 30 goals in 1974–75, despite a sorry Rangers performance in the regular season. He retired at the end of the 1977–78 season and a year later became the first Ranger to have his number retired. He finished his career with 406 goals and 1,021 points in 1,065 career games and was elected to the Hall of Fame in 1982.

Which player holds the NHL record for most points registered in a game?

From the moment the Toronto Maple Leafs were born, their hallmark has been an abundance of quality centermen. Check the Hockey Hall of Fame: Joe Primeau, Syl Apps Sr., Ted Kennedy, and Max Bentley. Each one of them contributed to former Leafs boss Conn Smythe's belief that the secret of winning hockey teams is "strength through the center."

Another Hall of Famer, Darryl Sittler, would continue the Leafs' tradition of great centers. In his first three National Hockey League seasons, Sittler's point total climbed from 18 (in 1970–71) to 32 to 77. His team-leading 84 points—38 goals, 46 assists—in the 1973–74 season was his best of all and confirmed the Toronto organization's faith in the 6'0", 190-pound farm boy. Sittler was drafted by the Leafs in 1970. When his contract ran out in 1972–73, the Maple Leafs, satisfied with Sittler's production, prepared a new pact. However, the WHA Toronto Toros also wanted Sittler and were prepared to unload something like $1 million to prove their sincerity. Sittler chose to stay with the Leafs.

Toronto finished fourth in 1973–74 after lodging in sixth the previous year, and Darryl clearly was the top center on the club. He finished 15 points ahead of veteran pivot Norm Ullman and an embarrassing—but not for Darryl—31 points ahead of one-time ace center Dave Keon.

On February 7, 1976, Sittler set an NHL record with ten points (six goals, four assists) in a single game. Many people believe that this record will never be broken. In

Which defenseman was posthumously inducted into the Hall of Fame after he was killed in a car accident?

On February 20, 1974, the Buffalo Sabres visited Toronto for a game with the Maple Leafs. Prior to the opening face-off, Buffalo trailed Toronto by seven points, a big but not insurmountable gap. A Sabres win would narrow the margin enough to make the homestretch interesting, and coach Joe Crozier planned accordingly. His plan was to start five bruising skaters and disrupt the Maple Leafs' aggressiveness, then beat the supposedly disorganized enemy. The plan looked good on paper but, alas, it failed in practice. Buffalo's big men hit the Leafs, to be sure, but they were handed two early penalties, which Toronto immediately converted into power-play goals.

After the game, manager Punch Imlach and defenseman Tim Horton took a stroll up Church Street in Toronto, near Maple Leaf Gardens. Tim had a badly bruised jaw and was depressed about the loss. The perennial optimist, Imlach tried to cheer his old pal. "You played only two periods," said Imlach, "and one shift in the third, yet you were picked as a star of the game. If all the guys played well, we'd have won going away."

Horton forced a smile and said, "Well, Punch, there's always tomorrow."

But for Tim Horton, there would be no tomorrow. En route to Buffalo in his sports car, Tim died early the next morning when he lost control of his automobile, and it crashed on the Queen Elizabeth Way. He was posthumously inducted into the Hall of Fame in 1977 after a brilliant 22-year career, most of which was spent as a member of the Leafs.

1981 he was traded to Philadelphia, where he spent three years, and he finished his career in Detroit in 1985. In 1989 Sittler was inducted to the Hall of Fame, and in 2003 the Maple Leafs permanently raised his number 27 to the rafters. In 1,096 career games, Sittler recorded 1,121 points.

Who was the center for Buffalo's trio known as "The French Connection"?

Hockey is far more than just a sport in the French-speaking province of Quebec, Canada. It is more like a religion. Stars such as Maurice "the Rocket" Richard, Jean Beliveau, and Bernie "Boom-Boom" Geoffrion have been worshipped as folk heroes. Now another name has been added to the list—Gilbert Perreault, the lyrical skater for the NHL's Buffalo Sabres and a man who has the most credentials to fill Beliveau's distinguished skates.

In his first four NHL seasons, Perreault won both the Calder and Lady Byng Trophies and almost immediately took over as leader of Buffalo's hockey club. He was an example of what scoring finesse was all about. In that sense, Perreault most resembled Beliveau when Jean was having his finest years with the Montreal Canadiens. "Like Beliveau," said Rangers general manager Emile Francis, "Gil has all moves and great range. There's no way to stop him if he's coming at you one-on-one."

Curiously, Perreault *was* stopped during the 1973–74 season but by one of his own teammates. In a game against the New York Islanders at Buffalo's Memorial Auditorium, defenseman Mike Robitaille fell on Perreault and fractured Gil's left ankle. As a result, Perreault missed 23 games and finished the season with a rather modest 18 goals and 33 assists for 51 points. Fortunately, his recovery was complete, and he seemed the same or better in 1974–75 when he had his best season, with 39 goals and 57 assists for 96 points.

Perreault spent his entire 17-year career with the Sabres and served as team captain for six of those seasons. In 1,191 career games, he tallied 1,326 points (512 goals, 814 assists). The Sabres retired his number 11 in 1990, the same year he was inducted into the Hall of Fame. He is the Sabres' all-time leader in games played, goals, assists, and points.

Who became the first Detroit Red Wing to score 50 goals in a season?

In a sense the 1973–74 season was a banner year for Mickey Redmond, the dashing 26-year-old Detroit right wing. For the second campaign in a row, he scored more than 50 goals and was the runner-up to Marcel Dionne as leading scorer of the Red Wings. But Mickey was less than exultant about those results. Even though he collected 51 goals and 26 assists for 77 points, the total represented a drop of 16 from his mark the previous season.

Redmond, 5'11" and 185 pounds, also got "the feeling" years earlier as an offensive prodigy playing his hockey on outdoor rinks in frigid northern Ontario. He was nurtured early in the whys and wherefores of shooting a puck and learned his lessons well. When Mickey was growing up in the city of Kirkland Lake, he and brother Dick would disdain the usual childhood pastimes to sharpen their puck-shooting skills in the compact "Redmond Arena"—otherwise known as the basement of Mickey's house. "Dick and I used to shoot by the hour in the cellar—when we weren't on the ice somewhere," the Red Wing star right winger reminisced.

Redmond grew up to break some hockey records. His 52 goals during the 1972–73 National Hockey League campaign set an all-time Detroit mark for most tallies in a single season. Considering that the record was formerly held by the legendary Gordie Howe, Mickey's milestone is all the more impressive. He joined the likes of Maurice Richard, Bernie Geoffrion, Bobby Hull, Phil Esposito, Johnny Bucyk, Rick Martin, Mike Bossy, and more recently Alex Ovechkin and Steven Stamkos—all of whom have netted 50 or more goals in one season. Redmond's forte was his overpowering shot, which was known to cause opposing goaltenders great distress. The superstar Redmond claims he acquired the shot by practicing with a metal puck while playing Junior A hockey for the Peterborough Petes.

Redmond would finish his career with 428 points in just 538 games played. After he retired in 1975–76, Redmond became a color analyst, primarily for the local Red Wings telecasts.

STARS BETWEEN THE PIPES

Which Hall of Fame goaltender was overshadowed by a fellow Hall of Famer and his brother for much of his career?

One thing the National Hockey League has never lacked is brother acts—the Bentley boys, Rocket and Pocket Rocket Richard, and the high-scoring Hulls, to name a few, all of them first-rate forwards and stars of their day. So when the Canadiens' Tony Esposito, 14 months the junior of brother Phil, made his league debut in goal against the Oakland Seals on November 29, 1968, hockey followers did not take special notice. No fanfare, no big buildup—Phil's "kid brother" was just another rookie netminder about to be painfully indoctrinated into the frozen world of ricocheting rubber.

Tony played sparingly for Montreal, and in June 1969, the Canadiens left him unprotected in the intraleague draft, and he was picked up by Chicago. Tony fit right in with the Hawks' scheme. Coach Billy Reay displayed a lot of confidence in him by starting Espo in the 1969–70 season opener versus St. Louis. Tony was bombed, 7–2, but Reay continued to give him the lion's share of the work while veteran goalie Denis DeJordy assumed the backup duties.

Led by Tony's goaltending, the Black Hawks would go on to face Phil's Bruins in the Stanley Cup semifinals. Needless to say, the Esposito brothers had their own personal affair to settle. Tony was determined to keep his older brother off the score sheet. But Phil put his seven-year NHL savvy to use and led the Bruins to a four-game sweep of the Black Hawks. Poor Tony manned the goal in each game.

Tony would go on to play another 14 seasons for the Black Hawks. He won the Calder and Vezina Trophies in 1970 and won a share of two more Vezinas in 1972 and 1974. He was elected to the Hall of Fame in 1988, and his number 35 was retired by the Chicago franchise in 1998.

Which NHL goalie won the Conn Smythe Trophy a full year before he won the Calder Trophy as Rookie of the Year?

Ken Dryden began his National Hockey League career in the limelight. Elevated by the Canadiens late in the 1970–71 season from the Montreal Voyageurs of the American Hockey League, Dryden played in only six regular season games. Then, as the Canadiens captured the Stanley Cup under Coach Al MacNeil, Dryden won the Conn Smythe Trophy as the most valuable player in the playoffs. Dryden posted a 2.24 goals-against average in 1971–72, his official rookie season (he was still considered a rookie because he had played fewer than 26 games the previous season), and was awarded the Calder Trophy as the best NHL freshman. The next season, his average climbed a hair to 2.26 as he played in 54 games, ten fewer than his rookie year. Dryden carted home the Vezina Trophy for this effort.

It was then that Ken dropped the verbal bomb. He announced he was quitting pro hockey to take a $7,000-a-year job as a law clerk in Toronto. Money was—and wasn't—

his object. He was willing to work for peanuts as a law clerk because the Habs weren't willing to meet his financial terms. Dryden's replacements were three relative novices—Wayne Thomas, Michel Plasse, and Michel "Bunny" Larocque. Many observers felt the Canadiens would fold without extra competence between the crossbars. Ultimately, they were right. Meanwhile, Ken enjoyed several activities, among them playing defense in a Toronto industrial league. He also did television commentary for the Toronto Toros of the World Hockey Association.

Naturally, the rumor mill flourished. Would Dryden jump to the WHA in 1974–75? It was no secret that he and Canadiens general manager Sam Pollock had their differences. Toros president John Bassett wanted to build a new arena and would need a drawing card. Evidently, Dryden would be able to choose between a five-year, $1 million WHA contract and a three-year, $450,000 Canadiens contract. All was resolved on May 24, 1974, when Dryden returned to Montreal to sign his new NHL contract. The McGill Law School graduate employed an old Cornell classmate, Arthur Kaminsky, as his agent. The contract was one of the highest ever for goalies, estimated at well over $100,000 a year. But Ken had a mediocre year in 1974–75 as the Canadiens were wiped out of the Stanley Cup playoffs by Buffalo.

Dryden's career was reasonably short, just eight seasons, but he is currently first all time in win percentage for a goaltender with 65 percent. He was inducted into the Hall of Fame in 1983, and his number 29 was retired by the Canadiens in 2007.

Which Hall of Fame goaltender backstopped the Flyers to two straight Stanley Cups?

The human rubber radar machine that is Bernie Parent of the Philadelphia Flyers climbed to the top rung as one of the best goaltenders in the National Hockey League, if not the world. Thanks to the French-Canadian from Montreal, the Flyers finished first in the West Division in 1974, first in the Lester Patrick Division in 1975, and then marched triumphantly to the Stanley Cup both years. Flyers captain Bobby Clarke once said, "Bernie is the most valuable player in all of hockey."

Nobody in Pennsylvania would deny that. Playing in 73 out of 78 regular season games in 1973–74—more than any other goalie—Parent produced a dazzling 1.89 goals-against average, best in the league. Unfortunately for Bernie, the Vezina Trophy is a team award, and the Flyers and Chicago Black Hawks finished with

Bernie Parent

identical 2.10 goals-against averages (Bobby Taylor played seven games for Philadelphia and compiled a 4.26 average). Consequently, there was a Vezina tie. Parent made up for that in the 1974 playoffs. While Chicago's Tony Esposito and his Black Hawks were bombed out of the semifinals by Boston, Bernie was virtually flawless in the Flyers' goal.

The decisive moment occurred on opening night in October 1973 against the Toronto Maple Leafs at Philadelphia's Spectrum. Parent had also played for Toronto and openly criticized the city at the time. Now the Maple Leafs were out for revenge. However, they didn't accomplish much. Nothing, in fact. The Flyers scored twice, and Parent shut out the Leafs. If it were possible, Parent improved as the season progressed. He compiled 12 shutouts, just three shy of a league record, and displayed the dexterity that reminded seasoned observers of the goaltending master, Jacques Plante. This was less than surprising, since it was the very same Plante who had taken Bernie under his wing when they alternated in goal for the Maple Leafs.

That good feeling was shared by Philadelphians, who summed up their reaction to their favorite goalie by buying thousands of bumper stickers with the apt description: "Only the Lord Saves More Than Bernie Parent!"

TOUGH GUYS FOR A TOUGH ERA

Which Hall of Fame defenseman perfected the "submarine body check"?

Brad Park played the game precisely the way it was meant to be played—hard but clean. He perfected the "submarine body check," which involved thrusting his hip into the path of onrushing opponents and catapulting them upside down to the hard ice. The check, rare in contemporary hockey, is a throwback to the days when the game was slower and defensemen had considerably more time to plan such devastating, yet clean maneuvers.

Park's submarine checks were not feared more than his fists. When suitably provoked, he retaliated with a barrage of lefts and rights that usually guaranteed him no less than a draw and often a victory over his enemies. During the 1971–72 season, when the Boston Bruins were intimidating most of the Rangers, it was Park who virtually single-handedly took on the bruising Bruins, whipping Ted Green and Johnny McKenzie and fighting awesome Bobby Orr to a draw.

Park made it to the NHL in 1968 with the Rangers. It was then that his toughness received its supreme test from the greatest hockey player of them all, Gordie Howe. During a game late in the 1968–69 season at Olympia Stadium in Detroit, Howe tried to circle around Park in the Rangers' zone. Brad crouched low and crunched his six feet and 190 pounds into the Detroit player's stomach. It was a textbook body check, hard but clean, and Howe was deftly removed from the play. Unfortunately for Park, he was still young and naïve about the ways and means of the NHL jungle. He assumed that Howe would respect a clever body block and quietly congratulate Park for his talent. Instead, he went after him and deposited Park to the ice with his stick.

During the 1973–74 season, Park led all the Rangers in scoring, but they finished third in the NHL's East Division and were wiped out of the Stanley Cup semifinal round after a brutal series with the Philadelphia Flyers. Philadelphia's Mean Machine singled out Park for considerable punishment. Leading the Flyers' assault was the super aggressive Dave Schultz, who dealt Brad several lumps—not all of them legal. Park fought back nobly but, when the series had ended, he stuck by his philosophy that hockey can be played tough but clean.

He was traded to the Boston Bruins in November 1975 and played eight seasons there. He finished his career with the Red Wings in 1985 and was elected into the Hall of Fame in 1988, his first year of eligibility.

Which Boston great was nicknamed "Bloody" O'Reilly?

For youngsters like Terry O'Reilly, the Boston Bruins' 1972 loss of key players to the WHA was a blessing. O'Reilly, a stocky right winger with a reddish-blond mane to match his Irish name, spent the 1971–72 season with the Boston Braves, an American Hockey League affiliate of the Bruins. Although he scored a paltry nine goals in 60 games, the six foot, 180-pounder earned a reputation as a rough 'n' ready roister who was not averse to doing his opponents bodily harm. He spent 165 minutes in the penalty box repenting for such transgressions.

The Niagara Falls, Ontario, native was placed on a line with rookie center Gregg Sheppard and three-year man Don Marcotte. Christened the "Kid Line" despite Marcotte's veteran standing, the trio hustled, dug, and battled their way into the hearts of the Bruins' fans and, even more important, Bruins management. Rarely a game went by when the line wasn't responsible for either scoring goals or preventing their opponents from mounting a consistent offense.

O'Reilly personally contributed five goals and 22 assists to the line's output, while logging 109 minutes in the sin bin. O'Reilly and then-teammate Derek Sanderson staged a bloody brawl in the Bruins' dressing room at Oakland in 1973–74. As a result, Sanderson eventually was traded to the Rangers.

O'Reilly spent his entire 14-year career in Boston and racked over 2,000 career penalty minutes. His number 24 was retired by the Bruins in October of 2002.

Who played right wing on a line with Phil Esposito for the Bruins in the late '60s and '70s?

Ken Hodge was Phil Esposito's right-hand man, literally. The 220-pound right winger received more than 400 assists in the nine years he and Phil had been teammates, many of them the result of aggressive play along the boards and in the corners. Along with left winger Wayne Cashman, his first thought had been getting the puck to super scorer Esposito somewhere near the slot. If, as many observers claim, hockey games were won in the corners, Hodge was one of the most valuable Bruins.

151

Sometimes it was dirty work, and it was usually a thankless assignment, but Hodge insists he never minded playing second fiddle to Phil. "Maybe I could have scored more if I just thought about myself personally," he said. "But in the years we've been together, each man on the Bruins has enjoyed his greatest season. So why change success? Especially when you've got a man in the slot who can score 76 goals one year and 66 the next?" Besides, Ken had plenty of moments in the spotlight. In 1969–70, he netted 105 points, and he twice went over the 40-goal mark in a season.

Ironically, it wasn't until he went to Boston that his scoring prowess was uncovered. Back in Chicago, coach Billy Reay employed him mainly as a policeman, a role he perfected when the Big Bad Bruins began their raucous climb to prominence in the late sixties. He was able to mix it up with any of the NHL's big boys and quite often did. But he was much more than a cop and a second fiddle. He was a winning hockey player, which pretty much says it all.

THE BROAD STREET BULLIES

Which player scored 30 goals and 34 assists his rookie season and still did not win the Calder Trophy in 1972–73?

Bill Barber was Philadelphia's first choice in the 1972 amateur draft. A native of Callander, Ontario, and one of five brothers, Bill was encouraged to play hockey by his father, who hoped that at least one of his sons would make it to the NHL.

"Just to make sure we had everything going for us, Dad built us a rink that was almost regulation size, had hydro poles put up, and lights strung out."

Barber was selected by the Flyers after he had spent three years with the Kitchener Juniors in the OHA. During that time he had 127 goals and 171 assists while playing both the center and wing spots. He expected to make the Flyers without any trouble, but he was farmed out to Richmond before the start of the 1972–73 season because his checking was not up to NHL standards. A month later, he was called up, and he was on his way to a fine major-league career, although he is disparagingly considered the most dangerous "swan-diver" in the NHL. Barber's 30 goals and 34 assists did not win him the Calder Trophy in 1972–73. But he did win the hearts of the Flyers' fans.

As part of the famed LCB line (with Reggie Leach and Bobby Clarke), Barber helped lead the Flyers to two straight Stanley Cups in 1973–74 and 1974–75. He also was a member of Team Canada during the 1976 Canada Cup and scored the tying goal in the final against Czechoslovakia, a game Canada would win in overtime.

He served as a team leader for nearly a decade, briefly captained the Flyers from 1981 to 1983, and was instrumental in the Flyers' record-setting thirty-five-game winning streak in 1979–80. Barber was forced to retire following the 1984–85 season after not being able to return from reconstructive knee surgery. His number 7 was retired by the Flyers in 1990, shortly after his induction into the Hall of Fame. Following his retirement, Barber enjoyed a short coaching career and was the Jack Adams Award winner in 2001, but he was fired in 2002. He currently sits second all time in scoring for the Flyers.

Which player was forced to retire after just five years due to a terrible eye injury?

One of the genuinely tragic figures of hockey, Barry Ashbee was struck down by a blazing slapshot during the 1974 Stanley Cup semifinals between the New York Rangers and the Philadelphia Flyers. Ashbee, who spent most of his fifteen-year career in the minors, didn't gain a regular NHL berth until 1970–71, when the Flyers signed him to a contract. He was the linchpin of Philadelphia's solid defense during

Bill Barber

the 1973–74 campaign, when the Flyers finished first in the West Division, and he guided Philadelphia to an opening-round victory over the Atlanta Flames.

On April 28, 1974, at Madison Square Garden, his career suddenly ended when Rangers defenseman Dale Rolfe shot at the Flyers' net. The puck hit Ashbee's right eye with all its force. He lost nearly all sight in the eye and retired to become a Flyers scout. "I'm not bitter," Ashbee insisted. "Some people strive for sixty years and they can't make it. I got what I wanted when I was thirty-four—a Stanley Cup win for the Flyers. I had thought about being a Cup winner since I was seven."

Ashbee would go on to become an assistant coach for the Flyers and helped guide them to their second straight Stanley Cup in 1975. In April 1977 Ashbee was diagnosed with leukemia and died just a month later. His number 4 was retired by the Flyers on October 3, 1977, and they named a trophy in his honor presented each year to the team's top defenseman.

Which one-time 50-goal scorer was a major part of the Flyers' 1974 and 1975 Stanley Cup championships?

It was March 8, 1974, a day after the Flyers dominated the Red Wings 6–1. On the front page of the paper was a picture of Rick MacLeish along with the headline: "NHL Cup Here? It May Happen!"

It did happen. And one reason why it happened was because of the deft shooting, stick-handling, and playmaking of the 5'11", 175-pound MacLeish. Time and again as the Flyers annexed first place in the NHL's West Division and marched along the trail to the 1974 Stanley Cup, the wrist-shooting native of Lindsay, Ontario, provided Philadelphia with essential goals. Significantly, MacLeish applied himself most diligently against the two tough challengers who confronted Philadelphia en route to the championship—the New York Rangers and Boston Bruins. MacLeish led the league in playoff scoring with 13 goals and 9 assists in 1974 and was equally important in the Flyers' Stanley Cup run in 1975.

Which Philadelphia Flyers legend won the Conn Smythe Trophy in 1976, despite losing the Cup?

A junior teammate of Bobby Clarke in Flin Flon, Manitoba, Reggie Leach became Clarke's linemate in Philly. Nicknamed "The Chief" for his ancestry, Leach was the third man chosen in the 1970 amateur selections, just ahead of Rick MacLeish. Both were originally chosen by the Bruins but later became integral parts of the Flyers' attack.

Clarke urged the Flyers to acquire Leach for the 1974–75 season, although there had been reports that Reg would be more of a hindrance than a help to the Philadelphia club. Leach responded by scoring 46 goals for the Flyers and appeared destined for a long career in Philly. His major weapon was a devastating shot that overwhelmed any stickhandling deficiencies. He starred on the famed LCB (Leach, Clarke, Barber) line, which helped lead the Flyers to the Stanley Cup in 1975.

He is currently tied with Finnish legend Jari Kurri for most goals in a playoff year with 19. In 934 NHL games, he scored 381 goals and notched 666 points. He was inducted into the Philadelphia Flyers Hall of Fame in 1992.

Who holds the record for most penalty minutes in a single season?

No athlete ever received more media attention for less talent than Dave Schultz, a pugnacious forward who burst into the NHL scene in 1971–72 for one game and became a regular a season later. A key member of the ferocious Philadelphia Flyers, Schultz worked hard to earn his nickname—"The Hammer." He led the NHL in penalty minutes during the 1972–73, 1973–74, and 1974–75 seasons (garnering an astronomical, record-breaking 472 penalty minutes in 1974–75), and in eight years as a pro, he spent the equivalent of 57 games in the penalty box. "I fought my way into the NHL and that's something I can't forget," the big left winger explained.

Schultz was certainly tough. On Philadelphia's "Mean Machine," he was the "baddest of the bad." He also developed some skill—and that made him twice as dangerous. He reached the 20-goal mark in 1973–74 and scored some key goals in the Flyers' successful 1974 Stanley Cup crusade. At one point, his "plus-minus" rating (team goals for and against while on the ice) was best of all the West Division forwards.

He is one of the biggest reasons the Philadelphia Flyers earned the nickname "The Broad Street Bullies," a nickname often still referred to today. In 535 career NHL games, he racked up an astounding 2,294 penalty minutes to just 200 points. His record of 472 penalty minutes in a single season is said to be a record that will never be broken.

Schultz also had a rule created for him known as "The Schultz Rule," which banned players from wrapping their hands in boxing tape, which Schultz was known for when he got into scrapes.

Who captained the Flyers to two straight Stanley Cups in 1974 and 1975?

In a roundabout way, it can be said that the Philadelphia Flyers' 1974 Stanley Cup was won on the ice of Moscow's Sports Palace in 1972. That was when Team Canada defeated the Soviet National Hockey Club, and Bobby Clarke, the diabetic kid from Flin Flon, Manitoba, emerged as the most sought-after player in the eyes of Russian hockey experts.

All professional scouts were aware that Bobby was a diabetic and, not surprisingly, scorned him as a potential NHL prospect. Even the Flyers overlooked him at first, but, under the prodding of scout Gerry Melnyk, they decided to take a gamble. Three years after Melnyk's recommendation, Bobby was voted the Flyers' captain, the youngest leader in the NHL at the time. He was the prime architect in the ascendency of Philadelphia as a hockey power.

In the spring of 1973, the Flyers reached the Stanley Cup semifinals for the first time but were eliminated by Montreal in five tough games. It was in this series that Clarke first gained attention as a combatant. The Canadiens thought he was downright dirty; the Flyers countered by saying he played the game extraordinarily hard.

In 1972–73 he returned from the series against Russia and completed the campaign with the most coveted prize in the NHL—the Hart Trophy. He would go on to win the trophy twice more in 1975 and 1976. He also won the Selke Trophy as the top defensive forward in 1977–78. He helped the Flyers "bully" their way to two straight Stanley Cups (the franchise's only Stanley Cups) in 1974 and 1975. After being the heart and soul of the Broad Street Bullies, he retired in 1984 after 15 seasons with the Flyers and went on to become the general manager of the team. He resigned in 2006 after the team's poor start but returned later that year as senior vice president. The Flyers retired his number 16 in 1984 and unveiled the Bobby Clarke Trophy, which is given every year to the

Bobby Clarke was a diabetic, yet he managed to become one of the most accomplished players of the 1970s.

What is the longest unbeaten streak in NHL history?

In a stretch from October 1979 to January 1980, the Philadelphia Flyers went 35 games without suffering a loss. The streak included 25 wins and 10 ties.

team's Most Valuable Player. He is currently the Flyers' all-time leader in points and assists and is second in goals.

Which former defenseman and coach was known as "the Irish Enforcer"?

Pat Quinn began his NHL playing career in Toronto, continuing to Vancouver and then Atlanta. In each city Pat was the policeman, "the Irish Enforcer." He is often best remembered for causing an all-out brawl in Boston after he laid a heavy hit on Bobby Orr. Neither the Boston players nor fans were happy about this, and Quinn had to quickly protect himself. He was eventually forced to seek sanctuary in the Toronto dressing room. It remains a question as to whether there was anything illegal about this hit. At the very worst, Quinn was guilty of a charge. Orr ended up in the hospital with a slight concussion and slight whiplash in his neck.

In 1972, Quinn was obtained by the Atlanta Flames, and his improvement as a backliner became obvious. During 1973–74, Pat collected a total of 32 points, indicating his growing confidence as a puck carrier and playmaker rather than a simple mayhem producer.

Upon retiring after the 1976–77 season, he went on to become the head coach of the Philadelphia Flyers. He twice led them to the quarterfinals and once to the Stanley Cup Finals, losing to the New York Islanders in 1980. The next season he was fired by the Flyers, and a few years later accepted the Los Angeles Kings coaching job, but he had little success in his three years behind the bench for the Kings. In 1990 he became head coach of the Vancouver Canucks and led them to the Stanley Cup Finals in 1994, which they would lose to the New York Rangers. He later went to Toronto and remained there until his retirement in 2006.

He won the Jack Adams Award as top coach twice (1980, 1992) and prior to his retirement, he was the winningest active NHL coach. Quinn died November 23, 2014, at the age of 71.

THE START OF SOMETHING BIG

Which player when he broke into the league was considered to be the "next Bobby Orr"?

New York Islanders defenseman Denis Potvin did a lot of growing up in 1973–74, his rookie big-league season. He may have started the year as a highly touted, wealthy 19-

year-old, but he certainly finished like a mature veteran. He made mistakes and suffered at least one major humiliation en route to the Calder Trophy as the National Hockey League's Rookie of the Year.

Bobby Orr, in 1966–67, had been the last defenseman to win the Calder Trophy. And Orr was the man with whom Denis has been most compared. Orr's records as an amateur defenseman in the Ontario Hockey Association's Junior A League had been obliterated by Potvin, a bilingual backliner from Hull, Quebec, just across the river from Ottawa. Potvin would be earning four times as much as Orr did in his rookie season. And the nineteen-year-old with the ferocious slapshot had built a reputation as a fighter with the Ottawa 67's Junior A team in the OHA. It was still an intimidating set of circumstances because of young Potvin's ballyhoo. But Denis was modest about his press notices heralding him as another Orr. "I'm not Bobby and I know it," he said. "You can't compare us anyway because our styles are different. I can't skate as well as Bobby, but I feel there are a couple of other things I do better—like hitting. That's a big part of my game. I just hope I can accomplish some of the things Bobby has done, but in a different way."

Potvin's sunny raves were temporarily obliterated by a black cloud of embarrassment on December 16, 1973. The Islanders were to play the Philadelphia Flyers that night at the Spectrum. Denis overslept and missed a 10 A.M. team bus from the Nassau Coliseum to Philadelphia. Coach Al Arbour was suitably furious, and the bus was ordered to leave without him. Instead of trying to find alternate means of transportation, Potvin remained home, and when the team returned and had its next practice at the Coliseum, Denis apologized to his teammates after being put through a grueling practice. The incident and its resultant bad press made him realize it is not just what you do, but who you are, especially when you're a rookie making well over $100,000 a year.

How much of an impact did Potvin have on the Islanders?

Potvin made an immediate impact in the league by winning the Calder Trophy, for most outstanding rookie, his first year and winning three Norris Trophies for most outstanding defenseman in 1976, 1978, and 1979. After the 1978–79 season, in which the Isles finished first in the NHL and were favorites to win the Stanley Cup but were ousted in the semifinal versus rival New York Rangers, then-captain Clark Gillies was relieved of his duties with the "C." Potvin took over the captaincy role prior to the start of the 1979–80 season. In his first year as captain, the Isles won their first of four straight Stanley Cups, and Potvin was a pivotal member of what became known as the team's "glory years." In the eight seasons he served as captain, the Islanders didn't miss the postseason once under the leadership of Potvin. He retired at the end of the 1987–88 season and held the records for the most goals, assists, and points by a defenseman prior to the records being broken by Ray Bourque, Paul Coffey, and others in the 1990s and 2000s. Potvin was elected into the Hall of Fame in 1991, and his number 5 was retired a year later.

Who was behind the bench during the Islanders' four Stanley Cups?

Alger Joseph "Radar" Arbour remains the winningest coach for the Long Island hockey team. Like many coaches, the Sudbury, Ontario, native played in the NHL, winning the Stanley Cup with the Red Wings, Black Hawks, and Maple Leafs. In the 1970–71 season with the Blues, he retired as a player 22 games in and coached the rest of the year. In 1973, Al was picked as the new head coach for the New York Islanders. After missing the playoffs in his first year with the team, he led the Islanders to 12 straight playoff appearances, four Stanley Cups, and 19 straight playoff series wins. He retired in 1986, but a poor start by the Isles in 1988–89 resulted in Arbour returning to the bench. In the 1993 playoffs, he led the Isles in a Game 7 win against the two-time defending champion Pittsburgh Penguins. He retired after the 1993–94 season but returned once more in 2007. On November 3rd, he coached one last game to make his career total an even 1,500. At age 75, Arbour became the oldest person to coach an NHL game. The Isles won 3–2 against the Penguins, giving him 740 all-time wins behind only Scotty Bowman in league history.

THE 1980s

THE ISLANDERS ERA

What is notable about the first fighting major in Islanders team history?

In a game between the Rangers and Islanders, Billy Smith decided to drop the gloves with Rod Gilbert. Smith was the Isles' goalie, however. He was known for his fiery temper and propensity for slashing anyone who stepped near his crease.

Why was the Isles' dismal first season a blessing in disguise?

While the team only recorded 12 wins in its first season, 1972–73, that allowed general manager Bill Torrey to draft Denis Potvin with the first pick of the 1973 draft.

What was Torrey's initial strategy for building a strong team?

Torrey knew that, while it would lead to a trying first few seasons, developing young players would be beneficial down the road. He aimed to draft players who "will be around for years rather than those who will not be with us after a year or two."

Which key players did Torrey and his team of scouts select in the 1972 entry draft?

In 1972, the Isles selected forwards Billy Harris, Lorne Henning, Bobby Nystrom, and Garry Howatt. Harris was a steady goal

Bill Torrey (right) with Billy Harris

159

Pound for pound, Garry Howatt (far right) was the Isles' best player of his day.

scorer who never missed a game in seven-plus seasons with the Islanders. The other three all played key roles in the run to the Islanders' first Stanley Cup championship.

What other crucial need did Torrey fill before the franchise ever played its first game?

In the 1972 expansion draft, Torrey selected a 21-year-old goaltender from the Los Angeles Kings by the name of Billy Smith. Smith, of course, went on to win four Cups during the Islanders' dynasty.

Whom did Torrey select in the 1974 amateur draft?

The Islanders selected Hall of Fame linemates Clark Gillies in the first round and Bryan Trottier in the second. They also added Swedish defenseman Stefan Persson, whom Torrey snagged with the 214th pick.

What element of coach Al Arbour's philosophy helped push the Islanders to greatness?

Arbour was known as a strict disciplinarian who never accepted anything but the best from his team. Bobby Nystrom, for example, remembered that on the opening day of training camp in 1973, Arbour promised his players a light skate. Two and a half hours later they were still on the ice.

Which Islanders took home major awards after the 1975–76 season?

Bryan Trottier, who set a rookie scoring record with 95 points, unsurprisingly took home the Calder Trophy. Denis Potvin claimed the Norris Trophy, and many surveys named Arbour the Coach of the Year.

When did the Islanders acquire the final piece to their impressive forward corps?

In 1977, Torrey picked Mike Bossy fifteenth overall; he was a pure goal scorer who would complete the "Trio Grande" line skating alongside Gillies and Trottier.

Why did Potvin reject an offer from the WHA to sign with the Islanders?

Potvin chose the NHL to fulfill his dream; he was quoted as saying, "I always wanted to play in the NHL and only the NHL."

Which two additions helped to push the Islanders to their first Stanley Cup championship?

With a month left in the 1979–80 season, U.S. defenseman Ken Morrow joined the team after winning gold in the Lake Placid Olympics. Torrey also traded during the season for Los Angeles Kings center Butch Goring, who bolstered the team's defensive efforts and penalty killing.

What two events helped serve as bonding experiences for the Isles during their quarterfinal playoff series against the Boston Bruins?

At the end of the first period of Game 2, a brawl broke out on the ice. Then in the locker room, defenseman Bobby Lorimer stood up and said that he would not be bothered by the opponent's physicality, and he was ready to go play. The team came together and refused to be intimidated by the Bruins.

What was the key to the Islanders' dynasty?

As best summed up by U.S. Olympic and New York Rangers coach Herb Brooks, the Islanders were a stable organization that brought in and developed players who

Butch Goring

161

complemented each other well. "They were a balanced team.... They played a good skating game, they played a real physical game, they had good goalkeeping, they played well without the puck, they played well with the puck," he said.

What was unusual about Game 6 of the 1980 Stanley Cup Finals?

Game 6 was the first U.S. network broadcast of an NHL game since 1975. Consequently, the game's start on Saturday, May 24 had to be moved to the afternoon in order to fit the CBS schedule.

What was the key to the Islanders' first NHL title?

Without a doubt, the Isles' special teams carried them to greatness. They scored 15 power-play goals in the six games of the finals. The penalty killers also pitched in, scoring seven short-handed goals throughout the course of the playoffs.

Who led the Islanders in scoring during their 1981 Stanley Cup run?

Mike Bossy set an NHL record that postseason by scoring 35 points (17 goals, 18 assists in 18 games) over the course of four rounds of play.

Which unlikely player took home the 1981 Conn Smythe Trophy?

While he was primarily known for his hard work and defensive play, Butch Goring found his scoring touch in the playoffs. He potted 20 points (10 goals, 10 assists) during the run to the Cup.

Which milestones dominated the Islanders' impressive 1981–82 regular season?

During the 1981–82 season, the team broke the Boston Bruins' record for the longest NHL winning streak by taking 15 in a row. Billy Smith earned the Vezina Trophy with a 2.97 goals-against average, and Mike Bossy recorded the most points ever by a right winger (147).

What records were set when the Islanders claimed their third straight Stanley Cup in 1982?

The Islanders were the first American franchise to win three straight titles. Mike Bossy, who would claim the Conn Smythe Trophy with 17 playoff goals, tied Jean Beliveau's finals record with seven goals in the Stanley Cup Finals.

To what did the Islanders attribute their ability to survive coming within six minutes of elimination in the first round of the 1982 playoffs?

Because they had finally found success after several trying seasons, the Islanders' locker room had developed a collective fear of losing. They knew what it was like to go home empty-handed and would do everything in their power to prevent it from happening again. The Islanders trailed underdog Pittsburgh by two goals late in the third period, but John Tonelli led them to a 4–3 overtime victory in Game 5 of the best-of-five series.

Billy Smith

Why did Billy Smith need to stand tall in the 1983 Stanley Cup Finals?

Not only were the Islanders facing Wayne Gretzky's Edmonton Oilers and one of the most intimidating offenses the league had ever seen, but they were exhausted from a grueling Wales Conference finals against the Boston Bruins. Over the course of the four-game series sweep, Smith proved he was more than worthy of the nickname "Battling Billy."

What elite company did the Isles join by winning four consecutive Stanley Cups?

The Islanders became only the second team to lift Lord Stanley's chalice that many times in a row; only the Montreal Canadiens had performed the feat before.

Which unlikely players led the Isles in scoring during the 1983 Stanley Cup Finals?

In a series between the Islanders and the Edmonton Oilers, offensive fireworks were expected. But Wayne Gretzky was held without a goal during the entire series, and the Sutter brothers, Duane and Brent, led all scorers with seven and five points, respectively.

Why was this Stanley Cup especially significant for Denis Potvin?

During the series, the star defenseman's father was near death. They had previously made an agreement, however, that Denis would fight for the Cup, and his father would fight for his life. Thankfully, the elder Potvin was in the arena to see his son claim the trophy.

What impact did the Islanders have on the Edmonton Oilers?

After being humbled on the ice, Kevin Lowe and Wayne Gretzky walked past the Islanders' locker room after the final game had ended. The young stars expected the Islanders to be in the midst of celebration but instead saw them quietly seeking treatment for their numerous injuries. This moment was crucial for the young Oilers as it showed them the sacrifices it took to become champions; they, of course, would go on to depose the Isles as the NHL's dominant dynasty.

What logistical change in the Stanley Cup Finals gave Edmonton the edge?

In previous seasons, the home ice shifted in a 2-2-1-1-1 format; for the 1984 playoffs, however, the league adopted a 2–3–2 format. This allowed Edmonton three straight home games, which they won after splitting the first two on Long Island. Mike Bossy believed the Isles needed to steal only one victory in Edmonton to claim the Cup, but the New York dynasty ended in the Northlands Coliseum.

How long had the Islanders gone without losing a playoff series?

When the dynasty was all said and done, the Isles had won 19 straight playoff series and four Stanley Cups. That is the longest streak in professional sports, barely beating the Boston Celtics basketball dynasty of the 1960s. The Isles also had to play four rounds of games each season to claim the Cup; while the Montreal Canadiens won four straight titles a decade earlier, they played just three playoff series a year.

OILERS NEAR DYNASTY

How did the Oilers set themselves up for success after joining the NHL?

After joining the league, it looked like the Oilers would lose Wayne Gretzky to the entry draft rule; the team was only able to protect two goalies and two skaters, and the Great One was ineligible for protections as an underaged player. Owner Peter Pocklington, however, signed him to a "personal services" contract, which bound him to the Oilers. With their star secured, the Oilers also drafted incredibly well under the leadership of general manager Glen Sather, adding Mark Messier, left wing Jari Kurri, defenseman Paul Coffey, goalie Grant Fuhr, and right wing Glenn Anderson.

What records did the Oilers set during the 1981–82 season?

In addition to Gretzky setting scoring marks by recording 92 goals and 120 assists for 212 points, the Oilers set a record for the most goals in a season with 417. On the defensive side of the ice, Fuhr set a rookie record with a 23-game undefeated streak. The club was also involved in the highest-scoring playoff game the league has ever seen, a 10–8 Edmonton victory over Los Angeles in the first round.

What "miracle" undid the Oilers' 1981–82 season?

After an impressive regular season that saw them finish with the second-best record in the NHL, the Oilers faced the Kings in the first round of the playoffs. With the best-of-five series tied 1–1, the Oilers took a 5–0 lead after two periods in Los Angeles; the Kings, however, scored five goals in the third period and won the game 6–5 in overtime. This comeback became known as the "Miracle on Manchester" (the Kings' arena, the Forum, was on Manchester Blvd.) and changed the tone of the series, as the Kings won in five games.

What made the Oilers so impressive during the 1982–83 season?

During the 1982–83 season, the Oilers had four skaters—Mark Messier, Wayne Gretzky, Glenn Anderson, and Jari Kurri—all break the 100-point plateau. Paul Coffey finished the year with 96 points. This offense carried the Oilers through the season, until they were swept by the Islanders in the Stanley Cup Finals.

What signs of success did the Oilers show in 1983–84?

During the regular season, Edmonton won a franchise-record 57 games by scoring an NHL-record 446 goals. The team was also

A statue of the great Wayne Gretzky was installed at Rexall Place (the Edmonton Coliseum) in 1989.

the first in league history to boast three 50-goal scorers (Wayne Gretzky, Jari Kurri, and Glenn Anderson). Paul Coffey finished the year with 146 points and became the second defenseman in history to score 40 goals.

Why was the Oilers' Stanley Cup victory significant for both the province of Alberta and Western Canada?

Edmonton became the first team from Alberta to win the Stanley Cup. Not only did the championship prove that the former WHA team was more than capable of thriving in the NHL, but it was Western Canada's first victory in the Stanley Cup Finals since the 1925 Victoria Cougars.

Why did the Oilers lack the same intensity in the 1984–85 regular season?

Prior to the season, eight Edmonton players were called into duty for the Canada Cup. Consequently, the team made a collective decision to pace themselves during the regular season; GM/coach Glen Sather even took a week off to go to Hawaii.

What scoring records did the Oilers set during the 1985 playoffs?

In the conference finals against Chicago, the Oilers scored 44 goals in six games; that still stands as a record for the most goals scored in a single round of the playoffs. Jari Kurri, Paul Coffey, and Wayne Gretzky all set individual scoring records, too. Kurri scored 19 goals, tying Reggie Leach for the most goals during a playoff run; Coffey potted 18 goals, the most ever by a defenseman in the playoffs; and the Great One set a new playoff scoring record with 47 points in 18 games.

165

What bad omens hung over the Oilers at the start of the 1985–86 season?

During June of 1985, left wing Dave Hunter was charged with impaired driving; while he was not formally convicted until February 1986, he served a week of jail time during the season. Mark Messier also faced legal trouble, as he crashed his car in September 1985. While he avoided jail time, he was charged with careless driving in addition to hit and run and had to pay a fine. The club also acquired center Craig MacTavish from the Boston Bruins, who had missed the entire 1984–85 season serving jail time for his vehicular manslaughter conviction.

How did the Oilers perform in the 1985–86 regular season?

Paul Coffey playing in the 2008's All-Star Legends game in Toronto.

Despite the potential distractions, the Oilers managed to claim the inaugural Presidents' Trophy with 119 points. They were led by Gretzky's record-setting 215 points, which included 163 assists. Paul Coffey set a record for the most goals by a defenseman with 48 and Jari Kurri led the NHL with 68 goals.

What unusual event demonstrated the intensity of the playoff series between the Oilers and Flames?

Given that the series was between two Alberta rivals, a great deal of physicality was to be expected. During a game in Calgary, though, Flames enforcer Nick Fotiu was so riled up that he attempted to climb into the Edmonton bench to go after Glen Sather.

How were the Oilers finally undone by the Flames?

In the third period of Game 7 in the second round, Edmonton defenseman Steve Smith attempted a breakout pass from behind his own net. The pass struck goalie Grant Fuhr's skate and deflected into the net, giving the Flames a 3–2 lead. To make matters worse, Smith had just given away the Stanley Cup-losing goal on his birthday.

How did the Oilers respond to their Stanley Cup disappointment?

Like all good teams, the Oilers returned to the ice for the 1986–87 season with a point to prove. While they struggled to beat the Flames, Edmonton still managed to claim a second consecutive Presidents' Trophy with a 50-win, 106-point season.

What crack in the Oilers' ranks emerged during the 1986–87 season?

As he was struggling with injuries, Paul Coffey became angry with coach and general manager Glen Sather. The defenseman did not always see eye-to-eye with Sather and felt he was held to a different standard than the other players; he would be traded to Pittsburgh following a monetary disagreement with Sather before the 1986–87 season.

Who unexpectedly gave the Oilers problems in the 1987 Stanley Cup Finals?

While their offense was as potent as ever, the Oilers struggled to solve the Flyers' rookie netminder, Ron Hextall. Edmonton took a commanding 3–1 series lead, but Hextall's superb play took the series to a seventh game, where he was finally overpowered in a 3–1 loss.

What did Wayne Gretzky do after raising the Stanley Cup following Game 7?

While the Great One received the Cup first as the team captain, he immediately passed it to Steve Smith, who had inadvertently given the Flames the playoff series a year earlier.

Why did the Oilers' Cup defense get off to a rocky start in 1987–88?

At the start of training camp, several key Oilers did not show up. Mark Messier held out while he was negotiating a new contract; center Kent Nilsson and defenseman Reijo Ruotsalainen both decided they would rather play in Europe than in Edmonton. Backup goalie Andy Moog refused to report to camp, saying he wanted a full-time job, while Glenn Anderson was AWOL until the season started. Paul Coffey, unhappy with his salary and treatment by Glen Sather, never showed up at all and was traded to Pittsburgh. Moog was also dealt, to the Boston Bruins.

What Stanley Cup tradition did Wayne Gretzky start after the 1988 finals?

Once he claimed the Cup, Gretzky called all the Oilers, including the coaches and management staff, to center ice for a team picture. This has been done by every championship team ever since.

What unusual event took place during the 1988 Stanley Cup Finals against Boston?

During Game 4, Boston Garden was struck by a power outage; with the score tied 3–3 in the second period, NHL president John Ziegler had no choice but to cancel the game due to darkness. While the stats from the suspended game still counted in the record

---

Who was the unlikely star of the 1987–88 Oilers?

While their offense was no longer the most powerful in the league, the Oilers still had a world-class netminder in Grant Fuhr; during 1987–88, he started a league-record 75 games and won 40 of them.

books, the series returned to Edmonton, and the Oilers swept the series in what would have been Game 5.

THE GRETZKY TRADE

Why did Kings owner Bruce McNall decide he had to trade for Wayne Gretzky?

After trading away Marcel Dionne to the Rangers in 1987, the Kings lacked a true star on the ice and a box office draw. McNall realized the one player people couldn't ignore was Gretzky, so he set out to obtain him at any price.

When everything was said and done, what did the Oilers receive in the Gretzky trade?

It is known simply as "The Trade." When the Oilers sent Wayne Gretzky, Marty McSorley, and Mike Krushelnyski to Los Angeles on August 9, 1988, they received $15 million (USD), Jimmy Carson, and Martin Gelinas in addition to the Kings' first-round picks for 1989, 1991, and 1993. The Oilers would then trade the 1989 pick to the Devils for Corey Foster; the 1991 pick was used to select Martin Rucinsky, and the 1993 pick was used on Nick Stajduhar.

How extreme was the Edmonton fans' reaction to the trade?

Understandably, the fans could not believe what had happened. They burned owner Peter Pocklington in effigy outside Edmonton's Northlands Coliseum. It was later revealed, however, that Pocklington knew Gretzky was likely to leave as a free agent, so he sought to get the best return possible rather than losing the star for nothing.

Pocklington had begun to shop Gretzky to other teams after the 1987–88 NHL season due to financial troubles with his other business ventures. After the trade was announced, Pocklington received death threats from outraged Canadians. The trade was so upsetting to Canadians that one member of the Canadian parliament demanded, albeit unsuccessfully, that the trade be blocked by the government. To this day, Pocklington maintains that he has no regrets about the trade because it was good for the Edmonton Oilers and good for hockey in general.

Wayne Gretzky, attending a film festival in 2005. When he was traded in 1988 to the Kings, Edmonton Oilers fans were furious.

How did the Oilers fare in their first season without Gretzky?

Without the Great One, the Edmonton offense struggled. The Oilers finished third in the Smythe Division, behind the Flames and Gretzky's Kings, and had to face their former star in the first round of the playoffs. After taking a 3–1 series lead, Edmonton fell to the Kings in Game 7 and was eliminated.

What personnel changes did the Oilers make for the 1989–90 season?

Before the season began, Glen Sather stepped down from coaching duties and was replaced behind the bench by his longtime assistant John Muckler. When the season began, things did not get any easier; Grant Fuhr had appendicitis and later injured his shoulder, forcing backup goalie Bill Ranford to start most of the season. Center Jimmy Carson felt that he could not handle the pressure of playing in Edmonton and was traded to Detroit; the deal, which involved six players and a draft pick in November 1989, brought forwards Adam Graves, Joe Murphy, and Petr Klima to the Oilers.

Who emerged as a force to be reckoned with during 1989–90?

While he had been named captain following Gretzky's departure and was always a very good player, Mark Messier announced himself as a star. During the regular season, he finished second in the NHL with 129 points; during the playoffs, he scored 31 points (nine goals and 22 assists in 22 games) and was an intimidating physical presence.

Who was the star of the 1990 Stanley Cup Finals?

Forced into action by Grant Fuhr's injuries, Bill Ranford led the Oilers to glory. Not only did he stand strong as Edmonton was vastly outshot in Game 1, allowing them to steal a victory in the third overtime period, but he stopped 29 of 30 shots in the title-clinching Game 5. He earned the Conn Smythe Trophy for his efforts, posting a 2.53 goals-against average and a .912 save percentage in the playoffs.

How many players were on all of Edmonton's Stanley Cup-winning teams?

Seven players raised all five of the Oilers' Stanley Cups: Mark Messier, Glenn Anderson, Jari Kurri, Kevin Lowe, Randy Gregg, Charlie Huddy, and Grant Fuhr.

SUPER MARIO AND THE PENGUINS

How desperate were the Pittsburgh Penguins to get Mario Lemieux?

After back-to-back seasons with the league's worst record, the Penguins' franchise was in dire straits. They knew, however, that landing the first overall pick in the 1984 draft would assure them Mario Lemieux, who could turn the franchise around. They were so desperate to get the first pick that they consciously tried to finish with the worst record.

While management was not exactly happy to do this, they knew missing out on Lemieux would probably be the end of the Penguins.

Which Calder Trophy winner tallied an astronomical 282 points in 70 games in the junior hockey league prior to being drafted number one overall?

In the 1984–85 season, the Penguins unveiled rookie sensation Lemieux, who tallied 43 goals and 100 points his rookie season and won the Calder Trophy. This followed his record-breaking season with the Laval Voisins of the Quebec Major Junior Hockey League. Despite a huge frame, Mario moved across the ice with ease. His passing and shooting were done with wonderful precision.

Did adding Lemieux and Paul Coffey turn things around for the Penguins?

While the additional talent undeniably helped, Pittsburgh continued to miss out on the postseason. In 1985–86 and 1987–88, they were eliminated from contention on the final day of the season; in 1986–87, they missed the playoffs by two games while four teams of comparable or worse records qualified.

How did the Penguins finally reach the playoffs?

Pittsburgh finally reached the playoffs during the 1988–89 season on the back of Lemieux's offense. He led the league in goals, assists, and points (85, 114, and 199 respectively). He was so unstoppable that he famously scored five goals, each of a different type (even strength, short-handed, power play, penalty shot, and empty net), on December 31, 1988, against the New Jersey Devils. To solidify their defense, the Penguins acquired star goaltender Tom Barrasso in a trade with the Buffalo Sabres on November 12, 1988.

Why did the Penguins look like an unlikely pick to win the Cup in 1990–91?

During the previous season, Lemieux's unfortunate health struggles had begun; he missed time with a herniated disc, and the Penguins missed the playoffs. They compensated, however, by adding veterans such as Bryan Trottier, Joe Mullen, Larry Murphy, Ron Francis, and Ulf Samuelsson to help carry the load.

How did the Penguins punctuate their Stanley Cup victory?

In Game 6 of the 1991 finals, the Penguins topped the Minnesota North Stars 8–0, setting the record for the largest margin of victory in a Cup final.

What distinction did the Penguins get for winning the Stanley Cup?

After their championship, the team visited President George H. W. Bush at the White House; while this is now an annual tradition, it was the first time a president had welcomed an NHL team.

What unfortunate coaching change were the Penguins forced to make following their championship?

In August 1991, Bob Johnson was hospitalized with a brain aneurysm and was diagnosed with brain cancer. While he kept tabs on the team from the hospital, he turned the coaching duties over to Scotty Bowman.

Why did the Blackhawks look to be a threat to the Penguins' chance at a second title?

During the regular season, Chicago had finished with 87 points, the same number as the Penguins. The Blackhawks also entered the 1992 Stanley Cup Finals on a 10-game winning streak, having dispatched the Blues, Red Wings, and Oilers.

Which players have both won the Hart Trophy and been Paul Coffey's teammate?

In the answer to a famous hockey trivia question, eight players who skated with Coffey also have been league MVP. They are: Bryan Trottier, Wayne Gretzky, Mario Lemieux, Mark Messier, Sergei Fedorov, Eric Lindros, Jaromir Jagr, and Joe Thornton.

How did Tom Barrasso get his start playing goalie?

When he was three years old, Barrasso joined the older kids in his neighborhood for a game of street hockey. Since the Boston native wasn't big enough to compete with the older players, he was forced into the net.

Which fellow NHL netminder did Barrasso play against when they were both children?

In a youth hockey Mosquito Tournament, Barrasso faced the North Shore All-Stars; their goaltender was a young Patrick Roy.

Which honors did Barrasso take home after his rookie season?

After allowing 117 goals and compiling a 26–12–3 record in his first NHL season,

Tom Barrasso

1983–84, Barrasso won the Vezina Trophy and the Calder Trophy. The Buffalo goalie also was named to the All-Rookie Team and the All-Star team.

What made Barrasso's start in the NHL so prodigious?

After being drafted fifth overall in 1983 by the Sabres, Barrasso jumped to the NHL straight from high school; that made him—at 18—the youngest goaltender to earn an NHL win since Hall of Famer Harry Lumley with Detroit in the 1940s.

Wha was the undeniable subplot of the 1992–93 season?

In news that shook the hockey world, Mario Lemieux was diagnosed with Hodgkin's disease; remarkably, though, he returned to the game two months after his

David Volek

diagnosis. While he played just 60 games, he still put up 160 points (69 goals, 91 assists) and had a career-best plus-55 rating to claim his fourth Art Ross Trophy. He led the way as the Penguins went on a 17-game winning streak to break the NHL record previously held by the New York Islanders.

Who ultimately ended the Penguins' season?

The Penguins came up against the Islanders in the second round of the 1993 playoffs; while the Penguins were the favorites, the series went to seven games. In overtime, David Volek scored the winning goal, ending the Pens' chances at a third consecutive title.

SUPERSTARS OF THE 1980s

Which all-time great retired in 1999?

Wayne Gretzky. His last season was 1998–99, when he played for the New York Rangers and reached one last milestone, breaking the professional goal-scoring record (regular season and playoffs) of 1,071, which had been held by Gordie Howe. His last NHL game in Canada was on April 15, 1999, a 2–2 tie with the Ottawa Senators, and the Rangers' second-to-last game of the season. Following the game, instead of the announcement of the game's three stars, Gretzky was named all three stars. Prior to the Rangers' final game of the season, at Madison Square Garden, Gretzky announced that he would be retiring at the end of the season. Gretzky ended his career as the game's all-time leader in points (2,857 in 1,487 regular-season games) and goals along with numerous other records. He is widely considered to be the greatest hockey player to ever play the game and is referred to by many as "The Great One."

Who was the last player to play in the NHL helmetless?

Craig MacTavish. During his 17-year career he played for the Boston Bruins, Edmonton Oilers, New York Rangers, Philadelphia Flyers, and St. Louis Blues. Not only is he remembered as the last player not to wear a helmet, but he was also the player to take the final face-off of Game 7 of the 1994 Stanley Cup Finals, in which the Rangers won their first Cup in 54 years, hanging on to beat Vancouver 3–2. In 1,093 games played, MacTavish recorded 213 goals and 267 assists for 480 points, plus 891 penalty minutes.

Who was the NHL's first black goalie?

Grant Fuhr was always overshadowed by teammates Wayne Gretzky, Mark Messier, and Jari Kurri, but he was extraordinary in net—the preeminent goaltender of the late 1980s. Despite drug problems, he was part of five Stanley Cup championship teams and became a First Team NHL All-Star. He led the league in miraculous saves, as he pulled puck after puck out of nowhere and became the sixth goalie in NHL history to win 400 games. Fuhr's career spanned from the 1981–82 season to 1999–2000, and he was inducted into the Hockey Hall of Fame in 2003.

Which young player was tragically killed after just five NHL seasons?

Philadelphia Flyers goaltender Pelle Lindbergh blossomed into the NHL's top goalie in 1984–85. The Swedish netminder went 40–17–7 and was awarded the Vezina Trophy. On November 10, 1985, he was tragically killed in a car crash; he was 26. At the time of his death, the Flyers were an impressive 12–2–0. Backup goaltender Bob Froese stepped in and played masterfully, recording five shutouts as the Flyers won seven out of nine games following Lindbergh's death.

Which son of Gordie Howe was recently inducted into the Hall of Fame?

Regarded as one of the most gifted forwards in North America, Mark Howe was the second—and youngest—of Gordie

Mark Howe, son of Gordie Howe, is shown here in 2011 getting ready for an alumni game with the Flyers.

173

Howe's sons to play major-league hockey. Mark was drafted by the WHA's Houston Aeros for the 1973–74 season and played left wing on a line with his father and Jim Sherrit, scoring 38 goals and 41 assists for 79 points. When Mark made the jump to the NHL with the Hartford Whalers, he switched to defense.

After an injury almost derailed his career, he was seen as damaged goods by the Whalers and was sent to the Philadelphia Flyers. He starred for the Flyers' defense for 10 seasons. He was a three-time runner-up for the Norris Trophy and was one of the forces behind the Flyers' terrific defensive play in the mid-'80s. He appeared in three Stanley Cup Finals but was never able to get his hands on Lord Stanley's cup.

He retired from the NHL following the 1994–95 season and was inducted into the Hall of Fame in 2011. Howe's number 2 was retired by the Flyers in 2012. He and Gordie became only the second father-son combination (Bobby and Brett Hull were the first) to have their numbers retired by NHL franchises.

Who has the most career goals, assists, and points by an NHL defenseman?

Ray Bourque was drafted by the Boston Bruins 8th overall in 1979 and went on to play 21 seasons with them. As a rookie in 1979–80, Bourque made an immediate impact on the team, scoring his first NHL goal in his first NHL game. That year he registered 65

Ray Bourque, at right, playing defense for the Bruins in 1979.

points, a record for rookie defensemen at the time, won the Calder Trophy, and was named a First Team All-Star selection, the first time in history a non-goaltender had achieved that distinction.

Though Paul Coffey overshadowed him at first, by the 1986–87 season, Bourque had become one of the best defensemen in the NHL. He had already annexed four Norris Trophies and also demonstrated many of Bobby Orr's qualities. He had an excellent offensive game and was a tremendous skater.

Upon the retirement of Terry O'Reilly in 1985, Bourque was named a co-captain along with Rick Middleton. Upon Middleton's retirement in 1988, Bourque wore the "C" permanently and continued to wear it for the remainder of his time in Boston. He became the franchise's longest-tenured captain. He was famous for his ability to contribute offensively at a higher level than most other defensemen in history. While he played for the Bruins, the team continued a North American professional record of 29 consecutive playoff appearances. In 1988 and 1990, the Bruins made it all the way to the Stanley Cup Finals but both times lost to the Edmonton Oilers.

The Bruins' playoff appearance streak was broken in 1997, and by 1999–2000, the Bruins had plummeted to the bottom of their division. Bourque ultimately requested a trade from the Bruins so he might have a chance to win the Stanley Cup. Originally, he wished to be traded to an East Coast team, but Bruins GM Harry Sinden secretly organized a trade with the Colorado Avalanche, saying that they were the best team for him to go to. On March 6, 2000, a trade to the Avalanche was finalized. In 2000–01, his only full season with the Avalanche, he was named an alternate captain. Despite being way

past his prime, Bourque led all Colorado defensemen in points with 59, playing alongside Adam Foote and later Rob Blake. Bourque played an instrumental part in the Avalanche's playoff run, and on June 9, 2001, the Avalanche won the Stanley Cup. After taking the Cup from Commissioner Gary Bettman, captain Joe Sakic immediately handed the Cup to Bourque to raise first. After 22 years, the longest drought by any Cup-winning player in the long history of the Stanley Cup had ended. Bourque retired that offseason.

In 1,612 career games, Bourque scored 410 goals and added another 1,169 assists. He is ranked number one all-time in points and goals for a defenseman. His 528 plus-minus rating is third all-time behind Larry Robinson and Bruins legend Bobby Orr. He won the Norris Trophy as

Bruins General Manager Harry Sinden

175

the top defenseman in the NHL five times. He was inducted into the Hall of Fame in 2004, and both the Bruins and Avalanche retired his number 77, making Bourque only the sixth player to have his number retired by multiple teams.

Who is the only player in NHL history to be named captain for two distinct terms with two separate franchises?

Ron Francis was drafted fourth overall in 1981 by the Hartford Whalers. During his 23-year career, Francis played for the Whalers, Pittsburgh Penguins, and Carolina Hurricanes. He was tremendously consistent and averaged more than a point per game over the course of his career.

Francis began his career playing for almost 10 seasons with the Whalers. He served as team captain for six of those and during his tenure in Hartford set nearly every offensive record in franchise history. In March of 1991, he was traded to the Penguins in one of the most lopsided trades in history. The players Hartford acquired in the trade never came close to the numbers or impact that Francis produced while in Pittsburgh. Francis centered a formidable second line behind star Mario Lemieux. Three months after the trade, he helped the Penguins capture their first Stanley Cup in franchise history. The following season, Francis truly showed his value with Lemieux injured and led the Penguins to a repeat as Stanley Cup champions. Francis spent seven seasons total in Pittsburgh, serving as team captain twice.

In 1998–99, he signed as a free agent with the Carolina Hurricanes, who had just moved from Hartford the previous year. He spent another five and a half seasons in Carolina, adding to his franchise records. He again served as team captain and helped lead the Hurricanes to a surprise visit to the 2002 Stanley Cup Finals, but the team lost to Detroit in five games. In an attempt to make one last run at the Stanley Cup, Francis was traded to the Toronto Maple Leafs, but he was unsuccessful. He retired prior to the 2005–06 season.

In 1,731 career NHL games, Francis registered 549 goals and 1,249 assists. He currently sits fourth all-time in career points behind Wayne Gretzky, Mark Messier, and Gordie Howe. His number 10 jersey was raised to the rafters of the Hartford Civic Center, former home of the Whalers, though it was not officially retired. The Hurricanes formally retired his number in 2006. He was named their general manager in 2014.

Which Hall of Fame defenseman became feared for his hard slapshot after splitting the mask of an opposing goaltender?

Al MacInnis, who played 23 seasons in the NHL for the Calgary Flames and St. Louis Blues, was drafted 15th overall by the Flames in 1981. While playing junior hockey for the Kitchener Rangers, he tied Bobby Orr's OHL record for most goals by a defenseman (the record has since been broken) with 38.

He made his debut with the Flames in 1981, playing only two games before being sent back to Kitchener. The next season he appeared in 14 games before again being sent back to Kitchener. In the 16 total games, he recorded only four points. In 1983–84, however, he played 51 games with the Flames, registering 45 points. That year he also appeared in 11 playoff games. The following season he registered points on a point-per-game pace and earned a spot in the All-Star Game.

From 1989 through 1991, he was a Norris Trophy finalist but did not win the trophy all three times. In 1989, MacInnis's 31 points in the playoffs led the Flames to their first Stanley Cup championship in franchise history. For his efforts in the playoffs, which included nine points in the finals, MacInnis was awarded the Conn Smythe Trophy. He was the first defenseman to lead the league in postseason scoring and registered a 17-game point streak, the longest by a defenseman. In 1990–91, he became just the fourth defenseman in NHL history to record a 100-point season.

Al MacInnis

In the summer of 1994, MacInnis signed an offer sheet with the St. Louis Blues after the Flames had failed to make it past the first round of the playoffs five straight seasons. He was limited to just 32 games his first year with the Blues and put up only 28 points. He returned to form and for the next eight seasons with the Blues averaged 72 games played. His production did dip, however, to an average of just 52 points over the course of those eight seasons. Only three times did he eclipse 60 points, whereas in 10 seasons with the Flames he failed to top the 60-point mark only once. Though his production offensively might have dipped, his defensive play did not. He was finally rewarded for his outstanding defensive play in 1999, winning the Norris Trophy. He played four more years in St. Louis before an eye injury forced him into retirement.

MacInnis currently ranks third in Calgary Flames history in points and is first in assists. He ended his career with 1,274 points in 1,416 games played, and he ranks third all-time in goals, assists, and points by a defenseman. As a member of Team Canada, he won the gold medal at the 2002 Olympic Games. He was inducted into the Hockey Hall of Fame in 2007, and the Blues retired his number 2 in 2009.

Which Hall of Famer captained the Calgary Flames to the Stanley Cup in his final NHL season?

A strapping Alberta farm boy, Lanny McDonald was the first-round draft choice of the Toronto Maple Leafs in the 1973 amateur player pool. McDonald's impressive junior career with the Medicine Hat Tigers was capped by the 1972–73 Western Canada championship. McDonald scored 62 goals and 77 assists that season, often seeing 40 minutes of ice time per game.

The Leafs picked Lanny fourth overall, and he was immediately tabbed a "can't miss" prospect. But a series of painful injuries limited McDonald's effectiveness during his rookie campaign, and he scored only 14 goals and 16 assists in 70 games. The youngster's tough luck continued into the postseason as a shoulder injury prevented him from playing in the 1974 Stanley Cup playoffs. The high point of his years with Toronto came in the 1978 playoffs, when he followed up a 47-goal, 40-assist regular season by scoring in overtime in Game 7 to upset the Islanders and send the Leafs to the semifinals.

In December of 1979, Toronto general manager Punch Imlach traded McDonald to the Colorado Rockies. He had only one full season in Colorado, in which he scored 35 goals and 81 points. In November of 1981, McDonald was traded to Calgary, and he remained there for the rest of his career. He captained the Flames to their first Stanley Cup championship in 1989 against Montreal in a rematch of the 1986 Stanley Cup Finals. McDonald retired following the Cup victory and is remembered as one of the greatest players in Flames history. He was inducted into the Hall of Fame in 1992, and his number 9 was retired by the Flames in 1990.

NON-CANADIANS REACH THE TOP

What was historic about the Islanders' 1980 Stanley Cup title?

There were two European players, Stefan Persson and Anders Kallur of Sweden, on the Islanders that season. Not only was this unusual for the NHL at the time, but the pair would become the first European players to lift the Stanley Cup.

Which player came within two goals of tying Wayne Gretzky's record of 92 goals in a season?

Gretzky's teammate, left wing Jari Kurri of Finland, scored an amazing 90 goals in the 1984–85 season. In addition, he tallied 19 playoff goals, which tied a record set by the Philadelphia Flyers' Reggie Leach in 1976.

Kurri and Gretzky together led the Ed-

Jari Kurri in an Avalanche jersey.

monton Oilers to the second-best record in the NHL and a Stanley Cup Finals victory over the Flyers.

What national milestone did Tom Barrasso accomplish in 1997?

As a member of the Pittsburgh Penguins, Barrasso recorded his 300th win, making him the first American-born goalie to reach that plateau.

Who was the first European-born and -trained player to captain a team to the Stanley Cup?

Nicklas Lidstrom, born in Sweden, was drafted by Detroit in 1989 and played his entire 20-year career with the Red Wings. For the final six seasons, he served as team captain.

Lidstrom made his debut for the Red Wings in 1991 and had an impressive rookie campaign, notching 60 points. Lidstrom played a large role in Detroit's dominance throughout the '90s. He helped lead the Red Wings to two straight Cups in 1997 and 1998. In 2002 Lidstrom again was key in Detroit's run to another Stanley Cup title. That year Lidstrom became the first European to win the Conn Smythe Trophy as playoff MVP.

In 2005–06 Lidstrom had the best year of his career, notching 80 points. At the end of the year, he was awarded the captaincy after longtime captain Steve Yzerman retired. The new captain led the Red Wings to the Stanley Cup title in 2008. He became the first European-born and -trained player to captain a team to the Cup.

Lidstrom again led Detroit to the finals in 2009 before losing to the Penguins in a rematch of the previous year's finals. Lidstrom officially retired following the 2011–12 season.

In his Hall of Fame career, Lidstrom won the Norris Trophy seven times, tied with Doug Harvey for second-most all-time. He was a 12-time NHL All-Star and four-time Stanley Cup champion. He was a big part in Sweden's run to the gold medal in the 2006 Olympics and with that gold medal became a member of the prestigious Triple Gold Club. His number 5 was retired by the Red Wings in March of 2014.

DROPPING THE GLOVES

Why was Paul Holmgren suspended for trying to fight Paul Baxter in 1981–82?

After exchanging slashes, Philadelphia's Holmgren and Pittsburgh's Baxter found themselves wrestling on the ice. Referee Andy Van Hellemond separated the two and assessed Holmgren a match penalty for an unprovoked assault. Holmgren responded by taking a swing at the referee; unsurprisingly, he was fined and suspended.

Why does Baxter think fighting could be on the way out of pro hockey?

Baxter simply sees it as a matter of "natural evolution." Says the former Penguin: "Between the game's current emphasis on speed, skill, and puck possession, and the increasing size of players, there could be a time in the near future when fighting is simply not worth the risk."

How does Cochrane feel about the current trend of small players taking on the role of agitator?

Cochrane does not appreciate them, especially since he feels they rarely face accountability for their actions on the ice. For example, he says that if Matt Cooke played during his playing days, he wouldn't have gone a period without being met by an enforcer. A 6'2", 200-pound defenseman, Cochrane averaged well over 200 penalty minutes per season with the Flyers in the early 1980s.

What did Craig Coxe do to solidify his reputation as a big-time enforcer?

In addition to fighting Bob Probert twice in his career, Coxe once fought both Probert and his fellow "Bruise Brother" Joey Kocur in the same game on their own home ice in Detroit.

Why was November 11, 1985, the most memorable night of Coxe's career?

While that was the evening he fought both Bob Probert and Joey Kocur, that was not the end of Coxe's involvement in the game. He also scored the game-winning goal for Vancouver.

What ultimatum was Tim Hunter given during his time in the Central Hockey League?

Like many enforcers, Hunter was told his path to success could go one of two ways. To earn ice time, he said he was told " that in order to play, I had to be the best defenseman or the meanest son of a bitch in the league." He chose the latter and went on to play almost 1,000 games at the NHL level.

Who does Hunter think the best enforcer in the modern game is?

He thinks Shawn Thornton of the Boston Bruins is the best around because of his versatility. While he is more than capable of dropping the gloves, Thornton can also skate a regular shift, chip in on offense, and not look out of place against any opponents.

What reality facilitated Kevin McClelland's change in his on-ice role?

During the early days of his career, Mc-Clelland thought he would find success as a grinder, who played with a physical edge but was still capable of taking a regular offensive shift. When he was traded to the Edmonton Oilers a couple of seasons into his career, though, they needed someone to protect Wayne Gretzky and his skilled teammates; McClelland accepted the role as the stars' protector.

How does McClelland feel about fighting today?

While McClelland made his success fighting, he does not advocate fisticuffs as a coach in the Central Hockey League. As far as he's concerned, the days of "true enforcers" have come and gone.

Former enforcer Tim Hunter later became coach of the Moosejaw Warriors in Canada's Western Hockey League.

What was the most unusual injury Jim Peplinski obtained during an on-ice altercation?

In the 1986 Stanley Cup Finals, Peplinski came together with the Canadiens' Claude Lemieux. Lemieux gouged Peplinski's eyes and bit his finger until the bone was exposed. The Flames' enforcer skated over to the referee to show him the wound and got a precautionary tetanus shot.

What type of enforcers did Richard Zemlak struggle with?

Despite being one of the toughest players on the ice, Zemlak had issues dealing with his anxiety as a player. While knowing his potential opponents for each game was a valuable part of his preparation, it still made him uneasy in the days before the game. Zemlak racked up 307 penalty minutes in just 54 games with the North Stars in 1987–88.

Which Vancouver Canucks player sparked a magical run to the 1982 Stanley Cup Finals?

Tiger Williams was known for the tenacious attitude and leadership he brought to the Canucks' locker room when he was traded in 1980 from the Toronto Maple Leafs. A prime example of how dedicated Williams was to the success of his teams, he once took a run at former Leafs teammate Lanny McDonald when the Canucks squared off against Calgary. When asked by then-coach Harry Neale to take it easy against his former friend,

181

Tiger retorted, "We're not f-ing friends tonight." Williams helped propel the Canucks to a surprise run to the 1982 Cup finals, where he chipped in 10 points … and 116 penalty minutes in the postseason alone! His work with Vancouver helped change the way people viewed the franchise and, for a time, made the Canucks relevant.

THE 1990s

EXPANSION TEAMS

What compromise by the NHL brought hockey back to Northern California after 14 years?

The Minnesota North Stars struggled through the last few years of the 1980s. Between 1984 and 1989, the North Stars finished only one season above .500, and in 1988 finished with an abysmal record of 19–48–13—the second-fewest wins in franchise history to this day.

Failing teams draw failing crowds. With fewer bodies in the arena than on the ice, flustered owners Gordon and George Gund, who were no strangers to failure, bolstered a plan to move the team to the Bay Area.

Back in the 1970s, the Gund brothers actually owned another franchise in the San Francisco Bay Area—the California Golden Seals—which had suffered from serious attendance problems of their own. In 1976, the Gunds responded by moving the team to their hometown in Cleveland to become the Cleveland Barons, after the popular American Hockey League team that had played in the city from 1929 to 1973.

Unfortunately for the Gund brothers, attendance issues persisted in Ohio. When they moved they had very little money for promoting the team. Therefore, they were never able to fill the arena in the two years they were in Cleveland. Their home at the time, the Richfield Coliseum, had the largest seating capacity in the NHL of 18,544. For much of their time in Cleveland, the Barons suffered through severe payroll difficulties. With the franchise on the verge of collapse, Barons players were actively being courted by other teams. Following the 1977–78 season, the Gunds tried to buy the Coliseum but were unsuccessful. In 1978, the brothers then decided to purchase the bankrupt North Stars and form an unprecedented merger between the two franchises. The team (as the North Stars) stayed in Minnesota but moved to the Barons' old spot in the Atlantic Division.

This would last until the 1990–91 season, when the Gunds sold the North Stars to a group, led by Howard Baldwin, Morris Belzberg, and Norm Green, that ironically had previously petitioned for a team in the Bay Area.

Finally, in 1991, after a tumultuous road trip through corn country, the Gund brothers returned to the Bay Area after 14 years of being away with the expansion San Jose Sharks, settling into the old Seals' Cow Palace just outside San Francisco. Two years later, the Gunds moved, one last time, just up the road into the SAP Center in San Jose. And in another ironic plot twist, that same year, Norm Green and the Minnesota North Stars headed south to Dallas, leaving Minnesota without hockey—rendering the entire compromise futile.

Which five teams did the NHL open its doors to in the early 1990s?

The Mighty Ducks of Anaheim, San Jose Sharks, Ottawa Senators, Florida Panthers, and Tampa Bay Lightning.

Which two teams were forced to relocate in the early 1990s because of a depreciating Canadian dollar?

In the wake of a failing Canadian economy, it was the small-market teams that suffered the most. The two smallest at the time, the Winnipeg Jets and the Quebec Nordiques, crumbled under the financial pressure and had few other options than relocation. In May of 1995, the Quebec Nordiques announced that they would be forced to relocate to Colorado after a proposed bailout was shot down by Quebec's provincial government. A year later, the Winnipeg Jets followed suit after an unsuccessful search for a local bidder and landed in Phoenix.

Believe it or not, in the early 1990s, NHL hockey in Canada was an ill-advised investment. The Canadian economy was struggling with a recession, and the Canadian dollar was steadily depreciating. By 1996, the exchange rate on the Canadian dollar reached $1.40 and continued to lose value. Competing in a recession with big-market teams, small-market teams—with lower stadium capacity, lower ticket prices, and less lucrative local television deals—were struggling to hold their own. To add insult to injury, with the league undergoing expansion, free agency ran rampant with few restrictions, giving players the bargaining chip to demand they get paid in U.S. dollars. For Canadian teams in this pre-salary cap era, this presented a huge problem. These teams, now having to pay salaries in U.S. dollars while still collecting revenue in Canadian dollars, found themselves on rocky financial footing, to say the least. And with no substantial revenue-sharing established in the league, small-market, Canadian teams became the vulnerable members of the pack. Quebec was the smallest market and was the first to go, with Winnipeg not far behind.

Who was the first-overall pick in the 1991 NHL Entry Draft who refused to sign with the team that picked him?

Eric Lindros was cited as one of the most-coveted prospects since Wayne Gretzky, earning him the moniker "The Next One." Quebec City, with the first-overall pick, had been slated very early to pick Lindros. However, he had made it abundantly clear that he did not want to go to Quebec City and released a public statement prior to the draft to that effect.

Quebec City would not offer the stud centerman the marketability that a player of his caliber could reach in another mar-

Eric Lindros in a 2014 photo.

ket. And for a young star like Lindros, that spelled a lot of missed opportunities financially. His mother, Bonnie Lindros, told the *Philadelphia Inquirer*: "Eric wants to play in the NHL. But it's big business, let's face it. The bottom line is the buck, so that's what it will come down to."

Come Draft Day, Quebec, unwilling to succumb to pressure, went ahead and drafted a less-than-pleased Lindros. When asked to wear the sweater for pictures as is done on Draft Day, he refused, and it became evident he had no intention of ever wearing it.

Quebec City, plagued by financial trouble, was a small market with no potential for marketability. Already the market disparity caused by the recession was leaving small-market teams in the dust, but Quebec, being an almost entirely monolingual francophone, was far-flung. With no English radio stations and only one privately owned English television station, the French-Canadian squad had no room to grow.

Lindros sat out the the season, refusing to sign with the Nordiques. After initially announcing that they would not give in and release Lindros, the team finally caved under mounting financial burdens. Quebec brokered not one, but two deals with New York and Philadelphia. Arbitrator Larry Bertuzzi ruled that the Flyers had reached the deal first, thus sending Lindros to Philadelphia, where in six years of captaining the squad, he never won a Cup.

Which American NHL team relocated in 1997?

The Hartford Whalers were plagued for most of their existence by the small-market curse, as the smallest American market. They struggled to compete with the neighboring big-market teams sandwiched between New York and Boston. Despite assurances in 1994 from new owner Peter Karmanos that the team would remain in Hartford through 1998, it was announced in 1997 that the Whalers would in fact relocate because of their inability to negotiate a reasonable construction and lease package for a new arena in Hartford.

On May 6, 1997, Karmanos officially announced that the team would move to the Research Triangle area of North Carolina. Due to the short amount of time and inability to hold a contest to decide the team name, Karmanos himself dubbed the squad the Carolina Hurricanes.

Which two Hall of Famers were part of the two biggest trades of the decade that brought a Cup to both destination cities?

The two biggest trades were marked by two of the biggest names in the history books: Mark Messier, who had led the Edmonton Oilers to five Stanley Cups at the time, and legendary goaltender Patrick Roy, who had two cups with Montreal, where he also became the youngest Conn Smythe winner in NHL history. In an effort to loosen their salary cap, the Edmonton Oilers traded captain Messier to the New York Rangers in 1991.

In New York, Messier earned the moniker "The Messiah" and won the hearts of both the fans and the media. The Rangers, who had not won a Stanley Cup since 1940 at the time, were desperate for leadership and scoring to end the dry spell. Messier provided both, scoring 107 points in just his first season. He went on to lead the Blueshirts to the long-sought-after Cup. He became the first and only NHL player to captain two different teams to the championship.

Roy, on the other hand, had a less than favorable exit in Montreal. After ten successful seasons with the Canadiens, Roy was pushed out after coming to blows with new head coach Mario Tremblay. Tremblay and Roy, who had once been teammates, did not get along. Tremblay openly mocked the goalie for his English skills, and Roy had a bit of a temper.

On December 2, 1995, halfway through Tremblay's first season behind the bench, the Montreal Canadiens suffered their worst loss at home in franchise history, an 11–1 defeat at the hands of the Detroit Red Wings. Roy had not had a good night, allowing nine goals in less than two periods. Coach Tremblay finally pulled Roy from the game with a few minutes left in the second frame. Skating back to the bench, he stormed past the coach and leaned over the bench to the team's president, Ronald Corey, and told him: "This is my last game in Montreal." Roy later told reporters that Tremblay had left him in the game for as long as he did simply to embarrass the goaltender. He was then suspended by the

Patrick Roy

team, and four days later, it was announced that he was traded to the new expansion team in Colorado.

With the Avalanche, Roy went on to win two more Cups. He also became the only player in NHL history to win the Conn Smythe Trophy a record three times with two different teams. He was inducted into the Hockey Hall of Fame in 2006.

Who holds the NHL record for most consecutive 70-point seasons?

Arguably one of the best players of the decade, Jaromir Jagr became Mario Lemieux's successor as the game's pre-eminent offensive talent. At 6'2" and a strong 216-pound frame, along with his now iconic 1990s mullet, Jagr arrested defenses with a dazzling combination of size, speed, and skill. After playing the role of Robin to Lemieux's Batman, Jagr claimed the scoring title in the 1994–95 season. He would follow that up with a 62-goal, 149-point runner-up effort in 1995–96 and go on to win four straight scoring titles from the 1997–98 season to the 2000–01 season. He now holds the league record for 70-point seasons with 15, from 1992 to 2003. That includes five campaigns when he posted over 100 goals.

After 11 seasons in Pittsburgh, Jagr was traded to Washington in 2001 and was traded again near the end of the 2003–04 season to the New York Rangers. He has since also had stints with the KHL's Avangard Omsk, Philadelphia, Dallas, Boston, New Jersey, and Florida. In 1550 career games, following the conclusion of the 2014–15 season, he has 722 goals and 1,080 assists for 1,802 points. He continues to be one of the game's best offensive players, but he will always be remembered for his glory years in Pittsburgh.

Dubbed one of the league's greatest offensive defensemen, who holds the second-best scoring record among defensemen?

Paul Coffey finished his 21-year career with 396 goals, 1,135 assists, and 1,531 points, all of which are second on the all-time list for defensemen. Only Ray Bourque has more with 410 goals, 1,169 assists, and 1,579 points.

One of the best offensive defensemen of all time, Coffey emerged as one of the key pieces of the Oilers dynasty in the 1980s. Playing alongside the likes of Wayne Gretzky, Mark Messier, Jari Kurri, and Glenn Anderson, Coffey excelled at joining the vaunted Oilers attack, giving support to the forwards by often playing the role of the trailing man on rushes.

The four-time Stanley Cup champion also won three Norris Trophies (1985, 1986, and 1995) and was selected to eight All-Star teams, solidifying his spot as one of the greatest defensemen the game has ever seen. Coffey was inducted into the Hockey Hall of Fame in 2004.

HABS' LAST CUP, ENTER DETROIT

Which NHL coach later became a member of the Canadian Senate, despite never learning to read or write?

Jacques Demers was one of the greatest coaches of the decade—maybe even in NHL history. Although his coaching resume includes Quebec, St. Louis, Detroit, Montreal, and Tampa Bay, under Demers, newly named captain Steve Yzerman and the Red Wings would flourish, finding consistent playoff success for the first time since expansion. In his four years with Detroit, they advanced to at least the third round three times, missing the playoffs only once—in his final year.

But success had not come easy for the French-Canadian. Struggling through a troubled childhood with a sick mother, an abusive father, and sisters to care for, Demers was forced to grow up quickly. Taking on the responsibility of tending to the chores, taking care of his mother, and even bearing the financial burden, Demers had little time for much else. Under the heavy stress and his father's psychological abuse, Demers had little energy to take his schooling seriously.

At the age of 15, Demers dropped out of school to work full-time so he could put food on the table and a roof over their heads. "It's not that I wanted to drop out of school. I wasn't learning anything," Demers said. "I wasn't going anywhere, so I went to help support. My dad would lose all of his jobs because he wouldn't report to work most of the time. At the time, it was just something I felt I had to do."

He got a job at a grocery store, where he got paid in food, and with the apartment building's custodial staff to get free rent. At the age of 17, Demers lost the beacon that guided him through those dark years—his mother died of cancer. But before she passed, she told him her dying wish was for him to be successful. From then on, Demers finally focused on his own dreams, determined to fulfill his mother's request.

Despite having never learned to read or write, Demers followed his dreams of coaching in the NHL, quickly rising through the ranks of junior and minor leagues to the WHA and, eventually, the NHL with the Quebec Nordiques and then the St. Louis Blues.

It was in Detroit, however, where he would see his greatest success. Taking over the "Dead Wings," a team that had finished dead last in the league in the 1985–86 season, Demers saw many similarities with the team and himself. "They were the

Jacques Demers

laughing stock in the NHL, as I was the laughing stock in school where kids made fun of me because we were so poor," Demers said. "That was a huge challenge, the Detroit Red Wings. When I was young I always challenged myself to get out of a bad situation and I think that really helped me."

Unlike many of the disciplinarian, screaming, hard-riding coaches of the day, Demers would guide the Red Wings with an unconventional coaching style. Injecting passion and emotion into his players, he became a father figure to his team—something he'd never had himself growing up.

Demers would later find more success with the team he grew up hating in Quebec: the Montreal Canadiens. He led them to the Stanley Cup in the 1992–93 season, his first year with the team. Demers coached Montreal for three more seasons before being fired early in the 1995–96 season. He coached Tampa Bay for two seasons before leaving the bench for good in 1999.

After leaving hockey, he finally broke the silence surrounding his illiteracy. With the help of writer Mario Leclerc, Demers detailed his struggles in a biography entitled *En toutes lettres,* meaning *All Spelled Out.*

What was the McSorley Blunder?

In Game 2 of the 1993 Stanley Cup finals between the Los Angeles Kings and Montreal Canadiens, the Kings were up 2–1 in the waning minutes of the third period. Having won Game 1, the Kings were close to assuming a commanding 2–0 series lead.

However, disaster would strike for the Kings. Montreal coach Jacques Demers fingered Los Angeles' Marty McSorley for using an illegal stick. After the officials' measurement confirmed Demers' accusation, the Canadiens wound up with a power play and a golden chance to tie the game.

Desperately needing a goal to tie, Demers pulled his goalie to get a 6-on-4 advantage. Sure enough, Montreal defenseman Eric Desjardins, who had the Habs' lone tally in the game, scored in dramatic fashion to force the game into overtime. Only 51 seconds into the extra session, Desjardins completed his hat trick to give the Canadiens a momentum-swinging victory.

Pouting over the loss, Los Angeles bench boss Barry Melrose said after the game: "If I was involved in the seventh game with the series on the line and I suspected Montreal was using an illegal stick, I would not call it. I never did, and I never will."

For Demers, however, it was simply a matter of listening to his players. "During Game 1, a few players noticed that he had an illegal stick, and they let me know," Demers said. "When you get started in the playoffs, that's when you really start noticing the real character players. Those guys are looking around and paying attention to everything."

Who was the unlikely winner of the Stanley Cup in 1993?

At the start of the 1992–93 playoffs, few had the Montreal Canadiens pegged as potential Stanley Cup contenders. Pittsburgh, the winners of the previous two Stanley Cups, had once again dominated the regular season, while the Habs had merely finished third in the Adams Division.

Playing against the Quebec Nordiques in the opening round, the Canadiens went down two games to none and hardly looked like contenders. With the Montreal papers calling for goaltender Patrick Roy to be traded in the off-season after two disastrous performances, Demers continued to have faith in his beleaguered netminder. A little bit of faith and patience can go a long way in the playoffs, and it did.

Montreal, led by Roy's heroics, roared back with four straight wins to dispose of the Nordiques. They would then ride their steam-rolling momentum into the next series against Buffalo, sweeping the Sabres in a 4–3 score in all four games—three of which were in overtime.

Instead of facing the vaunted Penguins in the conference finals, the Habs instead squared off against an upstart Islanders squad that had upset Pittsburgh in the last series. Thanks to some outstanding goaltending from Roy, who especially shined in Game 2's double-overtime win, Montreal would dispose of the Islanders in five games to reach the finals.

Meeting the Los Angeles Kings in the Stanley Cup Finals, Montreal would lose the first game of the series before rattling off three consecutive overtime victories. Even with the Kings sending wave after wave of shots against Roy during the overtime sessions, the Canadiens' goalie stood tall, soon earning the Conn Smythe Trophy as playoff MVP. Montreal would win Game 5 in a convincing 4–1 fashion to win the Stanley Cup.

For the Canadiens, the triumph was deliciously appropriate. Montreal's 24th franchise championship just so happened to coincide with the centennial of Lord Stanley's mug.

Who was "The Captain" who led the Rangers to their 1994 Stanley Cup?

Mark Messier won five Stanley Cups with the Edmonton Oilers in 1984, 1985, 1987, 1988, and once more in 1990 after earning his captaincy. Following the 1990 Cup-winning season, the Oilers, suffering in a small market, were forced to deal Messier to the New York Rangers.

Despite being ousted in the second round of the 1992 playoffs by Jaromir Jagr and the Pittsburgh Penguins, Messier celebrated a personal victory in the form of a Hart Trophy in his first year with the team.

The second year there was even more of a disappointment, as the Rangers missed out on the playoffs and it was the first time

Mark Messier

in Messier's career he wasn't in the postseason. After bringing in Mike Keenan as the head coach, Messier and the Rangers knew they were capable of winning a Stanley Cup. After finishing first overall in the regular season, the Rangers knew it was Stanley Cup or bust for them. They easily knocked off the Islanders and Capitals in the opening two rounds, but the task got tougher as they had to face their rival, and a strong team at the time, the New Jersey Devils, in the Eastern Conference finals. While trailing 3–2 in the series with their backs to the wall, Messier famously confronted the New York media and guaranteed the Rangers a victory in Game 6. Not only did the Rangers win the game 4–2, but the captain himself scored a natural hat trick in the third period of the game and carried the Rangers to a Game 7. The Rangers went on to win Game 7 in a thrilling, nail-biting finish where unlikely hero Stephane Matteau scored on a wraparound in double overtime. The Rangers went on to the Stanley Cup finals, where they defeated Pavel Bure and the Vancouver Canucks in seven games, making Messier the first and, still, only player to date to captain two separate teams to Stanley Cup victories.

Who were the Russian Five?

The name Russian Five actually refers to two separate but related units composed of five Russian hockey players. The first unit played for both the CSKA Moscow team and the Soviet National Hockey teams during the 1980s. That unit was comprised of Viacheslav Fetisov, Alexei Kasatonov, Sergei Makarov, Igor Larionov, and Vladimir Krutov. The five dominated international hockey before splitting up and heading to the NHL in the 1990s.

The second unit, also known as the Red Army or "The Wizards of Ov," played for the Detroit Red Wings throughout the 1990s. The Red Wings' Russian Five was comprised of Sergei Fedorov, Vyacheslav Kozlov, Vladimir Konstantinov, Igor Larionov, and Viacheslav Fetisov. Fedorov, perhaps the best known of the bunch, won the Hart and Selke Trophies in 1994, and Konstantinov was runner-up to the Norris Trophy in 1997.

The unit played a huge role in Detroit's incredible success throughout the 1990s. During the 1997 playoffs, the Red Wings had a record of 16–0 in games in which one of the five notched a point, and conversely, a record of 0–4 in games in which none of them earned a point.

The unit would break apart shortly after the 1997 championship season when Konstantinov was involved in a career-ending limousine accident. Fetisov was also injured in the accident but was able to return to action. Fedorov and Larionov would go on to be a major part of the Red Wings Stanley Cup championship in 2002.

Who was the longest-serving captain in NHL history?

After being chosen fourth overall in the 1983 NHL draft, Steve Yzerman immediately became one of the NHL's elite offensive stars. However, it was more than his skill level that would lead him to the distinction of being the longest-serving captain in NHL history.

Wings general manager Jim Devellano originally wanted to draft Detroit native Pat LaFontaine, but when he was taken 3rd overall, the Red Wings were forced to "settle" on Yzerman. Steve was so impressive during rookie camp that the Red Wings decided to not

191

Four of the five "Russian Five" are (clockwise from top left) Viacheslav Fetisov, Igor Larianov, Alexei Kasatonov, and Sergei Makarov. Not pictured is Vladimir Krutov.

send him back to juniors like they had originally planned. During his rookie season, Yzerman scored 39 goals and 87 points and finished second in the Calder Trophy voting.

After Detroit lost then-captain Danny Gare to free agency in the 1986 off-season, head coach Jacques Demers needed someone new to take over the role. In his words, he needed a captain "with the Red Wings crest tattooed on his chest."

While the 21-year-old Yzerman was young, Demers felt he was ready for the responsibility. After all, he had already spent three years in the league and served as an assistant captain for two of those. Still, it proved to be a learning experience for Yzerman at first, learning to command the respect of the room with guys who had been around quite a bit longer than him.

Dave Lewis, who played with Yzerman and later coached him, said that a knee injury suffered late in the 1987–88 season had proved to be a big moment for the youngster's career. His aggressive take on the rehabilitation of that injury would help shape the mindset he would take on as a leader.

"To accomplish what needed to be done, Steve was as focused and determined as anyone I've ever known. Was he a vocal guy in the locker room? Not really. He didn't say a lot, but when he did, people listened to him," Lewis said. "When he was upset with his performance or a breakdown on the ice, he would react coming back to the bench, often breaking a stick. He didn't have to say a word. It was a reaction that said, 'You can't do this and expect to win.'"

While he became a much respected captain amongst his teammates, Detroit's lack of Stanley Cup success would lead to the press calling for a trade, criticizing his one-dimensional offensive game. In time, under Scotty Bowman, he would redefine his game into that of an elite, two-way forward. He went on to lead the Red Wings to consecutive Stanley Cups in 1997 (when he won the Conn Smythe Trophy) and 1998. Yzerman's play began to decline in 2001, however, due to a nagging knee injury that eventually required surgery. Despite tremendous pain in his knee, Yzerman finished sixth in team scoring and again led the Red Wings to the Stanley Cup in 2002, the last of his playing career.

Yzerman captained the Red Wings for 19 years and over 1,300 games before hanging up the skates at the end of the 2005–06 season. He had played a total of 1,514 games, third in franchise history behind only Gordie Howe and Nicklas Lidstrom. Yzerman ranks ninth in NHL history with 692 goals and seventh in overall scoring with 1,755 points. In addition to this, Yzerman ranks second in almost every major offensive category in Red Wings history, behind only Gordie Howe. In 2007 the Red Wings retired Yzerman's number 19 and in the corner of the banner, they added a "C" to forever commemorate him as "The Captain." He was inducted into the Hockey Hall of Fame in 2009.

After spending his career both leading on the ice and on the charts, it's only right that he continued to lead in the front office. After he retired in July 2006, he spent nearly four more years with the Detroit organization as a vice president. In May 2010, he left Detroit for the first time in two decades to claim the title of general manager of the Tampa Bay Lightning. He also served as the GM of Team Canada for the 2010 and 2014 Winter Olympic games, both times winning gold.

DEVELOPMENT OF THE DEVILS

What significant impact did Lou Lamoriello have on college hockey?

During the summer of 1983, Lamoriello and the athletic directors of Boston University, Boston College, Northeastern, and New Hampshire formed the Hockey East Association. Lamoriello served as the Hockey East commissioner until 1987, when he resigned to become the president of the New Jersey Devils. In his honor, the Hockey East champion receives the Lamoriello Trophy.

What surprising move did Lamoriello make after being named president of the Devils?

Upon being named president, Lamoriello also named himself the club's general manager. While many doubted that he had the necessary knowledge about the professional ranks, over time, he proved himself to be one of the best in the business.

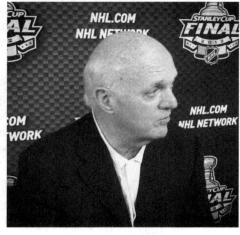

Lou Lamoriello

How has Lamoriello fared in his brief coaching stints?

Lamoriello has found himself behind the bench three times in his NHL career. After Larry Robinson resigned midway through the 2005–06 season, Lamoriello led the Devils to an Atlantic Division title. The following season after relieving Claude Julien of his duties late in the season, Lamoriello once again took over for the eventual Atlantic Division champions. He last took over during the 2014–15 season after firing Peter DeBoer, who had led the Devils behind the bench since the 2011–12 season.

Which two players were key in New Jersey's 1995 sweep of the Red Wings in the Stanley Cup finals?

Despite facing a potent Red Wings attack, Martin Brodeur only allowed seven goals during the four-game sweep. On the other end of the ice, Claude Lemieux led the team's offensive attack; he finished the playoffs with a league-leading 13 goals and claimed the Conn Smythe Trophy as playoff MVP.

SUPERSTARS OF THE 1990s

Which U.S. hockey star was nicknamed "The Golden Brett"?

Brett Hull, the son of Hall of Famer Bobby "The Golden Jet" Hull, became known as one of the game's greatest snipers. Hull was first eligible for the NHL Entry draft in 1982 but was not selected until 1984, when the Calgary Flames took him 117th overall. The following year, Hull chose to play college hockey at the University of Minnesota-Duluth and as a freshman scored 32 goals and won the Rookie of the Year award. In 1985–86, Hull broke the school record of 49 goals in a season by netting 52 that year.

As a result, he was named a finalist for the prestigious Hobey Baker Award. Following his sophomore season, he signed a professional contract with the Flames.

He spent the first year of his career in the American Hockey League, where he scored 50 goals in 67 games for the Moncton Golden Flames. In 1986, he made his NHL debut and scored his first NHL goal, which ended up being the game winner. In 1987–88 he earned a permanent spot on the Flames' roster, registering twenty-five goals and 50 points in 52 games. However, on March 7, 1988, Hull was traded to the St. Louis Blues.

Hull played 11 of his 19 NHL seasons with the Blues. At the start of the 1989–90 season, Hull was paired with Adam Oates on the top line. From 1989–90 to 1991–92, Hull scored 228 goals, the second-highest three-season total in NHL history behind Wayne Gretzky. He scored 50 goals in 50 games in 1990–91, becoming only the fifth player in NHL history to do so. He then repeated the feat the next season. He notched 86 total goals during the 1990–1991 season, the third-highest total ever. No one has even come close to scoring that many goals since. For his efforts that season, he was awarded the Hart Trophy as league MVP.

Oates departed in the middle of the 1991–92 season, and though Hull's numbers dropped slightly, he still recorded his fourth and fifth seasons of 50 or more goals, scoring 70 or more three times during that five-year span. After the 1993–94 season, Hull surpassed the 40-goal mark just twice. In 1998, he signed a three-year deal as a free agent with the Dallas Stars, where he would win his first Stanley Cup by scoring the series winner in triple overtime of Game 6 of the Cup Final against the Buffalo Sabres. Following his time in Dallas, he signed a two-year contract with the Detroit Red Wings in 2002. He scored 30 regular season goals and added another 10 in the postseason en route to his second Stanley Cup in his first season in Detroit. Following the 2004–05 lockout, Hull briefly attempted a comeback with the Phoenix Coyotes before ultimately retiring in October 2005.

Though his father was Canadian and a member of Team Canada in international play, Brett chose to represent Team USA and led them to a silver medal in the 2002 Olympic Games. He also won a gold medal in the 1996 World Cup of Hockey and a silver in the 1991 Canada Cup. In 1,391 career games, Hull scored 741 goals, third highest in NHL history. He was inducted into the Hall of Fame in 2009, and his number 16 jersey was retired by the Blues. His nickname "The Golden Brett" is a spin-off of his father Bobby's nickname, "The Golden Jet." He currently serves as executive vice president of the St. Louis Blues.

Which defenseman became known, and feared, for his vicious body checks?

Scott Stevens was originally drafted 5th overall in 1982 by the Washington Capitals. Stevens went on to play 22 seasons in the NHL, eight with the Capitals, one with the St. Louis Blues, and 13 with the New Jersey Devils. He served as captain of the Devils for 12 of his 13 years in New Jersey.

Stevens made the team his first year with the Capitals at the ripe age of 18. He immediately made an impact on the squad, scoring his first NHL goal in his first game, on

Scott Stevens was the first Devil to have his number retired, as shown here in the 2006 ceremony.

his first shot on net. He managed to end his rookie year with 25 points and finished third in the Calder Trophy voting. During his rookie year, the Capitals made their first-ever appearance in the postseason. The following year Stevens nearly doubled his numbers from his rookie campaign. He then enjoyed a breakout year in 1984–85, scoring 21 goals, a team record for defensemen. After eight seasons in Washington, however, Stevens felt it was time to move on. He signed a four-year deal worth just over $5 million with the Blues. The Capitals chose not to match the offer sheet. Upon his arrival in St. Louis, he was named captain. His time there, however, only lasted one year. The Blues had signed former Devils star Brendan Shanahan to an offer sheet, and the two parties could not decide on appropriate compensation. The Devils wanted Stevens in the deal, who the Blues did not want to give up. An arbitrator eventually ruled in favor of the Devils, and Stevens was on his way to the Garden State.

At first Stevens refused to report to the Devils' training camp. Many fans and players wanted General Manager Lou Lamoriello to trade Stevens again as a result. Stevens eventually reported to camp and went on to finish fifth on the team in scoring. Following his first season in New Jersey, he was named captain, an honor he would hold for the remainder of his career. During his time as a Devil, he captained the team to four Stanley Cup Finals appearances, three of which they won. In the playoffs Stevens had huge, memorable hits on Vyacheslav Kozlov of the Detroit Red Wings, Eric Lindros of the Philadelphia Flyers, and Paul Kariya of the Anaheim Ducks. The hits on Lindros and Kozlov concussed both players and essentially ended Lindros's career.

The 2003–04 season would ultimately be the last of Stevens's career. Early in the season, he was diagnosed with post-concussion syndrome due to a taking a puck to the head. When the lockout of 2004–05 forced the NHL to cancel the season, Stevens decided to retire. Despite his success as a shutdown defender, Stevens never won the Norris Trophy as the league's top defenseman.

Stevens ended his career as the longest-reigning captain in Devils franchise history. At the time of his retirement, he held the NHL record for most games played by a defenseman. He currently sits number two in the category behind Chris Chelios. In 2006 the Devils honored him by raising his number 4 to the rafters of the Prudential Center, the first player in team history to achieve the honor. He was inducted into the Hockey Hall of Fame in 2007. Many people consider Stevens, or "Captain Crunch" as some called him, to be the one of, if not *the,* hardest-hitting players of all time. Stevens currently serves as an assistant coach for the Devils.

Which goaltender started his legendary career in the 1990s and went on to win more games than any other goalie in NHL history?

Martin Brodeur started for the New Jersey Devils and made his NHL debut on March 26, 1992, a 4–2 victory over the Boston Bruins at the Meadowlands. He would take hold of the starting job for New Jersey in 1993–94 and won the Calder Memorial Trophy as Rookie of the Year. Brodeur won the Stanley Cup the following season and would go on to win two more Cups in 1999–2000 and 2002–03. He won the Vezina Trophy as the league's top goalie four times, the William M. Jennings Trophy for fewest goals against five times, and would break nearly every goaltending record, most notably for most victories with 691 career wins.

Who was the first goaltender to win the Hart Trophy multiple times?

Dominik Hasek, a native of the Czech Republic, played sixteen NHL seasons with the Black Hawks, Sabres, Red Wings, and Senators. He was originally drafted 199th overall by the Chicago Black Hawks in 1983 and became one of the best goaltenders in the NHL.

Hasek arrived in the NHL in 1990 at the age of 25. For two years, Hasek served as backup for Ed Belfour in Chicago. He was traded in 1992 to the Buffalo Sabres, where he first served as a backup for Grant Fuhr. However, due to an injury, Hasek took over the starting goaltender spot and soon developed into his elite form. He won his first Vezina Trophy for the league's top goaltender in 1994 and was the runner-up for the Hart Trophy as NHL MVP. In 1997 he played in a career-high 72 games, posting a 33–23–10 record and a 2.09 goals-against average. In 2001 Hasek was traded to the Detroit Red Wings, where he won the Stanley Cup in 2002. He retired after that season but returned to the Wings in 2003–04, where he was injured most of the season. Following the NHL lockout of 2004–05, Hasek signed with the Ottawa Senators. Hasek returned yet again to the Red Wings and played two seasons before he retired for good. He won his second Cup with Detroit in 2008.

Hasek was a superstar in the 1998 Olympic Games in Nagano, Japan, where he allowed only six goals en route to a gold medal. Perhaps the highlight of his Olympic games was a shootout victory over the heavily favored Canadian team in the semifinals, where he stopped Theo Fleury, Ray Bourque, Joe Nieuwendyk, Eric Lindros, and Brendan Shanahan in the shootout. He also won a bronze medal in the 2006 Olympic Games.

Hasek won the Vezina Trophy six times, twice won the Hart Trophy (1997, 1998), and was a finalist another three times. In 735 career games, Hasek had a goals-against average of 2.13 and a save percentage of .922. He currently has the highest career save percentage of all time.

How many players have won a gold medal, Stanley Cup, Memorial Cup, and World Junior Championship title?

Only one player has pulled off such a feat: Scott Niedermayer. He won a gold medal at the 1991 World Junior Championship with Canada, the 1992 Memorial Cup with the Kamloops Blazers, and Olympic gold medals in 2002 and 2010 with Canada. He was also a four-time Stanley Cup champion with the New Jersey Devils after the 1994–95, 1999–2000, and 2001–02 seasons and the Anaheim Ducks after the 2006–07 season.

Which defenseman holds the record for most games played by an American-born player?

Chris Chelios, from Evergreen Park, Illinois, was not heavily recruited by U.S. colleges. After moving to California, he attended U.S. International University to play at the NCAA level but was ultimately cut from the team. After adding a few inches and muscle, he ended up playing for the Moose Jaw Canucks of the Saskatchewan Junior Hockey League, where he tallied 87 points. Chelios was eventually drafted 40th overall by the Montreal Canadiens in the 1981 NHL draft. After being drafted, Chelios completed his amateur eligibility by playing at the NCAA level for the University of Wisconsin.

After only playing 12 regular season games in 1983–84, Chelios became a full-time player the next year. He notched 55 helpers to go along with 9 goals and was runner-up to the Calder Memorial Trophy. In 1985–86 he won his first Stanley Cup with the Canadiens. Chelios broke out during the 1988–89 season, notching a career-high 73 points. In 1990–91, he was traded to the Blackhawks. He remained with Chicago until 1999, when, at the age of 37, he was traded to the Detroit Red Wings, with whom he finished the 1998–99 campaign and then played nine more seasons with them. In 2008 Chelios broke Patrick Roy's record for the most career playoff games played. After a brief stint with the the Atlanta Thrashers, Chelios officially announced his retirement in August 2010.

Chelios was an 11-time All-Star and won three Norris Trophies and three Stanley Cups. In 1,651 regular season games played, he notched 948 points and logged 2,891 penalty minutes. He is also tied with Gordie Howe for most seasons played with 26. He was inducted into the Hall of Fame in 2013.

Chris Chelios

Who was the first American-born hockey player to record 1,000 NHL points?

In 16 NHL seasons, Joe Mullen played for the St. Louis Blues, Calgary Flames, Pittsburgh Penguins, and Boston Bruins. He was a member of three Stanley Cup championship teams, winning with the Flames in 1989 and the Penguins in 1991 and 1992.

An undrafted player, Mullen played for the Boston College Eagles and was a two-time First Team All-American, prior to being signed by the Blues.

He was the first American-born player to score 500 goals and to reach 1,000 points. Mullen was inducted into the United States Hockey Hall of Fame in 1998 and the Hockey Hall of Fame in 2000. After his career, he served as an assistant coach in Pittsburgh and briefly was the head coach of the Wilkes-Barre/Scranton Penguins of the American Hockey League. He is currently an assistant coach for the Philadelphia Flyers.

Which Finnish-born legend notched 76 goals his rookie season for a record that's said will never be broken?

Teemu "The Finnish Flash" Selanne was drafted 10th overall by the Winnipeg Jets in the 1988 NHL draft. But Selanne played four more years for the Jokerit club of the SM-liiga club before arriving in Winnipeg in 1992. He took the NHL by storm, scoring a franchise record of 76 goals and adding another 56 helpers for another franchise record of 132 points. His 76 goals and 132 points were also both NHL records for rookies, two records

199

that many say will likely never be broken. Not surprisingly, Selanne captured the Calder Memorial Trophy that year.

Midway through the 1995–96 season, Selanne was traded to the Mighty Ducks of Anaheim, where he spent another five seasons. In those five seasons, Selanne twice surpassed both the 100-point mark and the 50-goal mark. In 2000–01, despite a team-high 59 points, the Ducks, who were in last place in the conference, traded Selanne to the San Jose Sharks, where he spent two more seasons. He then signed a one-year contract with the Colorado Avalanche in 2003 but was hampered by injuries. After the 2004–05 lockout, Selanne returned to Anaheim, and he remained there until his retirement after the 2013–14 season. In 2006–07, he helped lead the Ducks to their first Stanley Cup championship.

Selanne is also a highly decorated international player. In 96 international games played, Selanne has recorded 54 goals and 48 assists. He has helped Finland win two bronze medals and one silver in the Olympics and has one of both in the World Championships. He is also currently the all-time scorer in the Olympics with 43 points.

Selanne would never quite reach the staggering numbers of his rookie season again but would be a 20-plus goal scorer for most of his 21-year career. In fact only in five of his NHL seasons did Selanne fail to score more than 20 goals. He played in five All-Star games and was four times named the Finnish ice hockey player of the year. This future Hall of Famer ranks among the best Finnish hockey players of all time.

Who was the first European player to lead the league in scoring?

Jaromir Jagr was selected fifth overall in the 1990 NHL draft by the Pittsburgh Penguins. With the Penguins, he won consecutive Stanley Cup championships in 1991 and 1992. In 1995, Jagr won his first of four consecutive Art Ross Trophies. The next year Jagr set an NHL record for most points ever scored by a European player with 149. During his career, Jagr has captained the Penguins and the New York Rangers and has also played for the Washington Capitals, Philadelphia Flyers, Dallas Stars, Boston Bruins, New Jersey Devils, and the Florida Panthers. He is also the only player to play in the Stanley Cup Finals as a teenager and at 40-plus years of age.

Who was the first American-born player to lead the NHL in goals?

Keith Tkachuk was drafted 19th overall by the Winnipeg Jets in 1990, after one year of college hockey at Boston University. Following his first Olympic appearance for Team U.S.A. in 1992, Tkachuk made his debut with the Jets scoring 8 points in 17 games, earning the captaincy the following season.

He starred for the Jets until 1996, when the franchise moved to Phoenix. During his time in Winnipeg, he twice eclipsed the 40-goal mark. Tkachuk continued his strong play for the first two seasons he was in Phoenix. Though his goal production began to dip in 1998, he still put up decent numbers.

Soon, he began struggling with injuries and was traded to the St. Louis Blues, where he made an immediate impact, scoring six goals in the final 12 games of the 2000–01

Keith Tkachuk

season. Tkachuk struggled with injuries in St. Louis as well, and in six years, passed the 30-goal mark only three times. He was traded in 2007 to the Thrashers but returned to the Blues the next season to finish out his career in St. Louis, retiring in 2010.

Tkachuk was one of the elite power forwards of the 1990s. He scored 30 goals 8 times in his career and had two 40- and two 50-goal seasons. He finished his career with 538 goals and 2,219 penalty minutes in 1,201 games.

Who has the most career goals and points by a Swedish-born hockey player?

Mats Sundin was drafted first overall in 1989 by the Quebec Nordiques, becoming the first European-born and -trained player to be the first pick. He played his first four NHL seasons in Quebec after making his NHL debut in 1990 in which he finished second on the team in points behind Joe Sakic with 59 points.

He continued to improve his point production, scoring 76 points his second season and a career-high 114 points in his third season. He played one more season for the Nordiques before being traded to the Toronto Maple Leafs in a deal that sent veteran Wendel Clark to Quebec.

Sundin went on to star for the Maple Leafs for 13 seasons, serving as team captain for 11 of those campaigns. In 1999, he led the Leafs to the Eastern Conference Final of

201

the playoffs. Then, with Sundin leading the way, the Leafs made the playoffs another six seasons and again made it to the Conference Final in 2002.

In 2008, Sundin became the Leafs' all-time leader in goals and assists by a forward and points by any position. That year, too, he became a free agent and ultimately signed with the Vancouver Canucks for two years for a lucrative $20 million offer. The next year, he announced his retirement.

In 1,346 NHL games, Sundin scored 564 goals and added 785 assists. He was inducted into the Hockey Hall of Fame in 2012 and had his jersey retired by the Leafs.

Which former Swedish star never had a season with a negative plus-minus rating?

Peter Forsberg, the sixth-overall pick in the 1991 draft, is considered to be one of the finest players of his generation. Forsberg was originally drafted by the Philadelphia Flyers but was quickly traded to the Nordiques in the Eric Lindros trade. He continued to play overseas for a few years before making his NHL debut following the 1994–95 lockout. Ironically, his first NHL game was against the Flyers, in which he registered his first NHL assist and point. He scored 50 points as a rookie, which at the time was second only to Joe Sakic, and he took home the Calder Trophy as the league's top rookie.

In 1995 the Quebec Nordiques moved to Colorado, and in their first year in Denver, Forsberg, along with Sakic, Adam Foote, and Patrick Roy, guided the Avalanche to their first Stanley Cup. Forsberg finished the season with a career-high 116 points. In 2001, he again led the Avalanche to a second Stanley Cup. And in 2003, he centered a highly productive line with Alex Tanguay and Milan Hejduk, leading the league in points with 106. For that effort, he was awarded the Hart Trophy as league MVP.

Following the lockout of 2004–05, the Avalanche were forced to let Forsberg go, and he signed a two-year deal with the Flyers. He played for two injury-prone years in Philly before being moved to the Nashville Predators. In 2008, he stated that he would not return to the NHL and ended up playing for Modo Hockey, the same team he played for prior to coming to the NHL. He attempted a comeback in 2010, but due to risk of injury, Forsberg was forced to retire from professional hockey altogether.

Forsberg ended his career with 885 points in 708 NHL games in his 13 injury-ridden years. He also had a tremendous amount of success internationally and is a member of the Triple Gold Club. In total, he has won 9 medals (4 goal and 5 silver), including two golds in each of the 1994 and 2006 Olympics. In 2011, the Avalanche retired his number 21 in a grand ceremony prior to their season opener. After retirement, he went on to serve as an assistant GM of the Modo Hockey club under former NHL star Markus Naslund.

Who is the only player in NHL history with over 600 goals and 2,000 penalty minutes?

Brendan Shanahan was originally drafted by the New Jersey Devils second overall in the 1987 draft. He made his debut with the Devils as an 18-year-old in 1987–88, scoring 26 points in 65 games. In just his third NHL season, he established himself as a point-per-game player, scoring 72 points in 73 games. By the time Shanahan was 22, he had already established himself as a scorer in the NHL.

In 1990–91, Shanahan signed a contract with the St. Louis Blues as a free agent, where he remained for four years—eclipsing the 50-goal plateau twice. He was eventually traded to the Hartford Whalers in exchange for Chris Pronger, where he stayed for only a year and scored a team-high 44 goals. Just two games into the 1996 season, he was traded to the Detroit Red Wings in exchange for Keith Primeau, an aging Paul Coffey, and a first-round pick.

Shanahan spent the next nine seasons in Detroit, where he scored 30 or more goals only twice. In 1997, he scored 47 regular season goals en route to Detroit's first Stanley Cup since 1955. The following season Shanahan posted just 57 points, but the Red Wings went on to repeat as Stanley Cup championships. In 2001–02, the Red Wings picked up future Hall of Famers Brett Hull, Luc Robitaille, and Dominik Hasek in the off-season. Despite the presence of these stars, Shanahan continued to shine, as the Red Wings dominated the regular season. He scored 37 regular season goals and added 19 playoff points as the Red Wings won their third Stanley Cup in six years. In 2006–07, he signed as a free agent with the New York Rangers, where he struggled for two years, again scoring under 30 goals each year. He subsequently returned to the Devils in 2008–09 but posted career lows in every category and ultimately retired prior to the 2009–10 season.

The power forward currently holds the record for most career Gordie Howe hat tricks (a goal, an assist, and a fight) with 17. He ended his career with 656 goals, 1,356 points, and 2,489 penalty minutes in 1,524 games. He is also a member of the elite Triple Gold Club, having won Olympic gold in 2002 and a World Championship gold in 1994. He has the second most goals of any left winger in history and was inducted into the Hockey Hall of Fame in 2013. Ironically, for three years, he served as president of the Department of Player Safety and Chief Player Disciplinarian. Due to the large number of suspensions he handed out, the media coined him the nickname "Shanaban." He went on to serve as president and alternate governor of the Toronto Maple Leafs.

Who is the highest-scoring left winger of all time?

Luc Robitaille was drafted by the Los Angeles Kings in the 9th round of the 1984 NHL draft. In three seasons of junior hockey, Robitaille amassed 155 goals and 424 points in just 197 games. He made his NHL debut in 1986 and scored 45 goals and added 39 assists, on his way to winning the Calder Memorial Trophy as the top rookie.

For the next seven seasons with the Kings, Robitaille scored 40 or more goals, three times eclipsing the 50-goal mark. In 1992–93, he scored a career-high 63 goals—a mark that, at the time, was the highest by a left winger (Alex Ovechkin broke that record in 2007–08). That same year, with captain Wayne Gretzky injured, Robitaille temporarily wore the "C" and helped lead his team to the playoffs. The Kings made it all the way to the Stanley Cup Finals but lost to the Canadiens in five games.

Luc Robitaille

In 1994, the Kings failed to make the playoffs, and Robitaille was traded to the Penguins in exchange for Rick Tocchet and a second-round pick. In Pittsburgh, he set career lows in both goals and assists, subsequently getting traded to the Rangers along with Ulf Samuelsson in exchange for Petr Nedved and Sergei Zubov. He had two more lackluster seasons before he was traded back to the Kings. And after struggling his first year back in L.A., he returned to his All-Star form, scoring at least 30 goals in three more seasons with the Kings. In 2001, however, he left the West Coast to sign a two-year deal to join the star-studded Detroit Red Wings, where he put up 30 goals and 50 points to help them win the Presidents' Trophy and the Stanley Cup. In 2003–04, Robitaille returned to L.A. for one final time. His numbers, however, were not up to par.

He played his final home game in April of 2006. For the game, he wore the captain's "C" and received an enormous standing ovation from the crowd after the game. He played his final NHL game two days later.

Robitaille finished his career as the highest-scoring left winger of all time with 668 goals and 726 assists in 1,431 NHL games. He is also the franchise leader in goals for the L.A. Kings and became only the second player in NHL history to record over 1,000 points after being drafted in the 9th round or lower. In 2007, his number 20 was raised to the rafters at the Staples Center, and two years later, he was inducted into the Hall of Fame. He went on to be named the Kings' president of business operations in 2007 and won a Cup with the Kings in 2012, their first ever, and went on to tally a second just two years later.

Which former Colorado star holds the record for most postseason overtime goals?

Joe Sakic was drafted by the Quebec Nordiques 15th overall in the 1987 NHL draft. He spent his entire 21-season career with the franchise and served as captain of the team for 16 of those seasons.

Sakic chose to play another year in junior hockey before making the jump to the NHL in order to further prepare himself but made his NHL debut in 1988, on pace to be the front-runner for the Calder Trophy before an injury forced him to miss 10 games and slip into a scoring slump. Despite this, he still finished his stellar rookie campaign with 62 points in 70 games and in both of the next two seasons eclipsed the 100-point mark.

He served as a co-captain in 1990–91 and in 1992 was named full-time captain of the team. In 1995, the Nordiques moved their franchise to Denver. That same year, Sakic led the team with a career-high 120 points and added another 34 in the playoffs en route to the franchise's first Stanley Cup and the city of Denver's first-ever major professional sports championship. For his efforts in the playoffs, Sakic was awarded the Conn Smythe Trophy. The next season, the Avalanche won their first-ever Presidents' Trophy as the league's top team, despite Sakic only playing 65 games.

As a free agent during the summer of 1997, Sakic signed a three-year, $21 million offer sheet with the New York Rangers, but the Avalanche ultimately matched the offer. Some injuries limited Sakic during the next few seasons, but he still managed to put up good numbers. In 2000–01 he scored a career-high 54 goals and added another 64 assists to again lead his team to the Stanley Cup championship. This time, instead of being the first to hoist the Cup, he performed perhaps one of the most famous hand-offs ever, giving the Cup to defenseman Ray Bourque, who had gone a record-breaking 22 seasons without a Cup. Sakic also took home the Hart Trophy as league MVP that year. In 2006, Sakic played in his last full NHL season and recorded his sixth 100-point season. He formally announced his retirement in 2009.

Sakic finished his career with an impressive 625 goals and 1,641 assists in 1,378 games. He is considered to be one of the greatest leaders in NHL history. When the Avalanche retired his number 19 prior to the 2009–10 season, they placed a "C" next to his name on the banner, recognizing his lengthy service as team captain.

OTHER STANLEY CUP WINNERS OF THE 1990s

1994–95 SEASON

What happened to the 1994–95 NHL season as a result of the lockout?

Due to a work stoppage, the league shortened the season from 84 games, the length of the previous two seasons, to 48. Further, it was the first and only time in league history that the regular season extended into May. It was also the first time that regular season games were limited to intraconference play. This situation would occur again in 2012–13.

How was the 1994–95 campaign a season of firsts?

The New Jersey Devils won their first Stanley Cup championship in franchise history. As the 5th seed, the Devils became the lowest seed ever to win the Stanley Cup (since eclipsed by the 2012 Kings who were 8th) and their regular season winning percentage was the lowest since the 1967 Toronto Maple Leafs.

Who were the key members of the 1994–95 Devils?

The 1994–95 Devils are remembered for head coach Jacques Lemaire's relentless neutral zone trap strategy. What it did was clog the middle of the ice and thereby diminish the impact of opposing offensive stars. Captain Scott Stevens led the defense, Stephane Richer and Neal Broten led the team in scoring, and Bill Guerin, Bobby Holik, Brian Rolston, and Scott Niedermayer were in the early stages of their careers. Goaltender Martin Brodeur, in just his second NHL season, produced a stellar .927 save percentage, 1.67 goals-against average, and three shutouts in the postseason as he started all 20 contests.

Scott Stevens

Why was the Devils' journey to the Stanley Cup Finals in 1995 like a Jekyll and Hyde season?

It was a tale of two contrasting seasons in New Jersey, as the Devils struggled in the first half of the regular campaign but improved drastically in the second half, ultimately earning a fifth seed in the Eastern Conference. As the playoffs approached, the Devils were playing their best hockey of the season. In the Conference Quarterfinals, they faced off against the Boston Bruins, prevailing in five games, including three shutout victories.

Next, the Devils triumphed over the Pittsburgh Penguins in five games to move on to the Eastern Conference Finals, where they faced the Philadelphia Flyers. The Devils defeated the Flyers in six games, advancing to the Stanley Cup Finals against the Detroit Red Wings in what was the first of nine consecutive finals with American-based franchises.

Why was the Devils' upset victory over Detroit in the 1995 Finals so unusual?

Overwhelming favorites to win the Stanley Cup, the Red Wings had dominated the Western Conference, posting a 12–2 playoff record en route to the Cup round. Led by legendary bench boss Scotty Bowman, Detroit sported six Hall of Fame players at the peak of their careers, including Paul Coffey, Sergei Fedorov, Steve Yzerman, Dino Ciccarelli, and Nicklas Lidstrom.

However, to the surprise of many, the Devils won the first two games in Detroit to take a 2–0 lead back to New Jersey for Game 3. The Devils dominated that contest, winning 5–2 with five different goal scorers to take a 3–0 stranglehold on the series and subsequently complete the sweep on home ice in Game 4. Claude Lemieux took home the Conn Smythe Trophy as playoff MVP, having led all skaters in playoff goals with 13.

To which city did the Quebec Nordiques relocate in 1995?

In May 1995, shortly after the Nordiques were eliminated from the playoffs, President and CEO Marcel Aubut announced that the team had been sold to COMSAT Entertainment Group, owner of the NBA's Denver Nuggets. COMSAT subsequently moved the team to Denver, where it was renamed the Colorado Avalanche.

Who were the key members of the Avalanche in 1995?

The Avalanche had built a strong team led by former Nordiques Joe Sakic, Peter Forsberg, Adam Foote, 1995 Conn Smythe winner Claude Lemieux, and head coach Marc Crawford.

Which future Hall of Famer was added to the Avalanche roster in the 1995 midseason, and what were the circumstances that led to the transaction?

Colorado was bolstered on December 6, 1995, when Avalanche general manager Pierre Lacroix added legendary goaltender Patrick Roy after the former Montreal Canadien was humiliated for being left in the net after allowing 9 goals during a game against the Red Wings.

Which player did the Canadiens receive in exchange for Patrick Roy?

He was traded to the Avs along with ex-Montreal captain Mike Keane in exchange for Jocelyn Thibault, Martin Rucinsky, and Andrei Kovalenko.

How did the Avalanche fare during the regular 1995–96 season?

The Avalanche coasted to a 47–25–10 record, easily won the Pacific Division, and finished second in the Western Conference. The team had a prolific offense, scoring 326 goals, an average of nearly 4 per game and four players—Joe Sakic, Peter Forsberg, Claude Lemieux, and Valeri Kamensky—who scored at least 30 goals.

Which teams did Colorado beat en route to the 1996 Stanley Cup?

In the playoffs, the Avalanche beat both the Vancouver Canucks and Chicago Blackhawks in six games to move on to the Western Conference Final, where they faced the Presidents'

What happened in Roy's first game against his former team?

On February 5, 1996, in his first game against his former team, Roy stopped 37 of 39 shots in a 4–2 win. After the game, Roy took the game puck and flipped it to Canadiens head coach Mario Tremblay as he left the ice.

Trophy winner, the Detroit Red Wings. Colorado defeated Detroit in a hard-fought six-game series and moved on to the Stanley Cup Finals against the Florida Panthers.

What happened during the 1996 Finals?

The Avalanche swept the series 4–0 in a series that is perhaps best remembered for Uwe Krupp's triple overtime winner in Game 4, after more than 100 minutes of play with no goals being scored to claim the franchise's first Cup.

Who won the Conn Smythe Trophy in 1996?

Joe Sakic was the playoffs' scoring leader with 34 points (18 goals and 16 assists) in 22 games to cap an incredible season that saw him take home both the Art Ross Tro-

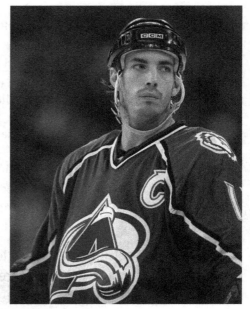

Joe Sakic

phy for leading the league in regular season scoring and the Conn Smythe Trophy, awarded to the most valuable player to his team during the playoffs.

1996–97

Who were the key members of the 1996–97 Red Wings?

The 1996–97 Detroit Red Wings were led by team captain Steve Yzerman, superstar Sergei Fedorov, bruising goal scorer Brendan Shanahan, and ace defenseman Nicklas Lidstrom.

What were some of the Red Wings' notable regular season moments during the 1996–97 season?

Detroit's campaign had many highlights, including Fedorov's five-goal performance in December versus the Washington Capitals and the Red Wings–Avalanche brawl in March that continued to fuel the rivalry between the teams.

Where did Detroit finish in the regular 1996–97 season?

The Red Wings finished second in the Central Division and went into the playoffs as the third seed in the Western Conference.

Which teams did the Red Wings defeat in the first two rounds of the 1997 playoffs?

In the first round, Detroit dispatched the Blues in six games and moved on to face Anaheim in the second round. Three of the games went to overtime, but the Red Wings swept the Ducks to move to the Western Conference final for the third straight season, where they would face the defending champion Colorado Avalanche.

What happened in the 1997 conference finals?

The Red Wings and Avalanche played a hard-fought series, with Detroit ultimately prevailing in six games to defeat the defending Stanley Cup champions.

What happened during the 1997 Stanley Cup Finals?

Detroit won the first two games to take a 2–0 series lead over Philadelphia and then won Game 3 decisively by a score of 6–1. Game 4 was best remembered for Darren McCarty's second-period tally, effectively sealing the series. The burly checker faked out Flyers' rookie defenseman Janne Niinimaa inside the blue line, swooped around him, then did a quick cutback in front of goaltender Ron Hextall before slipping the puck into the net. Eric Lindros would score his lone goal of the series with 15 seconds to play. The 2–1 win brought Detroit its eighth Stanley Cup and its first in 42 seasons.

Who led Detroit in scoring during the post-season, and who was awarded the 1997 Conn Smythe trophy?

Sergei Fedorov led the Wings in playoff scoring with 20 points. Detroit goaltender Mike Vernon, who had been in net during the Wings' failed 1995 playoff run and relegated to the bench the year before, earned vindication and his first Conn Smythe Trophy as playoff MVP by holding Philadelphia to six goals in four games.

1997–98 SEASON

Entering the 1997–98 season, what were the dominant storylines for the Red Wings?

The 1997–98 Detroit Red Wings entered the season looking to become the first team to repeat as Cup champions since the 1990–91 and 1991–92 Pittsburgh Penguins. In the wake of the brain injury that ended Konstantinov's career the previous off-season, the Red Wings dedicated the 1997–98 season to him.

What tragedy beset the Red Wings after the 1997 Stanley Cup Final?

Six days after winning the Stanley Cup, defensemen Vladimir Konstantinov and Viacheslav Fetisov, as well as massage therapist Sergei Mnatsakanov, were involved in a limousine accident. The driver, who later said he fell asleep, had a suspended license for previous drunk-driving convictions. Fetisov would recover from his injuries, while the accident ended Konstantinov's career.

What happened with Fedorov during the off-season?

After a lengthy holdout to start the season, Fedorov, a restricted free agent, signed an offer sheet with the Carolina Hurricanes, but the Red Wings matched it on February 26, 1998, ending the holdout.

How did Detroit do during the regular 1997–98 season?

For the second straight year, Detroit finished the regular season second in the Central division and entered the playoffs as the third seed in the Western Conference. The Red Wings were an extremely

Chris Osgood (pictured) replaced Mike Vernon as the Red Wings goalie in 1998.

well-balanced squad. Detroit had a prolific front line, finishing 2nd in the NHL in goals, despite not having a single player average a point per game.

Who replaced Mike Vernon as the Red Wings goaltender?

After winning the Conn Smythe Trophy the previous season, Mike Vernon had been replaced as the regular Wings goaltender during the season by the younger Chris Osgood.

What was the Red Wings journey to the 1998 Finals like?

Detroit triumphed over the Phoenix Coyotes in the first round in six games, then dispatched the St. Louis Blues for the second consecutive season in six games to set up a matchup against Brett Hull and the Dallas Stars in the Western Conference Finals. The Red Wings went on to defeat the Stars in six games, moving on to their second straight Cup Finals against the Eastern Conference champion Washington Capitals.

What happened in the 1998 Finals?

The Wings won the Stanley Cup in another sweep, and Vladimir Konstantinov came out onto the ice in his wheelchair on victory night to touch the Cup and celebrate with his former teammates.

Who won the 1998 Conn Smythe Trophy?

Red Wings captain Steve Yzerman netted six goals and added 18 assists for 24 points in 22 games and was awarded the Conn Smythe Trophy as playoff MVP.

What special distinction does that 1997–98 Red Wings team currently hold?

That Detroit sextet was the last team to successfully defend its Stanley Cup championship.

**What exception did NHL commissioner
Gary Bettman make after the Finals?**

Commissioner Bettman arranged for Konstantinov's name to be engraved on the Cup, despite his not being on the official roster.

1998–99 SEASON

Who were the key members of the 1998–99 Dallas Stars?

The Stars were led by Mike Modano, Brett Hull, Joe Nieuwendyk, captain Derian Hatcher, and goaltender Ed Belfour.

How did Dallas finish during the regular season?

The Stars dominated the regular season with a record of 51–12, won the Pacific Division, and earned the Presidents' Trophy with the NHL's best record. The club entered the 1999 playoffs as the prohibitive favorite to take home Stanley.

What road did Dallas take to reach the Western Conference Finals?

In the first round, the Stars swept their budding rival, the Edmonton Oilers, in four tightly contested, one-goal games, and then won a hard-fought, six-game series against the St. Louis Blues to set up a heavyweight Western Conference Finals matchup with the Colorado Avalanche.

What happened in the 1999 Conference Finals?

After the teams split the first four games, the series shifted back to Dallas, where the Avalanche won Game 5 to take a 3–2 series lead. The Stars responded with a Game 6 win to even the series at three games apiece and dominated Game 7, building a 4–0 lead and ultimately winning by a score of 4–1 to advance to their first Cup Finals since 1991, when they were the Minnesota North Stars.

Which team did Dallas face in the 1999 Stanley Cup Finals?

The Stars faced the Eastern Conference champion Buffalo Sabres, who were led by captain Michael Peca, coach Lindy Ruff, and goalie Dominik Hasek.

What happened during the Stanley Cup Finals of 1999?

The teams split the first two games, and the series moved back to Dallas, where Ed Belfour made 23 saves to shut out the Sabres and give Dallas a 3–2 series lead. Game 6 remained tied until 14:51 of the third overtime period, when Brett Hull scored off a rebound from inside the crease over a sprawling Hasek to end the series and award Dallas their first

Stanley Cup. It was the longest Cup-winning game in Finals history and the second-longest Finals game overall.

Which player took home the 1999 Conn Smythe Trophy?

Joe Nieuwendyk was awarded the Conn Smythe Trophy as playoff MVP, scoring 11 goals and adding 10 assists in 23 games, as well as tallying 6 game-winning goals.

What was the lasting legacy of the 1999 Stanley Cup final?

Brett Hull's controversial Stanley Cup-winning goal is synonymous with the phrase "no goal," because his foot appeared to be illegally in the crease, but the puck was

Dominic Hasek

not. Subsequent to the series-ending goal, the NHL sent out a memo clarifying the "skate in the crease" rule that allowed goals in instances where the scorer maintained control (not possession) of the puck prior to entering the crease. On this play Hull kicked the puck with his left skate, while still outside of the crease, into a shooting position. NHL officials maintained that Hull's two shots at the net constituted a single possession of the puck since the puck deflected off Hasek, and that ruling stood.

1999–2000 SEASON

How will the late 1990s and early 2000s be remembered?

The 1999–2000 NHL season marked the pinnacle of the "dead puck" era and was the first non-lockout NHL regular season since 1967–68 expansion in which no player reached the 100-point plateau.

What in-season coaching change did the Devils make?

Larry Robinson was promoted from assistant coach to head coach, replacing Robbie Ftorek, with only eight games left in the regular season. Ftorek stayed on as a scout for the rest of season, and the NHL allowed his name to be included on the Stanley Cup.

Where did the Devils finish during the regular season?

The Devils finished the regular season in second place in the Atlantic Division, behind only the Philadelphia Flyers, and entered the playoffs as the two-seed in the Eastern Conference.

Which teams did New Jersey defeat in the first two rounds of the 2000 playoffs?

In the first round, they swept the Florida Panthers and subsequently defeated the Toronto Maple Leafs in six games to set up a Conference Finals matchup against the first-seeded Philadelphia Flyers.

What was special about the Devils' performance in Game 6 of the second round against Toronto?

The Devils' defense, spearheaded by captain Scott Stevens, Ken Daneyko, Scott Niedermayer, Vladimir Malakhov, and rookies Colin White and Brian Rafalski, held the Maple Leafs to an NHL modern record-low six shots on goal in the game in a 3–0 New Jersey victory.

What transpired in the Eastern Conference Finals?

After splitting the first two games in Philadelphia, the Flyers won Games 3 and 4 in New Jersey to take a commanding 3–1 series lead heading back to Philadelphia. The Devils won the fifth game by a score of 4–1 to force a Game 6 back in New Jersey. The Devils prevailed at home 2–1 and forced a decisive Game 7 back in the City of Brotherly Love. In a tightly contested matchup, New Jersey ultimately finished the Flyers off by a score of 2–1 to move on to the Stanley Cup Finals.

Which team did the Devils face in the 2000 Stanley Cup Finals?

In the Western Conference Final, the defending Stanley Cup champion Dallas Stars had defeated the Colorado Avalanche in a classic seven-game series to set up a New Jersey–Dallas match in the Stanley Cup Finals.

Who had home-ice advantage in the 2000 Finals?

Despite New Jersey being a lower conference seed (4) than Dallas (2), New Jersey (103) had earned one more regular season point than the Stars (102), giving them home-ice advantage in the series.

How did the 1999–2000 Finals shape up during the first five games?

The teams split the first two games in New Jersey, but the Devils won the following two games in Dallas to take a command-

Ken Daneyko

213

ing 3–1 series lead. The Stars fought off elimination with a triple-overtime win in Game 5 in New Jersey, and the series shifted back to Dallas for a pivotal Game 6.

What was the defining moment of the series?

For the second straight year, the Stanley Cup was awarded after extra sessions. Game 6 moved into double overtime before New Jersey won the Cup on a Jason Arnott one-timer after he received a perfect pass from linemate Patrik Elias.

Jason Arnott

What else made the 2000 Stanley Cup Finals unique?

This was the first time since the New York Islanders lost to the Edmonton Oilers in 1984 that a defending Stanley Cup champion lost in the Finals.

Who was awarded the Conn Smythe Trophy that year?

Devils captain Scott Stevens was named playoff MVP. The future Hall of Fame defenseman scored three goals, including two game-winners, and added eight assists in 23 games. He also played stellar defense, regularly matching up against the opponent's top line.

ENFORCERS

Who is the toughest fighter Mike Hartman ever crossed paths with?

Believe it or not, Hartman's toughest opponent was not even a hockey player but a boxer. During one off-season in the '90s, he sparred with James "Lights Out" Toney, who was a two-weight world champion.

Who was the one exception to Tim Hunter's on-ice policy of fight, forgive, forget?

While Hunter understood the nature of his work and did not hold grudges, he made an exception for Marty McSorley, who jumped Hunter and scratched his eye when the game was out of reach. The two settled their accounts in a grudge match in October 1991.

What does Hunter think of the notion of "The Code" amongst enforcers?

Hunter calls it "a crock of s**t," the only code that he abided by offering an opponent a rematch to make up for a previous defeat.

How did Kevin Kaminski earn his nickname?

Despite his small stature (5'10", 190 lbs.), Kaminski never backed down from a fight, earning himself the alliterative nickname "Killer."

Which two stars did Kaminski model his play after?

Growing up, Kaminski admired Bryan Trottier and Wendel Clark and strived to play a similar, physical, defensively responsible game.

How did Darin Kimble burst onto the NHL scene?

In his NHL debut, Kimble's Quebec Nordiques faced off against the New Jersey Devils. Kimble not only dropped the gloves twice but even added a goal.

What reality of life as an enforcer did Kimble find the most challenging?

Kimble found waiting to be called into action particularly tough; as an enforcer, he would often spend most of the game on the bench before being called into action.

What aspect of being an enforcer did Jeff Odgers enjoy?

For all the physical punishment, Odgers appreciated the fact that he got to meet and play against some of the men he idolized, such as Wayne Gretzky and Ray Bourque.

How did Cam Russell describe a fight with Bob Probert?

He called an engagement with Probert "a notch in your belt," as it was something you could always remember as a point of pride.

What does Russell have to say about the risk of injuries that enforcers face?

While injuries are part and parcel with life as an enforcer, Russell took them as a "badge of honor"; getting hurt was simply part of doing his job on the ice.

What motivated Jason Strudwick to drop the gloves in his first NHL game?

Besides the obvious intention to prove his worth at the highest level, Strudwick figured that fighting would at least give him a story to tell if he did not make it as a pro.

What rule did Sabres enforcer Rob Ray force the NHL to create?

Since hockey fights are largely an attempt to gain a grip on the opponent to exert leverage, Ray would remove his jersey before or during a fight to gain an advantage. In response, the league passed the "Rob Ray Rule," which penalizes players for removing or failing to properly secure their jerseys.

How did Tamer show respect for opponents off the ice?

Despite the nature of their work, enforcers hold no ill will towards each other beyond the final horn. Early in his career, Tamer fought Brad May; after the game, they found themselves in the same restaurant, and Tamer bought his opponent a beer.

What aspect of his career did Rocky Thompson find the most stressful?

While he was not afraid of losing or getting hurt, Thompson felt personal pressure to be the best enforcer he could be. He never wanted to sit in the penalty box, knowing someone had performed better than him.

What does Tony Twist think is the key to becoming a great fighter?

Twist believes that the key to greatness is fighting through illness, injuries, and the urge to avoid dropping the gloves. He claims that the best push through the challenges because they truly enjoy fighting.

How does Twist feel about those who criticize enforcers?

He thinks that they cannot understand the realities of life as an enforcer; as long as a player is willing to fight and a team is willing to employ him, Twist has no issues.

How does Twist sum up the role of an NHL enforcer?

In simplest terms, Twist says that enforcers exist to tell other players, "Hey, don't act stupid."

What lesson did Ryan VandenBussche learn the hard way?

Early in his career, VandenBussche wanted to fight Stu Grimson and spent an entire shift chasing him around the ice. Grimson allowed his opponent to tire himself out before engaging and easily won the fight. From then on, VandenBussche would never drop the gloves at the end of a shift again.

What was the biggest challenge of Doug Zmolek's career as an enforcer?

During his first season in the NHL, Zmolek had to learn to pick and choose his fights. He was not always in control of his emotions and consequently was able to be drawn into fights he had little chance of winning.

Whose punch was known throughout the league to crack the helmets of those he squared off with?

Joey Kocur was known to have a devastating right-hand punch, so much so that it led to a deteriorated use of it from the repeated blows on helmets and teeth. Former NHL heavyweight Donald Brashear openly admitted that during various bouts with Kocur, his helmet was cracked from the right-handed thrusts, and despite having the helmet, Brashear would still experience pain in his gums on both sides of his face and could not eat for days. Other such feared players who had their worlds shaken by Kocur include Brad Dalgarno of the New York Islanders, who had his orbital bone, cheekbone, and jaw fractured by a Kocur punch. Also known to have a

Troy Crowder

flair for the dramatic, Kocur also scored goals in both the 1997 and 1998 Stanley Cup Finals series, which were both won by his Detroit Red Wings.

Which former Devils tough man bloodied Bob Probert in their first encounter?

Bob Probert has a reputation as being one of the most feared fighters in NHL history. However, in his first bout with young gun Troy Crowder, then a member of the New Jersey Devils, Probert was bloodied into a pulp, raising eyebrows and enticing gasps across the hockey world.

THE 2000s

Which team filed for bankruptcy in 2009?

The Phoenix Coyotes. In 2008 it was reported that the Coyotes were suffering massive losses, and the NHL was paying the team's bills. In 2009 previous owner Jerry Moyes put the team into bankruptcy just hours before Gary Bettman was to present him an offer to sell the team to Chicago Bulls and White Sox owner Jerry Reinsdorf. Moyes intended to sell the team to Canadian billionaire Jim Balsillie, who intended to relocate the team to Hamilton, Ontario. The NHL responded by stripping Moyes of his remaining owner- ship authority.

From May until September 2009, the NHL held a series of hearings to determine the Coyotes' fate. After several bids to buy the team failed, the NHL was forced to take full control of the team and negotiate a temporary lease with the city of Glendale until they were able to find a new owner for the team.

What team was Scotty Bowman coaching in 2002 when he earned his final Cup as a coach?

In 1993–94, Peterborough native Bowman accepted the coaching job for the Detroit Red Wings. His first year he led them to a first-place finish in the Western Conference, but the Wings were quickly ousted by the San Jose Sharks. In 1995 Bowman led the Red Wings all the way to the Stanley Cup Finals, their first appearance in the Finals in 29 years. Unfortunately for Bowman and Co., they were quickly swept aside by the New Jersey Devils, despite being the universal favorite. The next season he led them to an NHL record 62 regular season wins, but they were ousted by the Colorado Avalanche in the Western Conference Finals.

In 1997 the Red Wings finally broke through under the coaching of Bowman and won the franchise's first Stanley Cup in 42 years by sweeping the Philadelphia Flyers. The next season, the Red Wings would repeat as Stanley Cup champions, sweeping the Washington Capitals. These would be followed by three disappointing, early playoff exits.

In the 2002 Stanley Cup playoffs, Bowman once again led the Red Wings to the Stanley Cup, defeating the Carolina Hurricanes. Following the clinching victory, Bowman announced his retirement. During the presentation of the trophy ceremony, Bowman donned an old pair of skates so that he could take a proper lap around the rink with the Cup. He is second all time on the Red Wings win list, second only to the legendary Jack Adams. He ended his NHL coaching career with a league-best 1,244 wins.

One of the best coaches in NHL history, Scotty Bowman is seen here at a 2006 awards ceremony in Vancouver.

Which referee was rumored to miss the beginning of a season due to a rule that would ruin his hair?

He would be none other than Kerry Fraser. After missing the start of the 2006–07 campaign from a broken toe, some joked that he really missed games because of the new rule requiring referees to wear helmets, which would ruin his hair. But, in all fairness, his legacy goes far beyond his bouffant hairdo. Entering the league in 1980, Fraser officiated over 1,900 games, 13 Stanley Cup Finals, and over 250 playoff games. In 2010, he officiated the NHL Winter Classic between the Flyers and Bruins at Fenway Park and reffed his final game on April 11 at the Wachovia Center when the Flyers hosted the Rangers. He currently runs a blog on TSN called "C'mon Ref," where he discusses controversial calls around the NHL.

When was the NHL's first outdoor hockey game, where was it played, which teams participated, and what was the result?

The NHL's first outdoor hockey game was in 2003 in what is now called the Heritage Classic. The game was played at Commonwealth Stadium in Edmonton, Alberta, between the Edmonton Oilers and the Montreal Canadiens. Over 57,000 fans took in the game, despite temperatures close to –18 degrees C°, –30 with the wind chill. The game was held on the 25th anniversary of the Edmonton Oilers joining the NHL in 1979 and the 20th anniversary of their first Stanley Cup in 1984. Over 2.7 million Canadian viewers watched the CBC television broadcast, the second most for a regular season NHL game, and it was also the first NHL game broadcasted in high definition.

First, there was a game played between some of the best former players of each team. This "megastars" game included former greats such as Wayne Gretzky and Guy Lafleur. Mark Messier, the only active player at the time, was given special permission from the New York Rangers front office to play in the game and was the only player to wear a helmet. The squad for the Oilers won the contest 2–0.

The second game, which featured the current squads for both teams, was won by the Canadiens 4–3. Richard Zednik of the Canadiens scored the first goal of the game and also scored the game winner. Montreal goaltender Jose Theodore wore a Canadiens tuque on top of his goalie mask for the game.

Which team traded its first overall draft pick and captain after the 2005 NHL lockout because of subpar playoff performances?

The Boston Bruins drafted Joe Thornton with the first overall pick in the 1997 NHL Entry Draft. In a decision that garnered much criticism, the Bruins named Thornton team captain in 2003. Thornton was criticized for his leadership style and character while also receiving scrutiny for not being able to elevate his level of play in the playoffs. After the 2005 NHL lockout, Thornton was traded to the San Jose Sharks in exchange for Marco Sturm, Wayne Primeau, and Brad Stuart.

Which two current NHL superstars won both the Hart and Art Ross Trophies in the first three years of their careers?

Washington Capitals winger Alexander Ovechkin and Pittsburgh Penguins center Sidney Crosby. Ovechkin was drafted first overall by the Capitals in the 2004 NHL draft. Ovechkin made his NHL debut on October 5, 2005, scoring two goals in a 3–2 victory over the Columbus Blue Jackets. He would go onto score 52 goals and 54 assists to lead all rookies with 109 points and edge Crosby to win the Calder Trophy as the top rookie. In 2007–08 he led the NHL with 65 goals and 112 points and captured the Rocket Richard and Art Ross Trophies. He was also voted as the Hart Trophy winner as league MVP.

Crosby broke into the NHL in 2005–06 after being the first overall pick in the 2005 NHL draft. He finished sixth in the league in scoring his rookie season. In 2006–07 he finished the season with a league-leading 120 points, winning the Art Ross Trophy as well as the Hart Trophy as league MVP, the second-youngest player to do so.

Joe Thornton

Which two teams participated in the first Winter Classic? Where was it played, and what was the result?

The first NHL Winter Classic took place during the day on January 1, 2008, between the Buffalo Sabres and the Pittsburgh Penguins. The game was played at Ralph Wilson Stadium in Orchard Park, New York, home of the NFL's Buffalo Bills. It was the first regular season NHL game to take place outdoors in the United States. A temporary ice rink was erected on the football field. An NHL attendance record of 71,217 people took in the game.

The teams wore vintage jerseys for the game. The Penguins wore powder blue jerseys for the first time since 1973, and the Sabres wore their old white jerseys, which they wore from 1978 to 1996. Both goaltenders wore custom, vintage-style goalie masks, and Sabres goaltender Ryan Miller wore a hockey sock on top of his mask.

After 60 minutes and an overtime period, the game was tied 1–1 on goals from Pittsburgh's Colby Armstrong and Buffalo's Brian Campbell. The game went into a shootout, where Penguins captain Sidney Crosby scored in the third round to give the Penguins the victory.

Which team was defeated in the Stanley Cup Finals and got revenge by beating the same opponent in the Finals the next year?

After falling to the Red Wings in the 2008 Finals, the Pittsburgh Penguins squared off against the Wings again in the 2009 Finals. While Detroit looked to repeat, Pittsburgh held them off and claimed the Cup in seven games as Marc-Andre Fleury stopped Niklas Lidstrom with two seconds remaining. Evgeni Malkin took home the Conn Smythe, making him the first Russian player to do so.

Which is the most recent Eastern Conference team to come back from a 3–0 series deficit?

The Philadelphia Flyers. They accomplished this feat in the second round of the 2009–10 playoffs against the Boston Bruins. Due to an injury to their starting goaltender, they were forced to play their backup, Brian Boucher, during the first playoff series. He outplayed Martin Brodeur to give the Flyers the series win over the Devils. During the series, the Flyers suffered key injuries to star players Jeff Carter and Simon Gagne, as well as top penalty killer Ian Laperriere, who went down with a gruesome facial injury after blocking a shot.

In the second round, the Flyers found themselves down 3–0 in the series. Gagne was able to return in Game 4 and scored the overtime winner to keep their season alive. The Flyers won the second game 4–0, despite Boucher suffering MCL sprains in both knees, forcing Michael Leighton into the net. The Flyers won the sixth game 2–1 in Philadelphia, setting up the deciding Game 7 in Boston.

The Flyers fell behind 3–0 early in Game 7 but were able to complete one of the greatest comebacks in all of sports. They became the third NHL team and fourth American sports team to come back from a 3–0 deficit in a series and win it. The Flyers went on to defeat the Canadiens in five games to advance to the Stanley Cup Finals, which they lost in six games to the Chicago Blackhawks.

Which general manager became known for trading away many future NHL stars?

Former New York Islanders general manager Mike Milbury became infamous for consistently being on the wrong side of a trade in his tumultuous 11-year stint on Long Island in the late 1990s and early 2000s. Players that Milbury traded who went on to have successful NHL careers included Wade Redden, Todd Bertuzzi, Zdeno Chara, Bryan McCabe, Tommy Salo, and Roberto Luongo to name a few.

Which Vezina Trophy-winning goaltender was MVP of the 2010 Olympics Games, despite failing to win gold?

Ryan Miller, from East Lansing, Michigan, was drafted 138th overall in the 1999 NHL draft by the Buffalo Sabres. Prior to being drafted, Miller enjoyed a very successful career at Michigan State and won the Hobey Baker Award as college's top hockey player in 2001. He set an NCAA record with 26 career shutouts.

After three seasons at Michigan State, Miller was assigned to the American Hockey League affiliate of the Sabres, the Rochester Americans. He played for the Americans for the better part of three seasons. He established himself at the Sabres' starting goaltender in 2005–06 and finished 11th among NHL goalies with 2.60 goals-against average and 9th in save percentage. In 2006–07 he led the Sabres to an incredible start, winning their first ten games in a row. In 2009–10 Miller was selected as a member of Team USA for the Olympic Games in Vancouver. Leading up to the Olympics, he had an exceptional GAA of 2.00. He was phenomenal in the Olympic Games, backstopping Team USA to the gold-medal game, before being heartbrokenly defeated by the Canadiens in overtime, courtesy of Sidney Crosby's game winner. He finished the regular season with a 2.22 GAA.

Ryan Miller

223

Miller is the Buffalo Sabres' franchise leader in career wins with 284 and most wins in a season, when he won 41 in 2009–10. He won the Vezina Trophy as the league's top goaltender in 2010 and was also a First Team All-Star.

Which player prior to being drafted was nicknamed "The Next One"?

Sidney Crosby. Crosby was one of the most highly regarded draft picks in hockey history, leading many to refer to the 2005 NHL draft as the "Sidney Crosby Sweepstakes." Crosby was selected first overall by the Pittsburgh Penguins.

In his first NHL season, Crosby finished sixth in league scoring with 102 points (39 goals, 63 assists) and was runner-up to the Calder Trophy, which was won by fellow phenom Alexander Ovechkin. By his second season, he led the NHL in points with 120 and captured the Art Ross Trophy, becoming the youngest player and only teenager to win a scoring title in any North American sports league. That same season he won the Hart Trophy and Lester B. Pearson Award as the NHLPA's choice for most outstanding player, becoming only the seventh player in history to win all three in one year.

Crosby was named captain of the Penguins at the start of the 2007–08 season and led them to the Stanley Cup Finals, where they were defeated by the Detroit Red Wings. The next year he again led them to the Stanley Cup finals against the Red Wings, and this time they won in seven games.

Internationally, Crosby has played for Team Canada in several tournaments, including the World Junior Championships, Junior World Cup, and the 2010 Winter Olympics in Vancouver, where he scored the overtime winner in the gold medal match against the United States.

Who is the only player in NHL history to play in three straight Stanley Cup finals for three different teams?

Marian Hossa is one of the major NHLers of the 2000s, and he participated in each Stanley Cup Finals between 2008 and 2010. In 2008 he reached the Stanley Cup finals with the Pittsburgh Penguins, but they lost to the Detroit Red Wings. The following off-season, he signed as a free agent with the Red Wings. Again, the Red Wings and the Penguins faced off in the Stanley Cup Finals. This time the Penguins won and again deprived Hossa of a chance to hoist Lord Stanley's Cup. On July 1, 2009, Hossa signed a 12-year, $62 million contract with the Chicago Blackhawks. The Blackhawks would go on to reach the finals and face the Philadelphia Flyers, who they defeated in six games. Captain Jonathan Toews accepted the Cup and handed it to Hossa, who, after two years of being so close, was finally a Stanley Cup champion.

Which NHL captain became the youngest member of the Triple Gold Club?

That would be Chicago's Jonathan Toews. Since bursting onto the NHL scene in 2007, Toews has been regarded as one of the best captains in the NHL and is already one of the most decorated at the tender age of 27. He was named the third-youngest captain in

NHL history by the Blackhawks entering the 2008–09 season, and he would go on to lead the team to Cup championships in 2010, 2013, and 2015. Toews would cement his reputation as a playoff performer with a Conn Smythe Trophy to his credit in 2010, the Hawks' first Stanley Cup since 1961. After winning gold in the World Championships with Canada, Toews added the first of two Olympic gold medals to his name and then his first Cup, becoming the youngest member of the Triple Gold Club, passing Peter Forsberg. Rounding out his resume are a Calder Trophy as the league's top rookie in his first year of service, the second youngest to do so, as well as the Frank. J. Selke Trophy in 2013. The trophy room is already full for Toews, but with his leadership and skill, the Blackhawks should remain a Cup contender for years.

Martin Brodeur

Which NHL coach returned from retirement to help a struggling team?

Jacques Lemaire, born in LaSalle, Quebec, in 1945, won eight Stanley Cups with the Montreal Canadiens and scored the Cup-winning goal in 1977 and 1979. He served as a player-coach in Switzerland before coaching with the Canadiens from 1983 to 1985. In 1993 he began his tenure with the New Jersey Devils. Utilizing young goaltender Martin Brodeur and legendary defensemen Scott Stevens and Scott Niedermayer, Lemaire crafted a defense-first, neutral zone trap playing style. The Devils reached the Eastern Conference Finals in the 1993–94 season but lost in seven games to the New York Rangers. The following year, they reached the Finals and surprised everybody by sweeping the offensive powerhouse Detroit Red Wings. Lemaire left after the 1997–98 season and became the first head coach for the expansion team Minnesota Wild in 2000. He held that position until April of 2009 and returned to the Devils after the dismissal of Brent Sutter. The Devils were ousted in five games by the Philadelphia Flyers in the first round of the playoffs, and Lemaire decided to call it a career. The following season, new Devils coach John MacLean was fired after 33 games, prompting a second return for Lemaire. In 49 games, the Devils went 29–17–3, narrowly missing the playoffs. Finishing his career with 617 wins and 11 total Stanley Cups, he is now working as a special assignment coach for the Devils.

2000–01 SEASON

Who were the key members of the 2000–01 Colorado Avalanche?

The Avalanche was led by captain Joe Sakic, Peter Forsberg, Rob Blake, Ray Bourque, Alex Tanguay, and goaltender Patrick Roy.

How did the Avs finish the regular season?

Colorado dominated the regular season, won the Presidents' Trophy, and, despite losing star forward Peter Forsberg to a ruptured spleen, entered the postseason as the Stanley Cup favorites.

Which teams did the Avs defeat in rounds one and two?

In the first round, the Avs swept the Canucks, then they beat the seventh-seeded L.A. Kings in a hard-fought, seven-game series to move on to the Western Conference Finals versus the St. Louis Blues.

What transpired in the Western Conference 2001 Finals?

The Avalanche dominated the first two games and took a 2–0 series lead back to St. Louis for Game 3, where Blues winger Scott Young scored the winner in the second overtime period. In the first period of Game 4, the Avalanche scored three goals in a span of a minute and 18 seconds and were in prime position to win on the road going into the second period with a three-goal lead. St. Louis came back to tie the game in the third, but Colorado winger Stephane Yelle won the game for his club on a deflection shot. Game 5 also went to overtime, and Colorado captain Joe Sakic scored the game-winning, series-clinching goal on the power play.

Which team did Colorado face in the 2001 Stanley Cup Finals?

In the Eastern Conference Finals, the defending champion Devils dispatched the powerful Penguins, led by Mario Lemieux. The Hall of Famer had a memorable return to hockey after three and a half years of retirement. Lemieux tallied 76 points in 43 games. Yet New Jersey defeated the resurgent Penguins in five games to set up a New Jersey–Colorado Stanley Cup Final.

Mario Lemieux playing in Buffalo in 2005.

What was unique about the Devils–Avalanche 2001 Finals?

It marked the first Finals since 1989 in which the number-one seeds in each conference met. Also, the Avalanche, which previously had relocated to Colorado from Quebec following the 1994–95 season, faced the former Colorado Rockies, which became the Devils when they relocated to New Jersey prior to the 1982–83 campaign.

How did the Avs win the 2001 Stanley Cup?

Colorado dominated Game 1 and prevailed 5–0 to take the early series lead. The Devils won Game 2 to tie the series at one going back to New Jersey. The two teams split Games 3 and 4 and the series went back to Colorado tied at two. The Devils dominated Game 5 and went on to win by a score of 4–1 with a chance to clinch on home ice in Game 6. However, the Avalanche had different plans, as Patrick Roy pitched a shutout and Colorado won 4–0 to send the series back to Denver for a winner-takes-all Game 7. Roy gave a legendary performance in the deciding game while Alex Tanguay scored a pair of goals, including the Cup winner, and the Avalanche clinched the Cup on home ice with a 3–1 victory.

Which player won the Conn Smythe in 2001?

Goaltender Patrick Roy was awarded the Conn Smythe Trophy for a record-breaking third time as the playoffs' Most Valuable Player.

What was the defining moment of the series?

The series is best remembered for a gesture made by Colorado captain Joe Sakic. When presented with the Cup by NHL commissioner Gary Bettman, Sakic was reluctant to raise it to the rafters and instead skated directly to Ray Bourque, who had just won the first and only Stanley Cup of his career. With tears streaming down his face, Bourque took a victory lap with the trophy and would retire from the NHL after the season.

2001–02 SEASON

What masterful roster changes did Red Wings general manager Ken Holland make prior to the 2001–02 season?

The 2001–02 Detroit Red Wings were to become one of the greatest teams in modern history. After the previous season's disappointing playoff exit, Holland went to the trade market to address Detroit's more glaring needs. He quickly filled them by trading for Hall of Fame goaltender Dominik Hasek and signing forwards Brett Hull and Luc Robitaille. These aces joined other future Hall of Fame talents: Chris Chelios, Sergei Fedorov, Igor Larionov, Nicklas Lidstrom, Brendan Shanahan, and Steve Yzerman, along with Pavel Datsyuk in his rookie season and legendary coach Scotty Bowman, who had decided to return for one more year.

How many future Hall of Famers were featured on the Red Wings team?

The squad featured 9 players who eventually would be Hall of Famers.

How did Detroit finish the regular 2001–02 campaign?

Detroit dominated the regular season, finishing with a record of 51–17–10–4 for 116 points. The Red Wings won the Central Division, their third Presidents' Trophy, and went into the postseason as overwhelming Stanley Cup favorites.

Which teams did the Red Wings face in the first two rounds of the 2001–02 postseason?

In the first round of the playoffs, the eighth-seeded Vancouver Canucks took the first two games in Detroit, after which Wings captain Steve Yzerman gave a closed-door speech to the team. Only the players in the locker room knew what was said, but the Wings headed to Vancouver and won the two games there before heading home to win two and take the series. After a quick series triumph over the division rival St. Louis Blues, Detroit met its longtime nemesis, the second-seeded Colorado Avalanche, in a highly anticipated Conference Final.

What happened in the Western Conference Finals?

Detroit and Colorado battled back and forth during the series, as each squad tied the series three times before reaching Game 7 in Detroit. The Wings came out firing and won the decisive seventh game, 7–0. As the final game in the series came to a close, the Neil Diamond song "Sweet Caroline" was played over the Joe Louis Arena loudspeakers, as the victorious Red Wings prepared to head off to a Stanley Cup-clinching series with the third-seeded victors of the Eastern Conference, the Carolina Hurricanes.

What happened during the 2002 Detroit–Carolina Stanley Cup Finals?

The Carolina Hurricanes took Game 1 in overtime to take the early series lead, but

Steve Yzerman, retired Red Wings captain, talks to reporters during his 2008 Michigan Sports Hall of Fame induction.

Nicklas Lidstrom raises the prized Cup.

the Red Wings won Game 2 by a score of 3–1 to earn a split as the series shifted to Raleigh. The third game went into triple overtime with multiple opportunities for both teams. At 14:47 of the third overtime period, Igor Larionov scored the game-winning goal to give the Wings the series lead. Game 4 was never in doubt as Detroit won 3–0 to take a commanding 3–1 series lead with a chance to clinch the Cup on home ice. In front of over 20,000 roaring fans at Joe Louis Arena, the Red Wings clinched their third title in six years.

What was unique about the 2002 Conn Smythe Trophy winner?

Nicklas Lidstrom was named playoff MVP, marking the first time in NHL history that the Conn Smythe Trophy was awarded to a player from outside North America.

2002–03 SEASON

Who were the key members of the 2002–03 Stanley Cup-winning New Jersey Devils?

The 2002–03 Devils were an extremely well-balanced team, with the likes of Scott Stevens, Scott Niedermeyer, Patrik Elias, Jamie Langenbrunner, Scott Gomez, and Joe

Nieuwendyk, as well as checkers John Madden and Jay Pandolfo and goaltender Martin Brodeur.

How did New Jersey finish during the regular season?

The Devils won the Atlantic Division and finished second in the Eastern Conference behind only the Presidents' Trophy-winning Ottawa Senators.

Which teams did the Devils defeat in the first two rounds of the playoffs?

In the first round, the Devils dispatched the Boston Bruins in five games, then defeated the Tampa Bay Lightning in five games, winning all six games on home ice, to set up a heavyweight Eastern Conference Final against the Ottawa Senators.

What happened in the Eastern Conference Finals?

The teams split the first two games in Ottawa, whereupon the series shifted back to New Jersey for Game 3. At that point the Devils won a defensive battle by a score of 1–0. New Jersey also won Game 4 and appeared to have the series in control with a commanding 3–1 lead, but Ottawa rebounded at home in Game 5 and staved off elimination with a 3–1 victory. Game 6 went to overtime, and Senators defenseman Chris Phillips scored the game-winning goal to hand New Jersey their first and only home loss of the playoffs. However, the Devils won Game 7 in Ottawa by a score of 3–2, on Jeff Friesen's series-winning goal with just over two minutes to play, to send New Jersey to the Stanley Cup Finals.

Which Devils player scored an unnoticed goal that wasn't counted in Game 3 of the Eastern Conference quarterfinals against the Senators on May 15, 2003?

Jay Pandolfo wristed one into the net with such force that it flew in and slid back out before anyone noticed. It wasn't until much later that an in-net camera discovered it. By then, it was too late for the goal to count. Regardless, New Jersey still won the game by, albeit, a slim margin of 1–0 off an earlier tap-in by Sergei Brylin.

Which team did the Devils face in the 2003 Stanley Cup Finals?

In the Western Conference, the Anaheim Mighty Ducks defeated the Minnesota Wild to set up the Stanley Cup Finals between the second-seeded Devils and the seventh-seeded Ducks.

What happened in the first four games of the final?

The series opened in New Jersey with the Devils dominating the first two games on two Martin Brodeur 3–0 shutout victories to take a 2–0 series lead to California. Game 3 was remembered for Brodeur's clumsy mistake. The normally focused Devils goalie accidentally dropped his stick when the puck came toward the net. The rubber then deflected off his fallen stick and into the net to give the Ducks a 2–1 lead. The Devils would tie the game but lose in overtime. Game 4 remained scoreless through the end of regulation, and once again Anaheim came out on top in overtime, winning 1–0, tying the series at two games apiece.

What was the defining moment of the 2003 Stanley Cup series?

After the Devils won Game 5 to take a 3–2 series lead, the defining moment of the series occurred in Game 6, when Ducks captain Paul Kariya was hammered in open ice by Devils captain Scott Stevens. Kariya lay motionless and was then escorted to the locker room but unexpectedly returned to the bench minutes later. About eleven minutes after the hit, he fired a slapshot that found the back of the net to help the Ducks win the game 5–2 and send the series to a seventh game.

Which team ultimately emerged as the Cup champion?

The Devils dominated Game 7 on home ice with a 3–0 victory to give New Jersey its third Stanley Cup.

Why was the 2003 MVP of the playoffs a unique choice?

For his stellar play throughout the playoffs and finals, losing netminder Jean-Sebastien Giguere was awarded the Conn Smythe Trophy as playoff MVP, becoming only the fifth player, and fourth goaltender, in NHL history to win the award as a member of the defeated team.

Jean-Sebastien Giguere

What record did the Devils establish on their way to the championship?

New Jersey went 12–1 on home ice in the postseason. Their 12 home wins are an NHL record.

2003–04 SEASON

Who were the key members of the Stanley Cup champion 2003–04 Tampa Bay Lightning?

The Lightning were led by captain Dave Andreychuk, Martin St. Louis, Cory Stillman, Brad Richards, Vincent Lecavalier, Dan Boyle, and goaltender Nikolai Khabibulin.

How did the Lightning finish the regular season?

Tampa Bay cruised to the Southeast title. No other team in the division sported a .500 record. They also clinched the first seed in the Eastern Conference.

Which teams did Tampa Bay face in the first two rounds of the playoffs?

The Lightning dispatched the eighth-seeded Islanders in five games, then went on to face the Montreal Canadiens, who had upset rival Boston in a thrilling, first-round, seven-game series. The Lightning had no trouble with the Habs, sweeping them in four games.

What happened in the Eastern Conference Finals?

The Lightning faced the third-seeded Philadelphia Flyers in the Conference Finals. After the teams split the first two games, Tampa Bay won Game 3 behind a dominant performance from goalie Nikolai Khabibulin. Game 4 saw the Flyers pull even with a critical 3–2 victory that tied the series, which would resume in Tampa Bay. The Lightning won Game 5 by a score of 4–2, but the Flyers won a thrilling Game 6 in overtime. The series went back to Tampa Bay for a Game 7, where the Lightning edged the Flyers 2–1 to move on to the Stanley Cup Finals.

Which team did the Lightning face in the 2003–04 Stanley Cup Finals?

In the Western Conference, the Calgary Flames emerged as the Cinderella story, defeating the third-seeded Vancouver Canucks and the Presidents' Trophy-winning Detroit Red Wings. Calgary then beat the second-seeded San Jose Sharks in the Conference Final to set up a Cup Final between the Lightning and the Flames.

What happened during the Lightning–Flames Final?

After splitting the first four games of the series, the Flames won Game 5 to take a 3–2 lead with a chance to clinch on home ice. During Game 6, with the score tied 2–2 in the third, Martin Gelinas of the Flames (who had scored the series-winning goals in the

Flames' three previous series) seemed to have scored the go-ahead goal. It appeared that before goalie Nikolai Khabibulin kicked the puck out, it had already crossed the goal line. The play was not reviewed and the game went into double overtime, whereupon Lightning winger and former Flame Martin St. Louis scored the overtime winner and broke the hearts of Flames fans everywhere. The Lightning went on to win Game 7 by a score of 2–1 and captured their first championship in franchise history.

Brad Richards

Who got the 2004 Conn Smythe Trophy?

Brad Richards of Tampa Bay was named playoff MVP with 12 goals and 26 points.

What other notable awards did Lightning players receive during the 2003–04 season?

In addition to Brad Richards winning the Conn Smythe Trophy, he also captured the Lady Byng Memorial Trophy. Martin St. Louis took home several awards including the Plus/Minus Award, the Art Ross Trophy for leading the NHL in scoring, the Hart Memorial Trophy for league MVP, and the Lester B. Pearson Award, voted by the players as their top player in the league.

2005–06 SEASON

What was unique about the 2005–06 NHL season?

This was the season after the 2004–05 work stoppage, which resulted in the cancellation of the entire NHL season due to a labor dispute between NHL ownership and the NHL Players Association over the Collective Bargaining Agreement between the league and its players.

In what ways was the 2005–06 season filled with firsts?

It featured the much-hyped debuts of Sidney Crosby (102 points) and Alexander Ovechkin (106 points). It was only the second time that two rookies had more than 100 points in a season (Teemu Selanne and Joe Juneau did it back in 1992–93).

233

Who were the key players on the Carolina Hurricanes' Stanley Cup-winning roster?

The Canes were led by captain Rod Brind'Amour, Eric Staal, Cory Stillman, Justin Williams, Erik Cole, Ray Whitney, and goaltenders Martin Gerber and Cam Ward.

How did the Canes finish in the regular season standings?

Carolina ran away with the Southeast Division title and finished second in the Eastern Conference, just one point behind the Ottawa Senators.

What was unique about the first round of the 2006 playoffs?

The Western Conference made history in the first round when all four series were won by the lower-seeded teams (conversely, all four series in the Eastern Conference were won by the higher-seeded teams).

Which teams did the Canes face in the first and second rounds of the playoffs?

The Hurricanes beat the seventh-seeded Canadiens in six games, then went on to defeat the third-seeded New Jersey Devils in five games.

Which team did Carolina meet in the 2006 Stanley Cup Finals?

In the Western Conference, the eighth-seeded Edmonton Oilers defied the odds and defeated the Anaheim Ducks in five games to advance to the Stanley Cup Finals.

What made the 2006 Cup Finals unique?

This series marked the first time that two former World Hockey Association teams played against each other for the Stanley Cup since they merged with the NHL in 1979. This was

---

What made the 2006 Eastern Conference finals a classic?

The Hurricanes faced off against the Buffalo Sabres and, after splitting the first four games and seeing goalies Cam Ward and Martin Gerber each get turns between the pipes, Gerber started Game 5. Two minutes into the second period, Toni Lydman scored, giving Buffalo a 3–1 lead, prompting Canes coach Peter Laviolette to once more make a mid-game switch, this time turning back to Ward. The Canes evened the score and sent the game into overtime, whereupon Cory Stillman beat Ryan Miller low to give Carolina an emotional 4–3 win. Game 6 also went to overtime, and Danny Briere sent the series to a seventh game by burying a shot that went off Ward's glove. In the seventh and deciding game, the Sabres took a 2–1 lead into the third period, but Carolina answered early in the third with a goal by Doug Weight, and captain Rod Brind'Amour scored the series winner on a power play with about seven minutes left to help the Hurricanes secure their second trip to the Stanley Cup Finals in four seasons.

also the first Stanley Cup Finals to be contested by two teams that had both missed the playoffs the previous season. Even more interestingly, it would also prove to be the first Finals contested by teams that would both go on to miss it in the following year's playoffs.

What happened in Game 1 of the 2006 Final?

In Game 1, Carolina tied the biggest comeback in Stanley Cup Finals history, overcoming a three-goal deficit to win, 5–4. Late in the final period, Oilers goalie Dwayne Roloson suffered a series-ending knee injury in a collision and was replaced with Ty Conklin. With 32 seconds to go in regulation, Conklin misplayed the puck, and it deflected off Jason Smith's stick to the front of the empty net, allowing Rod Brind'Amour to score the winning goal. Following Roloson's injury, Jussi Markkanen started for the Oilers in Games 2 and 3.

Rod Brind'Amour

How did the series play out after the Roloson injury?

The Hurricanes won Game 2 by a score of 5–0. In Game 3, Edmonton's Ryan Smyth scored the winning goal after crashing into Cam Ward inside the crease as they both tried to get control of a rebound. Hurricanes head coach Peter Laviolette and many other Carolina players complained that Smyth should have been penalized for interference, but no penalty was called since the referees felt that he did not make enough contact with Ward to prevent him from attempting a save. Carolina won Game 4 and entered Game 5 with a commanding 3–1 series lead. However, Edmonton battled back to win Games 5 and 6 to force the series back to Carolina for a deciding Game 7.

What happened in the all-or-nothing Game 7?

In Game 7, Aaron Ward and Frantisek Kaberle gave Carolina a 2–0 lead before Fernando Pisani scored for Edmonton at 1:03 of the third period to cut the lead in half. With a minute and a half to go in regulation, the Oilers pulled goalie Jussi Markkanen in hopes of tying the game. Seconds later, a loose puck wound up on the stick of Eric Staal, who fed it to Justin Williams. Williams sprinted down the ice and tapped the puck into the empty net at 18:59 of the third period, sealing the Stanley Cup for the Hurricanes.

Why was the Cup victory especially sweet for Cory Stillman?

Stillman earned a Stanley Cup title for the second straight season, having won in 2004 with the Tampa Bay Lightning, becoming the first player to win back-to-back titles with different teams since Claude Lemieux (1995 New Jersey Devils, 1996 Colorado Avalanche).

Who earned the 2006 Conn Smythe and why was it special this time?

Cam Ward became the first NHL rookie goalie to win a Stanley Cup Final series since Patrick Roy led the Montreal Canadiens in 1986. Ward was also the first rookie since the Philadelphia Flyers' Ron Hextall in 1987 to be awarded the Conn Smythe Trophy as Most Valuable Player in the playoffs.

2006–07 SEASON

What major acquisition did Anaheim make prior to the start of the 2006–07 season?

The Ducks acquired defenseman Chris Pronger in a trade from the Edmonton Oilers. Pronger was dealt for forward Joffrey Lupul, prospect Ladislav Smid, Anaheim's 2007 first-round draft choice, and conditional first- and second-round picks in 2008.

Who were the key members of the 2006–07 Anaheim Ducks?

The team was led by captain Scott Niedermayer, Chris Pronger, Teemu Selanne, Corey Perry, Ryan Getzlaf, and goaltender Jean-Sebastien Giguere.

How did Anaheim finish during the regular season?

The Ducks clinched their first Pacific Division title in team history with 110 points and finished second in the Western Conference, just three points behind the Detroit Red Wings.

Which teams did the Ducks face in the first two rounds of the playoffs?

Anaheim beat the Minnesota Wild in five games in the first round, then eliminated the Canucks in five games to move on to the Western Conference Final against the top-seeded Detroit Red Wings.

What happened in the first four games of the 2007 Western Conference Finals?

Detroit opened the series at home in Game 1 with a 2–1 victory. In Game 2, Scott Niedermayer scored in overtime to tie the series. Game 3 at Honda Center featured a one-sided contest as the Red Wings blanked the Ducks 5–0 to take a 2–1 series lead. Chris Pronger was suspended by the NHL for Game 4 for elbowing Detroit forward Tomas Holmstrom, despite the fact that he did not receive a penalty for the hit during the game. In Game 4, the Ducks prevailed by a score of 5–3 to even the series at two games.

How did the 2007 Detroit–Anaheim series ultimately play out?

The Red Wings dominated the play in Game 5 but were only able to score once because of the strong play of Ducks goaltender J. S. Giguere. Finally, after over 59 minutes of play, the Ducks found the back of the net via a power-play goal by Scott Niedermayer with just 47 seconds left in the game. Halfway into overtime, Andreas Lilja was making a routine breakout play behind his net when forechecking pressure by Andy McDonald caused Lilja to turn the puck over to Teemu Selanne, who lifted a backhander above a sprawled Dom Hasek to give the Ducks a stunning 2–1 overtime victory and a 3–2 series lead going back to Anaheim. After the drama of Game 5, the Ducks won Game 6 to advance to the Stanley Cup Final for the second time in their history.

Which team did Anaheim face in the 2007 Stanley Cup Finals?

In the Eastern Conference Finals, the Ottawa Senators defeated the Presidents' Trophy-winning Buffalo Sabres in five games to advance to the Stanley Cup Finals.

Who won the 2007 Stanley Cup?

Anaheim took Games 1 and 2 and the series shifted back to Canada's capital, where the Senators won 5–3 to cut the Ducks' series lead in half. Ducks defenseman Chris Pronger was suspended for Game 4 because of an elbow he delivered to the head of Ottawa's Dean McAmmond in Game 3. Without Pronger, the Ducks won the fourth

Teemu Selanne

237

> ### How did Jim Agnew encounter
> ### "gentlemanly-ness" during a fight on the ice?
>
> At one point in his career, Agnew squared off against Al May; the pair had roomed together in juniors. Before the fight, they agreed to wager $50 on the fight, and they asked how each others' parents were during their five minutes in the penalty box.

game 3–2 to take a commanding 3–1 series lead. Back in California, the Ducks dominated Game 5, ultimately winning 6–2 to claim the first Stanley Cup in franchise history.

What did the Anaheim Ducks accomplish that no other California-based NHL team had?

The Ducks became the first California-based team to win the Stanley Cup.

Which player won the 2007 Conn Smythe Trophy?

Scott Niedermayer, who previously had won three Stanley Cups with the New Jersey Devils, was named playoff MVP.

What profession did Jim Agnew transition to after his career as an enforcer?

Within hours of each other in 2006, Agnew received his U.S. citizenship and finished the interview process for the deputy sheriff's position in Missoula, Montana.

How did Ken Belanger leave the NHL?

In 2006, Belanger walked away from the game, despite having offers on the table from several teams. He no longer liked fighting and hated the anxiety that it caused him.

How did Gordie Dwyer feel about going toe-to-toe with Bob Probert for the first time?

As he skated to the penalty box, Dwyer specifically remembers a feeling of pride and privilege; he fought not only a worthy opponent but arguably one of the best enforcers that hockey has ever seen.

What was Dwyer's reaction when Andrew Peters broke his nose during a fight?

In the locker room, Dwyer was told he had two choices: fix his nose immediately, or wait until after the game. He chose the former option and, with four men holding the enforcer down, doctors inserted two metal pins into his nose. When he got back on the ice, Dwyer challenged Peters to a rematch; Peters declined.

What are Reed Low's lasting feelings about his career as an enforcer?

While it was a tough way to make a living, Low is nothing but grateful that he had the honor of playing in the NHL.

What does Reid Simpson have in common with Flyers great Bobby Clarke?

Not only did both men embrace the physical side of the game, but they also share a hometown: Flin Flon, Manitoba.

Does Simpson think conventional enforcers, like John Scott, can continue to survive in the current NHL?

Simpson believes that today's enforcers need to be able to take a regular shift in order to remain relevant. If they cannot, coaches will not be able to use them, and they will eventually become obsolete.

Whose reaction was Brendan Witt afraid of when he accidentally broke Craig Berube's jaw?

During training camp, Witt checked his former rival and mentor Berube into the boards, breaking his jaw. While Berube understood that accidents happen on the ice, his wife was less sympathetic toward Witt.

Which Maple Leafs enforcer made a name for himself for fighting a fan during the game?

Tie Domi had a reputation for being an enforcer, but he did not hit the big spotlight until he was traded to the Toronto Maple Leafs. In a game against his former club, he sucker-punched Ulf Samuelsson and received an eight-game suspension and fine. That season, 1994–95, he broke the single-season penalty-minute record for the Maple Leafs with 365 penalty minutes, passing the benchmark held by Tiger Williams. During an incident in the 2000–01 season, Domi sprayed a heckler with his water bottle while seated in the penalty box in Philadelphia. Domi was screaming and climbing the glass to get at him when the glass gave way and the fan fell into the box, prompting a scuffle between the two.

Tie Domi

239

THE 2010s

How long of a Cup drought did the Bruins end in 2011?

Despite being one of the league's most storied franchises, the Bruins had not won a Stanley Cup since 1971–72. Thanks to the Conn Smythe-winning play of veteran goaltender Tim Thomas, Boston outlasted the Canucks in seven games. The victory also preserved another drought: a Canadian club had not won a Stanley Cup since the Canadiens in 1993.

In 2012 which team became the first-ever eighth seed to win the Stanley Cup?

Prior to the start of the 2011–12 season, the Los Angeles Kings made a blockbuster trade for Philadelphia Flyers captain Mike Richards in an effort to shore up their depth down the middle. After a terrible start in which they were 12–13–4, the Kings fired head coach Terry Murray and eventually replaced him with Darryl Sutter. Just before the trade deadline, GM Dean Lombardi orchestrated another big trade, acquiring Jeff Carter from the Columbus Blue Jackets in exchange for defenseman Jack Johnson. The trade reunited Carter with Richards, who were teammates and close friends while playing for Philadelphia. Aided by the acquisition of Carter, the Kings managed to squeak into the playoffs as the eighth-seeded team.

The Kings went up against the Presidents' Trophy-winning Vancouver Canucks in the first round. The Kings beat the Canucks in five games to advance to the conference semifinals, where they promptly swept the St. Louis Blues. With that, the Kings became the first eighth-seeded team to defeat both the first- and second-seeded teams in the playoffs. The Kings took on the Phoenix Coyotes in the Western Conference Finals and won in five games to reach the Stanley Cup Finals for just the second time in franchise history. They beat the New Jersey Devils in six games to win their first-ever Stanley Cup. Goaltender Jonathan Quick won the Conn Smythe Trophy as the playoff MVP with a 16–4 record, a 1.41 GAA, a .946 save percentage, and three shutouts.

L.A. Kings captain Mike Richards (center) with Marian Gaborik (left) and Jeff Carter at the 2014 Stanley Cup parade.

How much of the 2012–13 season was lost to a lockout?

The 2012–13 NHL lockout officially began at 11:59 p.m. on September 15 and lasted until a Memorandum of Understanding was signed on January 12, 2013. The work stoppage lasted 119 days; consequently, each team played a 48-game regular season before playing a regular playoff schedule. The All-Star Game in Columbus and the Winter Classic in Ann Arbor were also canceled and made up during the 2013–14 season.

What coach won the Jack Adams trophy in his first year as a head coach?

Patrick Roy did. After a Hall of Fame career as a goalie playing for both the Montreal Canadiens and Colorado Avalanche—during which he won two Stanley Cups with each franchise—Roy took over the reigns behind the bench for the Avalanche at the beginning of the 2013–14 season. After finishing 29th in the league the prior year and receiving the number-one overall pick in the draft, there wasn't much expected from a young, rebuilding Colorado team. However, not only were they able to prove the doubters wrong, they were one of the best teams in the league. After receiving just 39 points in a 48-game, lockout-shortened season the prior year, they nearly tripled that total in the 2013–14 season, coming in third place in the whole NHL with a point total of 112. The team set a franchise record with 52 wins and came in first in the Central Division.

Who was the only player to capture 100 points in the 2013–14 season?

While it may be a surprise to some that only one player reached the 100-point plateau, it won't surprise many that it was Sidney Crosby. Arguably the face of the NHL since entering the league in 2005, he tallied 36 goals and 68 assists to become the only NHL player in 2013–14 to surpass 100 points.

What team earned its second Stanley Cup in three years?

After making their mark on the league in 2012 by capturing the franchise's first-ever Stanley Cup, the Los Angeles Kings solidified their respected presence in the league by taking home their second Stanley Cup in three years. Although a tight series in which four games were decided by one goal—three of which were decided in overtime—the Kings, led by all-star goaltender Jonathan Quick, were able to defeat the New York Rangers in five games. Defensemen Alec Martinez put home a rebound off Rangers goalie Henrik Lundqvist 14:43 into the second overtime in front of his home crowd at the Staples Center.

Who was the NHL's only 50-goal scorer in 2013–14?

Alexander Ovechkin tallied 51 goals, which was good enough to win him the "Rocket" Richard Trophy, the award given to the player with the most goals scored in the NHL. It was the fifth 50-goal season in eight years for "Alexander the Gr8," who entered the NHL in 2005–06.

What was the biggest rule change heading into the 2013–14 season?

While there are many rule changes that are added prior to the start of every NHL season, there is always that one that sticks out or has more of a consequence than any oth-

Alexander Ovechkin

ers. The most notable rule change prior to the start of the 2013–14 season was the addition of hybrid-icing. The NHL had used the touch-icing system for more than 70 years prior to the switch. The main purpose of the switch was to protect players and reduce potentially damaging collisions along the end boards.

What player captured three trophies at the NHL's annual awards ceremony?

"Sid the Kid"—Sidney Crosby—won three awards at the 2013–14 NHL awards ceremony. As the only player in the NHL with 100+ points, he was awarded the Art Ross Trophy for the most points scored in the league. Crosby was also awarded the Hart Memorial Trophy, which is given out to the "player most valuable to his team." The third and final trophy Crosby won was the Ted Lindsay Award, which is given out to the "the most outstanding player during the regular season" and is voted on by members of the NHLPA.

Who won his fourth "Rocket" Richard trophy in eight years?

As the only player to score 50+ goals in 2013–14, Alexander Ovechkin was awarded the Maurice "Rocket" Richard trophy for the player with the most goals scored in the year. It was the eight-year veteran Ovechkin's fourth time winning the award and his fifth time tallying at least 50 goals. The four times winning the award are the most for a single player since the award debuted in the 1998–99 season.

Who became the youngest player to win the Calder Trophy in the 2013–14 season?

Upon getting drafted first overall in the 2013 NHL entry draft by the Colorado Avalanche, Nathan MacKinnon became the youngest player to dress for the franchise when he made his NHL debut on October 2, 2013. He tallied two points in his first game and scored his first NHL goal 10 days later on October 12 versus the Washington Capitals. MacKinnon went on to tally 63 points—24 goals and 39 assists—that season and helped lead the Avalanche to a franchise-record 52 wins. On June 24, 2014, MacKinnon was awarded the Calder Trophy for the NHL's Rookie of the Year. At 18 years old, MacKinnon became the youngest player to win the award.

Duncan Keith

What defenseman captured his second Norris Trophy in the last five years?

While some names usually associated with this trophy include Nicklas Lidstrom, Zdeno Chara, and more recently Erik Karlsson and P. K. Subban, one name that often flies under the radar is Duncan Keith of the Chicago Blackhawks. However, if he

What was the Stadium Series?

The Stadium Series was a set of four outdoor NHL games that first took place during the 2013–14 season. The series was created in response to the increasing popularity of the Winter Classic and Heritage Classic. The four games that season took place at three of the most famous stadiums across the country. As with the Winter and Heritage Classics, each team, except the Devils, wore specially designed uniforms, and the goalies wore specially painted masks. The Devils wore throwback uniforms with their old-school, green and red color scheme.

The Anaheim Ducks faced off against the Los Angeles Kings at Dodger Stadium. At the time of puck drop, the temperature was measured in the '60s. The Ducks came out on top, shutting out the Kings 3–0. The next two games featured the New York Rangers facing off against the New Jersey Devils and then against the New York Islanders. Both of those games were played at Yankee Stadium. The Rangers defeated the Devils 7–3 and then came out victorious against the Islanders 2–1. The last of the Stadium Series games was between the Chicago Blackhawks and the Pittsburgh Penguins. The Blackhawks won the game by a score of 5–1.

didn't capture the believers his first go-around when he won the trophy in 2010, he certainly did so in 2013–14, taking home his second Norris in five years after tallying 61 regular season points and helping lead the Blackhawks back to the Western Conference Finals prior to losing to the Kings. He also won the Conn Smythe Trophy in 2015, as the Blackhawks defeated the Tampa Bay Lightning in the Stanley Cup Finals.

Which future Hall of Fame defenseman's career was ended prematurely by a lingering concussion?

Chris Pronger, a native of Dryden, Ontario, was drafted number two overall by the Hartford Whalers in the 1993 NHL entry draft after two dominant years in juniors, playing for the Peterborough Petes.

Pronger made his NHL debut in 1993–94, when he played in 81 games with the Whalers and earned a spot on the NHL All-Rookie Team. After just two seasons in Hartford, he was traded to the St. Louis Blues in exchange for Brendan Shanahan. In 1997, his third season with the Blues, he was elected team captain after Brett Hull departed as a free agent. In 1999–2000 Pronger had the best year of his career. He finished with 62 points and a plus-minus rating of +52. He grabbed the Norris Trophy as the league's top defenseman and became the first defenseman since Bobby Orr to win the Hart Trophy, barely edging Jaromir Jagr.

Following the 2004–05 NHL lockout, Pronger was traded to the Edmonton Oilers and helped guide them to the Stanley Cup Finals in 2006 before losing to Carolina. Afterward, Pronger requested a trade out of Edmonton, citing family matters. He was traded to Anaheim and again helped guide his team to the Stanley Cup Finals, this time winning. In 2009 Pronger was traded on draft day to the Philadelphia Flyers. The same season he played a huge role in the Flyers' surprise run to the Stanley Cup Finals, but they eventually lost to Chicago in six games. In 2011 he was named captain of the Flyers after previous captain Mike Richards was traded. However, he would suffer several blows to the head, including a terrible eye injury, and his career came to an end as he would never quite recover from post-concussion syndrome. As of the end of the 2014–15 season, Pronger had not officially retired yet, but he remained on long-term injured reserve with little hope of playing again. In 2013 Pronger stepped down as captain, allowing Claude Giroux to take over the reins.

Pronger played for Team Canada in four different Olympic Games and twice won gold (2002, 2010). He is also a member of the Triple Gold Club. In addition to his terrific defensive play, Pronger was also a very tough player who would often deliver huge hits. After Pronger was traded from the Blues, he made the playoffs with every other team he played for and in every season he played in. He also reached the Stanley Cup Finals with those teams. Despite only winning the Norris Trophy once, Pronger is considered to be a lock for the Hall of Fame.

Who is the Ottawa Senators' all-time leader in goals, assists, and points?

Daniel Alfredsson, born in Sweden, was originally drafted 133rd overall in the 1994 NHL entry draft. He served as captain of the Senators from 1999 to 2013 and finished with 426 goals, 682 assists, and 1,108 points in 1,178 games as a Senator.

Alfredsson was largely unheralded going into his first training camp. He made his debut with the Senators in 1995–96 and recorded 61 points en route to winning the Calder Trophy as top rookie. In 1998 he was named team captain after previous captain Alexei Yashin was stripped of the captaincy for refusing to honor his contract. In 2005 Alfredsson was joined by Jason Spezza and Dany Heatley on a line forming the "CASH" line. He also became the first team captain to score a goal in a shootout. He finished the 2005–06 season with a career-high 103 points, which tied him for the team lead with Heatley. Alfredsson led the Senators to the Stanley Cup Finals in 2007 before falling to the Anaheim Ducks. After much debate as to whether he was going to retire, in 2013, Alfredsson decided to leave the Senators, and at the age of 40 he signed a one-year deal with the Detroit Red Wings. He would later sign a one-day contract with Ottawa to retire a Senator.

Alfredsson is a 13-time 20-plus goal scorer and twice eclipsed the 40-goal mark. He served as an alternate captain for Team Sweden in the 2006 Olympics, scoring five goals and adding another five assists en route to a gold medal. He was named to the All-Star Game six times.

Which future Hall of Famer is the Calgary Flames' all-time leading scorer?

Jarome Iginla, a native of Edmonton, Alberta, was originally drafted 11th overall by the Dallas Stars, but he was traded to the Calgary Flames before his rookie season began. He was a member of the Kamloops Blazers, won two Memorial Cups, and was named Western Hockey League Player of the Year in 1996.

Iginla made his debut with the Flames in the 1996 Stanley Cup playoffs and became the first 18-year-old to play for the Flames since Dan Quinn in 1983. He played his first full season with the team in 1996–97 and was named to the NHL All-Rookie Team, finishing the season with 50 points. In 2001–02 he set a career high with 52 goals, earning him the Art Ross and Maurice Richard Trophies. In 2003–04 he was named the 18th captain in Flames history. He registered his second career 50-goal season in 2007–08 and set a new career high in points with 98. In 2009 he passed Theo Fleury as the Flames' all-time leading scorer. In 2012 Iginla was traded to the Pittsburgh Penguins and the next year signed with the Boston Bruins as a free agent. He signed a three-year contract with the Colorado Rockies in 2014.

Iginla is the seventh player in NHL history to record 11 consecutive seasons with 30-plus goals. He is the Calgary Flames' all-time leader in points, goals, and games played. He twice represented Canada at the Olympic Games, winning gold both times. He is considered to be one of the most prominent power forwards of the past decade. Iginla is still in pursuit of his first Stanley Cup championship. He was the longest-tenured captain in Flames history, having worn the "C" for 10 seasons. In 1,219 games as a Flame, he registered 525 goals and 570 assists for 1,095 points.

Who is the tallest man to ever play in the NHL?

Slovakia native Zdeno Chara, defenseman and captain for the Boston Bruins, stands at 6'9". Chara was originally drafted 56th overall by the New York Islanders in 1996. After being a defensive force on the blue line for the Islanders, he was traded to the Ottawa Senators during the 2001 NHL draft in a deal that sent Russian forward Alexei Yashin to the Islanders. Chara played for Ottawa for another four years, where he developed into a reliable two-way defenseman along with his partner Wade Redden. In 2002–03 he was selected to his first All-Star game appearance. In 2005–06 Chara and Ottawa were unable to come to terms on a new contract, and Chara instead signed a deal with the Boston Bruins, who almost immediately named him the team captain. In 2007–08 Chara set a new career high in points with 51 and the following year set a career high in goals with 19. Both years he was named an NHL All-Star. In 2010–11 Chara led the Bruins to the ultimate glory, defeating the Vancouver Canucks in an exciting seven games to take home their first Stanley Cup since 1972. In 2013 he again was a physically dominant force on the blue line, leading his team to another Stanley Cup Final before falling to the Chicago Blackhawks in 6 games.

Chara won the Hardest Shot competition in the All-Star Game five times, setting an NHL record in 2012 of 108.8 MPH. He won the Norris Trophy in 2009 as the league's top defenseman and was twice more named a finalist. He is set to compete in his third Olympics. In 2010 he was team captain for Slovakia and will again serve as captain in 2014.

Zdeno Chara (center) with Miro Satan (right) and Tomas Kopecky (left) celebrating their Olympic silver medals during a 2012 parade in Bratislava, Slovakia.

Which franchise relocated in 2011 and to where did they relocate?

The Atlanta Thrashers relocated to Winnipeg, Manitoba. It was reported in October of 2009 that there were rumors of True North Sports & Entertainment, the company that owned both Winnipeg's MTS Centre and the American Hockey League's Manitoba Moose, intending to purchase the Thrashers and relocate them to Winnipeg.

On May 28, 2011, a deal was reached to bring the Thrashers to Winnipeg, and all that was left was for the NHL to decide the right time to officially announce the relocation. The league denied the report but acknowledged that advanced negotiations were underway and that commissioner Gary Bettman supported the move.

On May 31, 2011, at a press conference held at the MTS Centre, Bettman confirmed the sale and relocation. Winnipeg's ownership chose to keep the team's new name a secret until the 2011 NHL entry draft held in St. Paul, Minnesota. Winnipeg's new owner, Mark Chipman, introduced their new GM, Kevin Cheveldayoff, to "make our first pick on behalf of the Winnipeg Jets"—This was True North's first official announcement of the franchise's new name.

In 2010 which team ended a 49-year Stanley Cup drought, the longest active streak at the time?

Prior to the 2009–10 season, the Chicago Blackhawks signed high-scoring winger Marian Hossa, veteran John Madden, and Tomas Kopecky in an effort to make a run at the Stanley Cup. The Hawks already boasted young stars such as Jonathan Toews, Patrick Kane, and Duncan Keith. In April of 2010, they won their 50th game of the season and set a franchise record for wins and points in a season. They finished the regular season with a 52–22–8 record. They defeated the Nashville Predators in six games to open the playoffs and advanced to face the third-seeded Vancouver Canucks. After knocking off the Canucks in six games, the Blackhawks went up against the top seed in the West, the San Jose Sharks. They swept the Sharks to reach the Stanley Cup Finals for the first time since 1992. They went up against the seventh seed in the East, the Philadelphia Flyers. The Blackhawks won the first two games at home. The Flyers were able to even the series, however, with two straight wins at home as well. The Blackhawks won Game 5 to pull within one win of their first Cup in 49 years. After the Flyers tied the game late to send it into overtime, Kane slid the puck under goaltender Michael Leighton's pads, ending the game and securing the Cup for Chicago. Hawks captain Toews received the Conn Smythe Trophy as playoff MVP, finishing second in playoff scoring behind Philadelphia's Danny Briere.

Which player recently surpassed Peter Forsberg as the youngest player to join the Triple Gold Club?

Chicago Blackhawks center Jonathan Toews was the third overall selection in the 2006 NHL entry draft. The Winnipeg native played his first full season with the team in 2007–08 and was nominated as a finalist for the Calder Memorial Trophy but lost the award to teammate Patrick Kane. The fol-

lowing season, he was named captain of the Blackhawks at the ripe age of 20. He was the quickest to be named captain of a team, having played just 64 games in a Blackhawks uniform.

As a member of Team Canada, Toews won gold medals at the 2006 and 2007 World Junior Championship, the 2007 IIHF World Championship, and the 2010 Olympics Games. He was also named the best forward in the tournament at the 2010 Olympics. In 2010 Toews led the Chicago Blackhawks to their first Stanley Cup victory in 49 years. Throughout that playoff run, Toews finished second to Philadelphia's Danny Briere in playoff points with 29 and was awarded the Conn Smythe Trophy as playoff MVP, the second youngest to do so. With this Stanley Cup victory, Toews became the youngest player to join the Triple Gold Club (winning gold

Jonathan Toews

249

at the Olympics and World Championship and the Stanley Cup) at the age of just 22. In 2013 he again led the Blackhawks to the Stanley Cup, becoming only the second player (Wayne Gretzky was the first) in NHL history to captain a team to two Stanley Cups before the age of 25. Toews's Blackhawks won the Cup again in 2015.

As a rookie Toews notched 24 goals and 30 assists, good for 54 points. He followed that up with 69 and 68 points respectively in the next couple seasons. In 2010–11 he notched 76 points in 80 games. During the 2012–13 lockout season, Toews registered 48 points in 47 games and a plus-minus rating of +28. He was awarded the Frank J. Selke Trophy as the league's top defensive forward in 2013.

What was the most important rule change/addition prior to the start of the 2014–15 NHL season?

Prior to the start of every NHL season, the NHLPA, the NHL board of governors, and all GMs meet in Florida for summer meetings. Discussion often centers around ways to improve the integrity and play of the game. Following approval, the league often announces any rule changes or additions about one month before the start of the season. A major change that occurred prior to the start of the 2014–15 season was the addition of a diving/embellishment penalty that also would result in a fine for the player. While the topic had been discussed in the past, nothing had ever been done to actively prevent diving in the game other than an occasional "embellishment" call. Now with the league applying stricter rules for divers, the call is made more often, and measures are being made to prevent players from being repeat offenders. Not only does the offense result in a penalty for the player, but repeat offenders will be fined.

What player had a career resurgence in the 2014–15 season?

When Jordin Tootoo came to New Jersey Devils camp strictly on a tryout basis, not many people thought he would make the team, let alone emerge into the player he became for the Devs. Tootoo was coming off arguably his worst year in the NHL and having his con-

What team went from finishing last in their division in 2013–14 to making the playoffs the next?

While many teams had big turnarounds in the 2014–15 season, perhaps none was bigger than that of the New York Islanders. After an underachieving 2013–14 season in which they finished last in the Metropolitan Division with a measly 79 points, the Islanders had a tremendous reversal the following season. After picking up the likes of Jaroslav Halak, Johnny Boychuk, and Nick Leddy, the Islanders bolstered their team up and down to make them a force around the league. Not only did they make the playoffs, but they also gained respect from their peers.

tract bought out by the Detroit Red Wings. He spent most of the 2013–14 season in the minors, only seeing 11 NHL games, and had a career-low 1 point, which came on an assist. However, when Tootoo was given the opportunity via a tryout to make the Devils' big club, he took full advantage of it. Tootoo earned a one-year, $550,000, one-way contract with the Devils due to his efforts and play during camp and the pre-season.

As a Devil, his contributions certainly didn't go unnoticed. While he only tallied 15 points—10 goals and 5 assists—many of them were huge for the team. He also brought physicality to the team, which the team had lacked coming into the year. One of his biggest moments in the season came in a game vs. the Pittsburgh Penguins on December 29, when he fought Pens defenseman Robert Bortuzzo twice in a game the Devils ended up winning 3–1. It is no coincidence this two-round bout came just three weeks after Bortuzzo had hurt then-Devils star Jaromir Jagr on a check into the boards. Not only did Tootoo win the fight, but he also gave his team a much-needed jolt that night to knock off the Penguins.

What player broke the Washington Capitals' all-time points and goals record in the same season?

The 2014–15 season was one for the ages for the Washington Capitals' Alexander Ovechkin. Not only did he help the Cap make it back to the playoffs after missing the prior year, but he also captured his fifth Rocket Richard Trophy in only his ninth NHL season by leading the league with 53 goals. However, those weren't the biggest headlines for Ovechkin in 2014–15. He also broke the Capitals' franchise record for points and goals during the season. Capitals great Peter Bondra had previously held both records. The points record was broken on November 4, 2014, when the Capitals hosted the Flames. In the 4–3 Caps' overtime loss, Ovechkin picked up two assists. The first assist came in the first period, when his shot from the left point was tipped in by linemate Nicklas Backstrom, tying the score at 1–1. It was Ovechkin's 826th career regular season point, and it catapulted him into first all time for Capitals' point getters. Amazingly, it took Ovechkin only 691 career games to reach this milestone, whereas it took Bondra 961.

Next up for "Alex the Great" was the all-time Capitals goals record. Ovechkin broke the record in the last week of the season. On April 2, 2015, Ovechkin scored two goals and led the Capitals to a 5–4 shootout win over the Canadiens. With the game tied 1–1 in the second period, Alex entered the zone on the left side and cut towards the middle from the top of the circle after making a brilliant move around the defender and sniped his 51st goal of the season and his 473rd of his career. In doing this, Ovechkin passed Bondra, who previously held the record with 472 goals over his Capitals career. Ovechkin also broke this record with considerably fewer games played than Bondra—756 for Ovechkin, 961 for Bondra.

What current NHLer moved into fourth all time in total points scored?

After 20 years in the league, Jaromir Jagr is officially the number-four scorer of all time. While catching the leader, Wayne Gretzky, may be challenging, the 43-year-old Jagr has

251

a reasonable shot at jumping up to number two; he is 48 points behind Gordie Howe and 85 points from Mark Messier. Jagr was planning to return for the 2015–16 season with the Florida Panthers. Jagr has said that he'd like to play until he's 50. As he puts it, "If I stay healthy, it's not going to be my last year in hockey. I want to play until I'm 50 and maybe longer. But I want to play in the NHL only if I'm good enough." Jagr tallied 47 points on 17 goals and 30 assists during the 2014–15 season.

Jaromir Jagr

Who became the Flames' youngest player in franchise history to score 30 goals?

When the Flames selected Sean Monahan sixth overall in the 2013 NHL entry draft, Calgary knew they had a great player on their hands but didn't know how quickly he'd be able to adapt to the NHL. However, if their questions weren't answered after he tallied 22 goals and 12 assists in his rookie year during the 2013–14 season, they certainly were the following year. Monahan entered the 2014–15 season poised to improve off his performance from the prior year. And he did exactly that, tallying 31 goals and 31 assists. Monahan became the youngest Flames player to score 30 goals surpassing Dan Quinn, as well as other Calgary notables, Theo Fleury and Joe Nieuwendyk. Not only was it an outstanding year for Monahan, but he was also one of the big reasons the Flames were able to greatly exceed expectations and make it back to the playoffs for the first time in six years.

How many new coaches were hired prior to the start of the 2014–15 season?

Six. Here is a list of the coaches and where they came from:

- Barry Trotz, Washington—After serving as the head coach for the Nashville Predators for the 15 years since their inauguration into the NHL in 1998, Trotz and the Preds decided to split ways after they hadn't been able to make much of a playoff push in a couple of years. He was then hired by the Capitals on May 26, 2014, to help guide the way for an already playoff-poised team.

- Willie Desjardins, Vancouver—After spending nine seasons in the WHL with the Medicine Hat Tigers and Saskatoon Blades, in 2012 Desjardins became head coach of the Texas Stars, the AHL affiliate of the Dallas Stars. In his second season there, Desjardins helped lead Texas to their first-ever Calder Cup Trophy. The Canucks hired him after they fired John Tortorella after just one season.

- Peter Laviolette, Nashville—Laviolette has been a head coach in the NHL since 2001, when he came in with the New York Islanders. After just two years there, which included two first-round playoff losses, he moved on to the Carolina Hurricanes in 2003. After missing the playoffs his first year there, he miraculously led the team to their first-ever Stanley Cup in the 2005–06 season, when the Hurricanes defeated the Edmonton Oilers in seven games. However, after missing the playoffs the next two years and getting off to a rough start in 2008–09, he was fired by the Hurricanes just 25 games into the season. He wasn't out of a job for long, as the Philadelphia Flyers brought him in the following year. He led the Flyers to their first Cup Finals appearance since 1997 but ended up losing to the Blackhawks in six games. After a few more years of high hopes but disappointments, Laviolette was fired just three games into the 2013–14 season. He took over Barry Trotz's role as head coach of the Predators on May 6, 2014.

- Mike Johnston, Pittsburgh—Prior to becoming the head coach for the Pittsburgh Penguins, Johnston had served as the coach and general manager for the Portland Winterhawks of the Western Hockey League from 2008–14. Before that, Johnston served as an assistant with the Vancouver Canucks and L.A. Kings from 1999 to 2007, when he took over the Portland job. Johnston was hired to replace former Pens coach Dan Bylsma.

- Gerard Gallant, Florida—Gallant first came into the NHL as a coach in 2003 when the Columbus Blue Jackets hired him. After missing the playoffs his first two seasons there, he was relieved of his duties just 15 games into his third season. After that, he served as an assistant with the Islanders in the 2007–08 season, becoming the head coach of the Saint Johns Sea Dogs of the QMJHL. After a successful stint there, Gallant was appointed an assistant coach for the Montreal Canadiens in 2012, where he served for two seasons prior to being hired by the Florida Panthers as their head coach on June 21, 2014.

- Bill Peters, Carolina—Peters' coaching career began in 1996, but it wasn't until 2011 that he got his first action in the NHL. Prior to that, Peters had served as head coach for the Spokane Chiefs of the WHL, as well as the Rockford Icehogs, the Chicago Blackhawks' AHL affiliate. However, in 2011 Peters was brought in by the Detroit Red Wings to serve as an assistant. He mainly worked with the defense group and the team's penalty-kill. He coached with the Red Wings for three seasons prior to being hired as head coach by the Hurricanes on June 19, 2014.

Why did Riley Cote retire in 2010 at the age of 28?

Fighting simply took too much of a toll on Cote. He said that while he wished his game were more versatile, allowing him to survive longer, fighting was a massive emotional drain.

What stereotype of enforcers does Cote contradict?

While many view enforcers as mindless brutes or robots who are only seeking destruction, Cote is an example of the preparation it takes to be successful. In addition to researching his upcoming opponents, he also trained in mixed martial arts to get any advantage he could on the ice.

STRANGE BUT TRUE

Who made up the New York Rangers' "Bread" Line?

One of the classiest players in NHL history, Frank Boucher, a former Royal Canadian Mounted Policeman, was a sparkling Ranger on what was called the "Bread" Line during the Great Depression years. Boucher's linemates were brothers Bill and Bun Cook, right wing and left wing, respectively. Considered one of the finest offensive units of all time, the Cooks and Boucher guided the Rangers to Stanley Cups in 1928 and 1933.

Bill possessed the hardest shot and usually did the scoring while Boucher was an adept playmaker. Like Bun, Boucher also could score, and the unit was famed for their dazzling skate work and pattern-passing plays.

After his playing days, Boucher coached and managed the Rangers. Frank hired Bill to coach the Blueshirts from 1951 through 1953. When Bun's playing days ended, he, too, wound up behind the bench. He gained fame in the American Hockey League, orchestrating a number of championship clubs with the Cleveland Barons.

Which NHL player had more Cups than birthdays by the end of his career?

Habs legend Henri Richard was better known as "The Pocket Rocket" as the younger brother of Maurice "The Rocket" Richard, who was 15 years his senior.

However, it was Henri who was better known for having the most Stanley Cups in NHL history as a player with 11 championships to his name. At the time of his retirement in 1975, the leap-year baby, born on February 29, technically had only nine birthdays—two fewer than the number of times his name was etched into the Stanley Cup!

Even more uncanny was the fact that Henri was relatively small by then-NHL standards and never was expected to gain an NHL berth. When the Pocket Rocket arrived at the Canadiens' training camp in 1955, he was dismissed as too small. In fact his older brother preferred that Henri either be sent back to junior hockey, from whence he came, or at least to a minor pro team.

But coach Toe Blake claimed that Henri was the best player on the ice at every single pre-season practice and had no choice but to retain him on the big club. It was a wise choice. During the Pocket Rocket's first five years in the NHL, he was on five Cup winners.

From time to time, his older brother would come to Henri's assistance when bigger foes would attack him, but the Pocket brushed Maurice aside and said he could handle his own battles. Sure enough, Henri became notorious as one of the best fighters, as well as one of the best forwards in the NHL.

Henri Richard

Did a former NFL quarterback ever convince an owner to bring a hockey franchise to a city?

In a sense this actually did happen at the start of the 1990s, when the Minnesota North Stars suffered from attendance problems and assorted other woes that inspired owner Norman Green to look elsewhere to locate his team.

In 1993 amid further woes at the gate, Green received permission from the NHL to move his franchise to Dallas after former Dallas Cowboys star quarterback Roger Staubach convinced him that Dallas would be a suitable market for an NHL team. The move was made official on March 10, 1993, and the Minnesota North Stars became the Dallas Stars.

Actually, Texas had a long history with pro hockey teams. Immediately after World War II, both Dallas and Houston featured thriving, minor-league clubs. But when Green moved his franchise to Dallas, there were doubts that an NHL club could survive in such a nontraditional hockey market. The naysayers were proven wrong.

When did a club have to borrow jerseys for the Stanley Cup Finals?

In the 1920 Stanley Cup series, the Ottawa Senators played Seattle for the championship in the Washington State metropolis. When the Senators arrived in Seattle, they discovered that their distinctive, red-white-and-black-striped sweaters were almost identical to those of the Seattle's sextet. As a result, the Senators were forced to borrow white jerseys for the series. The substitute jerseys had no effect on the quality of the visitor's game. Ottawa went on to win the Cup wearing generic jerseys.

How did an influenza epidemic affect a Stanley Cup championship?

At the conclusion of the 1918–19 National Hockey League season, the Montreal Canadiens defeated Ottawa for the right to go west and challenge the Seattle Metropolitans for the Stanley Cup. The series opened on March 19, 1919, in Seattle, and the home club easily triumphed, 7–0, but Montreal rebounded in the second match and won it, 4–2. Seattle took the lead again in the third game, winning 7–2, setting the stage for what NHL historian Charles L. Coleman has described as "the greatest match ever played on the Pacific Coast."

Neither team scored in regulation time. One hour and 40 minutes of sudden-death overtime was played before the game was called a draw. When the teams met again four nights later, the score was 3–3 going into overtime, but this time the Canadiens prevailed after 15:57 of extra play on a goal by Odie Cleghorn.

The game was significant for several reasons. For one thing, it made abundantly clear the fact that the Canadiens had retained their flair for coming from behind, a trait that remained with them through the 1979 Stanley Cup playoffs, exactly 50 years later. For another thing, there was an incident that caught the eyes of some spectators as the teams battled for the winning goal. "Bad" Joe Hall, who in earlier games had battled vehemently with Seattle's Cully Wilson, appeared to lose his zest and finally left the ice and made his way to the dressing room. Unknown to all the onlookers, it was to be the last time Joe was ever to step on a hockey rink.

Hall was rushed to the hospital, stricken with the flu bug that was causing an epidemic throughout North America. Immediately after the game, several other Canadiens were bedded with the influenza, but not as bad as Hall. The belief was that the Montreal players had contracted the disease while sightseeing in Victoria, British Columbia, but this was never definitively ascertained.

With the series tied at two apiece, an attempt was made to finish the playoff for the Stanley Cup. Montreal's manager, George Kennedy, requested permission to "borrow" players from Victoria to finish the series, but the hosts declined the bid, and the playoff was cancelled without a winner.

Six days after he stumbled off the ice, Joe Hall died of influenza in a Seattle hospital. "His death," said teammate Joe Malone, "was a tragic and shocking climax to one of the most surprising of all Stanley Cup series."

Which team won the Stanley Cup by using three goaltenders over the course of the playoffs and who were they?

The Chicago Blackhawks of 1938 employed Mike Karakas, Alfie Moore, and Paul Goodman in goal. At the start of the playoffs, Chicago's chances of winning the Stanley Cup were considered no better than 100–1. To begin with, the Hawks were the only one of six qualifying teams to have less than a .500 record (14–25–9), and their first-round opponents were the Montreal Canadiens, who had a considerably more respectable

257

18–17–13 mark. Further complicating matters for Chicago was the fact that two of three games would be played in the Montreal Forum. Predictably, the Canadiens won the first match, 6–4. But when the series shifted to Chicago, Karakas shut out the Montrealers, 4–0. Suddenly, the Blackhawks were coming on strong. The final game was tied, 2–2, after regulation time. It was decided in Chicago's favor when Lou Trudel's long shot bounced off Paul Thompson and into the Montreal cage, although some observers insist that the puck was shot home by "Mush" March.

Now the Blackhawks were to face the equally aroused New York Americans sextet that had just routed its arch rivals in Manhattan, the Rangers, in three games. Once again, the Hawks would have the benefit of only one home game in the best-of-three series. The Americans opened with a 3–1 victory at Madison Square Garden. But when the series shifted to Chicago, Karakas took over again, and the team battled to the end of regulation time without a score. The game was settled in sudden-death overtime by Cully Dahlstrom. Chicago clinched the series with a third-period goal by Doc Romnes in the third game. The final score was 3–2, and the Black Hawks advanced into the Stanley Cup Finals against the Toronto Maple Leafs.

By now the betting odds had dropped considerably in Chicago's favor. But they soared again when it was learned that Karakas had suffered a broken big toe in the final game with the Americans. Karakas didn't realize the extent of the damage until he attempted to lace up his skates for the game with Toronto. He just couldn't make it, and the Hawks suddenly became desperate for a goaltender.

The Leafs were not in the least sympathetic to the Blackhawks' problem and summarily rejected requests for goaltending assistance. So the Chicago brass finally unearthed Alfie Moore, a minor-league, free-agent goalie, who reportedly was quaffing liquid refreshments in a Toronto pub when he was drafted to play goal for the Chicagoans. Moore answered the call and went into the Chicago nets on April 5, 1939, defeating Toronto, 3–1, in the opening game of the series at Maple Leaf Gardens. For the second game, the Hawks decided to try their luck with Paul Goodman, another minor-league goaltender. But this time Toronto rebounded with a strong 5–1 victory. It was obvious that if the Hawks were to win, they urgently required the services of Karakas. This was accomplished when he was outfitted with a special shield to protect his broken toe. The Hawks won the game before a crowd of 18,496 at Chicago Stadium on goals by Romnes and Carl Voss. The score was 2–1. By now the Leafs were reeling, and Chicago applied the *coup de grace* with relative ease in the fifth game, routing Toronto 4–1.

Walter "Turk" Broda of the Toronto Maple Leafs was renowned as one of the most successful clutch goalies of all time. How did he get the nickname "Turk"?

Born in Brandon, Manitoba, on May 15, 1914, Broda received his unusual nickname as a result of an English history lesson and his mass of freckles. At school one day, Broda listened intently as his teacher told a story about an English king who, behind his back, was called "Turkey Egg" by his intimates because of the huge freckles that dotted his round face. Shortly after the class was dismissed, one of Broda's schoolmates detected a similarity between his pal and the king. "Hey, look at Broda," the youngster laughed. "He looks like a turkey egg, too." The nickname, "Turkey Egg," caught on, but soon it was abbreviated to "Turk," and that was how Broda became known for the rest of his life. Neither his nickname nor his freckles ever negatively affected Turk's play. He won the Stanley Cup for Toronto in 1942, 1947, 1948, 1949, and 1951 before he retired.

Who was the Canadian sports editor who owned an NHL team while working for a newspaper?

Tommy Gorman, one of the most colorful hockey men in the game's history, was that man. In 1916, during the height of World War I, thousands of Canadians were marching off to war. At the time, Gorman was sports editor of the *Ottawa Citizen*. One day his newspaper ran a picture of a row of men—blocks long—lined up for their Stanley Cup playoff tickets. The *Citizen* indignantly inquired as to why these able-bodied men weren't overseas fighting for king and country.

The businessmen who owned the Ottawa club were appalled at the negative publicity conjured up by the *Citizen* photo and made an appointment with the sports editor, Gorman, whereupon they offered the team for sale. All they wanted Gorman to do was to pick up the debts, amounting to $1,400. Gorman dug up the money and eventually brought the Ottawa Senators into the NHL for the league's first season in 1917.

"Gorman," wrote *Vancouver Sun* columnist Jim Taylor, "had a couple of things going for him. He owned the team, and he ran the sports page. You'd be surprised at the coverage they got."

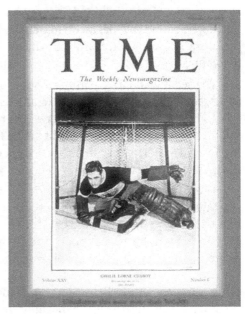

Which NHL club tried to "manufacture" a Jewish player in order to appeal to potential Jewish hockey fans?

A year before the Rangers became the second National Hockey League team in New York City, the Blueshirts were preceded by the New York Americans. The team called the Amerks arrived in 1925 to play in the 1925–26 season at the newly built Madison Square Garden. MSG then was located on Eighth Avenue between 49th and 50th Streets just off Times Square.

The Americans, who became an instant hit at the Garden, had to pay rent to the arena, which was fine during the club's

Lorne Chabot was given the name Chabotsky to make him seem Jewish; as shown here, he also made the cover of *Time* magazine on February 11, 1935, and was the first hockey player to do so.

first season, since the Amerks had no competition. But the arena ownership decided that it wanted its own MSG team, and that's how the Rangers were born.

Since the Amerks had cornered the market on NHL fans, the Rangers' brass turned to a boxing press agent named Johnny Bruno to help get fans. Bruno's advice to Blueshirts boss Lester Patrick was that his club needed both a Jewish player and an Italian player in order to lure Jewish and Italian fans to see the Rangers. Bruno scanned Patrick's roster and decided that goalie Lorne Chabot, a French-Canadian, could be palmed off as a Jew by changing his name to Chabotsky. While he was at it, Bruno picked out the name of Oliver Reinikka, a defenseman with Finnish roots. Bruno changed Oliver's name to Rocco and advertised him as an Italian.

Remarkably, the New York papers fell for the ruse and in their game box scores listed Chabot as Chabotsky and Reinikka as Rocco. Furthermore, it lasted all season, during which the Rangers fattened up on their own fan base—Jews, Italians, and many others who liked their winning style. But the hockey-savvy Canadiens didn't fall for Bruno's gimmick and always listed Lorne and Oliver by their correct names.

When was a coffin placed in an NHL club's dressing room prior to a Stanley Cup series?

In March 1922, the Toronto St. Patricks and Ottawa Senators staged a season-long battle for first place with the skaters from Canada's capital city finally taking the prize. However, the rivalry retained a razor-sharp consistency as the teams met in the opening playoff round that began on March 11, 1922, before a full house of 8,000 roaring fans in Toronto's Mutual Street Arena. The St. Pats surprised Ottawa in the opener, winning the game, 5–4, in what then was a two-game total-goals series.

The second and final game was scheduled for March 13 in Ottawa. The favored Senators required a two-goal lead to win the series from the St. Pats, but Toronto was carrying a hot hand in their nervous, restless rookie goalie, John Ross Roach. Yet, try as they might, the Senators could not beat goalie Roach. With Roach holding fast, Toronto held the formidable Senators to a 0–0 tie, good for a 5–4 goals advantage and the right to meet Vancouver for the Stanley Cup.

The city of Toronto was euphoric over the triumph and St. Pats players were overwhelmed with well-wishers when their train arrived in Union Station. When they arrived at their home arena, they found an elaborate coffin in the middle of their dressing room. "It was supposed to contain the last remains of the Ottawa team," wrote Foster Hewitt in his book *Hockey Night in Canada: The Maple Leafs' Story*. "The scene was dimly lighted with candles, from empty bottles that had served another purpose .... On the casket was a faded wreath, tagged with sympathy from Montreal Canadiens; nearby was a megaphone, painted in Ottawa colors and bearing a note to indicate that it had come from the Senators' coach, had served its purpose, and was now St. Patricks property. All through the dressing room, long green streamers trembled in the gentle breeze."

What NHL team won and lost the Stanley Cup on the same day?

In 1924, the Montreal Canadiens had defeated Ottawa, Vancouver, and Calgary in the playoffs to capture the league championship and, as a tribute to the winners, the citizens of Montreal hailed the Cup kings with a public reception. Following the reception, the Canadiens retired to the home of club owner Leo Dandurand for an informal get-together. Georges Vezina, Sprague Cleghorn, Sylvio Mantha, and Dandurand climbed into a Model-T Ford to make the trip. Climbing the Cote St. Antoine Road hill in Westmount, the Ford stalled, and all the occupants but the driver climbed out to give a push. Cleghorn, who had been carrying the hard-won Stanley Cup in his lap, deposited it on the curb at the roadside before joining in with the others pushing the car up the hill. When they reached the top, they got back into the car and resumed the trip. However, when they reached Dandurand's home, they all at once realized they didn't have the Cup.

Dandurand recalled the situation: "Sprague and I drove hurriedly back to the spot almost an hour after we had pushed the car up the hill. There was the Cup in all its shining majesty, still sitting on the curb of the busy street!"

Who was the NHL manager who nearly strangled one of his forwards to death?

When Tommy Gorman was running the Montreal Maroons, he was obsessed with the idea that too many veterans were carrying the puck behind the net before heading for enemy territory. His lectures on the subject proved fruitless, and finally, Tommy decided that a more drastic measure had to be taken. So, just prior to a practice session, he walked out onto the ice armed with a couple hundred yards of thick rope. With the help of a rink attendant, Gorman attached the rope to the goal net and extended it to each of the sideboards, thereby creating what amounted to a roadblock from the goal line to the end boards. The theory was simple: players were not to skate behind the net before orbiting on a rush.

Unfortunately, Gorman neglected to inform his players of the scheme, and Herb Cain, who was first on the ice, had no idea a barricade had been erected. Typical of an enthusiastic skater, Cain leaped on the ice and pursued the puck, which happened to be sitting a few feet from the rope. By this time Cain had picked up speed and was hurtling at about twenty miles an hour when he started what was to be a circling of the net with the puck. Cain never made it as his neck caught the rope with his entire body wrapped around it. Luckily, Cain was not seriously injured.

What is the "Curse of Muldoon"?

Some say the story is apocryphal, but it did appear in print, so others believe that it did happen. The "curse" is all about a fired coach seeking revenge against the boss who canned him and the team he had coached.

Pete Muldoon had been hired by the Chicago Blackhawks to be their new head coach in 1926–27. The club performed well, finishing third in the American Division and making the playoffs. The team scored the most goals in the NHL (115) but also allowed the most goals (116). Despite making the play-offs Muldoon was stunned when Blackhawks owner "Major" Frederic McLaughlin fired him at the start of the 1927–28 season.

That's the reality part. According to veteran Canadian columnist Jim Coleman, who for years wrote for the *Globe and Mail* in Toronto, Muldoon was so enraged that he supposedly yelled, "You'll see. I'll make sure you never win an NHL title!" at McLaughlin as he stormed out of the Blackhawks office.

If there was such a "curse," it certainly held. Chicago did not win a title while Muldoon was alive. Although the "curse" became a part of hockey lore, many insiders believe that it was a figment of Coleman's fertile imagination. Either way, it made for a good story.

A 1912 photograph of Pete Muldoon, who coached the Blackhawks in the 1920s. He supposedly cursed the team after being fired from the organization.

How did a trip to the movies result in Conn Smythe becoming the boss of the Toronto Maple Leafs instead of the New York Rangers?

In the decade following World War I, professional hockey enjoyed one of the most robust periods of expansion in its history. One city that participated in this growth was New York City. First the Americans, owned by bootlegger "Big" Bill Dwyer, caught on, inspiring a move to bring a second team to Madison Square Garden. Colonel John Hammond, an executive of the Garden, asked for a recommendation for a man to organize a group of players, which would become the New York Rangers.

Charles F. Adams, owner of the Boston Bruins, told Col. Hammond that the best available man for the recruitment job was Conn Smythe, a Torontonian who had been much decorated in World War I. Smythe had later managed the University of Toronto hockey clubs and would shepherd his club to Boston, where the Toronto skaters wowed Beantown fans. "Smythe is your man," said Adams. "You won't find any better."

Col. Hammond signed Smythe to a contract and, during the summer of 1926, Conn signed players for the new Rangers franchise. His choices, to say the least, were superb and included many who ultimately would be inducted into the Hockey Hall of Fame, including Bill Cook, Frank Boucher, and Murray Murdoch. When the players gathered at a Toronto hotel for pre-season training, Smythe felt content. His team, he believed, would be at or near the top of the standings at season's end.

One night after meeting at the training camp hotel, Smythe decided to take the night off and go to a movie with his wife. Why not? The club was in order, and everyone seemed content. But when Mr. and Mrs. Smythe returned from the theater, Col. Hammond was sitting in the lobby. He beckoned to Smythe.

"Where have you been?" Col. Hammond demanded. Smythe wasted no time telling his boss that he had taken his wife out to dinner and a movie. Col Hammond was unimpressed. "Well, that night out has just cost us one of the greatest players in the game. The Toronto St. Pats just sold Babe Dye to Chicago. We could have had him for $14,000." Less than penitent, Smythe shot back: "I wouldn't want Babe Dye on my team no matter what price. He's not the type of player we need."

Fit to be tied at both Smythe's impudence and confidence in himself, Col. Hammond phoned Barney Stanley, coach of the Blackhawks, and related Smythe's appraisal of Dye. "Why that Smythe must be crazy," shouted Stanley. "It only proved how little he knows about hockey players. I can't understand, Colonel, why you keep a man like that when there's an outstanding hockey man like Lester Patrick loose and ready to be signed."

With that, Col. Hammond hung up, summoned Smythe to his office, and told him that his services were no longer required by the Rangers. "Smythe was flat on his back," said his pal broadcaster Foster Hewitt, "and few would have blamed him if he had stayed down. But that wasn't his way of fighting. He was determined to convince himself, as well as others, that Hammond had made a big mistake. He told his friend that he would go out and organize another team that would beat the pants off the one he had organized for New York."

Smythe went about the business of trying to purchase the Toronto St. Patricks so that he could proudly re-enter the NHL. It took him one year from the time the Rangers had fired him for Conn to come through the front door of the major leagues again. In 1927 the St. Pats were put up for sale, and on February 14, 1927, a group headed by Smythe and J. P. Bickell bought the team with Smythe taking over as club governor. The name St. Patricks was officially dropped, and the team became known as they are today, the Toronto Maple Leafs. And all because Mr. and Mrs. Smythe went to dinner and a movie!

As for Babe Dye, the man Col. Hammond had so desperately wanted for his Rangers, he became injury-riddled as a Blackhawk, missed the entire 1927–28 season, and played only one more NHL game before being permanently shipped to the minors.

What two professional hockey teams clashed in the Duck Pond–Cow Barn series?

Moose Jaw and Weyburn, Saskatchewan. There were splendid hockey rivalries among the 13 senior clubs in Saskatchewan during the Depression years, but none was as wild as the meetings between Moose Jaw and Weyburn. During those years, they held a series called the Duck Pond–Cow Barn Series because the Moose Jaw team called the Weyburn rink a duck pond and the Weyburn team described the Moose Jaw rink as a cow barn.

They had to add special trains to accommodate the fans for that series, but the rinks could not pack in all of the avid Saskatchewan fans. Those who made it in were treated to viewing the Weyburn coach's duck hunting suit at his home rink while decoys were thrown on the ice. In Moose Jaw, his team came out leading a cardboard cow on wheels, which one player squatted beside and milked to the delight of the large crowd.

Which hockey brother act prompted a New York writer to pen a poem about them?

Hall of Famers Bill and Bun Cook and Frank Boucher formed the New York Rangers' Bread Line from 1926 to 1937.

The Cook Brothers, Bun and Bill. Few sportswriters were as droll as Harold C. Burr, who covered the Rangers for the *New York Sun* and later the *Brooklyn Eagle*. A tall, delightful man, Burr occasionally was moved to verse in describing Lester Patrick's Blueshirts during the Thirties. Burr's favorites were the Cook Brothers, Bill and Bun. One night, dazzled by their footwork, Burr composed the following bit of doggerel about his heroes:

> Old adages live because they are true;
> If they weren't, they wouldn't survive.
> But once in a while there are few
> That shouldn't be kept alive.
> In hockey, where speed and grit hold forth,
> Some sayings sound awfully funny.
> "Too many cooks spoil the broth."
> Did you ever meet Bill and Bunny?

What was the most turbulent Christmas night game in National Hockey League history?

When it comes to riotous hockey games, few could match the collision between the Boston Bruins and Philadelphia Quakers at Boston Garden on December 25, 1930. "It provided some of hockey's wildest scenes," said former Bruins publicist Herb Ralby, and "shattered all those Yuletide preachings about 'Peace on Earth, Good Will to All.' Actually, the game started out very Christmas-like until George Owen of the Bruins and Philly's Hib Milks squared off." Soon, everyone on the ice was slugging away, and the reserves joined the fray by jumping over the boards to get into the act.

"Philadelphia had a rookie defenseman called D'Arcy Coulson," Ralby recalled. "He was the son of an Ottawa millionaire and a player who was building up something of a record for himself when it came to fighting. He was in the penalty box when it all started. He leaped out and grabbed Eddie Shore as his opponent."

One of the most one-sided fights involved Boston's Dit Clapper and Wally Kilrea of Philadelphia. Boston goalie Tiny Thompson kept picking Kilrea up, and Dit kept knocking him down. "They didn't have a three knock-down rule for fights in those days," said Bruins trainer Win Green. "Dit must have knocked him down a dozen times."

Boston's riot police was summoned to the Garden to restore order. "When they finally got some peace and quiet," said Ralby, "there was one sad figure on the Boston bench. That was Marty Barry, a pretty good guy with his fists who somehow never got into the brawls. Bruins coach Art Ross seemed aware that Barry had felt left out. "If it will make you feel better," said Ross, "get out there and when the referee drops the puck, take a punch at their center." It so happened that Philadelphia's center was Jerry Lowrey, a battler himself and somewhat of a nut case, as things turned out. "Lowrey didn't wait for the referee to drop the puck," said Ralby, "as he lined up opposite Barry and suddenly dropped his stick and smacked the surprised Bruins right in the mouth, and the battle was on again."

Which hockey player was assessed a penalty while unconscious?

Stanley Crossett was handed a penalty while out cold during his brief, one-year career in 1930–31. Crossett was a defenseman for the Philadelphia Quakers who apparently didn't listen too well. The rookie was warned about trying to split the Detroit Falcons' defensive pairing of Reg Noble and Harvey "Rocky" Rockburn, whose specialty was sandwiching unsuspecting attackers.

In the second period of a Quakers–Falcons contest, Crossett tried to split the defensive duo but was nailed hard. He went flying into the end boards and was knocked unconscious by the ensuing collision with the boards when his stick was driven into his chin.

Meanwhile, Crosett had unknowingly gained revenge on Rockburn. While in midair, his stick had slashed Rocky over his eye, resulting in a bloody gash for the Falcons' blueliner and a five-minute major penalty to Crossett, who lay in a daze on the ice.

When was a hockey manager thrown out of a game only to be saved by the owner of the opposing team?

On March 15, 1932, the Toronto Maple Leafs were playing the Boston Bruins at Boston Garden. The referee was Bill Stewart, a popular, major-league umpire who later would coach the Chicago Blackhawks. With the score tied, in the first period, Stewart gave Toronto goalie Lorne Chabot a two-minute penalty for tripping Cooney Weiland of the Bruins. In those days, the goaltender himself had to leave the ice and sit out his penalty in the penalty box. Chabot skated to the sin bin, and his place in the nets was taken by defenseman Red Horner. Within a minute, the Bruins scored on Horner, but Chabot had to remain in the penalty box because 1932 rules held that the player must serve his full term no matter how many goals are scored.

At the time, the Leafs were managed by Conn Smythe and coached by Dick Irvin. Unhappy with Horner, Irvin replaced him in the nets with Alex Levinsky, but in no time at all, the Bruins beat Levinsky, and Chabot's penalty had not yet elapsed. Next, Irvin moved King Clancy between the pipes, and again, Boston scored. Like Irvin, Smythe was getting more and more furious behind the bench, and when Stewart skated near the Toronto bench, Smythe leaned over the dasher boards and grabbed the referee's sweater.

Stewart ordered Smythe to leave the bench, but the Leafs manager refused. Stewart then summoned Boston Garden police and told them to get Smythe out of there. The Toronto players would have none of that, and they formed a corporal's guard around Smythe.

At this point it appeared that a full-scale riot was about to be detonated, and nobody realized it more than Charles Adams, president of the Bruins. Swiftly, Adams descended upon the combatants, conferring with the police and referee Stewart. Soon, cooler heads prevailed, and everyone remained in the same seat he had occupied before the brouhaha had begun.

When did a skating bear invade Madison Square Garden ice?

One of the funniest men connected with the New York Rangers organization was Tom Lockhart, president of the Amateur Hockey Association of the United States throughout the forties, fifties, and sixties. During the thirties, Lockhart was supervising the amateur hockey games at Madison Square Garden and was also managing the New York Rovers, a first-rate, amateur team. He spiced up the Sunday afternoon hockey intermissions with ice-skating exhibitions, featuring a young Norwegian artist. The petite charmer was Sonja Henie, who went on to become a millionaire star of movies and ice shows.

"Some of my promotions were a little bizarre," Lockhart recalled. "Once when the Hershey Bears were coming to town I was told about a live bear that could skate. So I thought it would be a great idea to have the animal lead the Bears hockey team onto the ice."

Lockhart explained that the bear was outfitted with a pair of skates and handled them well. But his trainer couldn't stand on his blades, and it caused an uproar among the crowd. "As soon as the bear stepped on the ice," Lockhart remembered, "the trainer fell flat on his face. The bear kept skating around pulling the trainer all over the ice."

Rudy Pilous, who coached the Blackhawks to a Stanley Cup in 1961 and a former player for Lockhart's Rovers, was an admirer of Lockhart's promotions. "One day I was sitting in the penalty box," said Pilous, "and I look up and see three fights going on in the stands. Tom was running over to the box to give it to the referees. All of the sudden, he looks up at the stands and sees all the fights going on. Then he turns to me and says, 'Gee whiz, there's too much action goin' on here for three dollars. I gotta raise the prices.'"

Hall of Famer Bill Chadwick, who played amateur hockey in New York, once said that Lockhart persuaded him to become a hockey referee in the late thirties. "Tom didn't pay much money," said Chadwick. "In fact, I remember handling four games a week and getting fifty-five dollars—and I had to pay all my expenses. It was then I realized that Lockhart was destined to be a great hockey executive."

In 1939, a dashing leading man made two movies—one in which he played hockey, and one in which he wore a mask. Who was he, and what were the movies?

Long before the invention of the goalie's mask, Louis Hayward played the banished twin brother of King Louis XIV in the movie *The Man in the Iron Mask*. In the same year, Hayward starred as the title character in *The Duke of West Point* whose ice heroics highlighted the film's climax, a hockey match against the Royal Military College of Canada. That episode was based on fact, since the Army team and its Canadian counterpart often met in those pre-World War II days.

Who was responsible for the first "lady's hat trick" in hockey history?

The hat trick—scoring three goals in a game—is a feat many players have accomplished in the game's history, but the first lady's hat trick was a genuinely unique event. It has been turned by only one player, Montreal Canadien Butch Bouchard. It happened this way. The wife of Montreal defenseman Glen Harmon owned a high-class hat shop in Montreal, and Mrs. Bouchard harbored a strong desire for one of Mrs. Harmon's higher-priced creations.

Glen Harmon—self-appointed delivery boy—explained to Bouchard that since his wife liked it so much, he should buy it for her. Bouchard got one look at the price tag and said, "No dice."

Did John Wayne ever play a hockey star in the movies?

The Duke, as Wayne was known, did star in the 1937 release "Idol of the Crowds." While it's doubtful he did his own skating, Wayne portrayed the team's star, who overcomes an injury to lead his team to victory.

Harmon then offered Bouchard the hat free of charge—if he scored two goals in the game that night. Bouchard, who tallied a grand total of four goals in the previous 40 games, rose to the occasion, leading the Habs to a 2–0 victory over the Detroit Red Wings and winning himself a pretty new hat.

It is, therefore, not only the only lady's hat trick, but the only hat trick turned with only two goals scored to win it.

Which NHL Hall of Famer played his entire career under an "assumed" name?

Stan Mikita. The smooth-skating Chicago Blackhawks center began his life as Stanislas Gvoth in Sokolce, Czechoslovakia. At that time, the country was divided into three provinces—Bohemia, Moravia, and Slovakia. Sokolce happened to be in Slovakia, which is now a republic. On Stan's birth date, May 20, 1940, the Nazi war machine was spreading its tentacles across Europe, and although the Slovaks were ostensibly running their own province, life was brutal under the Nazi fist.

Sokolce was a depressing village during the occupation, and nothing about the Gvoth home did much to alleviate the dismal atmosphere. Four-year-old Stanislas and his family shared the house with four other families. "Each of us had two rooms, bedroom, all in one. And we had a little kitchen area in the other. The kitchen was down the driveway a piece."

Almost two months to the day before Stanislas' fourth birthday, the Czechoslovak government-in-exile broadcast from London, ordering its people to join "an army uprising." He didn't realize the Nazi occupation forces were casting a wary eye on the Eastern front, where the massive hardware of the Soviet Union had begun rolling toward the Slovakian border.

Once the German forces had surrendered, for the Gvoths, one war ended and a new one began. The Russian conquerors permitted the Czech government-in-exile to return to its homeland, but they lopped off Ruthenia, Czechoslovakia's easternmost province, and added it to the Soviet Union.

The relentless Russian demands continued until February 25, 1948, when the communists seized complete control of the government. Czech president Edvard Benes resigned June 7, following a parliamentary election in which the communists and their allies were unopposed.

Unknown to Stanislas, his aunt and uncle, Anne and Joe Mikita, who lived in St. Catharines, Ontario, had written to the

Stan Mikita at the 2009 Blackhawks Convention opening ceremony.

Gvoths early in the war and half humorously, half seriously suggested that they adopt Stanislas. Unable to bear children of their own, the Mikitas felt that perhaps the Gvoths would allow them to bring Stanislas back to Canada with them.

To the Gvoths, the family reunion in their homeland would be a time where the Mikitas would be taken through the countryside, renewing old acquaintances. They would drink good Czech Pilsner beer, sing, have fun, and allow Stanislas and his older brother, George, to meet their relatives from far-off Canada.

But unknown to Stanislas, the Mikitas had not forgotten the innocent exchange of letters early in the war. The Gvoths' depressing life weighed on their minds, and they considered their desire to adopt Stanislas.

The Gvoths agreed to the adoption. "Because of the restriction," Stan admitted, "that was the only way they could get me out of Czechoslovakia. My parents and my uncle and aunt had told me what was what and I promised I wouldn't cry."

Thus, Stanislas Gvoth became Stan Mikita, National Hockey League center who helped Chicago win the 1961 Stanley Cup.

Which Hall of Famer, who became a minor-league club owner, fancied himself a chiropractor, referee-baiter, and amateur boxer?

That man was NHL Hall of Fame defenseman Eddie Shore, who starred for the Boston Bruins and later the New York Americans. After Shore retired as a player, he bought the Springfield Indians of the American Hockey League. Notorious for his eccentricities, Shore took a personal interest in the physical well-being of his players as his goaltender, Jacques Caron, once discovered.

"Shore considered himself a capable chiropractor," said Caron. "One night I'd played well and he phoned me about 1 A.M. and told me to get right over to the rink. I asked why and he said he'd noticed me move funny on the last goal I let in and he wanted to adjust my spine. So I went there in the middle of the night and cracked me.

"Eddie liked to try that on other players but they all didn't go for it. We had another guy on the team, Wayne Larkin, and Shore wanted to crack him but Wayne said there was no way he'd even let him touch him. So during the game, Shore sneaked up behind him on the bench and snap, crack, he adjusted Wayne before he knew what hit him. Another guy on our club was walking down the street minding his own business, when Shore ran across through traffic, grabbed him right on the spot and cracked his spine. Said he was walking strangely."

When Shore owned the Indians, they played in a quaint, old building in West Springfield called the Eastern States Coliseum. Shore ruled the club from the Coliseum in the manner of a king on his throne, and Heaven help the man who crossed him, especially the referee and ice cops from other clubs.

"If he didn't like the officiating," Caron went on, "Eddie would go into the announcer's booth, grab the microphone and give the referee hell. One time Ian Cushenan from Buffalo fought with one of our guys who didn't put up much of a battle. Shore jumped on the ice, chased Cushenan all over and took him on. And Shore had to be well into his '60s at the time."

Name the hockey writer whose son became rock star Neil Young.

The columnist-author was Scott Young, one of the best writers on hockey. A journalist who graced the pages of Toronto's *Globe and Mail*, Young was also sports editor of the late *Toronto Telegram*. Although many regard Scott's most notable achievement as fathering Neil Young, the rock star and one-time member of Crosby, Stills, Nash, and Young, the elder Young did well for himself, co-authoring Leafs coach Punch Imlach's books. Scott was sharpest when taking on the NHL stuffed shirts. He was once banned from Montreal's Forum—although he managed to sneak into the arena. The Habs' bosses were upset about negative remarks Young had written about their team. After sneaking into the arena, Young seated himself behind Canadiens manager Frank Selke, Sr.—who was the one who had banned him from the Forum in the first place. Another time, Young described a Chicago Blackhawks' $1 million offer for Toronto's Frank Mahovlich as "hokum and bunkum." Shortly thereafter, the NHL invoked a few other unofficial sanctions against Young. A prolific writer on many subjects, Young later left the sports pages to write a general column for the *Globe and Mail*.

Which NHL forward changed his name to accommodate newsmen who couldn't spell it in the first place?

Steve Wojciechowski. There may have been other NHL players with 13 letters in their last name, but only Steve W-O-J-C-I-E-C-H-O-W-S-K-I of Fort William, Ontario, had his name changed so that writers and broadcasters could more easily pronounce and write it. Now, if you were Steve Wojciechowski, what would you change it to—Smith? Well, Steve became *Wochy*. By the way, he played right wing for the Detroit Red Wings in 1944–45 and had a fair year, 19 goals and 20 assists for 39 points in 49 games. Then, World War II ended, and the better players returned from service. Steve played in the Red Wings farm system and enjoyed a brief NHL comeback in 1946–47. By that time a lot of people could pronounce his name, but, alas, Steve couldn't score anymore. In five NHL games during his second time around, Wochy got exactly no goals, no assists, no points, no penalties. He did, however, thrive in the minors thereafter—with Indianapolis, Philadelphia, and Cleveland. Who knows how he would have fared had he remained Wojciechowski?

Who was the NHL trainer who played goal for three different big clubs?

Ross "Lefty" Wilson. In the old, pre-expansion days, when NHL teams carried only one regular goalie, a substitute was occasionally needed when the first-liner was seriously injured. Lefty Wilson, a Toronto native who played amateur hockey during World War II for the Toronto Navy team, was one such sub. Lefty played pro hockey briefly in the Detroit Red Wings system, but the Wings promoted him by hiring him as a trainer—and spare goalie. He appeared between the pipes for Detroit (1953–54), Toronto (1955–56), and Boston (1957–58), allowing only one goal in what amounted to one and one-half games played. After that, Lefty stuck to the trainer's job, which included yelling at referees and linesmen every ten minutes on the minute. Wilson was very good at that, possessing perhaps the most grating voice in NHL annals.

Which Hall of Fame goaltender blew a prediction and thereby inspired a sardonic poem?

Bill Durnan, the Montreal Canadiens Hall of Famer. During the 1947 playoffs, Durnan delivered a quote ridiculing the Habs' 1947 Cup Final foes, the Toronto Maple Leafs. Since his Montrealers were heavily favored to beat the Leafs, Durnan wondered out loud, "How did the Maple Leafs get into the playoffs?" Shortly thereafter, Toronto columnist Jim Coleman wrote a ditty to Durnan after the Leafs eliminated the Canadiens and won the Cup. It went as follows:

> A goalie should eschew prediction
> Regardless of any predilection
> For teacup leaves or crystal balls
> Window-tappings or psychic calls
> Durnan—Willyum—forget the muck!
> And simply try to stop the puck!

Which hockey player was booed out of his home rink and, eventually, his uniform?

It was Allan Stanley who, ironically, would eventually be voted into the Hall of Fame. A star defenseman with the Providence Reds of the American Hockey League, Stanley was obtained by the New York Rangers in 1948–49 for the then astronomical $60,000 worth of players and cash. Except for one season, the Rangers never had a good team while he was with them, but it wasn't Stanley's fault. The only time they had been in the playoffs in 14 years was his second season with the team. Eventually, he was named team captain, but then the Rangers couldn't win anything for four years, and the Madison Square Garden crowd became extremely hostile toward the thoughtful, clever, but lumbering Stanley. He became the scapegoat for the 15,000 faithful.

Allan Stanley in a Maple Leafs jersey.

271

"They got to me all right," Stanley admitted, "and I began running all over the place instead of playing my regular game. It got so that when the coach looked down the bench for substitutions, I'd find myself ducking behind the other players. I didn't want to play. It wasn't that I was afraid of the crowd, I just didn't feel like playing and didn't think I'd do the team any good."

Rangers manager Frank Boucher was sensitive about his defenseman's problem and, finally, decided to play Stanley only in road games to protect him from the Garden boo-birds. That annoyed the Garden bosses and, finally, Boucher traded Stanley—and Nick Mickoski—to Chicago for Bill Gadsby and Pete Conacher. "The fans," said Boucher, "booed him right out of a Ranger uniform. Stanley was a fine player but the customers didn't like his style." Others did and Stanley remained in the NHL for more than a decade and a half after he left New York.

Ironically, Allan's game seemed to improve wherever he played. When Punch Imlach brought Stanley to Toronto at the start of the 1960s, Allan was instrumental in helping the Maple Leafs win three straight Stanley Cups in 1962, 1963, and 1964. Once, when he returned to Madison Square Garden to face his former team, the Rangers, Stanley played yet another stellar game. Following the contest, a young New York fan followed Allan down 49th Street and finally ran up to him with a question: "Mister Stanley," the lad said, "how come you didn't play so good for us when you were a Ranger?" Stanley looked plaintively at the youngster and calmly, almost sadly, replied, "But I did, young man, I *did*."

Which all-time great's career almost came to an early end in the 1950 playoffs?

As a result of a collision with Toronto's Ted Kennedy in Game 1 of the 1950 Stanley Cup Semifinals, Gordie Howe's career almost ended when he suffered a skull fracture. Miraculously, he bounced back, and the following year won the Hart Trophy. He would continue to play pro hockey for another 30 years.

Who was the Stanley Cup hero who became the sports editor of a Canadian newspaper?

Pentti Lund was a defensive-oriented left wing who played for the New York Rangers during the 1949–50 season. Although he was born in Finland, Lund learned his hockey in Canada and played minor-league hockey for the Boston Olympics before reaching the National Hockey League.

In the playoffs held in March 1950, Lund's Rangers met the favored Montreal Canadiens. New York coach Lynn Patrick assigned Lund the dubious chore of guarding Montreal's high-powered Maurice "Rocket" Richard. Lund not only checked Richard to a standstill but wound up as the scoring star of the series, as his Rangers upset Montreal four games to one. The likeable Lund continued to star for New York in the Stanley Cup Finals against Detroit, which lasted seven games and went into double overtime in Game 7 before the Red Wings won. In over a dozen playoff games, Pentti scored six goals and five assists. Later, he was traded to the Boston Bruins. Lund eventually became sports editor of the Thunder Bay *Times-News* in Thunder Bay, Ontario.

What accomplished TV producer-director once played goal both for and against the New York Rangers?

During the late 1950s, Brooklyn-born Arnee Nocks, an amateur goaltender from the Manhattan Beach section of Brooklyn, had become an eminent television producer and director, handling such shows as *Kraft Television Theatre, Captain Video and His Video Rangers*, and *The Mike Wallace Interview*.

Nocks developed his passion for goaltending at the Brooklyn Ice Palace and eventually befriended many Rangers players, who appreciated his style and enthusiasm. When the NHL club needed a practice goalie, Nocks was contacted. His competence was applauded by such Hall of Fame Rangers as Bill Gadsby and Andy Bathgate. After he became the franchise's official practice goalie he, in a sense, played both for and against the Blueshirts.

What are some unusual birthplaces of well-known hockey stars?

Hockey Star	Birthplace
Ken Hodge	Birmingham, England
Willi Plett	Asuncion, Paraguay
Rick Chartraw	Caracas, Venezuela
Rod Langway	Taipei, Taiwan
Nick Fotiu	Staten Island, New York
Ivan Boldirev	Zrenjanin, Yugoslavia
Ed Kea	Weesp, Netherlands
Stan Mikita	Sokolce, Czechoslovakia
Walter Tkaczuk	Emsdetten, Germany
Bobby Nystrom	Stockholm, Sweden

Which coach piloted his team to the seventh game of the Stanley Cup Finals, quit his job, and signed with a minor-league team but started the next season coaching another NHL club?

Lynn Patrick was coach of the New York Rangers during the 1949–50 National Hockey League season. Although the Broadway Blueshirts had a modest record during the regular season, finishing fourth, they upset the Montreal Canadiens in the playoff semifinals and then extended the favored Detroit Red Wings to double overtime in the seventh and final game.

Lionized as a hero on Broadway, Patrick nonetheless was unhappy in New York and had actually made up his mind before the playoffs had begun that he would quit the Rangers' job. "I didn't want to live in New York City anymore," Patrick explained. Following the playoffs, Lynn resigned from the Rangers and signed to coach the Victoria Cougars of the Pacific Coast Hockey League, a team owned by his father, the venerable Silver Fox of hockey, Lester Patrick.

According to Lynn, he was fully prepared to lead the Victoria sextet, but two months after he had resettled his family in British Columbia, he received a call from Boston Bruins manager Art Ross with an offer to take the team's head coaching job. "I wouldn't have taken the job with Lester if I really thought I was in line for the Boston job," said Lynn. "Right up to the time Art called me, I had no desire to take another post in the East. But Ross was persuasive, and he made a great salary offer—

Lynn Patrick

twelve thousand dollars, which was big money then—and I accepted right there over the phone. Lester understood. I think he was expecting something like this to happen."

Who was the restaurateur who helped a hockey team win games with a potion?

The bistro owner was Manhattan's Gene Leone, who operated Mama Leone's restaurant on West 48th Street around the corner from the then Madison Square Garden on Eighth Avenue. An ardent Rangers fan, Leone was disappointed in the club's performance during the 1950–51 season and offered his friend, team manager Frank Boucher, an idea. Gene promised to concoct a potion that, after drinking, would enable the Rangers players to win more games.

The strange liquid soon became known as Leone's Magic Elixir, and a *World-Telegram* sportswriter named Jim Burchard wrote profusely about it. At the time of the elixir's first concoction, the Rangers' record was well below .500 by early December, and unless some sort of miracle could be produced, the future appeared bleak. That's when Leone distilled some of his delectable juices, mixed them with vintage wine from his cellar, and produced the "wonder drink" for the Rangers.

Leone perfected his formula and poured it into a large, black bottle about three times the size of a normal whiskey bottle. With appropriate fuss and fanfare, "Leone's Magic Elixir" was carried into the Rangers' dressing room, where such heroes as Don "Bones" Raleigh, Pentti Lund, Frankie Eddolls, Neil Colville, and Zellio Toppazzini quaffed the brew.

To say the results were amazing would be an understatement. They were hallucinatory. After drinking the mixture, the Rangers began to win and win and win. By early January they had lost only two of their eleven games, but observers insisted the real test would come when the Blueshirts visited Toronto, where they hadn't had a victory for ages.

Now the fun started. Leone demanded that the magic elixir, whose formula was so secret that he wouldn't even trust it to paper, be prepared at the last possible moment. This was done on a Saturday afternoon. When the elixir was ready, Leone turned it over to Burchard, who boarded a plane for Toronto. The plan was for Jim to arrive just before game time and present the potion to the Rangers.

The Rangers went out on the ice and performed like supermen. Within seven minutes of the first period, they scored three goals and coasted to a 4–2 win.

Did an NHL club ever play all its "home" games of the Stanley Cup Finals on the road?

Due to an annual invasion of Madison Square Garden by the Ringling Bros. and Barnum & Bailey Circus, the Rangers were forced to play two of their "home" games of the 1950 Stanley Cup Finals on the neutral ice of Maple Leaf Gardens in Toronto. Their opponent—the Detroit Red Wings—had captured the opener 4–1 at their own Olympia Stadium. The second and third games were played to a packed house in Toronto. The supposedly neutral Toronto boosters "adopted" the Rangers as their own and rooted for New York as passionately as they would have done so for the Leafs.

The Rangers split the two Toronto contests, winning 3–1, losing 4–0. The Blueshirts were now in a dilemma: Detroit led two games to one with all remaining games to be played on rival Detroit ice. The Rangers evened the series on Don Raleigh's overtime score, then took a 3–2 lead in games when Raleigh slipped the disc behind the Detroit netminder Harry Lumley for a 2–1 victory.

The Wings were not about to fold, however. They tied the series at three after their sixth-game win and set the stage for Game 7. In the second overtime, Pete Babando took a George Gee pass and whizzed the puck past goalie Charlie Rayner. The low screen shot accounted for the lone Detroit goal, but it defeated the Blueshirts for the Stanley Cup. The embattled Rangers, though playing valiantly, had to accept defeat—on the road, thanks to the circus.

Which National Hockey League team believed that it once had a "contract" with Santa Claus?

Even when they were a bad team, the Rangers loved to play games on Christmas Day night because they felt that Santa Claus was on their side. In the days prior to the NHL expansion and the formation of a players' association, it was traditional for teams to play games on Christmas night. During Christmas night games through the early 1950s, the Rangers almost never lost a game on December 25. Pretty soon General John Reed Kilpatrick, president of the Rangers, got the distinct impression that Santa Claus and his club had a "contract."

Once, the general had read an editorial in the old *New York Sun* that stated without equivocation that there *was* a Santa Claus, and being a reader of long standing, he had come to believe in that newspaper's slogan: "If it's in *The Sun*, it's so!" That being the case, he was willing to go along with Santa, and the record proved that Kris Kringle was especially good to his men. There was one stretch indeed, from 1930 to 1950, when the Rangers didn't lose once on Christmas night.

During the early 1950s, the Blueshirts' press agent Herb Goren made the most of it. "You couldn't tell The General," said Goren, "or the legion of Ranger followers, that this was pure coincidence! Of course not. This was Santa at work, seeing to it that the Rangers would not be disappointed by his presentation, casting a spell over the opposition in such a way that made everyone in New York believe the big city was Santa's favorite."

When did British royalty attend an NHL hockey game?

The date was October 13, 1951. The place: Toronto's Maple Leaf Gardens. The time was a Saturday hockey night in Canada. Everybody there was just a trifle on the jittery side as the pending royal visit to the Carlton Street hockey temple drew closer.

The advance planning had been made and carried out. The royal box, in which Princess Elizabeth and the duke of Edinburgh would sit, had been specifically equipped with correct flags and new chairs, plus a fresh coat of paint. A half hour before the royal arrival, the arena was filled with nervous tension and apprehension.

In the Maple Leafs dressing room, Captain Ted Kennedy sat wringing his hands, pondering the protocol of a formal introduction to the royal pair. There were a great number of perplexing questions. How to bow, what to say, what to call them. Teeder wasn't the only Leaf going through this agony. The Chicago Blackhawks' boss Bill Tobin and his captain, defenseman Jack Stewart, were experiencing the same nervous qualms, as game time drew near.

But as it turned out, there was no need for the anxiety. Princess Elizabeth and the duke—Prince Philip—quickly put everybody at ease. When they entered the royal box, the duke insisted that Conn Smythe sit with the princess while he sat directly behind with Reg Shaw, acting potentate of the Rameses Shrine.

With the husky Royal Canadian Mounties and Toronto police heavily in attendance, the game began. After only a few minutes, it appeared that the royal visit would extend past the original estimate of fifteen minutes. The princess, who had looked tired and weary upon arriving, started to come alive with the commencement of the game. Her eyes sparkled as she intently followed the play, she recoiled slightly at heavy checks, and she smiled and talked frequently with Mr. Smythe.

She was enjoying herself, and so was the duke. They were spellbound by the action on ice, and as each minute on the clock ticked off, the spell became deeper and deeper. The royal visit turned out to be a smashing success. The royal pair were captivated by the game of hockey, and the fans in the Garden were equally thrilled by the royal pair and their attendance at a Toronto home game.

How did a defenseman help a referee throw a fan out of a game?

One night, in the early fifties, during a game in Boston Garden, referee Bill Chadwick called a penalty on Jim Thomson of the Toronto Maple Leafs; the call led to some heated words between Thomson and Chadwick and resulted in a misconduct penalty for the irate Leaf. Still smoldering, Thomson finally climbed into the penalty box to serve his time. Not long after Chadwick called one against the Bruins, and as he skated over to the scorers' bench to report the misdeed, a Boston fan belted him on the head with a heavy object, knocking him to the ice.

Chadwick, dazed from the blow, scrambled to his feet and challenged the fan. It looked to be the beginning of a red-hot rhubarb, when a player suddenly grabbed Chadwick from behind and told him to cool down or he'd get into trouble and advised him to call the cops and have the fan ejected from the arena.

Calm overtook Chadwick's furor, and he proceeded to take the wise action, and the fan was removed. Later, Chadwick realized it had been his recent antagonist, Jim Thomson, who had jumped in and prevented him from taking personal action against the garbage-throwing spectator.

Did an octopus ever figure in the outcome of an NHL game?

Yes. This bizarre episode occurred in the 1952 Detroit Red Wings' playoff series at Olympia Stadium. The Wings had already won their first seven playoff games, and two diehard fans wanted to ensure the Wings' eighth consecutive victory.

Red Wings boosters Pete and Jerry Cusimano had a father who owned a Detroit fish store, and that fact of life led them to thinking, "Why don't we throw an octopus on the ice for good luck? It's got eight legs and that might be good for eight straight wins." Hence, on April 15, 1952, Pete and Jerry heaved a live octopus over the protective glass at Olympia Stadium and it landed on the ice with a loud SPLAT! Detroit went on to win the game and the Stanley Cup.

The octopus episode inspired such a wave of publicity that each time the Red Wings made the playoffs, more octopi reached the Olympia ice. And when the Olympia was razed and replaced by Joe Louis Arena, the eight-tentacled tradition continued and still is in vogue.

Which skater flunked as an NHL regular but made the grade as a hockey interpreter?

Adolph Frank "Aggie" Kukulowicz was the aspiring big-leaguer. When the New York Rangers were floundering near the bottom of the National Hockey League in the early fifties, they frequently looked to their junior affiliates in and around Winnipeg, Manitoba, for potential regulars. In 1952–53, Rangers manager Frank Boucher believed he had found such a phenom in Aggie Kukulowicz.

Sure enough, the tall, gangly forward produced a goal in his very first start with the Rangers and appeared capable of bigger and better things. However, Kukulowicz

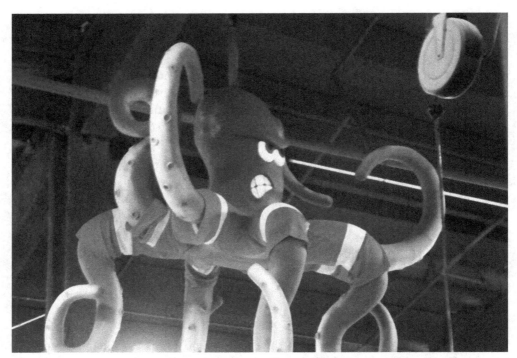

Al the Octopus is the Detroit Red Wings mascot. Al is named after Al Sobotka, the head ice manager at Joe Louis Arena; and the octopus was chosen because of the tradition of throwing the sea creatures onto the ice rink for good luck.

never scored again. Boucher dropped him after three games in 1952–53 but gave Aggie another trial a year later. Once more, Kukulowicz missed the boat and returned to the minors. He later took a job with Air Canada, which stationed him in Moscow, Russia.

Kukulowicz eventually gained hockey fame but in a different way. Whenever Canadian teams came to Moscow for hockey tournaments, Aggie always managed to be on hand as their official translator, thereby gaining more newspaper publicity than he ever did as a player. Aggie's presence also was noted during the 1979 Challenge Cup series in New York City between the Soviet National Team and the NHL All-Stars. Interpreting both for the media and the players, Kukulowicz did more talking than the entire Soviet team.

Who was the NHL defenseman whose name was fractured by Brooklynites?

Benedict Francis "Benny" Woit symbolized the unobtrusive, workmanlike defenseman who helped build the Detroit Red Wings' power team of the early fifties. Woit meshed well with the flashier and more skilled Hall of Fame defensemen Red Kelly and Marcel Pronovost. Benny also hit hard and supported his goaltender. He broke in with the Red Wings (1950–51) and remained with them through 1954–55, when he was dealt to the then-hapless Chicago Blackhawks. That was enough to ruin anyone's career. In two years he was out of the Bigs. Brooklynites pronounced his name "Wert." Once, when Benny was injured at Madison Square Garden, somebody from Brooklyn shouted, "Wert got hoit!"

What caused fans in Montreal to provoke a very destructive, full-scale riot in 1955?

The roots of the riot actually were traceable to a late-season game between the Canadiens and Bruins. During the bitterly fought contest, some Boston players went out of their way to outhit the Canadiens more than usual. During the game, former Montreal defenseman Hal Laycoe crashed into the Habs' best scorer, Maurice Richard, causing a large, bloody gash to open on his scalp. Richard responded to this by challenging Laycoe to a fight. After Laycoe retreated, Richard skated after him only to be grabbed by both teammates and linesman Cliff Thompson, who once had been a Bruins defenseman.

Instead of calmly buffeting Richard away from Laycoe, Thompson decided to use an assortment of antagonizing holds that only made the already bad situation even worse. Eventally, the irate Richard and Thompson ended up on ice. Following the situation, NHL president Clarence Campbell responded by suspending Richard for the remainder of the regular season and the playoffs, which thoroughly enraged Montreal fans, who regarded Campbell's suspension as an outrageous injustice.

On St. Patrick's Day night, March 17, Campbell planned to attend the Forum game between the Canadiens and Detroit Red Wings since the teams were in a neck-and-neck race for first place. When Campbell and his secretary, Phyllis King, arrived at their seats—in full view of the audience—the fans became further inflamed. Some of the angry spectators reacted by throwing rotten fruit and vegetables at Campbell. Another tried to punch the NHL president before he was escorted to safety. Elsewhere in the arena, an unidentified fan exploded a tear gas bomb, causing complete chaos to ensue. The *New York Times* dubbed the incident the "Richard Riot."

The game was forfeited to the Red Wings while rioting erupted outside the Forum and continued along the main drag, Ste. Catherine Street West. Only after Richard himself took took to television and radio to plead for calm did the rioting abate. As a result of the forfeit, the Canadiens lost their chance for first place, and Richard lost his bid for his one and only scoring championship. P.S.: Detroit won the Stanley Cup!

Which hockey championship trophy was stolen and never returned?

In 1955 the Penticton Vees, Canada's entry into the World Hockey Championship, defeated the Soviet Union representative and thereby annexed the title. As a result, the skaters from the interior of Canada's British Columbia province were given a huge hunk of silver otherwise known as the world championship cup.

However, once the photographers had completed their bulb-flashing and the players prepared for their triumphant journey back to Canada, the trophy crumbled into three distinct parts. Billy Warwick, who played for the Penticton sextet, recalled the episode.

"The trophy," said Warwick, "was in three pieces and it like looked like somebody had thrown it against a cement wall. The Russians must have been mad about losing it and heaved it and smashed the thing. I was so mad, I said, 'They'll never see this thing again.'"

Warwick was eminently sincere. The Vees gathered the trophy pieces and stashed them in an equipment bag that accompanied them on the flight back to Montreal. When they made their way through Customs, nobody bothered looking in the bags. Warwick later removed the pieces and had the trophy appraised by a jeweler friend. He was told that the trophy—19 inches high and 10 inches in diameter—was valued at about $7,500.

At the time, Warwick owned a restaurant in Penticton and figured the trophy would look good displayed behind the counter. He had it repaired and then hired a Vancouver trophy-maker to build a facsimile, which was done for only $60. "When the phony trophy was finished," said Warwick, "I had it shipped over to Europe with Canada's 1956 entry, the Kitchener-Waterloo Dutchmen. Nobody could tell the difference.

"It was the year of the Olympics. I saw the Russians skating around, holding up my phony trophy, and I knew they had fallen for it. The story came out a couple years later, but I've still had the real trophy. They'll never get it back. I ought to put it in my will. I've had offers for it, cold cash. But I won't sell it. If anybody gets it, it'll be the Hockey Hall of Fame."

Which superstar of the 1950s and 1960s nearly died as a result of a light body check in practice?

The near-fatal collision involved Bernie (Boom-Boom) Geoffrion of the Montreal Canadiens. On January 28, 1958, Geoffrion was participating in a scrimmage being handled by Habitants coach Hector (Toe) Blake. In the midst of the scrimmage, the Boomer collided with third-string forward Andre Pronovost. When the Boomer fell to the ice, his teammates reacted as if Geoffrion were perpetuating one of his numerous japes. "We didn't do a thing," said Tom Johnson, "because we thought Boomer was joking."

As the players gathered around the fallen right wing, they could hear him moan, *"J'etouffe, J'etouffe"* (I can't breathe). Forum physiotherapist Bill Head was summoned and ordered Geoffrion transported to the hospital. A day later the *Montreal Gazette* ran a banner headline: "Hockey Star Bernie Geoffrion Fights for His Life in Hospital." What had seemed at first to be a gag turned into a near disaster. Geoffrion had suffered a ruptured bowel, and only the quick work of Head at the Forum and surgeons at the hospital saved his life.

Who was the Hall of Famer who won the National Hockey League scoring championship one year, despite the fact that he played a good portion of the season with a broken wrist?

Montreal Canadiens left wing Dickie Moore produced that remarkable achievement in 1958. Moore, Andy Bathgate of the New York Rangers, and Henri Richard of the Canadiens were locked in a tight race for the scoring title with three months remaining in the season. It was then that Moore broke his left wrist, and the Canadiens' management feared that he would be lost for the season. But Moore had other ideas: "How 'bout putting a cast on my arm?" he suggested. "Let me take care of the rest."

Sure enough, when the Canadiens faced off in their next game, there was Moore on the ice, handcuffed with a bulky, plaster cast on his left arm. Gone was the ability to stick handle and the possibility of flicking a wrist shot, but nothing dampened Moore's spirit. He played in every game right through the end of the schedule and came up with 36 goals—tops in the league—with 48 assists for a league-leading total of 84 points. Perhaps the most amazing aspect of the effort was that Moore had spent most of the season playing right wing—a position that was unfamiliar for him.

What many experts wondered was what Moore could accomplish if he were free of injuries. The answer was provided the following season, when Moore played on the left side again. He was the scoring champion again, beating Gordie Howe's scoring record of 95 by one point.

Not surprisingly, Moore was a key component of Montreal's outstanding club that won five straight Stanley Cups from 1956 through 1960. Unfortunately, he was over-shadowed by more flamboyant French-Canadian stars such as Maurice Richard, Bernard Geoffrion, and Jacques Plante.

Without the knowledge of his team's doctors, a Montreal Canadiens superstar had a teammate saw open and remove the cast from his injured knee so he could perform in a playoff game. Who was the player with the cast and who did the sawing?

During the 1961 Stanley Cup playoffs between the Chicago Blackhawks and Montreal Canadiens, the Habs' ace right wing was suffering from an injured knee, which doctors had encased in a heavy, plaster cast. Although he was considered *hor de combat*, Bernie Geoffrion accompanied his teammates to Chicago for the sixth game of the Stanley Cup playoffs.

Sitting in his compartment on the railroad train as it sped westward, Geoffrion brooded over his misfortune until he reached a conclusion: no matter how serious the injury, he would attempt to play in the upcoming game at Chicago Stadium. Geoffrion concluded that he could not remove the plaster cast by himself, so he enlisted the aid of teammate Doug Harvey.

"Look, Doug," he said, "one more loss, and we're eliminated from the playoffs. Let's cut the cast." Harvey, the Canadiens' captain, realized the severity of the right wing's request. Nevertheless, Harvey obtained a knife and beckoned Geoffrion into the Pullman's washroom, where he delicately removed the hard plaster. Geoffrion's knee was blotched with red. "It hurt so much I couldn't sleep," he said. "But I wanted to play."

On the day of the game, Geoffrion informed his coach, Toe Blake, of what he had done and his intention to play. Blake allowed the club doctor to freeze Geoffrion's leg with

281

painkillers. Shortly after the Canadiens ace took his first turn on the ice, he was hit hard by two Chicago players. He tried to get up but collapsed as if his knee was stuffed with cardboard. Later, he again attempted to play, but the knee was useless. Without Geoffrion, Montreal lost the game and missed the Stanley Cup Finals for the first time in eleven years.

Who stole the Stanley Cup from its glass case in Chicago Stadium?

The culprit was a Montreal fan named Ken Kilander. An amateur player from Montreal, Kilander achieved notoriety in 1962, when he attended a Stanley Cup game at Chicago Stadium between the Canadiens and Blackhawks. Kilander walked through the Stadium corridor until he came upon a glass case holding *the* Stanley Cup itself. He studied the silver mug and the glass case with the intensity of a safecracker about to launch a great heist. The temptation proved too much for him, so he did it. He opened the glass case and when, to his supreme amazement, neither gongs nor sirens nor any form of warning buzzer sounded, he gingerly reached in and plucked the Cup off its stand.

Still not a sound. There was just one thing to do: leave. And he did. Nursing the Cup with affection, Kilander sauntered through the lobby of Chicago Stadium and headed for the exit doors. It was almost too good to be true. Kilander was just a few yards from freedom when a cop spotted him and asked why he happened to be carrying the Stanley Cup out of Chicago Stadium.

Kilander's retort never earned him entrance into *Bartlett's Familiar Quotations*—abridged or unabridged—but it deserved a prize for sheer sincerity. "I want to take it back to where it belongs," he explained. "To Montreal." Being a Chicagoan, the cop disagreed. He returned the Cup to the glass case where it belonged, and Kilander was urged to permit Cup movements to be decided on the ice.

What goalie once lost a Stanley Cup playoff game when he lifted his head off his "cushion"—the puck?

On April 5, 1962, the Toronto Maple Leafs and New York Rangers were tied in sudden-death overtime. The best-of-seven semifinal series was tied at two wins apiece, and this game at Maple Leaf Gardens would go a long way toward deciding which team would reach the final round. With little more than four minutes gone in the extra session, Frank Mahovlich of Toronto shot the puck at Gump Worsley of the Rangers. Worsley made the save, but the puck fell behind him, just in front of the goal line. Worsley shot his head back and rested his cranium atop the puck as one would rest on a cushion. Worsley impatiently awaited the referee's whistle stopping play but heard no whistle. Mistakenly thinking that the whistle had blown but he just didn't hear it, Worlsey lifted his head, whereupon the passing Toronto center Red Kelly easily pushed the puck into the net at 4:23 of the sudden-death period, giving the Maple Leafs the win.

Who scored in overtime while playing on a fractured ankle?

During the 1963–64 Stanley Cup Finals against the Detroit Red Wings, Toronto Maple Leafs defenseman Bobby Baun suffered an ankle injury and was carried off the ice on a stretcher. Baun returned, however, in overtime and scored the winning goal for the Leafs, sending the series to a seventh and deciding game. Baun skated in the Leafs' 4–0 seventh-game victory and then consented to have the ankle X-rayed. The pictures proved that Baun had been playing with a broken bone in his ankle.

Which hockey player quit playing in the NHL in his prime?

Carl Brewer, at the age of 26, quit the Toronto Maple Leafs to study at the University of Toronto. He campaigned successfully to regain his amateur status, then performed with the Canadian National Team. His professional career included ten NHL seasons with the Leafs, Red Wings, and Blues.

A prime reason for Brewer's premature retirement was his constant feuding with Maple Leafs general manager and coach Punch Imlach. Carl disagreed with Imlach's *martinent* tactics as did other teammates such as Frank Mahovlich. But Brewer took action and upped and left. Carl later became an active mover and shaker with the NHL Players' Association.

What three National Hockey League personalities were also superstar lacrosse players in British Columbia?

Former Boston Bruins defenseman Jack Bionda is generally regarded as the greatest box lacrosse player ever to hit the floor. John Bowie Ferguson, former left wing for the Montreal Canadiens, once was Most Valuable Player in the Western Lacrosse Association. Tom McVie, a former NHL coach, also was a lacrosse All-Star in British Columbia.

What intellectual radio personality gained fame as a hockey poet?

John Kieran, a panelist on the radio program *Information, Please!*, wrote a poem called "Give Me Hockey—I'll Take Hockey—Anytime." Kieran's ditty goes like this:

I'm a fairly peaceful man and a long-time baseball fan,
Always eager when the umpire cries: "Play ball!"
And I jump with joy or terror at each hit and slide and error
Till some game-deciding tally ends it all.
But the diamond sport is quiet to that reeling rousing riot,
To a splashing game of hockey at its prime;
It's a shindig wild and gay, it's a battle served frappe,
Give me hockey—I'll take hockey—any time.
Once, while crazy with the heat, I coughed up to buy a seat,
Just to watch a pair of boxers grab a purse.
It was clinch and stall and shove, and "Please excuse my glove,"
What I thought of them I couldn't put in verse.
But for fighting fast and free, grab your hat and come with me;
Sure, the thing that they call boxing is a crime;
And for ground and lofty smacking and enthusiastic whacking;

Give me hockey—I'll take hockey—any time.
I've an ever-ready ear for a roaring football cheer,
And I love to see a halfback tackled low;
It's a really gorgeous sight when the boys begin to fight.
With a touchdown only half a yard to go.
But take all the most exciting parts of football, baseball, fighting,
And then mix them up to make a game sublime;
It's the hottest thing on ice; you don't have to ask me twice;
Give me hockey—I'll take hockey—any time.
Yes, for speed and pep and action, there is only one attraction,
You'll see knockouts there a dozen for a dime,
When the bright steel blades are ringing and the hockey
Sticks are swinging,
Give me hockey—I'll take hockey—any time.

When did the roof of an NHL arena collapse, causing that home team to play its "home" games on the road?

In mid-February 1968, during the NHL's first grand expansion of the post-World War II period, high winds tore a huge hole in the top of the Philadelphia Spectrum, home of their Flyers. The collapse occurred during a performance of the Ice Capades at the Broad Street side of the building. Although 11,000 spectators were in the building at the time, no serious injuries were reported and, shortly thereafter, repairs were made. But on March 1, 1968, the roof collapsed again, and the building was closed indefinitely following an inspection tour by Mayor James Tate together with other city and Spectrum officials. This presented serious problems for the Flyers, who had a home game scheduled for March 3 against the Oakland Seals. The Spectrum remained closed, and the Flyers agreed to play their next "home" game that Sunday afternoon at Madison Square Garden.

About 200 fans journeyed from Philadelphia to see the matinee oddity, but they were outcheered by the New Yorkers in attendance who, for inexplicable reasons, cheered loudly for the Seals. The game ended in a 1–1 tie, and the Flyers yearned for the friendly confines of the Spectrum once more. Unfortunately for them, they were not to play a home game for some time. Delays piled upon delays in fixing the roof, and the problem turned

The Spectrum arena in Philadelphia is shown here being demolished in 2011. Much earlier, in 1968, the Flyers' home lost its roof during a windstorm. The team now plays at the Wells Fargo Center.

into a political football, as well as a hockey headache. Manager Bud Poile of the Flyers realized that his club would have to play more "home" games on the road, but he did not want to return to New York because of the hostility betrayed by Rangers fans.

On March 16, 1968, more than 300 Flyers fans stormed Philadelphia's City Hall demanding that the Spectrum roof be repaired promptly so their team could return. Meanwhile, the Flyers kept winning—or trying—and were kept in the running for first place. Surely they would make the playoffs, but when they did, where would they play their Stanley Cup games?

When the Spectrum was finally reopened, the Flyers had already played 14 of their last games on the road during the homestretch run for the championship. After repairs were completed, the Flyers faced the St. Louis Blues in the playoffs. Despite the fact that they played four of the seven playoff series *at* the Spectrum, Philadelphia lost the series to St. Louis.

Who was the player who died on the first day of New York Rangers training camp?

One of hockey's saddest pre-season tragedies involved a player who was hoping to reach the NHL. His name was Wayne Larkin; he had spent eight seasons in the American Hockey League. Everything about Larkin's eventual death was bizarre. The day was Friday the 13th—September 13, 1968.

The New York Rangers shuffled past the Holiday Inn bulletin board on their way to the usual workout at their Kitchener, Ontario, training site. Nobody seemed to notice their sign that warned "Beware of Friday the 13th!" as members of the Rangers and their farmhands from the Buffalo Bisons scrambled out of the motel en route to the Kitchener Memorial Auditorium.

On the ice, Bisons coach Fred Shero had a workout for Rangers prospects and old pros who were destined for the Buffalo and Omaha farm teams. Larkin, a chunky, balding 29-year-old forward pushed himself to keep up with the crowd but betrayed a determination that lifts borderline players into the major leagues when other assets are wanting.

Larkin completed his rush and then skated behind the old net with its filthy grey webbing draped around the weathered, gray piping. Shero was in the corner preparing a short lecture about the next exercise. At first, Larkin seemed to be standing in the traditional "at ease" hockey pose: his left blade jammed into the ice with his toe facing the ceiling. A few seconds later, he moved toward the face-off circle where a couple of teammates were standing.

Suddenly, he fell sideways and crumpled to the ice. At first, it appeared that the Winnipeg native was pulling a prank. "Wayne was a very funny guy," said his roommate, Guy Trottier. "At first I thought this was just one of his jokes." But it didn't take long for the skaters to realize that Larkin was in trouble. When he collapsed, his head hit the ice, and a gash opened on his forehead. At the time, Rangers coach Bernie Geoffrion was being interviewed by a Canadian Broadcasting Corporation reporter at ice level.

"I heard somebody yell 'get a doctor,'" Geoffrion recalled. "I turned around and saw him on the ice so I jumped over the boards and ran over to see what I could do. I had had plenty of injuries during my career and I knew the first thing to work on was the heart."

Buffalo goalie Eddie Chadwick untied Larkin's skate-laces while Rangers assistant trainer Jim Young fetched smelling salts. Players, newsmen, and railbirds milled around wondering how serious Larkin's condition was. But Geoffrion knew. He had begun a steady rhythmic pumping of Larkin's chest that was to last for 15 minutes.

"For a few seconds I thought I had brought him back," said Geoffrion, "but then I lost him." Still, Geoffrion kept pumping for a sign of life. The call for a doctor didn't produce immediate results, but a fireman who had been watching the workout rushed to the ice and leaned over Larkin. He placed his mouth on the fallen player's mouth and began the resuscitation process. Soon, an ambulance arrived, and a stretcher was wheeled across the ice. A plastic tube was inserted in Larkin's mouth, an oxygen machine was connected, and the life-giving material was fed to him. Still no response.

"Here comes the doctor," somebody shouted. "Help him down the ice." Dr. Felice Viti, the Rangers' team physician, trundled down the steps and climbed over the boards. He leaned over Larkin, who was still clothed in his Rangers jersey. Viti made a fist and pounded Larkin's chest several times. He put his stethoscope to his ears and listened. More pounding. Viti removed his stethoscope and beckoned to general manager Emile Francis. Ten seconds later, he motioned to have the player removed to the hospital.

At 12:30 P.M., a doctor walked out of the room. "Is Mr. Hunt here?" he asked. Buffalo manager Fred Hunt walked across the corridor. They talked briefly. Hunt walked into the anteroom. Within a minute he was out and dashed to the telephone. The doctor followed him. "He's dead," he told the group in the corridor. "It's just a matter of getting a coroner's autopsy."

Word flashed to the rink. Francis, who had been told by Viti that there was no hope, cancelled the workout. Everybody returned to the Holiday Inn. Nobody really knew what to say. In the afternoon, Francis was summoned by the hospital, where he identified the body for the coroner. The Rangers' manager had phoned Larkin's brother in Winnipeg, Manitoba, and informed him of the tragedy. Barry Larkin would then break the news to the player's wife, Winona, who had two children and a third on the way.

Who was the prominent vocalist who became the good luck charm of an NHL team?

On December 11, 1969, the Philadelphia Flyers decided to play a recording of popular 1930s and 1940s vocalist Kate Smith singing "God Bless America" instead of the national anthem. As luck would have it, the Flyers would go on to win the game. Some wondered whether the Philadelphia club had a good luck charm in the making, because soon it became apparent that the Flyers would win more on nights that "God Bless America" was sung than not.

Eventually, with owner Ed Snider's approval, Kate Smith officially became the team's good luck charm. In 1974 when the Flyers won their first Stanley Cup, Kate was actually invited to the Spectrum to sing "God Bless America" in person. After eight years of invoking the Smith magic, the Flyers won 49 games and lost only six when "God Bless America" was played.

After Kate's death, the Flyers continued playing "God Bless America," employing a video of her singing, along with their current singer, Lauren Hart, during home games. While Lauren never claimed to be another Kate Smith, her beautiful voice and ebullient personality made her a fan favorite as well, if not as effective a good luck charm.

A statue of Kate Smith stands in Philadelphia. Her rendition of "God Bless America" was played for years at Flyers games for good luck.

Which NHL record holder was banned from professional hockey in the sport's most publicized gambling scandal?

His name was William Taylor, and he had been a star junior-league player in Canada before reaching the NHL with the Toronto Maple Leafs. Known as Billy the Kid during his playing days, the popular forward later starred for the Detroit Red Wings. He enjoyed his best season in 1946, finishing third in league scoring and tallying seven assists in a single game, which then was an NHL record. Two years later, Taylor's career was ruined by a gambling scandal. Soon after the Kid had been traded from Boston to New York, a Detroit bookmaker mentioned Taylor's name during a police wiretap. After an investigation by NHL president Clarence Campbell, Taylor and his former roommate, Don Gallinger, were barred from organized hockey for life by the league Board of Governors, who concluded that the two had placed bets on games. Taylor was out of hockey for over 22 years when Conn Smythe helped convince the NHL owners that both players had done more than enough penitence for their sins, and the ban was lifted in 1970. The reinstated Taylor became a respected member of the hockey community as a scout with the Washington Capitals.

Which major-league hockey players had speaking roles in the Canadian movie *Face-Off*?

The 1971 production was about a hockey player who falls in love with a rock singer. NHL stars Derek Sanderson and George Armstrong had lines in the film, defenseman Jim McKenny skated for the leading man, and the Toronto Maple Leafs provided the manpower for the hockey sequences.

287

What NHL player was arrested as a suspected bank robber?

While a member of the Boston Bruins, hulking defenseman Carol Vadnais was arrested in Philadelphia when he was mistaken for a holdup man then at large. He was quickly released with apologies all around.

Who was the only American picked to participate with Team Canada in 1972?

He wasn't a hockey player, but he was well known in the NHL as Frosty Forristall, a pudgy Boston Bruins trainer. He happened to be the only U.S. representative on Team Canada, giving the series a "Yankee touch," according to Hall of Fame goalie Ken Dryden. "He has been around Canadian hockey players so long that he now thinks like a Canadian. If things go bad, we can blame it on him."

What forward had his career lengthened thanks to chicken wire?

The Cleveland Arena, home of the American Hockey League's famed Cleveland Barons, had one distinctive characteristic that separated it from common pro hockey rinks: It had chicken wire running around the top of the boards instead of the modern plexiglass. When the World Hockey Association's Cleveland Crusaders replaced the Barons, one Crusader, Gary Jarrett, took expert advantage of the chicken wire.

Jarrett could play the mesh better than anyone else in the league. He knew exactly where the soft rebounds would land and parked himself accordingly near the net. When the Crusaders left Cleveland for a new arena in Richmond, Ohio, they left the mesh behind. Jarrett couldn't catch up with the faster rebounds off the glass in the new rink and as his point production dropped off consistently, he quit.

What big-league forward went for his collegiate Ph.D while skating in the NHL?

Morris Mott was regarded as the most erudite professional hockey player during the NHL's early expansion years. A native of Creelman, Saskatchewan, Mott became a pro in 1972–73 with Salt Lake City in the Western League. A year later he reached the NHL with the California Golden Seals. However, Mott is better known for having pursued a doctorate in history at Queens University in Kingston, Ontario. The point–counterpoint of playing hockey and pursuing a degree presented problems for Morris. "When I was in class, I'd be thinking of being on the ice. It took me about four years to work it out."

What eight former NHL players were of Native American heritage?

Jimmy Jamieson, a defenseman, played one game for the New York Rangers in 1943–44; Fred Sasakamoose, from Sandy Lake Reserve, Debeden, Saskatchewan, played in eleven games for the Chicago Blackhawks in 1953–54; Jimmy Neilson, a half Dane, half Cree from Big River, Saskatchewan, played for the New York Rangers, California Golden Seals, and Cleveland Barons and the WHA Edmonton Oilers; George Armstrong, son of a Scottish father and Cree mother, played twenty seasons for the Toronto Maple Leafs and was inducted into the Hall of Fame in 1975; Henry Boucha, a Minnesota-born Chippewa Indian, played for the Detroit Red Wings, Minnesota North Stars, Kansas City Scouts, Colorado Rockies, and the WHA Minnesota Fighting Saints before retiring due to a nagging eye injury; Gary Sargent, another Minnesota Chippewa, played defense for the Los Angeles Kings before signing as a free agent with his hometown North Stars; Reggie Leach, born in Riverton, Manitoba, roared up and down the right wing for the Philadelphia Flyers and had his best season in 1975–76 when he scored 80 goals—61 in the regular season and another 19 in playoff competition; and Stan Jonathan, a member of the Tuscarora tribe, skated on the left wing for the Boston Bruins.

When did a bat invade a Stanley Cup playoff game?

During the 1975 Stanley Cup Finals between the defending champion Philadelphia Flyers and the Buffalo Sabres, a live bat buzzed over the Buffalo rink while the teams were locked in action. During a time-out prior to a face-off, Sabres forward Jim Lorentz pursued the winged creature and literally batted it down with his hockey stick.

"It came down," Lorentz explained, "and began flying around a couple feet above the ice. I don't know whether the bat was brought into the building in a paper sack and let loose or whether it lived in there. But it showed up about ten minutes into the first period.

Our goalie, Gerry Desjardins, took a swing at it with his stick and missed. I took my swing at it during a face-off. We were down 2–0 at the time. Maybe that had something to do with it. The bat didn't help its own cause either. It flew in a straight line—sick, maybe, or suicidal. It fell in front of Rick MacLeish of the Flyers. No one else wanted anything to do with it, but he took it over to the penalty box—and in his bare hand, what's more."

For his efforts, Lorentz was given a silver bullet by a policeman, while a concerned naturalist suggested that the anti-bat Jim be jailed. Many people wrote letters in protest. A trout fisherman, Lorentz was upset with the negative reaction his bat-swatting re-

---

What English film director who popularized the auto chase in his first American production became so attracted to hockey while in America that he included ice sequences in a subsequent movie?

Peter Yates is credited with starting the streak of car chases in the cinema of the 1970s in *Bullitt* (1969). In *The Friends of Eddie Coyle* (1973), starring Robert Mitchum, Yates shot footage during an actual NHL game at Boston Garden with Mitchum huddling in the stands with a hood (Peter Boyle), while the Bruins played below.

289

ceived. "Whenever I go fishing," he explained, "I release almost every fish I catch. I love animals. I wish it hadn't happened." P.S.: So did the bat!

Which player had a 5-point game in his first NHL appearance but still couldn't make the team?

On February 14, 1977, in Philadelphia, rookie Al Hill skated onto the Spectrum ice and stunned a capacity crowd by scoring 2 goals and 3 assists. Philadelphians were even more surprised when the first-year player was sent back to the minors 9 games later.

Who was the "athlete" who "played" for the Detroit Lions and Boston Bruins?

George Plimpton. The adventurous author of *Paper Lion* donned the uniforms of these professional teams in an ego-journalistic search of the contemporary athlete's psyche. In 1977 Plimpton had a successful, five-minute "trial" as the Boston Bruins goaltender during an exhibition game against the Philadelphia Flyers.

Which hockey movie allegedly cost a team a league championship?

Slap shot, starring Paul Newman as Reggie Dunlop, player-coach of the fictional Charlestown Chiefs, to this day is regarded as a niche classic flick. Many consider it the most realistic hockey movie ever to come out of Hollywood, and there's good reason for that.

What *Slap Shot* did was trace the lives, games, and off-ice adventures of a real minor-league team. In actuality, the Chiefs were the Johnstown (Pa.) Jets, which then played in the raucous Eastern Hockey League. To make the film even more realistic, actual players on the Jets were employed in the film. Because the players worked out for the production as much as twelve hours a day, Jets coach Jim Cardiff claimed that his team's playoff performance was adversely affected. "Our guys were just too tired to give their best. The result was no title and plenty of angry fans."

That said, the film itself gave the game of hockey a tremendous amount of publicity. Paul Newman's character was meant to portray veteran, minor-league tough guy and coach John Brophy, and Newman did the role perfectly. Former Eastern League player Buzz Deschamps, who played for the Long Island Ducks against Johnstown, later said that no movie ever depicted minor-league hockey better than *Slap Shot*.

Who is the only owner of a professional franchise ever to offer a refund to a season ticket holder if his team did not perform as well as the fan believed it should?

In the summer of 1978, Abe Pollin, owner of the NHL Washington Capitals, promised fans an improvement in his club during the 1978–79 season. Pollin guaranteed that anyone shelling out $380 for a season ticket who didn't like the way his Caps performed could get back 20 percent of his or her money, $76, simply by asking for it at the end of the season.

Why was goalie Gary Smith nicknamed "Suitcase"?

He was big, he was hilarious, and he was well-traveled. Goalie Gary Smith, who mid-way through the 1978–79 season found a home with the NHL-bound Winnipeg Jets, found many, many homes in his five-year pro career—twelve in all. In fact, Smith was the travelling salesman of professional hockey during that bygone era.

Gary Smith around 1962.

Gary started out in Rochester (AHL), then went to Tulsa (CHL), Victoria (WHL), Toronto (NHL), Oakland (NHL), Chicago (NHL), Vancouver (NHL), Minnesota (NHL), Hershey (AHL), Fort Worth (CHL), Indianapolis (WHA), and finally the Winnipeg Jets, Avco Cup champions of the WHA.

It meant many homes and much packing and unpacking for the often zany goalie. Through it all, the amazing aspect of Suitcase's career is that he played a competent game of goal wherever he was assigned. But as Smith learned, sometimes other elements come into play when judging a goaltender. In this case, travels overshadowed puck-stopping.

Who was the woman whose marital future depended on the outcome of a hockey game?

For Debbie Callahan, the 1978–79 Avco Cup finals in the WHA meant more than the usual thrill and spills of playoff hockey; in fact, her future marriage to Edmonton Oilers' radio broadcast-man Rod Phillips depended on the Oilers upsetting the powerful Jets of Winnipeg. It all started one night at the home of Oilers GM Larry Gordon, when club owner Peter Pocklington queried Phillips on his plans to marry Callahan. Pocklington told Phillips that if he married Debbie at center ice on the night the Oilers won the Avco Cup, he would send them to an island off the coast of Morocco for two weeks, expenses paid. Under pressure from two or three other friendly kibitzers, Phillips agreed. Despite the fact that Winnipeg won the Avco Cup, many Edmontonians were sure that Phillips would do the "gentlemanly" thing and wed Debbie Callahan.

What New York Ranger was involved in a bank hold-up?

In April of 1979, while the Rangers were embroiled in a heated Stanley Cup semifinal series with their hottest rivals, the Islanders, left winger Pat Hickey found himself among a bank full of startled depositors when three men charged in and, at gunpoint, ordered everyone to freeze. These guys came in just like in the movies," recalled Hitch. "They had guns in their hands, hoods over their heads. I was standing there reading a newspaper when this guy pointed his gun at me, so I froze—all except my knees, they started knocking." The bandits escaped with some loot but were later arrested by the police.

What seven brother combinations were active during the 1978–79 season, and for which teams did they play?

Brothers	Teams
The Esposito Brothers	Phil, who skated at center for the New York Rangers, and Tony, goaltender for the Chicago Blackhawks.
The Maloney Brothers	Dave, defenseman and captain of the New York Rangers, and Don, rookie left winger, also on the Rangers.
The Mulvey Brothers	Grant, right wing for the Chicago Blackhawks, and younger brother Paul, rookie left for the Washington Capitals.
The Murdoch Brothers	Bob, right wing on the St. Louis Blues, and Don, right wing on the New York Rangers.
The Seiling Brothers	Rod, a veteran defenseman who spent the 1978–79 season with the Atlanta Flames, and younger brother Ric, right wing on the Buffalo Sabres.
The Potvin Brothers	Jean, who spent the 1978–79 season with the Minnesota North Stars, and Denis, the award-winning defenseman on the New York Islanders.
The Smith Brothers	What list would be complete without a pair of brothers named Smith? Oddly enough, it is the only such pairing in the NHL, with Gordie playing defense for the Washington Caps, and fiery Billy minding the nets for the New York Islanders.

Which team was labeled a "Mickey Mouse" organization by Wayne Gretzky when The Great One played for the Edmonton Oilers?

The New Jersey Devils of the early 1980s were bedeviled with roster problems and lost a lot more games than they won. On a visit to Edmonton, the Oilers, led by Wayne Gret-

---

What lucky Canadian family boasted two sons who were the top goalies in both the NHL and WHA in one year?

Murray and Lucille Dryden were the lucky parents of Ken and Dave Dryden, First Team All-Stars in the NHL and WHA respectively in 1979. Mr. and Mrs. Dryden not only gave hockey two of its best goalies, Dave of the Edmonton Oilers and Ken of the Montreal Canadiens, they also founded a philanthropic group, Sleeping Children Around the World. The group was dedicated to providing mattresses, sheets, pillows, and pillowcases to underprivileged children.

zky, trounced the visitors from the Garden State. As it happened, one of the Devils was goalie Ron Low, who had been a close friend of Gretzky.

The Great One was so embarrassed about the manner in which the Devils had played in front of his pal Low that Wayne criticized the opponents in a post-game media scrum. Among other verbal jabs, Gretzky labeled the Devils a "Mickey Mouse organization."

Such a dig was out of character for the usually mild-mannered Gretzky. As a result, his critique soon was noted throughout North America and especially in New Jersey. When Wayne realized how much it hurt the Devils players, he modified his comments and, essentially, apologized.

Which teams played in a game that became known as the "Easter Epic"?

The New York Islanders and Washington Capitals were playing a seventh and deciding game in the 1987 Patrick Division Semifinal. When fans had left the arena in Landover, Maryland, six hours later, they had witnessed one of the most memorable hockey games of the 1980s—a four-overtime epic in which the Islanders prevailed 3–2.

Goalies Bob Mason of Washington and Kelly Hrudey of the Islanders played spectacularly, going save for save. Referee Andy Van Hellemond overlooked many overtime infractions, preferring to "let the players decide," and they liked that. Finally, at 1:56 a.m. on Easter Sunday, Pat LaFontaine's slapshot ended the Caps' misery. The Islanders lost their next series to the Flyers, but the talk of the 1987 playoffs was definitely the "Easter Epic."

What made the series-winning goal so unusual was the play before the climactic score. Once the puck entered the Washington zone, Islanders defenseman Gord Dineen took a big gamble. He left his position at the offensive blue line and rushed into the corner, deep behind the Capitals' net. Somehow, Dineen captured the puck and sent it skimming out to the blue line, where LaFontaine was stationed. Without seeking accurate aim, Patty slapped the puck goalward. Mason, who was screened on the play, stood upright in order to track the rubber but never got a look at the biscuit. In fact, Mason looked mummified after the puck sailed into the net.

When were the first women allowed at hockey games?

Prior to the 1920s, women were not seen at hockey matches because the game was considered too rough for them to view. However, a promoter induced the governor general of Canada to come to a game and he, in turn, brought along Princess Patricia. Once the princess had made her appearance at a hockey arena, women considered the act of being a hockey spectator acceptable.

Which player went 20 years between Olympic appearances?

In 1994, Petr Nedved was a member of the Canadian Olympic team that claimed a silver medal in Lillehammer, Norway. A good 20 years later, he returned to the Olympic stage, skating for the Czech Republic's team in Sochi, Russia.

How many players over the age of 40 appeared in the 2014 Winter Olympics?

The Sochi Olympics saw five "grandpas" take the ice: Latvian Sandis Ozolinsh, Czechs Jaromir Jagr and Petr Nedved, Swede Daniel Alfredsson, and Finn Teemu Selanne.

Who scored the first Stanley Cup-winning overtime goal in NHL history?

Harold "Mush" March lit the red light in the second overtime of Game 4 to help the Chicago Blackhawks claim the 1934 Stanley Cup. The Blackhawks won the game 1–0 and the series three games to one.

Which U.S. hockey team member is of Slovakian descent?

Paul Stastny of the St. Louis Blues—originally with the Colorado Avalanche—is of Slovakian heritage. His father, Hall of Famer Peter Stastny, defected from what then was Czechoslovakia to Canada. It is noteworthy that Peter always considered himself a Slovakian, not a Czech, even when the country was known as Czechoslovakia. Paul himself has dual citizenship from both Canada and the United States.

When was an NHL game canceled because of darkness?

On May 24, 1988, the Edmonton Oilers were facing the Boston Bruins in the Stanley Cup Finals. Since Boston Garden was built without air conditioning, the warm outside temperature caused the arena to be filled with haze. To make matters worse, all the arena lights went out late in the second period. As a result, the NHL had no choice but to postpone the game and reschedule it to another night after the electricity was restored.

How did the "Muldoon Voodoo" originate?

At the end of the 1926–27 season, the Chicago Blackhawks finished third in their division. The club's owner, Major Frederic McLaughlin, thought the team had enough talent to finish first and fired head coach Pete Muldoon. As Muldoon was leaving McLaughlin's office, though, he told the Major that the franchise had not seen the last of him, as he was placing a curse on the team. Sure enough, the Blackhawks never finished in first as long as McLaughlin was alive.

When did the first line composed of three African-Canadian players make its appearance in an American arena?

On February 27, 1949, the Sherbrooke Red Raiders played the New York Rovers in a

Peter Stastny

Quebec Senior League tilt at Madison Square Garden. The Red Raiders sent out a line of Manny McIntyre, Herbie Carnegie, and Ossie Carnegie, all of whom were of African-Canadian descent. They came to be known as the "Black Aces" and gained notoriety throughout North America and Europe.

Herbie Carnegie, a Toronto native, was the best of the trio, while McIntyre was the hardest hitter of the unit. At one time, Herbie was being sought by the NHL's New York Rangers. Apparently, manager Frank Boucher wanted to sign him to a contract and first send him to the club's American Hockey League club in New Haven. Although the episode received very little publicity, Carnegie is said to have refused the offer. In those days, players in the Quebec Senior Hockey League were able to make more money than some in the NHL. As a result, Herb finished his career in the minors and never got another shot at a big-league job.

Which ex-Flyer tried his hand in state politics as a candidate for the New Jersey state assembly?

Brian Propp, a five-time NHL All-Star, better known for playing in five Stanley Cup Finals games without once lifting the Cup, found out his luck was not much better in politics.

In 2007, Propp, a Philadelphia Flyers hero, ran for a seat in the New Jersey General Assembly in the 7th Legislative District. Although he was a left winger on the ice, Propp ran as a right-wing Republican. Ultimately, as with the five Cup Finals over the course of his NHL career, he lost.

ALL-TIME
AWARD WINNERS

Which player was so clean that he was perpetually given the Lady Byng Trophy by Lady Byng herself?

Frank Boucher was one of the cleanest players in the history of the game. He won it so many times—seven in eight seasons—that Lady Byng gave him the trophy to keep for himself. She then struck another trophy to give the future winners.

Boucher eventually became coach of the Rangers and led them to their third Stanley Cup triumph in 1940. During World War II, he briefly returned to the club's lineup as a player beause so many of his players had enlisted in the Canadian and American armed forces.

Following World War II, Boucher succeeded Lester Patrick as manager of the Rangers and held that job through the 1954–55 season. By that time, he had developed a fast farm system for the franchise. One of those farm teams, the junior level Guelph (Ontario) Biltmore Mad Hatters, became one of the best amateur clubs in Canada.

During what year did the Art Ross Trophy make its debut and what did it honor?

The Art Ross Trophy had its premiere in 1947–48, when the NHL still was a six-team league. It was designated for the player who finished the season with the most total points based upon the total of goals and assists.

Who was Art Ross?

Art Ross, a former defenseman, executive, and coach, donated the trophy in his name. Known as the "thinking man's hockey man," Ross was responsible for many innovations. One of them was a goal net designed to prevent pucks from quickly bouncing in and out so fast that even the goal judges couldn't tell if it was a legal score. Ross' craftily designed net was adopted by the NHL as its official net and was known as "The Art Ross

Net." Among other Ross creations was a more refined style of hockey puck that is still used in the NHL today.

As coach and later manager of the Boston Bruins, Ross developed a number of stars who eventually made it to the Hall of Fame. These included defenseman Eddie Shore and the famed Sauerkraut Line that included Milt Schmidt, Bobby Bauer, and Woody Dumart. From the late 1920s through the start of World War II, Shore's Bruins remained one of the classier and most successful NHL teams.

"Red" Kelly Defense

DETROIT RED WINGS

Red Kelly's 1954 trading card.

What was the James Norris Memorial Trophy awarded for, and who was the first recipient?

The Norris Trophy, which debuted in 1953–54, is awarded each year to the NHL's foremost defenseman. Red Kelly, an adroit Detroit Red Wings blueliner, was the first recipient of the award. Kelly was an appropriate choice since he was skilled in his own zone but also was a defenseman who would go on the attack if the situation warranted such a move. In later years, Bobby Orr of the Boston Bruins became a regular Norris Trophy winner.

The award is named after James E. Norris, owner of the Red Wings from 1932 to 1952. He bankrolled the Detroit franchise during the Great Depression and—with the help of his manager, Jack Adams—helped create some of the finest teams in NHL history.

Which NHL award first appeared in 1973–74, and who was its first recipient?

The Jack Adams Award, which is given to the NHL's top coach, appeared on the hockey scene in 1973–74. The Philadelphia Flyers' Fred Shero was the first coach to receive the silverware.

Adams was a player before becoming manager and coach of the Detroit Red Wings in the early 1930s, when the Motor City sextet was known as the Falcons. Fiery behind the bench and astute as a member of the franchise's high command, Adams developed such superstars as Gordie Howe, Terry Sawchuk, and Ted Lindsay.

A tight-fisted executive, Adams also was explosive while running his team. During the 1942 Stanley Cup Finals against the Toronto Maple Leafs, Adams punched referee Mel Harwood after Game 4 and was suspended by NHL president Frank Calder for the remainder of the playoffs. As a result, the Red Wings were vanquished in seven games after holding a 3–0 lead in games.

Among Shero's feats was his ability to steer the Flyers to a Stanley Cup in 1994. This was a landmark achievement since the Flyers became the first post-war expansion team to win the championship. Under Shero, the Flyers won another Cup a year later and went to the Cup Finals against Montreal in 1976 before losing to the Canadiens.

Who is the only player to win the Conn Smythe Trophy in consecutive seasons?

Philadelphia Flyers goaltender Bernie Parent in 1973–74 produced a dazzling 1.89 goals-against average, the best in the NHL. The goaltender led the Flyers into the Stanley Cup Finals against the vaunted Bruins and in the sixth and final game shut out the Bostonians to win the Cup. He won 12 games and finished with two shutouts.

The following post-season, the Flyers once again came out on top, defeating the Buffalo Sabres four games to two in the Final. Parent finished with a 1.89 goals-against average in the postseason, winning ten playoff contests on the way to his second consecutive Conn Smythe Trophy.

Parent was regarded as the single most important component of a Flyers machine that was otherwise known as the Broad Street Bullies. In an era when goalies still employed a "stand-up" style, Parent was revered for his form as much as for his ability to stop pucks. His career was tragically shortened by an eye injury.

Who was the oldest player to win the Calder Trophy, thus causing the league to change the qualifications for the award?

In 1989, former Soviet ace Sergei Makarov was given permission by Russian authorities to join the National Hockey League and play for the Calgary Flames. At the age of 31, Makarov won the Calder Trophy as the league's top rookie during the 1989–90 season.

Since Makarov arrived in the NHL after more than a decade of international hockey experience, the lords of hockey decided that it was unfair for a skater with such vast experience to compete for the freshman award against players almost half his age. As a result, the so-called Makarov Rule was put into place. The rule allowed for only players under the age of 26 to qualify for the Calder Trophy. Makarov played six years in the NHL for the Flames and the San Jose Sharks.

Which father-son combination became the first to win the Hart Trophy?

Bobby Hull and his son Brett Hull were similar in many ways as offensive threats. Both were hard-shooters and colorful performers. During the 1964–65 and 1965–66 seasons, playing for the Chicago Blackhawks, left wing Bobby Hull won the Hart Trophy as the NHL's Most Valuable Player. In both seasons, he recorded at least 39 goals and 71 points. More recently during the 1990–91 season, playing for the St. Louis Blues, Brett won the Hart Trophy by scoring 86 goals (third most all time in one season) and 131 points.

Which NHL player won the Conn Smythe Trophy three times, with two different teams, in three different decades, and was the youngest to win it?

Patrick Roy, a Hall of Fame goaltender, won the Conn Smythe Trophy three times, more times than any other player in NHL history. As a 20-year-old, he became the youngest winner of the trophy as he back-stopped the Montreal Canadiens to an un-expected Stanley Cup title in 1986. At the time, Roy not only was hailed for his dar-ing and competent play but also for his use of the then rarely used "butterfly" style of goaltending.

During the 1992–93 season, he again led his underdog Montrealers to a Stanley Cup title and claimed the Conn Smythe for

Brett Hull, son of Bobby Hull

the second time in his career. After ten years with the Canadiens, he was traded to the Colorado Avalanche, where he led them to a Stanley Cup title in 1996.

At the apex of his career in the 2000–01 season, Roy led the Avalanche to the best record in the NHL and another Stanley Cup title. This time, Roy went up against the de-fending champion New Jersey Devils goalie Martin Brodeur. Thanks to the manner in which Roy bested Brodeur, his Colorado club triumphed, and Patrick won his third and final Conn Smythe Trophy.

Who was the first American-born player to win the Conn Smythe Trophy?

Brian Leetch was awarded the Most Valuable Player trophy for his brilliant play during the New York Rangers' run to the Stanley Cup in 1994. A crafty performer behind his blue line, Leetch also was a speedy attack-defenseman with a knack for scoring goals and creating them.

Learning the ice game in Connecticut, Leetch went on to star for the Blueshirts and became the first non-Canadian to win the Smythe Trophy. In fact, he was the only American to do so until 2011, when Bruins goalie Tim Thomas captured the prize. Leetch is only one of two players in league history to win the Calder Trophy, the Norris Trophy, and the Conn Smythe Trophy in their careers. The only other player to accom-plish that feat was the outstanding Boston defenseman Bobby Orr.

In 1992 Leetch became the fifth defenseman in history to record 100 points in a season and is the only American to do so. He is also the last defenseman to make that claim to fame. He served as captain of the Rangers from 1997 to 2000 after Mark Messier departed for the Vancouver Canucks. Brian would eventually hand the captaincy back to Messier when Mark returned to New York in 2000.

Following retirement, Leetch remained a figure in New York as a member of the Madison Square Garden Network's hockey television commentating team.

From 1981 to 2001, only three different players won the Art Ross Trophy. Who were they?

Jaromir Jagr, Wayne Gretzky, and Mario Lemieux were the only scoring leaders in that span of two decades. During that era, Gretzky won the trophy ten times, Lemieux won it six times, and Jagr five times. Gretzky won the trophy seven

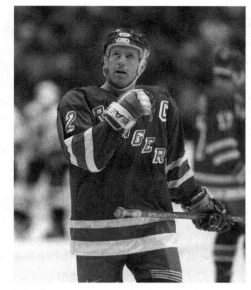

Brian Leetch

straight years, during which four of those years, he eclipsed the 200-point mark, including an NHL record 215 points in 1985–86. Lemieux won back-to-back trophies in 1991–92 and 1992–93 with at least 160 points. Jagr claimed the trophy every year between 1997 and 2001 with an average of 108 points.

Interestingly, each of the trio has been acclaimed as the best player of his time when in his prime but for different reasons. Gretzky was the original goal machine, starting with his years as an Edmonton Oiler, while Lemieux—much bigger and stronger—succeeded The Great One as an inimitable forward. Jagr, a Pittsburgh protege of Lemieux, was built like his mentor and played a similar style, which put the accent on puck control, as well as scoring. But given his druthers, Jagr preferred setting up goals more than scoring them.

Which two current NHL superstars won both the Hart and Art Ross Trophies in the first three years of their careers?

Washington Capitals right wing Alexander Ovechkin and Pittsburgh Penguins center Sidney Crosby turned the tricks. Ovechkin was drafted first overall by the Capitals in the 2004 NHL entry draft and has proven to be one of the most electrifying forwards in the NHL annals. He made his NHL debut on October 5, 2005, scoring 2 goals in a 3–2 victory over the Columbus Blue Jackets. He would go on to score 52 goals and 54 assists to lead all rookies with 106 points, beating out Crosby to win the Calder Trophy as the top rookie.

In 2007–08, the man who became known as The Big 8 led the NHL with 65 goals and 112 points and would capture the Rocket Richard and Art Ross Trophies. He was also voted as the Hart Trophy winner as league MVP.

Crosby broke into the NHL in 2005–06 after being the first overall pick in the 2005 NHL entry draft. Like Ovechkin, Sid the Kid almost immediately became the new face of the NHL. He finished sixth in the league in scoring during his rookie season. In 2006–07, he finished the campaign with a league-leading 120 points, winning the Art Ross Trophy, as well as the Hart Trophy as league MVP, the second-youngest player to do so.

After recovering from a concussion that threatened to end his career, Crosby once again was the Penguins' leader, although he won only one Stanley Cup with Pittsburgh. On the other hand, Ovechkin's style broadened when Barry Trotz began coaching the Capitals during the 2014–15 season. Concentrating on defense as well as offense, the Big 8 was a more versatile asset than ever before.

What two teams participated in the longest NHL game ever played?

On March 24, 1936, the Detroit Red Wings and the Montreal Maroons played the longest game in NHL history. The playoff game lasted well into the ninth period. The game went on so long that both teams were beginning to fatigue beyond recovery.

At one point, serious thought was given to calling off the game and having it played over another night. However, that idea was rejected, and the teams played on past midnight. By then, fatigue had become such a factor that the rival coaches began using skaters with the most stamina. They happened to be the youngest and previously least-used stickhandlers.

One of those players was Modere "Mud" Bruneteau of the Red Wings, who had been more a bench-warmer than a regular. Nevertheless, Detroit coach Jack Adams finally decided to use Bruneteau, and his move finally paid dividends. At the 16-minute mark of the ninth period, Mud fired the puck past Maroons goaltender Lorne Chabot. After 116 minutes and 30 seconds of overtime, the Red Wings finally defeated the Maroons.

How many consecutive playoff series did the Islanders win, setting an NHL record?

The New York Islanders opened the 1980s with four consecutive Stanley Cup championships from 1980 to 1983. Led by Mike Bossy, Bryan Trottier, Clark Gillies, and Denis

---

Has a team ever won or tied every game played on home ice in one season?

In 1929–30, the Boston Bruins, led by tough defenseman Eddie Shore, won all 22 of their home games at Boston Garden. In 1943–44, the Montreal Canadiens won or tied all of their games at the Montreal Forum on their way to the Stanley Cup championship. Neither arena exists as an NHL venue today. Both have been replaced by more modern NHL buildings.

Potvin, the Islanders were considered to be one of the greatest teams of all time, as they won 19 consecutive playoff series, a record that still stands today. Their run ended at the hands of the Oilers in the 1984 Cup final.

What helped make the Islanders' 19-series run so amazing was that they had to play their archrival Rangers among those series. In fact, the Islanders' defeat of the Rangers in the 1984 playoffs is considered one of the most exciting, well-played post-season challenges of all-time.

Many believe that the Nassau men might have made it five straight Cups had NHL president John Ziegler not rearranged the 1984 playoff schedule for the final round. The Islanders opened with two home games in Uniondale but then were forced to play three consecutive games in Edmonton, an arrangement that only was used that year.

Who holds the NHL record for most consecutive games scoring a goal?

In 1921–22, Ottawa's Harry "Punch" Broadbent scored goals in 16 straight games. During that season, he also won the NHL scoring title with 32 goals and 46 points.

Before Darryl Sittler accomplished the feat with the Toronto Maple Leafs, who previously held the record for most points in a single hockey game?

With five goals and three assists on December 28, 1944, Maurice Richard set the mark of eight points in a game. The victims of this scoring splurge were the Detroit Red Wings in a game played in Montreal. Bert Olmstead, also of the Montreal Canadiens, tied the mark with four goals and four assists against Chicago at the Montreal Forum ten years later.

Which two players are tied for the NHL rookie record for most goals in one game?

Howie Meeker of the Toronto Maple Leafs on January 8, 1947, and Don Murdoch of the New York Rangers on October 12, 1976. Both tallied five. Decades later, Meeker's record was challenged by then-teammate Wally Stanowski, a defenseman who claimed that he actually scored one of the goals credited to Meeker.

Who is the oldest player to record a hat trick in NHL history?

Jaromir Jagr notched three goals at the Prudential Center for the Devils against the Flyers on January 3, 2015, at the age of 42. The Czech ace was enjoying a remarkable season and, what's more, vowed that he would play in the NHL until he was 50. Shortly before the 2015 trade deadline, he was dealt to the Florida Panthers for a second-round draft pick and a conditional third-round pick. Meanwhile, Jagr continued to excel for the Panthers and was re-signed for the 2015–16 campaign.

Who set an NHL record with 95 points during the 1952–53 season?

In 1952–53 Gordie Howe of the Detroit Red Wings set an NHL record with 95 points. Howe finished the season just one goal shy of Maurice Richard's record of 50. For his ef-   303

Who scored the quickest hat trick in NHL history?

Bill Mosienko, a speedy winger for the Chicago Blackhawks, etched his name into the record books on March 23, 1952, when he scored three goals in 21 seconds against the New York Rangers at Madison Square Garden.

There were several hitches to Mosienko's accomplishment: 1. The goalie he beat was Lorne Anderson, a third-stringer elevated to the NHL from the minor-league Atlantic City Seagulls; 2. The undermanned Rangers pressed defenseman Hy Buller into action, and he played, despite a broken foot; 3. Mosienko went around Buller each time to score his goals.

As a humorous footnote to Mosienko's record-breaking hat trick, he almost made it four goals in 26 seconds. Following Bill's third red light, his center, Gus Bodnar, took the face-off and passed the puck off to Mosienko. Bill broke free again and went one-on-one with Anderson. Mosienko actually beat the goalie, but his shot hit the left post and caromed safely into the corner. When Mosienko returned to the Chicago bench, his coach—tongue-in-cheek—chided him with these words: "Bill, are you in a SLUMP!"

forts, Howe won the Hart Trophy for a second straight year as the NHL's Most Valuable Player. In addition to this, he won three consecutive scoring titles, an NHL first.

One of the most remarkable aspects of Howe's career is that he had recovered from a near-fatal fractured skull, suffered in Game 1 of the 1950 Stanley Cup semifinals between Detroit and the Toronto Maple Leafs. Doctors subsequently insisted that Howe never would play hockey again, but he was back in the Red Wings' lineup for the 1950–51 season, performing better than ever.

So dominant was Howe that he earned the nickname Mister Hockey and eventually skated in the World Hockey Association for the Houston Aeros and New England (Hartford) Whalers. Stickhandling for Houston, Gordie actually skated on a line with his sons, Mark and Marty. After Gordie retired, Mark went on to a starry NHL career as a defenseman and, like his dad, was voted into the Hockey Hall of Fame.

Which one-time Rangers defenseman holds the NHL record for most penalty minutes in one period?

Jim Dorey, who played briefly in New York during the 1971–72 season, holds the mark with 44 minutes in the sin bin during one period. Dorey, who also starred for the Toronto Maple Leafs, did not have to actually sit out those minutes, since the penalties included a game misconduct. Dorey was a rushing defenseman with a low boiling point who eventually jumped to the World Hockey Association, where he played for the New England Whalers, among other clubs.

Which NHL player became the highest-scoring rookie in Stanley Cup playoff history in 1979?

During the Stanley Cup playoffs in the spring of 1979, the New York Rangers exploded into prominence as a real threat to dethrone the Montreal Canadiens as Cup champs. At that point, the Canadiens had won three Stanley Cups in a row, directed by the brilliant coach Scotty Bowman.

Meanwhile, the challenging Rangers were led by veteran Phil Esposito and ace checking center Walter Tkaczuk. Pacing the younger Blueshirts was rookie Don Maloney. In 18 playoff games, the left winger scored 7 goals and added 13 assists for a total 20 points, a new high among rookie NHLers. This record since was broken by Dino Ciccarelli in 1981 and Ville Leino in 2010.

Which "seemingly unbreakable" record was set during the 1981–82 season?

Wayne Gretzky earned the nickname "The Great One" for many reasons but mainly for his scoring and playmaking prowess. During the 1981–82 season, the Edmonton Oilers center accomplished the unthinkable, scoring an incredible 92 goals and adding another 120 assists. Gretzky's record likely will never even come close to being matched. His 92 goals completely shattered the previous mark of 76 set by Phil Esposito. His 212 points broke his own NHL record by an amazing 48 points. During the season, Gretzky recorded ten three-goals-or-more hat tricks.

Among the many astonishing aspects of Gretzky's career was his physical stature. Unlike most players in the league, he was thinner than most and apparently more fragile. Yet, despite these shortcomings, he was able to dodge most of the bigger, more physical, foes and stay out of fights. In Edmonton he was further protected by the likes of enforcers such as burly Dave Semenko. An unwritten rule had it that if an opponent took liberties with The Great One, a teammate such as Semenko would intervene and battle the one who harassed Gretzky.

Which player holds the record for most career penalty minutes?

Dave "Tiger" Williams was the most penalized player of all-time. Throughout his career, he racked up a total of 3,966 penalty minutes. That is the equivalent of spending a long weekend in the penalty box. In 1980–81, the Vancouver left wing was penalized 343 minutes. In the following season, he sat for another 341 penalty minutes. His highest single-season total was 358 minutes in 1986–87 while a member of the Kings.

Williams was one of a unique blend of scorers who boasted offensive talent to go with his offensive behavior on the ice. During the 1982 Stanley Cup Finals between the Canucks and New York Islanders, Williams frequently would harass New York scoring threat Mike Bossy. "I took a lot from Tiger," said Bossy, "and just kept on playing my game." As a result, the Islanders won the Stanley Cup in four straight games.

305

Who holds the record for most goals as a rookie?

In 1992–93, Teemu Selanne, "The Finnish Flash," broke into the NHL with the Winnipeg Jets by scoring an amazing 76 goals and winning the Calder Memorial Trophy. Selanne was the 10th overall draft pick of the Jets and three years later made his major-league debut. Throughout his 25-year career, he has scored 50 goals three times and amassed 100 points four times while playing for the Jets, San Jose Sharks, Colorado Avalanche, and Anaheim Ducks.

The essence of Selanne's game was a blend of speed, savvy, and shooting skill matched by a precious few. Teemu easily adapted to the North American-style game, as well as the language. His sweet personality made him a favorite of interviewers and, in time, he became one of the most popular players on the continent.

Mike Gartner

Who holds the NHL record for most 30-plus goal seasons?

The National Hockey League's speed demon of his time, Mike Gartner owns that coveted record. For most of his career, the amiable Mike skated under the radar as a player. Gartner was selected fourth overall in the 1979 NHL draft by the Washington Capitals and enjoyed a solid rookie season in 1979–80, winning the Caps' Rookie of the Year and MVP awards. He led the team with 36 goals.

Gartner was traded to the North Stars in 1989. When he left the team, he was their all-time leader in career goals, assists, and points. Gartner never won the Stanley Cup or even played in the Cup Finals. He never won any major NHL award and was never named to the postseason All-Star team. He is one of the few players with this distinction to make it into the Hockey Hall of Fame. Gartner is tied with future Hall of Famer Jaromir Jagr for most consecutive 30-goal seasons with 15.

Who holds the record for most overtime goals in a season?

Steven Stamkos broke the record by scoring the overtime winner on goaltender Ondrej Pavelec of the Winnipeg Jets during the 2011–12 season. Less than a week before this game, Stamkos had broken Vincent Lecavalier's franchise (Tampa Bay Lightning) record for most goals in a season when he scored his 53rd goal. The overtime winner he scored so happened to also be his 60th on the season, making him the 20th player in history to do so. He is also the sixth player to record multiple 50-goal seasons prior to his 23rd birthday.

After the Lightning drafted Stamkos first overall in 2008, Steve immediately became the face of the franchise. Unfortunately, too much pressure was put on the rookie at the time, and he required a few more years to hone his game to sharpness, which he did. Stamkos now is regarded among the elite forwards in the NHL.

Who is the youngest player to be named captain of an NHL team?

At the start of the 2012 season, the Colorado Avalanche named 19-year-old Gabriel Landeskog the fourth captain in team his-

Steven Stamkos

tory. He is only 11 days younger than Sidney Crosby, who was the youngest captain prior to Landeskog. The second overall selection in the 2011 NHL draft, Landeskog had a terrific rookie season in which he was tied for the league in points among rookies with 52 and won the Calder Trophy as the league's top rookie.

Who are the only two players in NHL history to captain their team to two Stanley Cup championships at the age of 25?

The first player to do so was Wayne Gretzky, who won the Stanley Cup in 1983–84 and 1984–85 with the Edmonton Oilers. The second player was current Chicago Blackhawks captain Jonathan Toews, who led the Blackhawks to Stanley Cup championships in the 2009–10 season and again in the lockout-shortened 2012–13 season.

What NHL goaltender holds the record for the longest undefeated streak?

In 1971–72, Boston Bruins goalie Gerry "Cheesey" Cheevers played 33 consecutive games without a loss. In those games, he recorded 24 wins and 9 ties. The only goaltender who comes close to this is Frank "Mister Zero" Brimsek, who during the 1940–41 season went 23 games without a loss, chalking up 15 victories and 8 draws.

The American-born Brimsek emerged in the pre-World War II NHL era as a young sensation, one of the rare Americans to break into hockey's major league at the time. During the 1939 Stanley Cup round, he was nicknamed Mister Zero.

Like Brimsek, Cheevers became a Beantown hero but for different reasons. Gerry was a fighting goalie, and during the 1980 playoffs against the New York Islanders, Gerry tangled with his New York counterpart, Battlin' Billy Smith, in what became one of the nastiest goalie fights in NHL annals. Gerry also earned renown for having scar marks

307

painted on his goalie mask. They represented places where the puck crashed into his mask. Cheevers estimated the number of stitches he would require in his face had he not been wearing the mask and then painted that number on his face protector.

How did goalie Gerry Cheevers decorate his signature goalie mask?

When Cheevers took a puck to the mask, Bruins trainer John "Frosty" Forrestal would draw black stitch marks on the spot with a marker. Before long, Cheevers' mask was almost completely covered with them. To this day, it is one of the most recognizable goalie masks ever worn.

Who holds the record for most saves in an NHL game?

Although more than 90 percent of the NHL goaltenders at the start of the 1940s were Canadian, there were some exceptions. One of them was Minnesotan Sam LoPresti, who played for the Chicago Blackhawks. On the night of March 4, 1941, LoPresti fronted an undermanned team against the powerful Bruins at Boston Garden. During the contest, LoPresti faced an incredible 83 shots on goal!

Frank Brimsek, the Boston netminder that night, faced only 18 shots throughout the entire game, while LoPresti met a barrage of 37 pucks in the first period alone, followed by 27 shots in the second, and 22 in the third. More amazing than the number of shots on goal was the number LoPresti directed out of danger that night. Only three goals got beyond LoPresti, and it wasn't until a late third-period score by Bruin Eddie Wiseman that the game was decided.

The final score: Boston 3, Chicago 2. "The Bruins didn't get the winning goal until near the end of the game," LoPresti recalled from his tavern in Eveleth, Minnesota. "Wiseman got it on a rebound." LoPresti remembered that the Blackhawks "couldn't do anything right from the opening face-off; just couldn't move the puck out of our own zone. They were shooting from every angle and I didn't see half the shots. They were bouncing off my pads, my chest protector, my arms, my shoulders. I lost between eight and ten pounds that night."

After his second big-league season, the same year LoPresti faced the 83-shot barrage, he joined the U.S. Navy on the theory that "it was safer to confront Nazi U-boats in the

North Atlantic than vulcanized rubber in North America." Despite his father's goaltending challengers, Pete LoPresti, Sam's son, decided to make a career of puck-stopping and also made it to the NHL with the Minnesota North Stars. Pete faced plenty of rubber but never as much as his dad did on that night in Boston.

Which goaltender holds the all-time record for career save percentage?

Although he had virtually been overlooked by head coach Mike Keenan when he was a backup goalie for the Chicago Blackhawks, Dominik Hasek eventually would establish himself as a legendary puck stopper in other venues. Over 16 NHL seasons, he played for the Chicago Blackhawks, Buffalo Sabres, Detroit Red Wings, and Ottawa Senators. During his time in Buffalo, he established himself as one of the league's finest goalies, earning him the nickname "The Dominator." He was one of the league's most successful goalies in the 1990s and early 2000s.

Establishing a unique, flopping-all-over-the-crease style, from 1992 to 2001 Hasek became legendary, winning six Vezina Trophies, second most all time, and won consecutive Hart Trophies in 1997 and 1998, becoming the only goaltender to win the award multiple times.

Soon to have his style emulated by other goalies, Hasek had a nickname, "Flopper," that well depicted how he handled the crease. He is best known for his concentration, foot speed, flexibility, and unconventional saves, such as using his head to stop a puck or covering the puck with his blocker rather than his trapper.

He holds the highest career save percentage of all time with .9223 and is seventh all time in goals-against average (first in the modern era) with 2.202. He is also third all time in highest single-season save percentage with .9366 in 1998–99. That record was broken by Tim Thomas in 2010–11 and then again by Brian Elliott in 2011–12.

Who is the NHL's all-time goaltending leader in wins, losses, shutouts, games played, and goals scored?

Martin Brodeur of the New Jersey Devils. He recorded 691 regular season wins—all but his final three wins (with the St. Louis Blues) were recorded with the Devils. Brodeur also has the distinction of having the most losses in NHL history. Brodeur lost 468 times in his career.

Brodeur blanked his opponent 125 times. All but one shutout came with New Jersey; his last shutout—also his last win—came as a Blue against Colorado.

The goaltender, affectionately called "Marty," played in 1,266 games in his NHL career. His final seven appearances were with St. Louis.

Brodeur also has the most career goals by a netminder with three. He scored his first goal on April 17, 1997, in Game 1 of the 1997 Eastern Conference Quarterfinals against Montreal by shooting the puck the length of the ice into the vacated net. Brodeur is also credited with two more goals by being the last player to touch the puck before his opponent accidentally shot the puck into his own empty net against the Flyers on February 15, 2000, and at Carolina on March 21, 2013.

How many goaltenders recorded at least 100 regular season wins in more than one arena?

Only one. Brodeur won 266 regular season games in his original home arena at the Meadowlands. He won another 112 regular season games in Newark at the Prudential Center, where the Devils moved prior to the 2007–08 season.

Which goaltender holds the record for the most shutouts posted in one season?

Montreal Canadiens goaltender George Hainsworth earned 22 shutouts along with a stellar .920 save percentage in the 1928–29 season.

Jacques Plante

Which American-born goaltender holds the record for most career shutouts?

Two Americans share the all-time record for shutouts. John Vanbiesbrouck and Frank Brimsek each posted 40 shutouts in their careers with seven NHL clubs combined.

Which goaltenders have won the most Stanley Cups?

Jacques Plante and Ken Dryden, both of the Montreal Canadiens, each have six Stanley Cup rings. Plante won six Cups with the Habs in the 1950s, while Dryden backstopped the Habs to another six Cups in the 1970s.

Which goaltender holds the record for most points scored?

American goaltender Tom Barrasso, who played most of his career with the Pittsburgh Penguins, holds the record for most points with 48. All of Barrasso's points were assists.

Which goaltender holds the record for most penalty minutes?

Philadelphia Flyers goaltender Ron Hextall spent 584 total minutes in the penalty box over thirteen seasons of NHL play.

Bibliography

Banks, Kerry. *Hockey Heroes—Curtis Joseph*. Vancouver: Greystone Books, 2001.

Bathgate, Andy, and Wolff, Bob. *Andy Bathgate's Hockey Secrets*. Englewood Cliffs, New Jersey: Prentice Hall, 1963.

Beddoes, Dick, Stan Fischler, and Ira Gitler. *Hockey: The Story of the World's Fastest Sport*. New York: MacMillian, 1971.

Beddoes, Dick. *Pal Hal: A Biography*. Toronto, ON: Canada Publishing Corporation, 1989.

Beliveau, Jean, Chris Goyens, and Allan Turowetz. *My Life in Hockey*. Toronto, ON: McClelland & Stewart, 1994.

Berger, Howard. *Maple Leaf Moments—A Thirty Year Reflection*. Toronto, ON: Warwick Publishing, 1994.

Blair, Wren. *The Bird—The Life and Times of Hockey Legend Wren Blair*. Etobicoke, ON: Quarry Press, 2002.

Bossy, Mike, and Barry Meisel. *Boss: The Mike Bossy Story*. Scarborough, ON: McGraw-Hill Ryerson Ltd., 1988.

Botte, Peter, and Alan Hahn. *Fish Sticks—The Fall and Rise of the New York Islanders*. New York: Sports Publishing, 2003.

Boucher, Frank. *When the Rangers Were Young*. New York: Dodd, Mead, 1973.

Brown, Babe, and Bill Kurelo. *A History of the Oshawa Generals,* Volume 2. Oshawa, ON: The William Frank Hayball Foundation, 1983.

Camelli, Allen. *Great Moments in Pro Hockey*. New York: Bantam, 1971.

Carpiniello, Rick. *Messier: Hockey's Dragon Slayer*. Tampa, FL: McGregor Publishing, 1999.

Chadwin, Dean. *Rocking the Pond—The First Season of the Mighty Ducks of Anaheim*. Vancouver, BC: Polestar Press, 1994.

Cherry, Don. *Quotations from Chairman Cherry*. Vancouver, BC: Arsenal Pulp Press, 1992.

Dew, Dick, and Phil Esposito. *Phil Esposito's Winning Hockey for Beginners*. Chicago: Henry Regnery, 1976.

Ellis, Ron, and Kevin Shea. *Over the Boards—The Ron Ellis Story.* Bolton, ON: Fenn Publishing, 2002.

Eskenazi, Gerald, and Phil Esposito. *Hockey Is My Life.* Cornwall, NY: Cornwall Press, 1972.

Esposito, Phil, and Tony Esposito. *The Brothers Esposito.* New York: Hawthorn Books, 1971.

Ferguson, John, Stan Fischler, and Shirley Fischler. *Thunder and Lightning.* Scarborough, ON: Prentice Hall Canada, 1989.

Finnigan, John. *Old Scores, New Goals—The Story of the Ottawa Senators.* Kingston, ON: Quarry Press, 1992.

Fischer, Red. *Hockey, Heroes, and Me.* Toronto, ON: McClelland & Stewart, 1994.

Fischler, Stan. *The All-New Hockey's 100.* Montreal, QC: McGraw-Hill Ryerson Limited, 1988.

———. *Bobby Clarke and the Ferocious Flyers.* New York: Warner Paperback Library, 1974.

———. *Bobby Orr and the Big, Bad Bruins.* New York: Dodd, Mead, 1969.

———. *The Flakes of Winter: The Zany Antics of Hockey's Most Colorful Characters.* Toronto, ON: Warwick Publicity Group, 2011.

———. *Garry Unger and the Battling Blues.* New York: Dodd, Mead, 1976.

———. *Golden Ice—The Greatest Teams in Hockey History.* Montreal, QC: McGraw Hill—Ryerson, 1990.

———. *Gordie Howe.* New York: Grosset and Dunlap, 1973.

———. *Make Way for the Leafs—Toronto's Comeback.* Scarborough, ON: Prentice-Hall Canada, 1989.

———. *The Rivalry: Canadiens vs. Leafs.* Whitby, ON: McGraw-Hill Ryerson, 1991.

———. *Stan Mikita—The Turbulent Career of a Hockey Superstar.* New York: Cowles Book Company, 1969.

———, and Shirley Fischler. *Who's Who in Hockey.* Kansas City: Andrews McMeel Publishing, 2003.

Goyens, Chris, and Allan Turowetz. *Lions In Winter.* Scarborough, ON: Prentice-Hall Canada, 1986.

Hadfield, Vic, and Tim Moriarty. *Vic Hadfield's Diary: From Moscow to the Play-offs.* Garden City, NY: Doubleday, 1974.

Harris, Billy. *The Glory Years—Memories of a Decade, 1955–1965.* Scarborough, ON: Prentice-Hall Canada, 1989.

Houston, William. *Ballard—A Portait of Canada's Most Controversial Sports Figure.* Toronto: Summerhill Press, 1984.

Howe, Colleen, Gordie Howe, and Tom DeLisle. *And … Howe!* Traverse City, MI: Power Play Publications, 1995.

Hull, Brett, and Kevin Allen. *Brett: Shootin' and Smilin'.* Scarborough, ON: Prentice-Hall Canada, 1991.

Hull, Dennis, and Robert Thompson. *The Third Best Hull (I Should Have Been Fourth but They Wouldn't Let My Sister Maxine Play).* Toronto: ECW Press, 1998.

Hunt, Jim. *Bobby Hull.* Chicago: Follett Publishing Company, 1966.

Hunter, Douglas. *Yzerman—The Making of a Champion.* Toronto: Doubleday Canada, 2004.

———. *Open Ice—The Tim Horton Story.* Toronto: Viking Penguin Books Canada Limited, 1994.

Iabon, John, and Peter Maher. *The Eternal Flames—The Inspiring Story of the Stanley-Cup Winning Season.* Toronto: The Canadian Publishers, 1989.

Imlach, Punch, and Scott Young. *Heaven and Hell in the NHL—Punch Imlach's Own Story.* Halifax, NS: Goodread Biographies, 1982.

Irvin, Dick. *The Habs: An Oral History of the Montreal Canadiens 1940–1980.* Toronto, ON: McCelland & Stewart, 1991.

Kallas, Kris. *Access Denied: Forgotten and Future Heroes of Hockey's Hall of Fame.* ON: Frosted Forest Northern Ontario Publishing, 2011.

LaFontaine, Pat, Ernie Valatis, Chas Griffin, and Larry Weisman. *Companions in Courage: Triumphant Tales of Heroic Athletes.* New York: Warner Books, 2001.

LaRochelle, Claude. *Guy Lafluer: Hockey's No. 1.* QC: Lotographic Inc., 1978.

Lindros, Eric, and Randy Starkman. *Fire On Ice.* New York: Harper Paperbacks, 1992.

Lowe, Kevin, Shirley Fischler, and Stan Fischler. *Champions: The Making of the Edmonton Oilers.* Scarborough, ON: Prentice-Hall Canada, 1988.

———, Shirley Fischler, and Stan Fischler. *Champions: The Making of the Edmonton Oilers.* Toronto, ON: Fawcett Crest, 1988.

MacInnis, Craig. *Remembering the Golden Jet—A Celebration of Bobby Hull.* Toronto, ON: Stoddart Publishing, 2001.

———. *Remembering the Rocket.* Toronto, ON: Stoddart Publishing Co., 1998.

MacSkimming, Roy. *Gordie—A Hockey Legend.* Toronto, ON: Greystone Books, 1994.

Magnuson, Keith. *None Against.* Cornwall, NY: The Cornwall Press, Inc., 1973.

Malcom, Andrew H. *Fury—Inside the Life of Theoren Fleury.* Toronto, ON: The Canadian Publishers, 1997.

McAllister, Ron. *Hockey Heroes.* Toronto, ON: McClelland & Stewart, 1949.

313

McDonald, Lanny, and Steve Simmons. *Lanny*. New York: McGraw-Hill Ryerson Limited, 1987.

McFarlane, Brian. *The Red Wings*. Toronto, ON: Stoddart, 1998.

———. *The Rangers—Brian McFarlane's Original Six*. Toronto, ON: Stoddart, 1997.

Melady, John. *Overtime, Overdue: The Bill Barilko Story*. Trenton, ON: City Print, 1988.

Mikita, Stan. *I Play to Win—My Own Story*. New York: Pocket Books, 1970.

———, and Bob Verdi. *Forever a Blackhawk*. Chicago: Triumph Books, 1970.

Molinari, Dave. *Best in the Game—The Turbulent Story of the Pittsburgh Penguins' Rise to the Stanley Cup Champions*. Champaign, IL: Sagamore, 1993.

Moriarty, Tim. *The Incredible Islanders*. Carle Place, NY: Sorkin-Levine Sports Agency, 1975.

Nanne, Lou, and Jim Braton. *A Passion to Win*. Chicago: Triumph Books, 2010.

O'Brien, Andy. *Firewagon Hockey: The Story of the Montreal Canadiens*. Toronto, ON: Ryerson Press, 1967.

———. *Rocket Richard*. Toronto, ON: Ryerson Press, 1961.

O'Malley, Martin. *Gross Misconduct—The Life of Spinner Spencer*. Markham, ON: Viking Penguin Books Canada, 1988.

O'Reilly, Don. *Mr. Hockey—The World of Gordie Howe*. Chicago: Henry Regnery Company, 1975.

Park, Brad, and Stan Fischler. *Play the Man*. New York: Warner Books, 1972.

Potvin, Denis, and Stan Fischler. *Power on Ice*. New York: Harper & Row, 1977.

Richard, Maurice, and Stan Fischler. *Les Canadiens sont la!* Scarborough, ON: Prentice-Hall of Canada, 1971.

Robinson, Dean. *Howie Morenz: Hockey's First Superstar*. Erin, ON: Boston Mills Press, 1982.

Robinson, Larry, and Chris Goyens. *Robinson: For the Defense*. Scarborough, ON: McGraw-Hill Ryerson, 1988.

Roche, Wilfrid Victor. *The Hockey Book—The Great Hockey Stories of All Time, Told by the Men Who Know the Game Best*. Toronto, ON: McClelland & Stewart, 1953.

Rossiter, Sean. *Hockey Heroes: Mario Lemieux*. Vancouver/Toronto/New York: Greystone Books, 2001.

Sanderson, Derek. *I've Got to Be Me*. Cornwall, NY: Cornwall Press, 1970.

Salming, Borje, and Gerhard Karlson. *Borje Salming—Blood, Sweat and Hockey*. Toronto, ON: Harper Collins, 1991.

Schultz, Dave, and Stan Fischler. *The Hammer—Confessions of a Hockey Enforcer*. Toronto, ON: Collins Publishers, 1981.

Semenko, Dave. *Looking Out for Number One.* Toronto, ON: Stoddart, 1989.

Simons, Dave, and Bernie Federko. *Blue Fire: A Season Inside the St. Louis Blues.* Champaign, IL: Sagamore Publishing, 1992.

Sloman, Larry. *Thin Ice—A Season in Hell with the New York Rangers.* William Morrow, 1982.

Smythe, Conn, and Scott Young. *Conn Smythe—If You Can't Beat 'Em in the Alley.* Toronto, ON: McClelland & Stewart, 1981.

Stamm, Laura, Stan Fischler, and Richard Friedman. *Power Skating the Hockey Way.* New York: Hawthorn Books. 1977.

Starkey, Joe, and Mike Lange. *Tales from the Pittsburgh Penguins Locker Room: A Collection of the Greatest Penguins Stories Ever Told.* Champaign, IL: Sports Publishing, 2013.

Stellick, Gord, and Jim O'Leary. *Hockey Heartaches and Hal.* Scarborough, ON: Prentice-Hall Canada, 1990.

Tattle, Thomas. *A Wild State of Hockey: The Minnesota Wild's First Season on the Ice.* Edina, MN: Beaver's Pond Press, 2001.

Villemare, Gilles, and Mike Shalin. *Tales from the Rangers Locker Room.* New York: Sports Publishing, 2002.

Vipond, Jim. *Gordie Howe—Number 9.* Chicago: Follett Publishing Company, 1968.

Weinberg, Mark. *Career Misconduct—The Story of Bill Wirtz's Greed, Corruption and the Betrayal of Blackhawks Fans.* Chicago: Blueline Publishing, 2001.

Terms to Know

Assist—The pass or passes that lead to a goal. No more than two assists may be awarded on a goal. The record for assists in a season is held by Wayne Gretzky: 125. The record for assists in an NHL career is held by Gordie Howe: 1,049.

Backcheck—Covering an opponent, usually a player's opposite—left wing on right wing, for example—in the defensive zone. Good back-checkers are referred to as "two-way players." Two of the sport's best ever were Bob Davidson of the 1940s Maple Leafs and Milt Schmidt of the 1940s Bruins.

Backhand—A shot or pass using the closed end (heel) of the stick from a player's "other" side. A right-handed shot would *take* a pass on the *back* of his stickblade, with the other stick to his right. To *make* the pass or shot his stick would move across his body from right to left in the direction intended by the shooter. Maurice "Rocket" Richard and Red Berenson had good backhand shots.

Back-Pass—A pass pushed backwards by the puck carrier, left for a teammate on either flank.

Blocker—The glove worn on the stickhand of the goaltender. It is used to deflect pucks shot high to the goaltender's stick side. Emile Francis is credited with the creation of the blocker.

Blue Line—There are two blue lines. Together with the center red line, they break up the ice surface into three, sixty-foot sections. The blue lines are located sixty feet from end goal lines. Lester and Frank Patrick are credited with the introduction of the blue lines in 1918.

Boards—Together with the glass, the boards enclose the playing surface. Boards are constructed of wood or fiberglass and are a standard forty-eight inches high. The Minnesota Fighting Saints of the WHA had transparent boards so spectators could see the pucks at all times.

Bodycheck—Hitting an opponent cleanly with a shoulder or hip is referred to as a bodycheck. Ching Johnson, Eddie Shore, Bill Ezinicki, Bob Plager, and Brad Park are examples of great bodycheckers.

Breakaway—A player skating in alone on the goaltender in an attempt to score.

Clearing the puck—Getting the puck away from in front of the net or sending the puck out of the defensive zone while killing a penalty.

Crease—An area four feet long and eight feet wide, marked by a red line, in front of the goal cage. No opposing player may enter the crease subject to a two-minute penalty for interference. Goaltenders Gerry Cheevers and Bill Smith believed that too many opponents invaded their territory, so they kept the crease clear by force.

Crossbar—The horizontal pipe across the top of the goal cage: four feet above the ice and six feet long.

Defenseman—A team puts two defensemen on the ice at a time. The defenseman follows the play up-ice and is primarily responsible for protecting his end of the ice and breaking up an opposing attack. Usually defensemen run the power play. There are two types of defensemen: offensive and defensive. Offensive defensemen, typified by Bobby Orr—who led the league in scoring for two years—and Doug Wilson, take more of a part in scoring goals. Defensive defensemen, typified by Mike Milbury and Ken Morrow, are concerned only with keeping their end of the ice free from opposing forwards.

Deflection—A puck is shot toward the goal and changes direction after striking a skate or stick. Many players practice deflecting the puck past the goaltender.

Deke—A fake executed by moving the puck from the forehand part of the stick to the backhand.

Diggers—Those forwards who work the boards and the corners in order to gain possession of the puck. They are best exemplified by Ted Kennedy of the 1940s Maple Leafs and John Tonelli of the New York Islanders.

Drop-Pass—A "pass" that leaves the puck where it is. The man with the puck leaves the puck behind him for a trailing member of his team to pick up. This differs from a back pass in that the puck is not moved backwards but is left where it is.

Face-off—A face-off occurs at the beginning of a game, after a goal, and after every stoppage of play. The two teams line up opposite each other and parallel to the goal lines. The puck is then dropped between the opposing centers. On important face-offs, coaches often put two centermen on the ice in case one gets thrown out of the face-off by the linesmen. Face-offs are also known as "draws." Two of the best faceoff men of recent years are Bobby Clarke and Bryan Trottier.

Face-off Locations—When the whistle blows after a penalty is called and there's a stoppage of play, the time on the penalty clock is set and the ensuing face-off will take place at one of the two face-off dots in the offending team's zone. There are four (4) exceptions to this application:

(1) When a penalty is assessed after the scoring of a goal, the face-off will be at center ice.

(2) When a penalty is assessed at the start or end of a period, the face-off will be at center ice.

(3) When the defending team is called and the other team has entered the defending zone past the outer edge of either faceoff circle, the face-off will be in the neutral zone.

(4) When the team not being penalized ices the puck, the face-off is in the neutral zone outside the blue line of the team icing the puck.

Forechecking—Checking by the offense in the offensive zone in order to gain possession of the puck is known as forechecking. Coaches develop elaborate systems for forechecking. Conservative forechecking systems send one forward into the zone to press for the puck. Less conservative systems call for two or three forwards to check for the puck. Wayne Babych, Bernie Federko, and Brian Sutter of the St. Louis Blues are excellent forecheckers.

Forwards—The players who attack in the offensive zone are known as forwards. Their primary responsibility is to score goals. There are three types of forwards: the left wing, who skates up the left side, the center, who is responsible for the middle of the ice, and the right wing, who covers the right side. Records for forwards are held by Gordie Howe, who scored 1,850 NHL points in his career, and Wayne Gretzky, who scored the most points ever in a season: 212. Those forwards who also concentrate on defense are called "defensive forwards." Some of the best players in this category have included Bob Gainey, Walt Tkaczuk, and Steve Gasper.

Glass—The glass along the boards encloses the playing surface. The glass is either Plexiglas, Herculite, unbreakable plastic, or real glass.

Goal—When the puck crosses completely over the goal line and into the goal cage, a goal has been scored. A goal is one point. The record for most goals in a career was set by Gordie How: 801 goals in 1,767 NHL games. The record for goals in a season is held by Wayne Gretzky: 92. The record for goals in a game is held by Joe Malone: 7.

Goal Cage—The goal cage is four feet high, six feet wide, and two feet deep. The crossbar and goal posts are painted red, and the posts are anchored in place by pipes that extend at least eight inches into the hollow posts. Mark Howe almost lost his life when he was impaled on the base of the net.

Goaltender—The player who protects the goal and attempts to prevent goals from being scored is the goaltender, or "goalie." When he stops the puck he is said to have made a save. Glenn Hall holds the goaltenders record for consecutive, complete games: 502. Terry Sawchuck holds the record for career shutouts: 103.

Green Light—Behind the glass at each end of the arena, red and green lights are suspended. The green light is lit to signify that time has expired. No goals may be scored after the green light has been lit.

Hat Trick—Scoring three goals in a game is called a hat trick. The record for most hat tricks in a career is held by Phil Esposito: 32. The record for hat tricks in a season is held by Wayne Gretzky: 10.

Head-manning—Passing the puck to a teammate up ice is called head-manning.

Icing—Shooting the puck from behind the center red line across the opponent's goal line is icing. Play is stopped and a face-off occurs back in the defensive zone. If a team is shorthanded, there is no icing. A linesman can "wave off," not call, the icing if he feels that the other team could have played the puck.

Linesmen—The officials charged with calling offsides and too many men on the ice. They drop the puck for all face-offs, excluding the ones that occur after a goal has been scored.

Neutral Zone—The area between the blue lines is called the neutral zone.

Offside—There are two types of offsides; both involve a player being ahead of the puck. First: a player is offside when he crosses the opposing blue line ahead of the puck. Second: a player is offside if the puck crosses two lines on a pass. For example: Player A is behind his own blue line. Player B is across the center red line. A passes to B. B is offside because the puck crossed two lines—the blue line and the center red line—before B received the pass.

Penalty Box—Where all penalties are served.

Penalty Killers—The players assigned by the shorthanded team to defend against the power play. This is also known as "killing off a penalty." Two of the finest penalty killers were Nick Metz of the 1940s Maple Leafs, and Derek Sanderson of the 1970s Bruins.

Period—Hockey is divided into three twenty-minute segments known as periods.

Playmaker—A forward, usually a center, who is able to create scoring opportunities by setting up plays with his skating and passing. Bobby Clarke and Stan Mikita are examples of playmakers.

Point—A spot just inside the opposing team's blue line, normally near the right or left boards, rather than center ice. Usually, a defenseman is stationed there to feed passes to forwards or to take a shot on goal. On the power play, a coach often designates a forward to play one of the points, or the team's most offense-minded defenseman.

Poke-Check—Using the stick to knock the puck off the puck carrier's stick by suddenly poking the puck away. The move was supposedly invented by Dickie Moore of the 1902 Montreal AAA club. Jacques Laperriere and Ken Morrow also excelled at this technique.

Power play—When a team has a one-man or two-man advantage because of penalties assessed on its opponents, that team is on a power play. The Montreal power play of the 1955–1960 Stanley Cup years was so formidable that their success forced the NHL to change the rules governing penalties. At that time, a player served the duration his penalty in the box, regardless of how many goals the other team scored. The Canadiens would often score two, three, or four times and effectively end the game within the two minutes. Subsequently, the NHL rearranged the rule so that the penalized player returns to the ice after one goal is scored against his team, returning the teams to equal strength. The team that has scored the most power-play goals in a season is the Pittsburgh Penguins. During the 1981–1982 season, the Penguins scored 99 power play goals.

Puck—The three-inch wide, one-inch thick rubber disc used in hockey. Art Ross is the man who "created" the NHL puck. He beveled the puck's edges to keep it from rolling. Because many people claimed that the puck was difficult to see on television, the WHA experimented with a red puck. They discarded it, however, because the chemical used in the red paint allowed the puck to bounce too much.

Pulling the Goalie—Removing the goalie for an extra skater. This is done by teams losing in the final minutes of the game. They then attempt to overpower the opposing defense and goaltender. This maneuver is also used during a delayed penalty.

Ragging the Puck—A player—or sometimes several—who holds onto the puck through fine stick-handling or passing. This is a defensive or penalty-killing technique used when defending against the power play.

Rebound—A puck that bounces off the goaltender or the boards. Good goaltenders control their rebounds.

Red Light—The red light is suspended behind the glass in the back of the net and is lit by the goal judge when a goal is scored.

Red Line—The center line that divides the ice. It is used for offsides and icing calls. It was introduced by Frank Boucher and signaled the beginning of hockey's modern era.

Referees—The men in charge of the game. They alone administer the rules and dole out the penalties. There is a single referee per game.

Rink—Where hockey games are played. Most NHL rinks are a standard 200 feet long and 85 feet wide. However, certain rinks, such as Boston Garden, are older and don't meet modern standards. The difference in size is made up by shortening the neutral zone. This keeps both areas inside the blue line at 60 feet.

Save—Stopping a shot from going into the goal. Usually only goaltenders make saves, but occasionally, when the goaltender is trapped out of position, an alert defenseman keeps the puck out of the net. Goaltender Sam LoPresti of the 1941 Chicago Blackhawks made the most saves in one game, 80, against the Boston Bruins. The Bruins won the game, 3-2.

Screen Shot—A shot on goal that comes to the net through a maze of players. Goaltenders say that screen shots and deflections are the most difficult to stop.

Shorthanded—A team is shorthanded when they are killing a penalty. The Boston Bruins of 1970–1971 hold the record for the most goals by a shorthanded team, and Marcel Dionne holds the season record for a player: 10.

Slapshot—A shot on goal taken by raising the stick to shoulder height, slapping the puck, and following through almost like a golf drive. Bun Cook is given credit for first using the slapshot consistently, but there are many other players who used it just as well. Included in that group would be Bernie "Boom-Boom" Geoffrion, Reed Larson, Doug Wilson, and Bobby Hull. Hull's slapshot was once times at 118 mph.

Penalties Glossary

There are three kinds of penalties in hockey: (1) The minor penalty: any penalty calling for two minutes in the penalty box. (2) The major penalty: any penalty that requires five minutes in the penalty box. (3) The misconduct penalty: misconducts are "awarded" for abuse of officials, obscene language, or refusing to obey the referee's instructions. A misconduct penalty is ten minutes long and is served by the offending player. His team is not shorthanded for the time he spends in the penalty box. Game misconducts serve to remove a player from the rest of the game, regardless of time remaining to play.

Boarding—A minor penalty: causing an opponent to be thrown violently into the boards.

Butt-ending—A major penalty: jabbing an opponent with the butt-end of the stick.

Charging—A minor penalty: taking more than two strides before hitting an opponent.

Covering up—When a player stops play by keeping the puck motionless, he is covering up. This term usually refers to goaltenders who stop play after making a save.

Delay of Game—A minor penalty assessed for deliberately stopping play by throwing the puck out of the rink or for refusing to obey a referee's call.

Delayed Penalty—A referee signals a delayed penalty by raising his arm and not stopping play. This is done because the non-offending team has possession of the puck and the delay allows them a chance to create a play. The second the offending team touches the puck, the referee whistles a stoppage of play and assesses the penalty.

Elbowing—A minor penalty: it is illegal to hit an opponent with an elbow.

Fighting—A major penalty: anyone who fights receives a penalty. A minor penalty, which is what usually causes the fight, is generally assessed with the fighting penalty.

Freezing the puck—See "covering up."

High Sticking—There are two types of high sticking. The first involves playing the puck with the stick above the shoulders. This is illegal and results in a face-off. The second type of high sticking involves injuring an opponent with the stick while it is carried above the shoulders. This results in a minor penalty.

Holding—A minor penalty: grabbing, clutching and holding an opponent so as to impede his progress is known as holding and is illegal.

Hooking—A minor penalty: impeding the progress of an opponent by using the stick.

Interference—A minor penalty: preventing the opponent from reaching and playing the puck.

Penalty shot—The referee awards a penalty shot to a player who is breaking in alone on the goaltender and is fouled from behind in such a way as to eliminate his chance of scoring. Penalty shots are very rarely seen and could be called much more often than they are.

Roughing—A minor penalty assessed when the referee decides that unnecessary force has been used in checking an opponent.

National Hockey League Teams

ANAHEIM DUCKS
City: Anaheim, CA
Arena: Honda Center (18,336 seats)
Founded: 1993 (Mighty Ducks of Anaheim)
Mascot: Wildwing
Nickname: Mighty Ducks
AHL Affiliate: San Diego Gulls
ECHL Affiliate: Utah Grizzlies
Fun Fact: The Mighty Ducks were initially named after the 1992 Disney movie *The Mighty Ducks*. When the Ducks (then the Mighty Ducks) came into the league in 1993, they were owned by the Walt Disney Corporation. The sale of the team to Henry Samueli in 2005 led to a name and logo change, which, according to Samueli, was in accordance to the fans' wishes.

ARIZONA COYOTES
City: Glendale, AZ
Arena: Gila River Arena (17,125 seats)
Founded: 1972
Previous Team: Winnipeg Jets
Mascot: Howler the Coyote
Nickname: 'Yotes, Desert Dogs
AHL Affiliate: Springfield Falcons
ECHL Affiliate: Gwinnett Gladiators
Fun Fact: The Great One, Wayne Gretzky, coached the Arizona (formerly Phoenix) Coyotes for four seasons. The 'Yotes are the only team that the legendary Hall of Famer coached in the NHL. He was fired after the 2008–2009 season after the Coyotes finished fourth in the Pacific Division with 79 points.

BOSTON BRUINS
City: Boston, MA
Arena: TD Garden (17,565 seats)

Founded: 1924
Mascot: Blades the Bruin
Nickname: B's, Bears, Spokes, The Black and Gold
AHL Affiliate: Providence Bruins
ECHL Affiliate: South Carolina Stingrays
Fun Fact: In the 1988 Stanley Cup Finals, the lights went out at Boston Garden during game four, causing the game to be suspended. It was resumed two days later in Edmonton. The Oilers eventually won Game 4 to complete the sweep of the Bruins and capture the Stanley Cup.

BUFFALO SABRES
City: Buffalo, NY
Arena: First Niagara Center (19,070 seats)
Founded: 1970
Mascot: Sabretooth
Nickname: Slugs, Swords
AHL Affiliate: Rochester Americans
ECHL Affiliate: Elmira Jackals
Fun Fact: The Buffalo Sabres were victims of one of the most infamous calls in NHL History. During the triple overtime of Game 6 of the 1999 Stanley Cup Finals, Brett Hull scored the Cup-clinching goal for the Dallas Stars. However, his skate was clearly in the crease when he scored the goal, and at the time the rules stated that a goal cannot be scored by a player in the crease.

CALGARY FLAMES
City: Calgary, AB
Arena: Scotiabank Saddledome (19,289 seats)
Founded: 1972
Previous Team: Atlanta Flames
Mascot: Harvey the Hound
Nickname: Flamers
AHL Affiliate: Stockton Heat
ECHL Affiliate: Adirondack Thunder
Fun Fact: In 2004, the Calgary Flames made a run to the Stanley Cup Final. That season, the NHL went back to teams wearing their colored jerseys at home. During the playoffs, nearly every Flame fan wore a red jersey with the "C" logo, giving the fans the nickname the "C of Red." The demand for Flames jerseys was so high during the playoffs that CCM stopped producing all other teams' jerseys to keep up with the demand.

CAROLINA HURRICANES
City: Raleigh, NC
Arena: PNC Arena (18,680 seats)

Founded: 1997

Previous Team: Hartford Whalers
Mascot: Stormy
Nickname: 'Canes
AHL Affiliate: Charlotte Checkers
ECHL Affiliate: Florida Everblades
Fun Fact: Paul Maurice was the Hurricanes' first head coach during the team's inaugural season in 1997–1998. He was 30 years old, making him the second-youngest coach in NHL history. Gary Green, 26, is the only younger person to be a head coach.

CHICAGO BLACKHAWKS

City: Chicago, IL
Arena: United Center (19,717 seats)
Founded: 1926
Mascot: Tommy Hawk
Nickname: 'Hawks
AHL Affiliate: Rockford IceHogs
ECHL Affiliate: Indy Fuel
Fun Fact: The Blackhawks get their name from an infantry division during World War I called the Blackhawk division. Initially, the name was Black Hawks, after the name of a Native American chief. However, in 1986, official documents were discovered revealing the division was actually called Blackhawk, and the Chicago hockey team changed their name accordingly.

COLORADO AVALANCHE

City: Denver, CO
Arena: Pepsi Center (18,007 seats)
Founded: 1995
Previous Team: Quebec Nordiques
Mascot: Bernie the St. Bernard
Nickname: Avs
AHL Affiliate: San Antonio Rampage
ECHL Affiliate: Fort Wayne Komets
Fun Fact: The Avalanche moved to Colorado from Quebec for the 1995–1996 season and won the Stanley Cup that year. They swept the Florida Panthers in Stanley Cup Finals. In their first season, the Avs acquired Patrick Roy in a trade from Montreal, and over the next 39 games Roy posted 22 wins.

COLUMBUS BLUE JACKETS

City: Columbus, OH
Arena: Nationwide Arena (18,144 seats)
Founded: 2000
Mascot: Stinger, Boomer the Cannon
Nickname: CBJ, Jackets

AHL Affiliate: Lake Erie Monsters
ECHL Affiliate: Kalamazoo Wings
Fun Fact: The Blue Jackets got their name after the franchise held a "Name the Team" contest in 1996. Over 14,000 people submitted ideas, and eventually the list was narrowed to "Blue Jackets" and "Justice." The name Blue Jackets was seen as the more suitable name.

DALLAS STARS
City: Dallas, TX
Arena: American Airlines Center (18,532 seats)
Founded: 1967
Previous Team: Minnesota North Stars
Mascot: Victor E. Green
Nickname: Sheriffs, Southern Stars, Yellow Stars
AHL Affiliate: Texas Stars
ECHL Affiliate: Idaho Steelheads
Fun Fact: Believe it or not, it wasn't until 1995 that a team erased a two-goal deficit in the final minute of regulation to win a game. The Stars scored three times in the final minute against the Boston Bruins to win 6–5.

DETROIT RED WINGS
City: Detroit, MI
Arena: Joe Louis Arena (20,027 seats)
Founded: 1926
Previous Team: Detroit Cougars, Detroit Falcons
Mascot: Al the Octopus
Nickname: Wings, The Winged Wheel
AHL Affiliate: Grand Rapids Griffins
ECHL Affiliate: Toledo Walleye
Fun Fact: The tradition of the throwing an octopus on the ice began during the playoffs of 1952. Pete and Jerry Cusimano hurled the first octopus onto the ice on April 15, choosing an octopus because the eight tentacles represented the eight wins needed, at the time, to win the Stanley Cup. Despite sixteen playoff wins being the new number for a Cup, the tradition lives on.

EDMONTON OILERS
City: Edmonton, AL
Arena: Rexall Place (16,839 seats). *Future Arena:* Rogers Place (18,641 seats)
Founded: 1972
Mascot: Harvey the Hound
Nickname: The Oil, Greasers
AHL Affiliate: Bakersfield Condors
ECHL Affiliate: Norfolk Admirals

Fun Fact: The Oilers were the first team to be awarded the Presidents' Trophy after the 1985–1986 season. They registered 56 wins and posted 119 points.

FLORIDA PANTHERS
City: Sunrise, FL
Arena: BB&T Center (19,250 seats)
Founded: 1993
Mascot: Stanley C. Panther
Nickname: Cats
AHL Affiliate: Portland Pirates
ECHL Affiliate: Cincinnati Cyclones
Fun Fact: The Panthers were the first team to have a game broadcast in Spanish, which occurred during their inaugural season in 1993. Since then, the Panthers have continued to add Spanish-language broadcasts, and for the 2014–2015 season all of their games after October 30 were broadcast in Spanish in southern Florida.

LOS ANGELES KINGS
City: Los Angeles, CA
Arena: Staples Center (18,230 seats)
Founded: 1967
Mascot: Bailey
Nickname: The Crown, Monarchs
AHL Affiliate: Ontario Reign
ECHL Affiliate: Manchester Monarchs
Fun Fact: The Kings became the first team in North American professional sports to win a championship as an eighth seed, when they won the 2011–2012 Stanley Cup. They were not the first team to reach the Finals as an eight seed because the Oilers did so in 2006 only to lose to the Carolina Hurricanes.

MINNESOTA WILD
City: St. Paul, MN
Arena: Xcel Energy Center (17,954 seats)
Founded: 1997 (first active season: 2000)
Mascot: Nordy
Nickname: Minny
AHL Affiliate: Iowa Wild
ECHL Affiliate: Quad City Mallards, Alaska Aces
Fun Fact: Minnesota was the first team in NHL history to come back from 3–1 deficits twice in the same playoff year. In 2003, they did so against the Colorado Avalanche and the Vancouver Canucks only to get swept by the Mighty Ducks of Anaheim in the Conference Final.

MONTREAL CANADIENS
City: Montreal, QC
Arena: Bell Centre (21,287 seats)
Founded: 1909
Mascot: Youppi
Nickname: Habs, Les Habitants, Le CH, Les Canadiens, Le-Bleu-Blanc-Rouge, Le Grand Club, Les Glorieux, La-Sainte-Flanelle
AHL Affiliate: St. John's Ice Caps
ECHL Affiliate: Brampton Beast
Fun Fact: The Habs own the NHL record for the most consecutive winning seasons, with 32. That streak ended in 1983–1984, when their record was 35–40–5.

NASHVILLE PREDATORS
City: Nashville, TN
Arena: Bridgestone Arena (20,000 seats)
Founded: 1998
Mascot: Gnash
Nickname: Preds
AHL Affiliate: Milwaukee Admirals
ECHL Affiliate: Cincinnati Cyclones
Fun Fact: The Predators chose their logo of a sabre-tooth cat because of an historic event that occurred in Nashville in 1971. A sabre-tooth cat fang was found as construction workers were digging a foundation for a new building in downtown Nashville. That marked only the fifth time sabre-tooth remains had been found in North America.

NEW JERSEY DEVILS
City: Newark, NJ
Arena: Prudential Center (18,711 seats)
Previous Team: Kansas City Scouts (1974–1976), Colorado Rockies (1976–1982)
Founded: 1982
Mascot: NJ Devil
Nickname: Devs, Jersey's Team
AHL Affiliate: Albany Devils
Fun Fact: The team got its name from a "Name the Team" fan contest similar to one in Columbus. The name comes from the legend of the New Jersey Devil, the thirteenth child of a woman who invoked the spirit of the Devil during painful hours of labor. The legend goes that the Devil-child escaped his family and set off to live in the New Jersey Pine Barrens, where he lurks to this day.

NEW YORK ISLANDERS
City: Brooklyn, New York, NY
Arena: Barclays Center (15,813 seats)
Founded: 1972

Previous Location: Long Island, NY (Nassau Coliseum 1972–2014)
Mascot: Sparky the Dragon
Nickname: Isles
AHL Affiliate: Bridgeport Sound Tigers
ECHL Affiliate: Missouri Mavericks
Fun Fact: The Islanders selected the franchise's leading scorer, Mike Bossy, in the 1977 NHL Draft. In 1981, Bossy scored 50 goals in his first 50 games, becoming only the second player to start a season in that fashion since Maurice "Rocket" Richard did so in the 1944–1945 season.

NEW YORK RANGERS
City: Manhattan, New York, NY
Arena: Madison Square Garden (18,200 seats)
Founded: 1926
Nickname: Blueshirts, The Broadway Blueshirts, Tex's Rangers
AHL Affiliate: Hartford Wolfpack
ECHL Affiliate: Greenville Road Warriors
Fun Fact: By winning the Stanley Cup in 1994, the New York Rangers became the first team in NHL history to have a Russian born hockey player win it all. In fact, it wasn't just one Russian to win Lord Stanley that year: Alexei Kovalev, the most popular Russian on the team completed the feat with fellow countrymen Sergei Nemchinov, Alexander Karpovtsev, and Sergei Zubov.

OTTAWA SENATORS
City: Ottawa, ON
Arena: Canadian Tire Centre (20,500 seats)
Founded: 1990 (first active season, 1992)
Mascot: Spartacat
Nickname: Sens
AHL Affiliate: Binghamton Senators
ECHL Affiliate: Evansville Icemen
Fun Fact: The Original Ottawa Senators left town in 1934, and they went out in style. In their final home game of 1933, the crowd threw an assortment of fruits and vegetables onto the ice, including carrots, parsnips, lemons, and oranges. The next day, the *Ottawa Evening Citizen* reported that the fans said they threw them "for no reason whatsoever."

PHILADELPHIA FLYERS
City: Philadelphia, PA
Arena: Wells Fargo Center (19,500 seats)
Founded: 1967
Mascot: None, formally Slapshot
Nickname: Broad Street Bullies, Orange & Black, Fly Guys

AHL Affiliate: Lehigh Valley Phantoms
ECHL Affiliate: Reading Royals
Fun Fact: The Flyers went 25–0–10 over 35 games during the 1979–1980 season. The streak of 35 games without a loss is the longest such streak by any North American sports team.

PITTSBURGH PENGUINS
City: Pittsburgh, PA
Arena: Consol Energy Center (19,758 seats)
Founded: 1967
Mascot: Iceburgh
Nickname: Pens, 'Guins
AHL Affiliate: Wilkes-Barre/Scranton Penguins
ECHL Affiliate: Wheeling Nailers
Fun Fact: The Pittsburgh Penguins logo features a penguin playing hockey on top of a gold triangle. This triangle represents the "Golden Triangle" of downtown Pittsburgh. This is the place where the Monongahela and Allegheny Rivers meet to form the Ohio River.

SAINT LOUIS BLUES
City: St. Louis, MO
Arena: Scottrade Center (19,260 seats)
Founded: 1967
Mascot: Louie the Bear
Nickname: Bluenotes, The 'Notes
AHL Affiliate: Chicago Wolves
ECHL Affiliate: Alaska Aces
Fun Fact: The Blues' namesake, as well as its logo, are both derived from the "Blues" genre of music that was extremely prominent in St. Louis during the early- to mid-1900s. When the Blues were first brought into the league as an expansion franchise in 1967, their original owner, Sid Saloman Jr., insisted the team be called the Blues because no matter where you went in the city someone was always singing. The logo followed the same path. A blue music note with wings coming off the end became the Blues' first logo. Since then, the note-with-wings logo remains.

SAN JOSE SHARKS
City: San Jose, CA
Arena: SAP Center
Founded: 1991
Mascot: SJ Sharkie
Nickname: Fins, Fish
AHL Affiliate: San Jose Barracuda
ECHL Affiliate: Allen Americans

Fun Fact: The ownership history of the Sharks is longer and more confusing than one might expect. Gordan and George Gund III were part owners of the California Golden Seals and helped to move that franchise to Cleveland, later merging the team with the Minnesota North Stars. The Gunds' attempt to have the North Stars moved to the Bay Area was denied in the late 1980s. Meanwhile, an owner of the Hartford franchise, Howard Baldwin, shared the vision of a Bay Area team. The NHL brokered a deal in which the Gunds sold their shares of the North Stars to Baldwin, and in return the Gunds were given the new franchise in San Jose.

TAMPA BAY LIGHTNING

City: Tampa Bay, FL
Arena: Amalie Arena (20,500 seats)
Founded: 1992
Mascot: Thunderbug
Nickname: Bolts
AHL Affiliate: Syracuse Crunch
ECHL Affiliate: Florida Everblades
Fun Fact: In 2015 the Lightning became the first team in NHL history to eliminate three straight original six teams in the playoffs. They defeated the Detroit Red Wings in the first round, the Montreal Canadiens in the second round, and the New York Rangers in the third round. They had a chance to beat a fourth-straight original six team but lost to the Chicago Blackhawks in the Stanley Cup Final.

TORONTO MAPLE LEAFS

City: Toronto, ON
Arena: Air Canada Centre (19,800 seats)
Founded: 1917 as the Arenas; named the St. Patricks from 1919–1926
Mascot: Carlton the Bear
Nickname: The Leafs, Bay Street Bullies
AHL Affiliate: Toronto Marlies
ECHL Affiliate: Orlando Solar Bears
Fun Fact: The Toronto Maple Leafs became the first NHL franchise to win three consecutive Stanley Cups, doing so in 1947–1949. That streak has since been bested as the Montreal Canadiens and New York Islanders, both of which won four consecutive Stanley Cups.

VANCOUVER CANUCKS

City: Vancouver, BC
Arena: Rogers Arena (18,630 seats)
Founded: 1945
Mascot: Fin the Whale
Nickname: 'Nucks
AHL Affiliate: Utica Comets

ECHL Affiliate: Kalamazoo Wings

Fun Fact: The name "Canucks" was actually adopted from a classic Canadian cartoon hero, Johnny Canuck, who first appeared as a political cartoon in 1969. The character was portrayed as a lumberjack, hockey player, and regular citizen. Although the Canucks had initially done away with their original Johnny Canuck logo, they recently brought back a lumberjack version of Johnny Canuck as one of the team logos.

WASHINGTON CAPITALS

City: Washington, DC
Arena: Verizon Center (18,277 seats)
Founded: 1974
Mascot: Slapshot
Nickname: Caps, Eagles, The Red Army
AHL Affiliate: Hershey Bears
ECHL Affiliate: South Carolina Stingrays
Fun Fact: The Capitals inaugural season in the NHL came in 1974–1975. They would go on to post the worst record in NHL history (8-67-5, for a total of 21 points), which still stands today.

WINNIPEG JETS

City: Winnipeg, MB
Arena: MTS Centre (15,004 seats)
Founded: 2012
Former Team: Atlanta Thrashers (1999–2012)
Mascot: Mick E. Moose
Nickname: The Airforce
AHL Affiliate: St. John's Ice Caps
Fun Fact: The Winnipeg Jets are the only NHL franchise that has been relocated, only to later come back to the same city with the same team name. The first Winnipeg Jets franchise played in the NHL from 1979–1996, when the team was sold to a group of investors who, hoping for better financial conditions, moved the team to Phoenix, where it became the Coyotes. However, the Winnipeg Jets came to life again when the now-defunct Atlanta Thrashers sold their team to a Winnipeg-based investment group due to financial problems.

Stan Fischler's Top 100 Hockey Players

Note: Years listed are the players NHL playing careers or in the event of a lockout years they remained under contract/active as NHL players. Years that are not included are years they played elsewhere—excluding lockout seasons—in the NHA, WHA, KHL, etc., or mid-career retirement.

#1 WAYNE GRETZKY (1961–)

Playing Career: 1979–1999
Position: Center
Teams: Oilers, Kings, Blues, Rangers
Achievements: Among his many accolades, he won ten Art Ross Trophies (1980–1981 / 1981–1982 / 1982–1983 / 1983–1984 / 1984–1985 / 1985–1986 / 1986–1987 / 1989–1990 / 1990–1991 / 1993–1994), five Lady Byng Trophies (1979–1980 / 1990–1991 / 1991–1992 / 1993–1994 / 1998–1999), two Conn Smythe Trophies (1984–1985 / 1987–1988), nine Hart Trophies (1979–1980 / 1980–1981 / 1981–1982 / 1982–1983 / 1983–1984 / 1984–1985 / 1985–1986 / 1986–1987 / 1988–1989), five Ted Lindsay Awards (1981–1982 / 1982–1983 / 1983–1984 / 1984–1985 / 1986–1987) and one Lester Patrick Trophy (1993–1994). He was a four-time Stanley Cup champion, all as a member of the Oilers. His number 99 is retired throughout the NHL. The leading scorer in NHL history with 2,857 points, Gretzky recorded more assists (1,963) than any other player totaled points, and he is the only NHL player to notch over 200 points in one season—a feat he accomplished four times. His 894 regular season goals are also a record. "The Great One" is the all-time career leader in playoff scoring, with 382 points, and is the all-time post-season leader in goals (122) and assists (260).

#2 BOBBY ORR (1948–)

Playing Career: 1966–1979
Position: Defenseman
Teams: Bruins, Black Hawks
Achievements: Orr won eight consecutive Norris Trophies (1967–1968 / 1968–1969 / 1969–1970 / 1970–1971 / 1971–1972 / 1972–1973 / 1973–1974 / 1974–1975) and three

consecutive Hart Trophies (1969–1970 / 1970–1971 / 1971–1972). "Number Four, Bobby Orr" also won the Calder Trophy (1966–1967), the Lester Patrick Trophy (1978–1979), the Ted Lindsay Award (1974–1975) and two Conn Smythe Trophies (1969–1970 / 1971–1972). He won two Stanley Cups with Boston and scored the Cup-winning goal both times. Orr remains the only defenseman to win the league scoring title with two Art Ross Trophies (1969–1970 / 1974–1975) and holds the record for most points (139) and assists (102) in a single season (1970–1971) by a defenseman.

3 GORDIE HOWE (1928–)
Playing Career: 1946–1971, 1979–1980
Position: Right Wing
Teams: Red Wings, Whalers
Achievements: "Mr. Hockey" won four Stanley Cups with Detroit. He suited up in 23 NHL All-Star games. He also won six Art Ross Trophies (1950–1951 / 1951–1952 / 1952–1953 / 1953–1954 / 1956–1957 / 1962–1963), six Hart Trophies (1951–1952 / 1952–1953 / 1956–1957 / 1957–1958 / 1959–1960 / 1962–1963), the Lester Patrick Trophy (1966–1967), and in 2007–2008 he won the NHL Lifetime Achievement Award. Howe played in the most NHL games in league history, with 1,767. He finished his career as the all-time points leader (1,850) but has since been surpassed by Wayne Gretzky and Mark Messier. Howe's 801 goals are second all-time and he ranks ninth in assists with 1,049.

#4 MARIO LEMIEUX (1965–)
Playing Career: 1984–1997, 2000–2006
Position: Center
Teams: Penguins
Achievements: Four-time Lester B. Pearson Award winner (1985–1986 / 1987–1988/ 1992–1993 / 1995–1996), six-time Art Ross Trophy winner (1987–1988 / 1988–1989 / 1991–1992 / 1992–1993 / 1995–1996 / 1996–1997), two-time Conn Smythe Trophy winner (1990–1991 / 1991–1992), three-time Hart Trophy winner (1987–1988 / 1992–1993 / 1995–1996), and a four-time Ted Lindsay Award winner (1985–1986 / 1987–1988 / 1992–1993 / 1995–1996). "Super Mario" also brought home the Calder Trophy (1984–1985), Bill Masterton Trophy (1992–1993) and Lester Patrick Trophy (1999–2000). His 1,723 career points rank eighth all-time. Lemieux became the third player (after Gordie Howe and Guy Lafleur) to appear in an NHL game after being inducted into Hockey Hall of Fame on December 27, 2000. Lemieux led Pittsburgh to two consecutive Stanley Cups in 1990–1991 and 1991–1992. He also led Team Canada to an Olympic gold medal in 2002, a championship at the 2004 World Cup of Hockey and a Canada Cup in 1987.

#5 MAURICE RICHARD (1921–2000)
Playing Career: 1942–1960
Position: Right Wing
Team: Canadiens

Achievements: He won the Hart Trophy in 1946–1947 and played in 13 All-Star games. Richard was a member of eight Stanley Cup championship teams including five straight between 1956 and 1960. The Trophy for the NHL's top goal scorer each season bears his name. Nicknamed the "Rocket," he was the first player in NHL history to score 50 goals in one season, accomplishing the feat in 50 games in 1944–1945, and the first to reach 500 career goals.

#6 DOUG HARVEY (1924–1989)

Playing Career: 1947–1969
Position: Defenseman
Teams: Canadiens, Rangers, Red Wings, Blues.
Achievements: With Montreal, Harvey won six Stanley Cups. He also took home seven Norris Trophies (1954–1955 / 1955–1956 / 1956–1957 / 1957–1958 / 1959–1960 / 1960–1961 / 1961–1962). He played in 13 All-Star contests.

#7 JEAN BELIVEAU (1931–2014)

Playing Career: 1950–1971
Position: Center
Team: Canadiens
Achievements: Beliveau won two Hart Trophies (1955–1956 / 1963–1964), and one Art Ross Trophy (1955–1956), as well as the inaugural Conn Smythe Trophy (1964–1965). He finished his career with 1,219 points, which is the second all-time in Canadiens history, and played on 10 Stanley Cup winners, which is tied for second all-time.

#8 BOBBY HULL (1939–)

Playing Career: 1957–1972, 1979–1980
Position: Left Wing
Teams: Black Hawks, Jets, Whalers
Achievements: He won the Hart Trophy twice (1964–1965 / 1965–1966), the Art Ross Trophy three times (1959–1960 / 1961–1962 / 1965–1966), the Lady Byng Trophy (1964–1965), the Lester Patrick Trophy (1968–1969), and he won one Stanley Cup with the Black Hawks in 1960–1961. Hull played in a dozen NHL All-Star games. His famous shot earned him the nickname "The Golden Jet."

#9 TERRY SAWCHUK (1929–1970)

Playing Career: 1949–1970
Position: Goaltender
Teams: Red Wings, Bruins, Maple Leafs, Kings, Rangers
Achievements: Sawchuk won 447 regular season contests and ranks second all-time with 103 shutouts. He won another 54 postseason games to go along with four Stanley Cups, three with Detroit and one with Toronto. He won the Calder Trophy (1950–1951), Lester Patrick Trophy (1970–1971) and four Vezina Trophies (1951–1952 / 1952–1953 / 1954–1955 / 1964–1965). Sawchuk played in 11 All-Star games.

#10 EDDIE SHORE (1902–1985)

Playing Career: 1926–1940
Position: Defenseman
Teams: Bruins, Americans
Achievements: A two-time Stanley Cup winner with Boston, Shore won the Hart Trophy four times (1932–1933 / 1934–1935 / 1935–1936 / 1937–1938), second only to Howe and Gretzky, and the Lester Patrick Trophy (1969–1970).

#11 GUY LAFLEUR (1951–)

Playing Career: 1971–1985, 1988–1991
Position: Right Wing
Teams: Canadiens, Rangers, Nordiques
Achievements: Lafleur became the first player in the NHL to score 50 goals and 100 points in six straight seasons. Cornerstone player of five Cup championships with the Canadiens, Lafleur is the franchise's all-time leading scorer, notching 1,246 points (518 goals and 728 assists) in his 14 years with the Habs. He also holds the franchise record for points in a season, with 136 in 1976–1977. He won the Art Ross three times (1975–1976 / 1976–1977 / 1977–1978), one Conn Smythe (1976–1977), two Hart Trophies (1976–1977 / 1977–1978), and three Ted Lindsay Awards (1975–1976 / 1976–1977 / 1977–1978).

#12 MARK MESSIER (1961–)

Playing Career: 1979–2004
Position: Center
Teams: Oilers, Rangers, Canucks.
Achievements: Messier is second all-time in regular season points (1,887), playoff points (295) and regular season games played (1,756). He won six Stanley Cups, five with the Oilers and one with the Rangers. "The Messiah" is the only player to captain two different professional teams to championships. He won the Hart Trophy two times (1989–1990 / 1991–1992), the Ted Lindsay Award twice (1989–1990 / 1991–1992), the Conn Smythe Trophy in the Oilers first run to the Stanley Cup title in 1983–1984, and one Lester Patrick Trophy (2008–2009). Messier suited up in 15 NHL All-Star games.

#13 JACQUES PLANTE (1929–1986)

Playing Career: 1952–1965, 1968–1973
Position: Goaltender
Teams: Canadiens, Rangers, Blues, Maple Leafs, Bruins
Achievements: Plante was an innovator as a goaltender when he was the first to wear a mask in net on a consistent basis. He won one Hart Trophy (1961–1962), six Cups with the Canadiens, including five straight from 1956–1960, and seven Vezina Trophies (1955–1956 / 1956–1957 / 1957–1958 / 1958–1959 / 1959–1960 / 1961–1962 / 1968–1969).

#14 Ray Bourque (1960–)

Playing Career: 1979–2001

Position: Defenseman

Teams: Bruins, Avalanche

Achievements: Bourque holds the record for most career goals (410), assists (1,169) and points (1,579) by a defenseman. Bourque played 21 seasons for the Bruins and was the team's longest-serving captain. He won his only Cup in his last season as a member of the Colorado Avalanche in 2000–2001. Bourque suited up in 19 All-Star contests. He won the Calder Trophy (1979–1980), King Clancy Memorial Trophy (1991–1992), Lester Patrick Trophy (2002–2003), and five Norris Trophies (1986–1987 / 1987–1988 / 1989–1990 / 1990–1991 / 1993–1994).

#15 Howie Morenz (1902–1937)

Playing Career: 1923–1937

Position: Center

Teams: Canadiens, Black Hawks, Rangers

Achievements: Morenz was a three-time Stanley Cup winner with the Canadiens. He won three Hart Trophies (1927–1928, 1930–1931, 1931–1932) and was a two-time Art Ross winner (1927–1928 / 1930–1931).

#16 Martin Brodeur (1972–)

Playing Career: 1991–2015

Position: Goaltender

Teams: Devils, Blues

Achievements: A three-time Stanley Cup champion with the Devils, Brodeur is the NHL's all-time goaltending leader in games played (1,266), wins (691) and shutouts (125). He has the most postseason shutouts with 24. His 113 playoff victories are second all-time. Brodeur scored an NHL record three goals in his career: two during the regular season and one in the postseason. He led the NHL in wins nine seasons, in shutouts five times, and in games played six times, including 10 consecutive seasons of 70 or more from 1997–98 to 2007–08. Brodeur's 48 wins in 2006–2007 are a single-season record. He won the Calder Trophy (1993–1994), five Williams Jennings Trophies (1996–1997 / 1997–1998 / 2002–2003 / 2003–2004 / 2009–2010), and four Vezina Trophies (2002–2003 / 2003–2004 / 2006–2007 / 2007–2008). He is also a two-time Olympic gold medalist with Canada (2002, 2010) and led his nation to the gold in the 2004 World Cup of Hockey.

#17 Stan Mikita (1940–)

Playing Career: 1958–1980

Position: Center

Team: Black Hawks

Achievements: Mikita is the only player in NHL history to win the Hart, Art Ross, and Lady Byng Trophies in the same season, doing so in consecutive seasons in 1966–1967 and 1967–1968. He won the Art Ross two more times (1963–1964 / 1964–1965). He won the Lester Patrick Trophy in 1975–1976. A winner of the Stanley Cup with the Black Hawks in 1960–1961, Mikita ranks first all-time in franchise history in assists (926) and points (1,467), and is second in franchise history in goals (541).

#18 PHIL ESPOSITO (1942–)

Playing Career: 1963–1981
Position: Center
Teams: Black Hawks, Bruins, Rangers
Achievements: Esposito won five Art Ross Trophies (1968–1969 / 1970–1971 / 1971–1972 / 1972–1973 / 1973–1974), two Hart Trophies (1968–1969 / 1973–1974), two Ted Lindsay Awards (1970–1971 / 1972–1973), and the Lester Patrick Trophy (1977–1978). He also played in ten All-Star games. In a career in which he played for three Original Six franchises, he was a two-time Cup winner with Boston (1969–1970 / 1971–1972).

#19 DENIS POTVIN (1953–)

Playing Career: 1973–1988
Position: Defenseman
Team: Islanders
Achievements: Potvin played 15 seasons in the NHL and was a member of all four Islanders Cup-championship teams during the dynasty from 1980 to 1983. He won the Calder Trophy (1973–1974) and three Norris Trophies (1975–1976 / 1977–1978 / 1978–1979). He was elected to the Hall of Fame in 1991.

#20 MIKE BOSSY (1957–)

Playing Career: 1977–1987
Position: Right Wing
Team: Islanders
Achievements: Bossy played 10 seasons in the NHL and was a crucial part of the Islanders' four-year reign as Stanley Cup champions from 1980 to 1983. He is the only player in NHL history to score consecutive Cup-winning goals, which he did in 1982 and 1983. Bossy remains the only player to record four game-winning goals in one series (1983 Conference Finals vs. Boston), is the NHL's all-time leader in average goals scored per regular season game, and is one of only five players to score 50 goals in 50 games. Bossy won the Calder Trophy (1977–1978), three Lady Byng Trophies (1982–1983 / 1983–1984 / 1985–1986), and the Conn Smythe Trophy (1981–1982).

#21 JAROMIR JAGR (1972–)

Playing Career: 1990–2008, 2011–
Position: Right Wing
Teams: Penguins, Capitals, Rangers, Flyers, Stars, Bruins, Devils, Panthers
Achievements: As of the conclusion of the 2014–2015 season, Jagr has the most goals (722), assists (1,080), and points (1,802) of any non-North American born player in NHL history. He is fourth all-time in NHL scoring. A two-time Cup winner with the Penguins

in his first two seasons, Jagr is the oldest player to record a hat trick, doing so with his 15th career trick on January 3, 2015, as a Devil at the age of 42. Jagr holds the league record for overtime goals (19) and game-winning goals (129). The Kladno, Czech Republic native has won five Art Ross Trophies (1994–1995 / 1997–1998 / 1998–1999 / 1999–2000 / 2000–2001), one Hart Trophy (1998–1999) and three Ted Lindsay Awards (1998–1999 / 1999–2000 / 2005–2006).

#22 TED LINDSAY (1925–)

Playing Career: 1944–1960, 1964–1965
Position: Left Wing
Teams: Red Wings, Black Hawks
Achievements: A four-time Cup winner with the Red Wings, Lindsay scored 851 points in his Hockey Hall of Fame career. He won the Art Ross Trophy in 1949–1950 and the Lester Patrick Trophy in 2007–2008. Lindsay also skated in 11 All-Star contests. Often referred to as "Terrible Ted," Lindsay helped to organize the National Hockey League Players' Association (NHLPA) in the late 1950s. He is the namesake of the Ted Lindsay Award, which is presented annually to the "Most Outstanding Player" in the NHL, as voted by fellow members of the NHLPA.

#23 RED KELLY (1927–)

Playing Career: 1947–1967
Position: Defenseman
Teams: Red Wings, Maple Leafs
Achievements: Kelly won eight Stanley Cups, four each with the Maple Leafs and Red Wings. He played in 13 All-Star games and won the first Norris Trophy (1953–1954) and four Lady Byng Trophies (1950–1951 / 1952–1953 / 1953–1954 / 1960–1961).

#24 BOBBY CLARKE (1949–)

Playing Career: 1969–1984
Position: Center
Team: Flyers
Achievements: Clarke captained the Flyers from 1973 to 1979, winning the Stanley Cup with them in 1973–1974 and 1974–1975. He won the Hart Trophy three times (1972–1973 / 1974–1975 / 1975–1976), the Bill Masterton Trophy (1971–1972), the Ted Lindsay Award (1973–1974), the Lester Patrick Trophy (1979–1980), and the Selke Trophy (1982–1983).

#25 KEN DRYDEN (1947–)

Playing Career: 1970–1979
Position: Goaltender
Team: Canadiens
Achievements: Dryden won the Conn Smythe Trophy in 1970–1971 before his official rookie season in 1971–1972, a year that culminated with him winning the Calder Tro-

phy. He won all six games he played during 1970–1971, but it did not qualify as an official rookie season. He won five Vezina Trophies (1972–1973 / 1975–1976 / 1976–1977 / 1977–1978 / 1978–1979) in a surprisingly short seven-year career. Dryden won six Stanley Cups.

#26 LARRY ROBINSON (1951–)

Playing Career: 1972–1992
Position: Defenseman
Teams: Canadiens, Kings
Achievements: Robinson is the NHL's all-time plus/minus leader, finishing his career +730. He is the Canadiens all-time leader among defensemen in goals (197), assists (686) and points (883). He played all but his final three seasons with Montreal and finished his career with 958 points. Robinson won the Norris Trophy two times (1976–1977 / 1979–1980), the Conn Smythe Trophy (1977–1978) and six Stanley Cups with Montreal.

#27 FRANCIS MAHOVLICH (1938–)

Playing Career: 1956–1974
Position: Left Wing
Teams: Maple Leafs, Red Wings, Canadiens
Achievements: Mahovlich won the Calder Trophy (1957–1958) and six Cups, four with the Maple Leafs and two with the Canadiens. He suited up in 15 All-Star games.

#28 PAUL COFFEY (1961–)

Playing Career: 1980–2001
Position: Defenseman
Teams: Oilers, Penguins, Kings, Red Wings, Whalers, Flyers, Blackhawks, Hurricanes, Bruins
Achievements: Coffey ranks second all-time among NHL defensemen in career goals (396), assists (1,135), and points (1,531). He won three Stanley Cups with the Oilers and a fourth with the Penguins. He won two Norris Trophies (1984–1985 / 1985–1986) with Edmonton and a third (1994–1995) with Detroit. He played in 14 All-Star games.

#29 MILT SCHMIDT (1918–)

Playing Career: 1936–1942, 1945–1955
Position: Center
Team: Bruins
Achievements: A two-time Cup winner as a player, Schmidt won the Art Ross Trophy (1939–1940), Hart Trophy (1950–1951) and Lester Patrick Trophy (1995–1996) during his 16-year career.

#30 HENRI RICHARD (1936–)

Playing Career: 1955–1975
Position: Center

Team: Canadiens

Achievements: Henri won 11 Stanley Cups, more than any other player in hockey history. He scored the Stanley Cup clinching goal at the 2:20 mark of the first overtime of Game Six in the 1966 Stanley Cup Finals against the Detroit Red Wings. In the 1971 Stanley Cup Finals, Richard scored the game-tying and Stanley Cup-winning goals in Game Seven against the Chicago Black Hawks. He played in a franchise-record 1,256 games for Montreal and won the Masterton Trophy in 1973–1974.

#31 BRYAN TROTTIER (1956–)

Playing Career: 1975–1992, 1993–1994

Position: Center

Teams: Islanders, Penguins

Achievements: Trottier won four Cups playing for the 1980–1983 Islanders dynasty and added another two Cups with the Penguins in 1990–1991 and 1991–1992. He won the Calder Trophy (1975–1976), Hart Trophy (1978–1979), Art Ross Trophy (1978–1979), Conn Smythe Trophy (1979–1980), and King Clancy Memorial Trophy (1988–1989).

#32 DOMINIK HASEK (1965–)

Playing Career: 1990–2008

Position: Goaltender

Teams: Blackhawks, Sabres, Red Wings, Senators

Achievements: Affectionately called the "Dominator," Hasek won two Stanley Cups with the Red Wings in 2001–2002 and 2007–2008. He led the Czech national ice hockey team to its first (and so far only) Olympic gold medal in 1998 in Nagano, Japan. Hasek won six Vezina Trophies, three Williams Jennings Trophies (1993–1994 / 2000–2001 / 2007–2008), two Hart Trophies (1996–1997 / 1997–1998), and two Ted Lindsay Awards (1996–1997 / 1997–1998). He finished his career with 389 wins and 81 shutouts in 735 games.

#33 TED KENNEDY (1925–2009)

Playing Career: 1942–1955, 1956–1957

Position: Center

Team: Maple Leafs

Achievements: Kennedy won five Stanley Cups and one Hart Trophy (1954–1955). He suited up in six All-Star games.

#34 NEWSY LALONDE (1887–1970)

Playing Career: 1917–1922, 1926–1927

Position: Center

Teams: Canadiens, Americans

Achievements: Lalonde started his career with the Canadiens in 1909–1910, while they were a member of the NHA, and continued to suit up for the Habs when they became a founding member of the NHL in 1917–1918. In 99 games in the NHL, one of which came with the Americans in 1926–1927, Lalonde, also known as the "Flying Frenchman," totaled 124 goals and 41 assists. He notched 21 goals and four assists in 12 NHL postseason games, all with the Habs. He led the NHL in points in 1918–1919 and 1920–1921. He won the Stanley Cup with Montreal in 1916.

#35 PATRICK ROY (1965–)

Playing Career: 1984–2003
Position: Goaltender
Teams: Canadiens, Avalanche
Achievements: Roy is the only player in NHL history to win the Conn Smythe Trophy three times (1985–1986 / 1992–1993 / 2000–2001). His number 33 jersey is retired by both Montreal, where he compiled 289 victories in 551 games, and Colorado, where he totaled 262 wins in 478 games. He ranks second in NHL history with 1,029 games played and 551 wins. In the postseason he sits second in shutouts with 23 but first in games played (247) and wins (151). He backstopped both the Canadiens and the Avalanche to two Stanley Cups each. He won three Vezina Trophies (1988–1989 / 1989–1990 / 1991–1992) and five Williams Jennings Trophies (1986–1987 / 1987–1988 / 1988–1989 / 1991–1992 / 2001–2002).

#36 CHARLIE CONACHER (1909–1967)

Playing Career: 1929–1941
Position: Right Wing
Teams: Maple Leafs, Red Wings, Americans
Achievements: Conacher led the NHL five times in goals and two times won the Art Ross Trophy (1933–1934 / 1934–1935). Over five seasons—from 1931–1932 to 1935–1936—Conacher was named to three NHL First All-Star teams and two NHL Second All-Star teams. He won one Cup in 1931–1932 with the Maple Leafs.

#37 MARCEL DIONNE (1951–)

Playing Career: 1971–1989
Position: Center
Teams: Red Wings, Kings, Rangers
Achievements: Dionne won two Lady Byng Trophies (1974–1975 / 1976–1977), two Ted Lindsay Awards (1978–1979 / 1979–1980), one Art Ross Trophy (1979–1980), and the Lester Patrick Trophy (2005–2006). He ranks fourth all-time in goals (731), tenth in assists (1,040), and sixth in points (1,771).

#38 JOE MALONE (1890–1969)

Playing Career: 1917–1924
Position: Center
Teams: Canadiens, Bulldogs, Tigers
Achievements: Malone is the only player in the history of the NHL to score seven goals in a single game. He won two Art Ross Trophies (1917–1918 / 1919–1920) and also led the league in goals both seasons. Malone totaled 175 points in 126 NHL games. He won

two Cups with the Bulldogs during their time in the NHA and one while in the NHL with the Habs in 1923–1924.

#39 BILL DURNAN (1916–1972)
Playing Career: 1943–1950
Position: Goaltender
Team: Canadiens
Achievements: The NHL passed a rule after the 1947–1948 season barring goaltenders from performing the duties of captain that became known as the "Durnan Rule." Durnan compiled 208 wins in 383 games, won the Vezina Trophy (1943–1944 / 1944–1945 / 1945–1946 / 1946–1947 / 1948–1949 / 1949–1950) in six of his seven seasons, and won two Stanley Cups.

#40 STEVE YZERMAN (1965–)
Playing Career: 1983–2006
Position: Center
Team: Red Wings
Achievements: Stevie Y captained Detroit from 1986 to 2006, the longest term as team captain in NHL history, and led the Red Wings to three Stanley Cups. He won the Ted Lindsay Award (1988–1989), Conn Smythe Trophy (1997–1998), Selke Trophy (1999–2000), Masterton Trophy (2002–2003), and Lester Patrick Trophy (2005–2006). In 1,514 games, Yzerman ranks ninth all-time with 692 goals, eighth with 1,063 assists, and seventh with 1,755 points.

#41 NICKLAS LIDSTROM (1970–)
Playing Career: 1991–2012
Position: Defenseman
Team: Red Wings
Achievements: Lidstrom won seven Norris Trophies (2000–2001 / 2001–2002 / 2002–2003 / 2005–2006 / 2006–2007 / 2007–2008 / 2010–2011) and one Conn Smythe Trophy (2001–2002), becoming the first European player to win the award for playoff MVP. He also became the first European to captain his team to the Stanley Cup title in 2007–2008, his fourth and final Stanley Cup. Lidstrom ranks first all-time among European defensemen in NHL history and first all-time by any defenseman in Red Wings history in games played (1,564), goals (264), assists (878), and points (1,142). He also played in 11 All-Star games.

#42 BERNIE GEOFFRION (1931–2006)
Playing Career: 1950–1968
Position: Right Wing
Teams: Canadiens, Rangers

Achievements: A six-time Cup winner with Montreal, "Boom-Boom" Geoffrion won the Calder Trophy (1951–1952), Hart Trophy (1960–1961), and two Art Ross Trophies (1954–1955 / 1960–1961). He played in 11 All-Star contests.

#43 FREDERICK WELLINGTON TAYLOR (1884–1979)

Playing Career: 1905–1923
Position: Rover/Forward
Teams: Vancouver Maroons, Vancouver Millionairs, Renfrew Creamery Kings, Ottawa Silver Seven, Portage Lakes Hockey Club
Achievements: "Cyclone" Taylor was one of the earliest professional hockey players and played in several leagues at the beginning of the 20th century. Towards the end of the 1905–1906 season, he was signed by the Portage Lakers of the International Hockey League, the first professional league in North America, and scored 11 goals in 6 games. The following season, he won the league title with Portage. He would go on to win two Stanley Cups, one with the Ottawa Silver Seven of the Eastern Canada Amateur Hockey Association in 1908–1909, and another in 1914–1915, when he played for the Vancouver Millionaires of the Pacific Coast Hockey Association. In 1945, he was elected to the Hockey Hall of Fame as a charter member.

#44 FRANK BOUCHER (1901–1977)

Playing Career: 1921–1922, 1926–1938, 1943–1944
Position: Center
Teams: Senators (1917), Rangers
Achievements: Boucher won an astounding seven Lady Byng Trophies (1927–1928 / 1928–1929 / 1929–1930 / 1930–1931 / 1932–1933 / 1933–1934 / 1934–1935). He won a pair of Stanley Cups with the Rangers. He was also a recipient of the Lester Patrick Trophy (1992–1993).

#45 TOE BLAKE (1912–1995)

Playing Career: 1934–1948
Position: Left Wing
Teams: Maroons, Canadiens
Achievements: Blake won three Stanley Cups, one with the Maroons and two with the Canadiens. He earned the Art Ross Trophy and the Hart Trophy in 1938–1939. He also won the Lady Byng Trophy in 1945–1946.

#46 KING CLANCY (1903–1986)

Playing Career: 1921–1937
Position: Defenseman
Teams: Senators (1917), Maple Leafs
Achievements: Clancy won two Stanley Cups with the Senators and a third with Toronto. He played in two All-Star games. He is the namesake of the King Clancy Memorial Trophy, which is an annual award given to the player who best exemplifies leadership qual-

ities on and off the ice and has made a noteworthy humanitarian contribution in his community. The winner is chosen by select members of the Professional Hockey Writers' Association and the NHL Broadcasters' Association.

#47 GILBERT PERREAULT (1950–)
Playing Career: 1970–1987
Position: Center
Team: Sabres
Achievements: Perreault is Buffalo's franchise leader in career regular season games played (1,191), goals (512), assists (814), points (1,326), and game-winning goals (81). He won the Calder Trophy (1970–1971) and the Lady Byng Trophy (1972–1973).

#48 DICKIE MOORE (1931–)
Playing Career: 1951–1963, 1964–1965, 1967–1968
Position: Left Wing
Teams: Canadiens, Maple Leafs, Blues
Achievements: Moorse notched 608 points in 719 regular season contests, and in the post-season he totaled 110 points in 135 games. He was a six-time Stanley Cup champion with Montreal. He won back-to-back Art Ross Trophies in 1957–1958 and 1958–1959.

#49 NELS STEWART (1902–1957)
Playing Career: 1925–1940
Position: Center
Teams: Maroons, Bruins, Americans
Achievements: In his rookie season with the Maroons, Stewart won the Art Ross Trophy, the Hart Trophy and the Stanley Cup. He won another Hart Trophy in 1929–1930. From 1925–1932 Stewart centered the Maroons legendary "S Line" with Hooley Smith and Babe Siebert flanking him. In 650 games he compiled 515 points.

#50 GLENN HALL (1931–)
Playing Career: 1952–1971
Position: Goaltender
Teams: Red Wings, Black Hawks, Blues
Achievements: Hall won the Calder Trophy (1955–1956), Conn Smythe Trophy (1967–1968), despite being on the defeated Blues team that fell in the Stanley Cup Finals, and won the Vezina Trophy three times (1962–1963 / 1966–1967 / 1968–1969). He played in 13 All-Star games and won the Stanley Cup with Detroit in 1951–1952 and with the Black Hawks in 1960–1961.

#51 TIM HORTON (1930–1974)
Playing Career: 1949–1974
Position: Defenseman
Teams: Maple Leafs, Rangers, Penguins, Sabres

Achievements: Horton won four Stanley Cups with the Maple Leafs, including three straight from 1961–1962 to 1963–1964. He played in seven All-Star contests. Horton ranks second all-time in Leafs franchise history, and first among Leafs defensemen, in games played with 1,185. His 458 points in a Leafs uniform ranks him third all-time among Toronto defensemen.

#52 GEORGE HAINSWORTH (1895–1950)

Playing Career: 1926–1937
Position: Goaltender
Teams: Canadiens, Maple Leafs
Achievements: Hainsworth won three Vezina Trophies (1926–1927 / 1927–1928 / 1928–1929). In 1928–1929 he set an all-time record with 22 shutouts as he posted a 0.92 goals against average while only playing 44 games, 22 of which he won. In 1930 he set another NHL record that still stands, going 270 minutes and 8 seconds without allowing a goal during the playoffs for the Canadiens. He backstopped the Canadiens to back-to-back Stanley Cups in 1929–1930 and 1930–1931.

#53 BILL COOK (1895–1986)

Playing Career: 1926–1937
Position: Right Wing
Team: Rangers
Achievements: Cook was the first captain of the New York Rangers, scored the first goal in franchise history, and led the team to two Stanley Cup championships. He was the Art Ross Trophy winner, with 37 points (33 of them goals) in his first season in the NHL, and did it again in 1932–1933.

#54 SYL APPS (1915–1998)

Playing Career: 1936–1943, 1945–1948
Position: Center
Team: Maple Leafs
Achievements: Apps won the Calder Trophy in 1936–1937 and also won the Lady Byng Memorial Trophy in 1941–1942. He notched 432 points in 423 games, winning three Stanley Cups.

#55 TURK BRODA (1914–1972)

Playing Career: 1936–1943, 1945–1952
Position: Goaltender
Team: Maple Leafs
Achievements: Broda led the league in wins in 1940–1941 and 1947–1948. He backstopped Toronto to five Stanley Cup championships, including the historic rally in the 1942 finals, when the Leafs stormed back to win the series after falling into a three-games-to-zero deficit. He won two Vezina Trophies (1940–1941 / 1947–1948).

#56 Scott Niedermayer (1973–)

Playing Career: 1991–2010
Position: Defenseman
Teams: Devils, Ducks
Achievements: Niedermayer won three Stanley Cups with New Jersey and another when he captained the Ducks to their first title in 2006–2007. He is a member of the Triple Gold Club, signifying he has won the Stanley Cup, the World Championship (2004), and an Olympic gold medal (2002, 2010). Niedermayer also played on gold-medal-winning squads at the 1991 World Junior Championship and the 2004 World Cup of Hockey, making him the only player in history to win every major North American and international championship available to a Canadian player. He won the Conn Smythe Trophy in 2003–2004 and the Norris Trophy in 2006–2007.

#57 Brett Hull (1964–)

Playing Career: 1986–2006
Position: Right Wing
Teams: Flames, Blues, Stars, Red Wings, Coyotes
Achievements: Hull totaled 1,391 points in 1,269 games. In the postseason he notched 190 points in 202 games, including the Cup-clinching goal for the Stars in 1999 against Buffalo. He won a second Stanley Cup in 2001–2002 with Detroit. He won the Lady Byng Trophy (1989–1990), Hart Trophy (1990–1991), and Ted Lindsay Award (1990–1991). On the international stage with the U.S. national team, he won the gold medal at the 1996 World Cup of Hockey and the silver medal at the 2002 Olympics.

#58 Max Bentley (1920–1983)

Playing Career: 1940–1943, 1945–1954
Position: Center
Teams: Black Hawks, Maple Leafs, Rangers
Achievements: Bentley won the Lady Byng Trophy (1942–1943), Hart Trophy (1945–1946), and two Art Ross Trophies (1945–1946 / 1946–1947). He was a three-time Stanley Cup winner with Toronto.

#59 Dit Clapper (1907–1978)

Playing Career: 1927–1947
Position: Right Wing and Defense
Team: Bruins
Achievements: Clapper was the right wing on the powerful "Dynamite Line," along with linemates Cooney Weiland and Dutch Gainor. Clapper was the first player in NHL history to play 20 seasons. He scored 474 points in 833 games. He won three Stanley Cups with Boston.

#60 Joe Sakic (1969–)

Playing Career: 1988–2009

Position: Center

Teams: Nordiques, Avalanche

Achievements: Sakic captained the Avalanche to two Stanley Cup championships in 1995–1996 and 2000–2001. He also won the gold medal with Canada at the 2002 Olympics. He finished his career with 625 goals, 1,016 assists, and 1,641 points (ninth in NHL history) in 1,378 games. He won the Conn Smythe Award in 1995–1996. In 2000–2001 he won the Lady Byng Trophy, Hart Trophy, and Ted Lindsay Award. He played in 12 All-Star games.

#61 BRAD PARK (1948–)

Playing Career: 1968–1985

Position: Defenseman

Teams: Rangers, Bruins, Red Wings

Achievements: In 1,113 games Park scored 896 points. He won the Bill Masterton Trophy in 1983–1984. Park played in nine All-Star games.

#62 CHRIS CHELIOS (1962–)

Playing Career: 1983–2010

Position: Defenseman

Teams: Canadiens, Blackhawks, Red Wings, Thrashers

Achievements: Chelios ranks fifth all-time and first among defensemen with 1,651 games played in the NHL. His 948 points rank tenth all-time among defensemen. He is a three-time Norris Trophy winner (1988–1989 / 1992–1993 / 1995–1996) and won the Mark Messier NHL Leadership Award in 2006–2007. Chelios suited up in 11 All-Star games. He won three Stanley Cups, one with Montreal and two with Detroit, and a gold medal at the 1996 World Cup of Hockey with the United States.

#63 PIERRE PILOTE (1931–)

Playing Career: 1955–1969

Position: Defenseman

Teams: Black Hawks, Maple Leafs

Achievements: Pilote played 890 games in the NHL, scoring 80 goals and 418 assists for 498 points. He won the Stanley Cup with Chicago in 1960–1961. Pilote took home three Norris Trophies (1962–1963 / 1963–1964 / 1964–1965).

#64 BERNIE PARENT (1945–)

Playing Career: 1965–1972, 1973–1979

Position: Goaltender

Teams: Bruins, Flyers, Maple Leafs

Achievements: During the 1973–1974 and 1974–1975 seasons, Parent backstopped the Flyers to consecutive Cup championships, winning the Vezina Trophy and Conn Smythe Trophy both seasons. He won 47 regulation games in 1973–1974, an NHL record.

#65 BILL COWLEY (1912–1993)

Playing Career: 1934–1947

Position: Center

Teams: Eagles, Bruins

Achievements: In 549 games, Cowley notched 195 goals and 353 assists for 548 points. He won one Art Ross Trophy and two Hart Trophies (1940–1941 / 1942–1943). With the Bruins, he won a pair of Stanley Cups.

#66 MATS SUNDIN (1971–)

Playing Career: 1990–2009

Position: Center

Teams: Nordiques, Maple Leafs, Canucks

Achievements: Sundin suited up in 981 games for Toronto and is the franchise's all-time leader in goals (420) and points (987). He ranks second in franchise history with 567 assists. A three-time Olympian with Sweden, Sundin ranks first all-time in NHL history among Swedish-born players in goals (564) and points (1,349). Sundin played in eight All-Star games and won the Mark Messier NHL Leadership Award in 2007–2008.

#67 TEEMU SELANNE (1970–)

Playing Career: 1992–2014

Position: Right Wing

Teams: Jets (1979), Ducks, Sharks, Avalanche

Achievements: The "Finnish Flash" is ranked first overall in NHL history among Finnish players in games played (1,451), goals (684), and points (1,457). He is second in assists among Finns with 773. Selanne ranks first all-time in Ducks franchise history in games played (966), goals, (457), assists (531), and points (988). Selanne broke into the NHL by scoring 76 goals in 1992–1993, a league record for a rookie, which ultimately earned him the Calder Trophy. He won the inaugural Maurice "Rocket" Richard Trophy in 1998–1999. He was named recipient of the Bill Masterton Trophy in 2005–2006. Selanne played in 10 All-Star contests. In 2006–2007 he won the Stanley Cup with the Ducks.

#68 FRANK BRIMSEK (1913–1998)

Playing Career: 1938–1943, 1945–1950

Position: Goaltender

Teams: Bruins, Black Hawks

Achievements: Brimsek led the NHL in wins with 33 in his rookie season, winning the Calder Trophy and Vezina Trophy, and leading the Bruins to the Stanley Cup. Brimsek won the Stanley Cup with Boston a second time in 1940–1941 and won the Vezina Trophy again the following season.

#69 SIDNEY CROSBY (1987–)

Playing Career: 2005–

Position: Center

Teams: Penguins

Achievements: In his rookie year of 2005–2006, Crosby finished sixth in league scoring with 102 points (39 goals, 63 assists), becoming the youngest player to notch at least 100 points. In his second season, he led the NHL with 120 points (36 goals, 84 assists), becoming the youngest player and only teenager to win the Art Ross Trophy. Crosby became the youngest person to captain his team to the Stanley Cup in 2008–2009, leading the league in postseason goals (15) along the way. He won a second Art Ross Trophy in 2013–2014. Also on his resume are two Hart Trophies (2006–2007 / 2013–2014), three Ted Lindsay Awards (2006–2007 / 2012–2013 / 2013–2014), the Maurice Richard Trophy (2009–2010), and the Mark Messier NHL Leadership Award (2009–2010).

#70 GRANT FUHR (1962–)

Playing Career: 1981–2000
Position: Goaltender
Teams: Oilers, Maple Leafs, Sabres, Kings, Blues, Flames
Achievements: Fuhr led the NHL in wins, with 30 in 1983–1984, and did so again with 40 in 1987–1988. He won the Vezina Trophy in 1987–1988 and the Williams Jennings Trophy in 1993–1994. He suited up in six All-Star games. Fuhr won five Stanley Cups with the Oilers.

#71 AUREL JOLIAT (1901–1986)

Playing Career: 1922–1938
Position: Left Wing
Team: Canadiens
Achievements: Joliat totaled 460 goals in 655 games with Montreal, winning the Stanley Cup three times. He played in two All-Star games. Joliat won the Hart Trophy in 1933–1934.

#72 BRIAN LEETCH (1968–)

Playing Career: 1987–2006
Position: Defenseman
Teams: Rangers, Maple Leafs, Bruins
Achievements: Leetch finished his career as the ninth-highest scorer among defensemen in the NHL with 1,028 points (247 goals and 781 assists). He won the Calder Trophy (1988–1989), two Norris Trophies (1991–1992 / 1996–1997), and the Lester Patrick Trophy (2006–2007), and he became the first American to win the Conn Smythe Trophy (1993–1994). He won the Stanley Cup in 1993–1994 with the Rangers.

#73 GEORGES VEZINA (1887–1926)

Playing Career: 1917–1926
Position: Goaltender
Team: Canadiens

Achievements: Vezina backstopped the team to the Stanley Cup in 1915–1916 and 1923–1924. Nicknamed the "Chicoutimi Cucumber" for his calm composure while in goal, Vezina won 103 of his 190 games in the NHL. In the postseason he was victorious in 10 of his 13 games, including five shutouts. Vezinas passed on March 26, 1926, and at the start of the 1926–1927 season the Canadiens donated the Vezina Trophy to the NHL, which was awarded to the goaltenders on the team with the fewest goals against until 1981–1982. Since then, the Trophy has been given to the goalkeeper judged to be the best at this position as voted by the general managers of all NHL clubs. When the Hockey Hall of Fame opened in 1945, Vezina was one of the original inductees.

#74 ELMER LACH (1918–2015)

Playing Career: 1940–1954
Position: Center
Team: Canadiens
Achievements: Lach was one-third of the "Punch Line" with Maurice Richard and Toe Blake. A three-time Stanley Cup champion, he retired as the league's all-time leading scorer in 1954 with 623 points in 664 games. Lach won the Hart Trophy in 1944–1945 and the Art Ross Trophy in 1944–1945 and 1947–1948.

#75 CY DENNENY (1891–1970)

Playing Career: 1917–1929
Position: Left Wing
Teams: Senators (1917), Bruins
Achievements: Nicknamed the "Cornwall Cult," he was a five-time Stanley Cup champion, four with Ottawa (1919–1920 / 1920–1921 / 1922–1923 / 1926–1927), and once with Boston (928–1929). Denneny recorded 333 points in 328 contests and was an Art Ross Trophy winner in 1923–1924. When he retired he was the league's all-time leader in points and in goals (248).

#76 MIKE MODANO (1970–)

Playing Career: 1989–2011
Position: Center
Teams: North Stars/Stars, Red Wings
Achievements: The first overall pick in the 1988 draft by the Minnesota North Stars (later known as the Dallas Stars following their relocation), Modano produced 561 goals, 813 assists, and 1,374 points in 1,499 regular season games. He ranks second all-time among American-born players in all four categories. He also suited up in seven All-Star contests. The face of the franchise led Dallas to the 1998–1999 Stanley Cup championship, notching 23 points in 23 games and was also a member of the champion U.S. national team in the 1996 World Cup of Hockey. Modano was inducted into the Hockey Hall of Fame in 2014.

#77 DOUG BENTLEY (1916–1972)

Playing Career: 1939–1954
Position: Left Wing
Teams: Black Hawks, Rangers
Achievements: Bentley led the NHL in goals twice (1942–1943, 1943,1944) and was an Art Ross Trophy winner in 1942–1943. That same season he made NHL history when he played on the league's first all-brothers line with Max and Reggie. Bentley played in five straight All-Star games from 1947–1951.

#78 ANDY BATHGATE (1932–)

Playing Career: 1952–1971
Position: Right Wing
Teams: Rangers, Maple Leafs, Red Wings, Penguins
Achievements: In 1,069 games, Bathgate notched 973 points. He won the Hart Trophy in 1958–1959. With Toronto, he won the Stanley Cup in 1963–1964. Bathgate played in eight All-Star games from 1957–1964. He is famous for contributing to one of the greatest innovations in NHL history: while a member of the Rangers, Bathgate was the player who forced Jacques Plante to put on a goalie mask after injuring the Montreal netminder with a shot to the face on November 1, 1959.

#79 JOE PRIMEAU (1906–1989)

Playing Career: 1927–1936
Position: Center
Teams: Maple Leafs
Achievements: Primeau became a full-time player for the Leafs in the 1929–1930 season. "Gentleman Joe" was a member of Toronto's "Kid Line" with Charlie Conacher and Busher Jackson. He won his only Stanley Cup as a player in 1931–1932 and won the Lady Byng Trophy that same season. During his NHL career, Primeau scored 66 goals and 177 assists for a total 243 points in 310 games.

#80 JOHN BUCYK (1935–)

Playing Career: 1955–1978
Position: Left Wing
Teams: Red Wings, Bruins
Achievements: Bucyk scored 556 goals and 813 assists for 1,369 points in 1,540 games. A two-time Cup champion with Boston, he won two Lady Byng Trophies (1970–1971 / 1973–1974) and the Lester Patrick Trophy (1976–1977). He suited up in seven All-Star games.

#81 PETER STASTNY (1956–)

Playing Career: 1980–1995
Position: Center
Teams: Nordiques, Devils, Blues

Achievements: In 977 games, Stastny was a scoring machine, producing 450 goals and 789 assists for 1,239 points. He tallied 33 goals and 72 assists in 93 postseason games. Stastny won the Calder Trophy in 1980–1981. He played in six All-Star games.

#82 ALEX DELVECCHIO (1931–)

Playing Career: 1950–1974
Position: Center
Team: Red Wings
Achievements: Delvecchio played in 1,549 games and amassed 456 goals and 825 assists for 1,281 points. He won the Lady Byng Trophy three times (1958–1959 / 1965–1966 / 1968–1969) and the Lester Patrick Trophy (1973–1974). He played in 13 All-Star contests and won three Stanley Cups.

#83 BILLY SMITH (1950–)

Playing Career: 1971–1989
Position: Goaltender
Teams: Kings, Islanders
Achievements: Smith was the Islanders' starting goaltender for their record run of 19 consecutive postseason series wins, and he won four Cups with New York. He won the Vezina Trophy (1981–1982), Williams Jennings Trophy (1982–1983), and the Conn Smythe Trophy (1982–1983). On November 28, 1979, against the Colorado Rockies, Smith was the first NHL goaltender to be credited with scoring a goal.

#84 DARRYL SITTLER (1950–)

Playing Career: 1970–1985
Position: Center
Teams: Maple Leafs, Flyers, Red Wings
Achievements: Sittler served as Maple Leafs captain from 1975–1981. On February 7, 1976, he set an NHL record that still stands for most points scored in one game: he recorded ten points (six goals, four assists) as the Leafs defeated the Bruins. On April 22, 1976, while playing against the Flyers, Sittler tied the playoff record for most goals in one game with five. Sittler went on to score 484 goals and 637 assists for 1,121 points in 1,096 games, a Hall-of-Fame-bound career. He played in four All-Star games.

#85 ALEX OVECHKIN (1985–)

Playing Career: 2005–
Position: Left Wing
Team: Capitals
Achievements: Ovechkin broke into the NHL with a Calder-Trophy-winning season in 2005–2006, scoring 52 goals and 54 assists. As of the conclusion of the 2014–2015 season, he has won an Art Ross Trophy (2007–2008), three Hart Trophies (2007–2008 / 2008–2009 / 2012–2013), three Ted Lindsay Awards (2007–2008 / 2008–2009 / 2009–2010), and five

Maurice Richard Trophies (2007–2008 / 2008–2009 / 2012–2013 / 2013–2014 / 2014–2015). Ovechkin has scored the most goals and points in Capitals history.

#86 CHRIS PRONGER (1974–)

Playing Career: 1993–2012
Position: Defenseman
Teams: Whalers, Blues, Oilers, Ducks, Flyers
Achievements: Pronger appeared in the Stanley Cup finals with three different teams (Edmonton, Anaheim, and Philadelphia), winning the Cup with the Ducks in 2006–2007. On the international stage with Canada, Pronger won the gold medal at the 2002 and 2010 Olympics and the gold medal at the 1997 World Championships. In 1999–2000 he won the Hart and Norris Trophies. He played in five All-Star games.

#87 SERGE SAVARD (1946–)

Playing Career: 1966–1983
Position: Defenseman
Teams: Canadiens, Jets (1979)
Achievements: Born in Montreal, Savard won the Conn Smythe Trophy (1968–1969) and the Masterton Trophy (1978–1979). He played in four All-Star games. With Montreal, Savard won seven Stanley Cups.

#88 ERIC LINDROS (1973–)

Playing Career: 1992–2007
Position: Center
Teams: Flyers, Rangers, Maple Leafs, Stars
Achievements: Drafted first overall in 1991 by the Nordiques, Lindros never played a game for Quebec. Traded to the Flyers, he was the center of the vaunted "Legion of Doom" line. In 1994–1995, he won the Hart Trophy and the Ted Lindsay Award. Lindros led the Flyers to two Eastern Conference Finals and the Stanley Cup Finals. In 760 career games, Lindros scored 372 goals and 493 assists for 865 points.

#89 FRANK NIGHBOR (1893–1966)

Playing Career: 1917–1930
Position: Center
Teams: Senators (1917), Maple Leafs
Achievements: A five-time Stanley Cup winner—once with Vancouver of the PCHA and four times with the Senators—Nighbor was considered the master of the "poke-check" with his invaluable two-way hockey. Nighbor was the first winner of both the Hart Trophy and Lady Byng Trophy, in 1923–1924 and 1924–1925 respectively. He won a second Lady Byng in 1925–1926.

#90 CLINT BENEDICT (1892–1976)

Playing Career: 1917–1930

Position: Goaltender

Teams: Senators (1917), Maroons

Achievements: Benedict played on four Stanley-Cup-winning teams, three with the Senators and one with the Maroons. He was the first goaltender in the NHL to wear a face-mask, which he briefly did during his time with the Maroons. He led the league in shutouts during each of his first seven NHL seasons, all of which were with Ottawa.

#91 CHARLIE GARDINER (1904–1934)

Playing Career: 1927–1934

Position: Goaltender

Teams: Black Hawks

Achievements: Gardiner won one Stanley Cup during his seven-year career. He won a pair of Vezina Trophies (1931–1932 / 1933–1934) and played in the 1934 All-Star game.

#92 HENRIK LUNDQVIST (1982–)

Playing Career: 2005–

Position: Goaltender

Team: Rangers

Achievements: As of the end of the 2014–2015 season, "The King" is the only goaltender in NHL history to record 30 wins in nine of his first ten seasons. Lundqvist leads all Rangers goalies in career wins (339), career shutouts (55), and career save percentage (.921). A Vezina Trophy winner in 2011–2012, he has played in three All-Star games. He won the gold medal with Sweden at the 2006 Olympics in Turin, Italy.

#93 SPRAGUE CLEGHORN (1890–1956)

Playing Career: 1918–1928

Position: Defenseman

Teams: Senators (1917), Saint Patricks, Canadiens, Bruins

Achievements: Cleghorn won a pair of Cups with the Senators and a third with Montreal. He was one of hockey's first offensive defenseman. At the time of his retirement, Cleghorn's 169 career goals were second most in professional hockey history by a defenseman.

#94 BABE DYE (1898–1962)

Playing Career: 1919–1931

Position: Right Wing

Teams: Saint Patricks, Tigers, Black Hawks, Americans, Maple Leafs

Achievements: He led the league in goals scored in the 1920–1921, 1922–1923, and 1924–1925 seasons, and won the Art Ross Trophy in 1922–1923 and 1924–1925. He led the Saint Patricks to the Stanley Cup championship in 1922, scoring a Stanley Cup Finals record nine goals in the five-game series against the Vancouver Millionaires. His 38 goals in the 30-game 1924–1925 season set a Saint Patricks/Maple Leafs franchise record that stood for over three decades until broken by Frank Mahovlich in the 70-game

357

1960–1961 season. Over his first six seasons in the NHL, Dye scored 176 goals in 170 games, a record until Wayne Gretzky broke into the NHL.

#95 SID ABEL (1918–2000)

Playing Career: 1938–1943, 1945–1954
Position: Center
Teams: Red Wings, Black Hawks
Achievements: A three-time Stanley Cup champion with the Red Wings, Abel won the Hart Trophy in 1948–1949. That season he led the NHL in goals with 28. Abel played in three All-Star games.

#96 RON FRANCIS (1963–)

Playing Career: 1981–2004
Position: Center
Teams: Whalers, Penguins, Hurricanes, Maple Leafs
Achievements: Francis is third in NHL history in games played (1,731), second in assists (1,249), and fifth in points (1,798). He scored 549 goals. A two-time Cup winner with Pittsburgh, he won the Selke Trophy (1994–1995), three Lady Byng Trophies (1994–1995 / 1997–1998 / 2001–2002), the King Clancy Memorial Trophy (2001–2002), and the NHL Foundation Player Award (2001–2002). Francis played in four All-Star contests.

#97 JOE MULLEN (1957–)

Playing Career: 1980–1997
Position: Right Wing
Teams: Blues, Flames, Penguins, Bruins
Achievements: In 1,062 games, Mullen totaled 1,063 points. He won two Lady Byng Trophies (1986–1987 / 1988–1989) and the Lester Patrick Trophy (1994–1995). A three-time Stanley Cup champion—one with Calgary and two with Pittsburgh—he played in three All-Star games.

#98 YVAN COURNOYER (1943–)

Playing Career: 1963–1979
Position: Right Wing
Team: Canadiens
Achievements: Nicknamed "The Roadrunner," Cournoyer won the Conn Smythe Trophy in 1972–1973 after scoring 15 goals and 10 assists for 25 points in 17 postseason games. He was named captain of the Canadiens in 1975, following the retirement of Henri Richard. In total, he won ten Cups as a player, which is a tie for second all-time.

#99 SCOTT STEVENS (1964–)

Playing Career: 1982–2004
Teams: Defenseman
358 *Teams:* Capitals, Blues, Devils

Achievements: Stevens suited up for the Capitals in his first eight NHL seasons before playing one year with the Blues. However, after becoming a Devil in 1991, he would find glory. He captained New Jersey to three Stanley Cup titles in 1994–1995, 1999–2000, and 2002–2003, winning the Conn Smythe Trophy in 1999–2000. He was the first Devil to have his number (4) retired in franchise history (on February 3, 2006). Feared because of his ability to deliver clean yet disastrous hits along the boards or in open ice, Stevens notched 908 points in 1,635 NHL games and never finished a season with a negative plus/minus, finishing +377. He also played in 13 All-Star games.

#100 BUSHER JACKSON (1911–1966)

Playing Career: 1929–1944
Position: Left Wing
Teams: Maple Leafs, Americans, Bruins
Achievements: Ralph Harvey "Busher" Jackson was a member of the famed "Kid Line" with Joe Primeau and Charlie Conacher. He won the Art Ross Trophy in 1931–1932 and was member of Toronto's 1931–1932 Stanley Cup winning team. He played in three All-Star games. On November 20, 1934, Jackson set an NHL record (since tied) when he became the first player in NHL history to score four goals in a period (third period in a 5–2 win against the St. Louis Eagles).

Index

Note: (ill.) indicates photos and illustrations.

365